This Country of Ours
by
H. E. Marshall

Table of Contents

Chapter 1 - How the Vikings of Old Sought and Found New Lands

In days long long ago there dwelt in Greenland a King named Eric the Red. He was a man mighty in war, and men held him in high honour.

Now one day to the court of Eric there came Bjarni the son of Heriulf. This Bjarni was a far traveler. He had sailed many times upon the seas, and when he came home he had ever some fresh tale of marvel and adventure to tell. But this time he had a tale to tell more marvelous than any before. For he told how far away across the sea of Greenland, where no man had sailed before, he had found a new, strange land.

But when the people asked news of this unknown land Bjarni could tell them little, for he had not set foot upon those far shores. Therefore the people scorned him.

"Truly you have little hardihood," they said, "else you had gone ashore, and seen for yourself, and had given us good account of this land."

But although Bjarni could tell nought of the new strange land, save that he had seen it, the people thought much about it, and there was great talk about voyages and discoveries, and many longed to sail forth and find again the land which Bjarni the Traveler had seen. But more than any other in that kingdom, Leif the son of Eric the Red, longed to find that land. So Leif went to Eric and said:

"Oh my father, I fain would seek the land which Bjarni the Traveler has seen. Give me gold that I may buy his ship and sail away upon the seas to find it."

Then Eric the Red gave his son gold in great plenty. "Go, my son," he said, "buy the ship of Bjarni the Traveler, and sail to the land of which he tells."

Then Leif, quickly taking the gold, went to Bjarni and bought his ship.

Leif was a tall man, of great strength and noble bearing. He was also a man of wisdom, and just in all things, so that men loved and were ready to obey him.

Now therefore many men came to him offering to be his companions in adventure, until soon they were a company of thirty-five men. They were all men tall and of great strength, with fair golden hair and eyes blue as the sea upon which they loved to sail, save only Tyrker the German.

Long time this German had lived with Eric the Red and was much beloved by him. Tyrker also loved Leif dearly, for he had known him since he was a child, and was indeed his foster father. So he was eager to go with Leif upon this adventurous voyage. Tyrker was very little and plain. His forehead was high and his eyes small and restless. He wore shabby clothes, and to the blue-eyed, fair-haired giants of the North he seemed indeed a sorry-looking little fellow. But all that mattered little, for he was a clever craftsman, and Leif and his companions were glad to have him go with them.

Then, all things being ready, Leif went to his father and, bending his knee to him, prayed him to be their leader.

But Eric the Red shook his head. "Nay, my son," he said, " I am old and stricken in years, and no more able to endure the hardships of the sea."

"Yet come, my father," pleaded Leif, "for of a certainty if you do, good luck will go with us."

Then Eric looked longingly at the sea. His heart bade him go out upon it once again ere he died. So he yielded to the prayers of his son and, mounting upon his horse, he rode towards the ship.

When the sea-farers saw him come they set up a shout of welcome. But when Eric was not far from the ship the horse upon which he was riding stumbled, and he was thrown to the ground. He tried to rise but could not, for his foot was sorely wounded.

Seeing that he cried out sadly, "It is not for me to discover new lands; go ye without me."

So Eric the Red returned to his home, and Leif went on his way to his ship with his companions.

Now they busied themselves and set their dragon-headed vessel in order. And when all was ready they spread their gaily-coloured sails, and sailed out into the unknown sea.

Westward and ever westward they sailed towards the setting of the sun. For many days they sailed yet they saw no land: nought was about them but the restless, tossing waves. But at length one day to their watching eyes there appeared a faint grey line far on the horizon. Then their hearts bounded for joy. They had not sailed in vain, for land was near.

"Surely," said Leif, as they drew close to it, "this is the land which Bjarni saw. Let it not be said of us that we passed it by as he did."

So, casting anchor, Leif and his companions launched a boat and went ashore. But it was no fair land to which they had come. Far inland great snow-covered mountains rose, and between them and the sea lay flat and barren rock, where no grass or green thing grew. It seemed to Leif and his companions that there was no good thing in this land.

"I will call it Helluland or Stone Land," said Leif.

Then he and his companions went back to the ship and put out to sea once more. They came to land again after some time, and again they cast anchor and launched a boat and went ashore. This land was flat. Broad stretches of white sand sloped gently to the sea, and behind the level plain was thickly wooded.

"This land," said Leif, "shall also have a name after its nature." So he called it Markland or Woodland.

Then again Leif and his companions returned to the ship, and mounting into it they sailed away upon the sea. And now fierce winds arose, and the ship was driven before the blast so that for days these seafarers thought no more of finding new lands, but only of the safety of their ship.

But at length the wind fell, and the sun shone forth once more. Then again they saw land, and launching their boat they rowed ashore.

To the eyes of these sea-faring men, who for many days had seen only the wild waste of waters, the land seemed passing fair. For the grass was green, and as the sun shone upon it seemed to sparkle with a thousand diamonds. When the men put their hands upon the grass, and touched their mouths with their hands, and drank the dew, it seemed to them that never before had they tasted anything so

8

sweet. So pleasant the land seemed to Leif and his companions that they determined to pass the winter there. They therefore drew their ship up the river which flowed into the sea, and cast anchor.

Then they carried their hammocks ashore and set to work to build a house

When the house was finished Leif called his companions together and spoke to them.

"I will now divide our company into two bands," he said, "so that we may explore the country round about. One half shall stay at home, and the other half shall explore the land. But they who go to explore must not go so far away that they cannot return home at night, nor must they separate from each other, lest they be lost."

And as Leif said so it was done. Each day a company set out to explore, and sometimes Leif went with the exploring party, and sometimes he stayed at home. But each day as evening came they all returned to their house, and told what they had seen.

At length, however, one day, when those who had gone abroad returned, one of their number was missing, and when the roll was called it was found that it was Tyrker the German who had strayed. Thereat Leif was sorely troubled, for he loved his foster-father dearly. So he spoke sternly to his men, reproaching them for their carelessness in letting Tyrker separate from them, and taking twelve of his men with him he set out at once to search for his foster-father. But they had not gone far when, to their great joy, they saw their lost comrade coming towards them.

"Why art thou so late, oh my foster-father?" cried Leif, as he ran to him. "Why hast thou gone astray from the others?"

But Tyrker paid little heed to Leif's questions. He was strangely excited, and rolling his eyes wildly he laughed and spoke in German which no one understood. At length, however, he grew calmer and spoke to them in their own language. "I did not go much farther than the others," he said. "But I have found something new. I have found vines and grapes."

"Is that indeed true, my foster-father?" said Leif.

"Of a certainty it is true," replied Tyrker. "For I was born where vines grow freely."

This was great news; and all the men were eager to go and see for themselves the vines which Tyrker had discovered. But it was already late, so they all returned to the house, and waited with what patience they could until morning.

Then, as soon as it was day, Tyrker led his companions to the place where he had found the grapes. And when Leif saw them he called the land Vineland because of them. He also decided to load his ship with grapes and wood, and depart homeward. So each day the men gathered grapes and felled trees, until the ship was full. Then they set sail for home.

The winds were fair, and with but few adventures they arrived safely at home. There they were received with great rejoicing. Henceforth Leif was called Leif the Lucky, and he lived ever after in great honour and plenty, and the land which he

9

had discovered men called Vineland the Good.

In due time, however, Eric the Red died, and after that Leif the Lucky sailed no more upon the seas, for his father's kingdom was now his, and he must needs stay at home to rule his land. But Leif's brother Thorvald greatly desired to go to Vineland so that he might explore the country still further.

Then when Leif saw his brother's desire he said to him, "If it be thy will, brother, thou mayest go to Vineland in my ship."

At that Thorvald rejoiced greatly, and gathering thirty men he set sail, crossed the sea without adventure, and came to the place where Leif had built his house.

There he and his company remained during the winter. Then in the spring they set forth to explore the coast. After some time they came upon a fair country where there were many trees.

When Thorvald saw it he said, "It is so fair a country that I should like to make my home here."

Until this time the Norsemen had seen no inhabitants of the land. But now as they returned to their ship they saw three mounds upon the shore. When the Norsemen came near they saw that these three mounds were three canoes, and under each were three men armed with bows and arrows, who lay in wait to slay them. When the Norsemen saw that, they divided their company and put themselves in battle array. And after a fierce battle they slew the savages, save one who fled to his canoe and so escaped.

When the fight was over the Norsemen climbed upon a, high headland and looked round to see if there were signs of any more savages. Below them they saw several mounds which they took to be the houses of the savages, and knew that it behooved them therefore to be on their guard. But they were too weary to go further, and casting themselves down upon the ground where they were they fell into a heavy sleep.

Suddenly they were awakened by a great shout, and they seemed to hear a voice cry aloud, "Awake, Thorvald, thou and all thy company, if ye would save your lives. Flee to thy ship with all thy men, and sail with speed from this land."

So Thorvald and his companions fled speedily to their ship, and set it in fighting array. Soon a crowd of dark-skinned savages, uttering fearful yells, rushed upon them. They cast their arrows at the Norsemen, and fought fiercely for some time. But seeing that their arrows availed little against the strangers, and that on the other hand many of their braves were slain, they at last fled.

Then, the enemy being fled, Thorvald, turning to his men, asked, "Are any of you wounded?"

"Nay," they answered, "we are all whole."

"That is well, " said Thorvald. "As for me, I am wounded in the armpit by an arrow. Here is the shaft. Of a surety it will cause my death. And now I counsel you, turn homeward with all speed. But carry me first to that headland which seemed to me to promise so pleasant a dwelling-place, and lay me there. Thus it shall be seen that I spoke truth when I wished to abide there. And ye shall place a cross at my feet, and another at my head, and call it Cross Ness ever after."

10

So Thorvald died. Then his companions buried him as he had bidden them in the land which had seemed to him so fair. And as he had commanded they set a cross at his feet and another at his head, and called the place Cross Ness. Thus the first white man was laid to rest in Vineland the Good.

Then when spring came the Norsemen sailed home to Greenland. And there they told Leif of all the things they had seen and done, and how his brave brother had met his death.

Now when Leif's brother Thorstein heard how Thorvald had died he longed to sail to Vineland to bring home his brother's body. So once again Leif's ship was made ready, and with five and twenty tall, strong men Thorstein set forth, taking with him his wife Gudrid.

But Thorstein never saw Vineland the Good. For storms beset his ship, and after being driven hither and thither for many months, he lost all reckoning, and at last came to land in Greenland once more. And there Thorstein died, and Gudrid went home to Leif.

Now there came to Greenland that summer a man of great wealth named Thorfinn. And when he saw Gudrid he loved her and sought her in marriage, and Leif giving his consent to it, Thorfinn and Gudrid were married.

At this time many people still talked of the voyages to Vineland, and they urged Thorfinn to journey thither and seek to find out more about these strange lands. And more than all the others Gudrid urged him to go. So at length Thorfinn determined to undertake the voyage. But it came to his mind that he would not merely go to Vineland and return home again. He resolved rather to settle there and make it his home.

Thorfinn therefore gathered about sixty men, and those who had wives took also their wives with them, together with their cattle and their household goods.

Then Thorfinn asked Leif to give him the house which he had built in Vineland. And Leif replied, "I will lend the house to you, but I will not give it."

So Thorfinn and Gudrid and all their company sailed out to sea, and without adventures arrived safely at Leif's house in Vineland.

There they lived all that winter in great comfort. There was no lack of food either for man or beast, and the cattle they had brought with them roamed at will, and fed upon the wide prairie lands.

All winter and spring the Norsemen dwelt in Vineland, and they saw no human beings save themselves. Then one day in early summer they saw a great troop of natives come out of the wood. They were dark and little, and it seemed to the Norsemen very ugly, with great eyes and broad cheeks. The cattle were near, and as the savages appeared the bull began to bellow. And when the savages heard that sound they were afraid and fled. For three whole weeks nothing more was seen of them, after that time however they took courage again and returned. As they approached they made signs to show that they came in peace, and with them they brought huge bales of furs which they wished to barter.

The Norsemen, it is true, could not understand the language of the natives, nor could the natives understand the Norsemen; but by signs they made known that

11

they wished to barter their furs for weapons. This, however, Thorfinn forbade. Instead he gave them strips of red cloth which they took very eagerly and bound about their heads. Thorfinn also commanded his men to take milk to the savages. And when they saw it they were eager to buy and drink it. So that it was said many of them carried away their merchandise in their stomachs.

Thus the days and months passed. Then one summer day a little son was born to Thorfinn and Gudrid. They called him Snorri, and he was the first white child to be born on the Continent which later men called the New World. Thus three years went past. But the days were not all peaceful. For quarrels arose between the newcomers and the natives, and the savages attacked the Norsemen and killed many of them.

Then Thorfinn said he would no longer stay in Vineland, but would return to Greenland. So he and all his company made ready their ship, and sailed out upon the seas, and came at length safely to Greenland.

Then after a time Thorfinn sailed to Iceland. There he made his home for the rest of his life, the people holding him in high honour. Snorri also, his son who had been born in Vineland, grew to be a man of great renown.

Such are some of the old Norse stories of the first finding of America. The country which Leif called Helluland was most likely Labrador, Markland Newfoundland, and Vineland Nova Scotia.

Besides these there were many other tales of voyages to Vineland. For after Leif and his brothers many other Vikings of the North sailed, both from Greenland and from Norway, to the fair western lands. Yet although they sailed there so often these old Norsemen had no idea that they had discovered a vast continent. They thought that Vineland was merely an island, and the discovery of it made no stir in Europe. By degrees too the voyages thither ceased. In days of wild warfare at home the Norsemen forgot the fair western land which Leif had discovered. They heard of it only in minstrel tales, and it came to be for them a sort of fairy-land which had no existence save in a poet's dream.

But now wise men have read these tales with care, and many have come to believe that they are not mere fairy stories. They have come to believe that hundreds of years before Columbus lived the Vikings of the North sailed the western seas and found the land which lay beyond, the land which we now call America.

Chapter 2 - The Sea of Darkness and the Great Faith of Columbus

In those far-off times besides the Vikings of the North other daring sailors sailed the seas. But all their sailings took them eastward. For it was from the east that all the trade and the riches came in those days. To India and to far Cathay sailed the merchant through the Red Sea and the Indian Ocean, to return with a rich and fragrant cargo of silks and spices, pearls and priceless gems.

None thought of sailing westward. For to men of those days the Atlantic Ocean was known as the Outer Sea or the Sea of Darkness. There was nothing to be gained by venturing upon it, much to be dreaded. It was said that huge and

12

horrible sea-dragons lived there, ready to wreck and swallow down any vessel that might venture near. An enormous bird also hovered in the skies waiting to pounce upon vessels and bear them away to some unknown eyrie. Even if any foolhardy adventurers should defy these dangers, and escape the horror of the dragons and the bird, other perils threatened them. For far in the west there lay a bottomless pit of seething fire. That was easy of proof. Did not the face of the setting sun glow with the reflected light as it sank in the west? There would be no hope nor rescue for any ship that should be drawn into that awful pit.

Again it was believed that the ocean flowed downhill, and that if a ship sailed down too far it would never be able to get back again. These and many other dangers, said the ignorant people of those days, threatened the rash sailors who should attempt to sail upon the Sea of Darkness. So it was not wonderful that for hundreds of years men contented themselves with the well-known routes which indeed offered adventure enough to satisfy the heart of the most daring.

But as time passed these old trade-routes fell more and more into the hands of Turks and Infidels. Port after port came under their rule, and infidel pirates swarmed in the Indian Ocean and Mediterranean until no Christian vessel was safe. At every step Christian traders found themselves hampered and hindered, and in danger of their lives, and they began to long for another way to the lands of spice and pearls.

Then it was that men turned their thoughts to the dread Sea of Darkness. The less ignorant among them had begun to disbelieve the tales of dragons and fiery pits. The world was round, said wise men. Why then, if that were so, India could be reached by sailing west as well as by sailing east.

Many men now came to this conclusion, among them an Italian sailor named Christopher Columbus. The more Columbus thought about his plan of sailing west to reach India, the more he believed in it, and the more he longed to set out. But without a great deal of money such an expedition was impossible, and Columbus was poor. His only hope was to win the help and friendship of a king or some other great and wealthy person.

The Portuguese were in those days a sea-faring people, and their ships were to be found wherever ships dared go. Indeed Prince Henry of Portugal did so much to encourage voyages of discovery that he was called Henry the Navigator. And although he was by this time dead, the people still took great interest in voyages of discovery. So at length Columbus determined to go to King John of Portugal to tell him of his plans, and ask for his aid.

King John listened kindly enough, it seemed, to what Columbus had to say. But before giving him any answer he said that he must consult his wise men. These wise men looked upon the whole idea of sailing to the west to reach the east as absurd. So King John refused to give Columbus any help.

Yet although most of King John's wise men thought little of the plan, King John himself thought that there was something in it. But instead of helping Columbus he meanly resolved to send out an expedition of his own. This he did, and when Columbus heard of it he was so angry that he left Portugal, which for more than ten years he had made his home. He was poor and in debt, so he left the country secretly, in fear of the King, and of those to whom he owed money.

When Columbus thus fled from Portugal, penniless and in debt, he was a man over forty. He was a bitterly disappointed man, too, but he still clung to his great idea. So he sent his brother Bartholomew to England to beg King Henry VII to help him, while he himself turned towards Spain. Bartholomew, however, reached England in an evil hour for his quest. For Henry VII had but newly wrested the crown from Richard III, and so had no thought to spare for unknown lands. Christopher also arrived in Spain at an unfortunate time. For the Spaniards were carrying on a fierce warfare against the Moors, and King Ferdinand and Queen Isabella had little thought or money to spare for any other undertaking. Therefore, although Ferdinand listened to what Columbus had to say, for the time being he could promise no help.

So years passed. Columbus remained in Spain. For in spite of all his rebuffs and disappointments he did not despair. As the court moved from place to place he followed it, hoping always that the day would come when the King and Queen would listen to him, and believe in his great enterprise.

Meanwhile he lived in want and misery, and just kept himself from starvation by making and selling maps. To the common people he seemed a madman, and as he passed through the streets in his worn and threadbare garments children jeered and pointed fingers of scorn at him.

Yet in spite of mockery and derision Columbus clung to his faith. Indeed it burned in him so strongly that at length he made others share it too, and men who were powerful at court became his friends.

At last the war with the Moors ended victoriously for Spain. Then these friends persuaded Queen Isabella to listen again to what Columbus had to say. To this the Queen consented, and when she heard how poor Columbus was she sent him some money, so that he might buy clothes fit to appear at court.

When Columbus heard the good news he was overjoyed. As quickly as might be he bought new clothes, and mounting upon a mule he rode towards Granada. But when Columbus arrived he found the court still in the midst of rejoicings to celebrate victory. Among the light-hearted, gaily dressed throng there was no one who had a thought to spare for the melancholy, white-haired dreamer who passed like a dark shadow amidst them. With his fate, as it were, trembling in the balance, Columbus had no heart for rejoicing. So he looked on "with indifference, almost with contempt."

But at length his day came. At length all the jubilation was over, and Ferdinand and Isabella turned their thoughts to Columbus. He came before them and talked so earnestly of his great project that they could not but believe in it. The day was won. Both King and Queen, but more especially the Queen, were willing to help the great enterprise. Now however Columbus himself all but wrecked his chances. He had dreamed so long about this splendid adventure, he was so filled with belief in its grandeur, that he demanded conditions such as would hardly have been granted to the greatest prince in the land.

14

Columbus demanded that he should be made admiral and viceroy of all the lands he might discover, and that after his death this honour should descend to his son and to his son's son for ever and ever. He also demanded a tenth part of all the pearls, precious stones, gold, silver and spices, or whatever else he might gain by trade or barter.

At these demands the grandees of Spain stood aghast. What! This shabby dreamer, this penniless beggar aspired to honour and dignities fit for a prince! It was absurd, and not to be thought of. If this beggarly sailor would have Spain assist him he must needs be more humble in suit.

But not one jot would Columbus abate of his demands. So the Council broke up, and Columbus, with anger and disappointment in his heart, mounted his mule and turned his face towards the Court of France. All the seven long years during which he had waited, and hoped, and prayed, in Spain had been wasted. Now he would go to the King of France, and make his last appeal there.

But Columbus had left friends behind him, friends who had begun to picture to themselves almost as vividly as he the splendours of the conquest he was to make. Now these friends sought out the Queen. In glowing words they painted to her the glory and the honour which would come to Spain if Columbus succeeded. And if he failed, why, what were a few thousand crowns, they asked. And as the Queen listened her heart beat fast; the magnificence of the enterprise took hold upon her, and she resolved that, come what might, Columbus should go forth on his adventure.

Ferdinand, however, still looked coldly on. The war against the Moors had been long and bitter, his treasury was empty. Whence, he asked himself, was money forthcoming for this mad scheme? Isabella, however, had done with prudence and caution. "If there is not money enough in Aragon," she cried, "I will undertake this adventure for my own kingdom of Castile, and if need be I will pawn my jewels to do it."

While these things were happening Columbus, sick at heart, was slowly plodding on the road to France. But he only went a little way on his long journey. For just as he was entering a narrow pass not far from Granada, where the mountains towered above him, he heard the thud of horses' hoofs.

It was a lonely and silent spot among the hills, where robbers lurked, and where many a man had been slain for the money and jewels he carried. Columbus, however, had nothing to dread: he carried with him neither gold nor jewels. He went forth from Spain a beggar, even as he had come. But if fear he had any, it was soon turned to incredulous joy. For when the horsemen came up they told Columbus that his friends had won the day for him, and that he must return.

At first Columbus hesitated. He found it hard to believe that truly at last he had his heart's desire. When, however, the messenger told him that the Queen herself bade him return, he hesitated no longer. Joyfully turning his mule he hastened back to Granada.

At last Columbus had won his heart's desire, and he had only to gather ships and men and set forth westward. But now a new difficulty arose. For it was out upon the terrible Sea of Darkness that Columbus wished to sail, and men feared to face its terrors.

Week after week went past and not a ship or a man could Columbus get. He persuaded and implored in vain: no man was brave enough to follow him to the unknown horrors of the Sea of Darkness. Therefore as entreaty and persuasion proved of no avail, Columbus sought help from the King, who gave him power to force men to go with him.

Even then all sorts of difficulties were thrown in the way. Columbus, however, overcame them all, and at length his three ships were ready. But it had taken many months. It was February when he turned back so gladly to Granada; it was the third of August before everything was in order.

Before dawn upon the day he sailed Columbus entered the church, in the little sea-faring town of Palos where his ships lay at anchor. There he humbly confessed his sins, received the Sacrament, and committed himself to God's all-powerful guidance. The crew, wild, rough fellows, many of them, followed his example. Then Columbus stepped on board his ship, the Santa Maria, and turned his face westward.

He was filled with exaltation. But all Palos was filled with gloom, and upon the shore a great crowd gathered to bid a last farewell to these daring adventurers. And as the ships spread their sails and sped forth in the morning light the people wept and lamented sorely, for they never thought again to see their loved ones, who were about to adventure forth upon the terrible Sea of Darkness.

Chapter 3 - How Columbus Fared Forth Upon The Sea of Darkness and Came to Pleasant Lands Beyond

At first the voyage upon which Columbus and his daring companions now set forth lay through seas already known; but soon the last land-mark was left behind, and the three little vessels, smaller than river craft of today, were alone upon the trackless waste of waters. And when the men saw the last trace of land vanish their hearts sank, and they shed bitter tears, weeping for home and the loved ones they thought never more to see.

On and on they sailed, and as day after day no land appeared the men grew restless. Seeing them thus restless, and lest they should be utterly terrified at being so far from home upon this seemingly endless waste of waters, Columbus determined to keep them from knowing how far they had really gone. So he kept two reckonings. One, in which the real length of the ships' daily journey was given he kept to himself: the other, in which the journey was given as much shorter, he showed to the sailors.

A month went past, six weeks went past, and still there was no trace of land. Then at length came signs. Snow birds which never ventured far to sea flew round the ships. Now the waves bore to them a rudely carved stick, now the ships ploughed a way through masses of floating weeds. All these signs were at first greeted with joy and hope, and the sailors took heart. But as still the days went past and no land appeared, they lost heart again.

16

The fields of weeds which they had at first greeted with joy now became an added terror. Would they not be caught in this tangle of weeds, they asked, and never more win a way out of it? To their fearful and superstitious minds the very breeze which had borne them softly onward became a menace. For if the wind always blew steadily from the east how was it possible ever to return to Spain? So Columbus was almost glad when a contrary wind blew. For it proved to his trembling sailors that one at least of their fears was groundless. But it made little difference. The men were now utterly given over to gloomy terrors.

Fear robbed them of all ambition. Ferdinand and Isabella had promised a large sum of money to the man who should first discover land. But none cared now to win it. All they desired was to turn home once more.

Fear made them mutinous also. So they whispered together and planned in secret to rid themselves of Columbus. It would be easy, they thought, to throw him overboard some dark night, and then give out that he had fallen into the sea by accident. No one would know. No one in Spain would care, for Columbus was after all but a foreigner and an upstart. The great ocean would keep the secret. They would be free to turn homeward.

Columbus saw their dark looks, heard the murmurs of the crews, and did his best to hearten them again. He spoke to them cheerfully, persuading and encouraging, "laughing at them, while in his heart he wept."

Still the men went sullenly about their work. But at length one morning a sudden cry from the Pinta shook them from out their sullen thoughts.

It was the captain of the Pinta who shouted. "Land, land, my lord!" he cried. "I claim the reward."

And when Columbus heard that shout his heart was filled with joy and thankfulness, and baring his head he sank upon his knees, giving praise to God. The crew followed his example. Then, their hearts suddenly light and joyous, they swarmed up the masts and into the rigging to feast their eyes upon the goodly sight.

All day they sailed onward toward the promised land. The sun sank and still all night the ships sped on their joyous way. But when morning dawned the land seemed no nearer than before. Hope died away again, and sorrowfully as the day went on the woeful truth that the fancied land had been but a bank of clouds was forced upon Columbus.

Again for days the ships sailed on, and as still no land appeared the men again began to murmur. Then one day when Columbus walked on deck he was met, not merely with sullen looks, but with angry words. The men clamoured to return. And if the Admiral refused, why, so much the worse for him. They would endure no longer.

Bravely the Admiral faced the mutineers. He talked to them cheerfully. He reminded them of what honour and gain would be theirs when they returned home having found the new way to India, of what wealth they might win by trading. Then he ended sternly:

"Complain how you may," he said, "I have to go to the Indies, and

I will go on till I find them, so help me God."

For the time being the Admiral's stern, brave words cowed the mutineers. But not for much longer, Columbus knew right well, would they obey him if land did not soon appear. And in his heart he prayed God that it might not be long delayed.

The next night Columbus stood alone upon the poop of the Santa Maria. Full of anxious thoughts he gazed out into the darkness. Then suddenly it seemed to him that far in the distance he saw a glimmering light appear and disappear once and again. It was as if some one walking carried a light. But so fearful was Columbus lest his fervent hopes had caused him to imagine this light that he would not trust his own eyes alone. So he called to one of his officers and asked him if he saw any light.

"Yes," replied the officer, "I see a light."

Then Columbus called a second man. He could not at first see the light, and in any case neither of them thought much of it. Columbus, however, made sure that land was close, and calling the men about him he bade them keep a sharp look-out, promising a silken doublet to the man who should first see land.

So till two o'clock in the morning the ships held on their way. Then from the Pinta there came again a joyful shout of "Land! Land!"

This time it proved no vision, it was land indeed; and at last the long-looked-for goal was reached. The land proved to be an island covered with beautiful trees, and as they neared the shore the men saw naked savages crowding to the beach.

In awed wonder these savages watched the huge white birds, as the ships with their great sails seemed to them. Nearer and nearer they came, and when they reached the shore and folded their wings the natives fled in terror to the shelter of the forest. But seeing that they were not pursued, their curiosity got the better of their fear, and returning again they stood in silent astonishment to watch the Spaniards land.

First of all came Columbus; over his glittering steel armour he wore a rich cloak of scarlet, and in his hand he bore the Royal Standard of Spain. Then, each at the head of his own ship's crew, came the captains of the Pinta and the Nina, each carrying in his hand a white banner with a green cross and the crowned initials of the King and Queen, which was the special banner devised for the great adventure. Every man was dressed in his best, and the gay-coloured clothes, the shining armour, and fluttering banners made a gorgeous pageant. Upon it the sun shone in splendour and the blue sky was reflected in a bluer sea: while scarlet flamingoes, startled at the approach of the white men, rose in brilliant flight.

As Columbus landed he fell upon his knees and kissed the ground, and with tears of joy running down his cheeks he gave thanks to God, the whole company following his example. Then rising again to his feet, Columbus drew his sword, and solemnly took possession of the island in the name of Ferdinand and Isabella.

When the ceremony was over the crew burst forth into shouts of triumph and joy. They crowded round Columbus, kneeling before him to kiss his hands and feet praying forgiveness for their insolence and mutiny, and promising in the future to obey him without question. For Columbus it was a moment of pure joy and triumph. All his long years of struggle and waiting had come to a glorious end.

Yet he knew already that his search was not finished, his triumph not yet complete. He had not reached the eastern shores of India, the land of spice and pearls. He had not even reached Cipango, the rich and golden isle. But he had at least, he thought, found some outlying island off the coast of India, and that India itself could not be far away. He never discovered his mistake, so the group of islands nowhere near India, but lying between the two great Continents of America, are known as the West Indies.

Columbus called the island upon which he first landed San Salvador, and for a long time it was thought to be the island which is still called San Salvador or Cat Island. But lately people have come to believe that Columbus first landed upon an island a little further south, now called, Watling Island.

From San Salvador Columbus sailed about and landed upon several other islands, naming them and taking possession of them for Spain. He saw many strange and beautiful fruits: "trees of a thousand sorts, straight and tall enough to make masts for the largest ships of Spain." He saw flocks of gaily coloured parrots and many other birds that sang most sweetly. He saw fair harbours so safe and spacious that he thought they might hold all the ships of the world.

But of such things Columbus was not in search. He was seeking for gold and jewels, and at every place he touched he hoped to find some great eastern potentate, robed in splendour and seated upon a golden throne; instead everywhere he found only naked savages. They were friendly and gentle, and what gold they had - but it was little indeed - they willingly bartered for a few glass beads, or little tinkling bells.

By signs, however, some of these savages made Columbus understand that further south there was a great king who was so wealthy that he ate off dishes of wrought gold. Others told him of a land where the people gathered gold on the beach at night time by the light of torches; others again told him of a land where gold was so common that the people wore it on their arms and legs, and in their ears and noses as ornaments. Others still told of islands where there was more gold than earth. But Columbus sought these lands in vain.

In his cruisings Columbus found Cuba, and thought at first it must be the island of Cipango, but finding himself mistaken he decided at length that he had landed upon the most easterly point of India. He could not be far, he thought, from the palace of the Grand Khan, and choosing out two of his company he sent them as ambassadors to him. But after six days the ambassadors returned, having found no gold; and instead of the Grand Khan having seen only a savage chieftain.

These ambassadors found no gold, but, had they only known it, they found something quite as valuable. For they told how they had met men and women with firebrands in their hands made of herbs, the end of which they put in their mouths and sucked, blowing forth smoke. And these fire-brands they called

19

tabacos.

The Spaniards also discovered that the natives of these islands used for food a root which they dug out of the earth. But they thought nothing of these things. For what were roots and dried herbs to those who came in search of gold, and gems, and precious spices? So they brought home neither potatoes nor tobacco.

So far the three little vessels had kept together, but now the captain of the Pinta parted company with the others, not because of bad weather, says Columbus in his diary, but because he chose, and out of greed, for he thought "that the Indians would show him where there was much gold." This desertion grieved Columbus greatly, for he feared that Pinzon might find gold, and sailing home before him cheat him of all the honour and glory of the quest. But still the Admiral did not give up, but steered his course "in the name of God and in search of gold and spices, and to discover land."

So from island to island he went seeking gold, and finding everywhere gentle, kindly savages, fair birds and flowers, and stately trees.

Chapter 4 - How Columbus Returned Home in Triumph

Christmas Eve came, and the Admiral, being very weary, went below to sleep, leaving a sailor to steer the ship. But this sailor thought he too would like to sleep, so he gave the tiller in charge of a boy.

Now throughout the whole voyage the Admiral had forbidden this. Whether it was stormy or calm he had commanded that the helm was never to be entrusted to a boy. This boy knew very little of how to steer a ship, and being caught in a current it was cast upon a sand-bank and wrecked. By good luck every one was saved and landed upon the island of Haiti. But Columbus had now only one little vessel, and it was not large enough to carry all the company. Many of them, however, were so delighted with the islands that they wanted to stay there, and they had often asked the Admiral's leave to do so.

Columbus therefore now determined to allow some of his men to remain to found a little colony, and trade with the Indians, "and he trusted in God that when he came back from Spain - as he intended to do - he would find a ton of gold collected by them, and that they would have found a gold mine, and such quantities of spices that the Sovereigns would in the space of three years be able to undertake a Crusade and conquer the Holy Sepulchre."

So out of the wreck of the Santa Maria Columbus built a fort, and from the many who begged to be left behind he chose forty-four, appointing one of them, Diego de Arana, as Governor. He called the fort La Navida or The Nativity in memory of the day upon which it was founded. The island itself he called Española or Little Spain.

Then on Friday the 4th of January, 1493, the Nina spread her sails and slowly glided away, leaving in that far island amid the unknown seas the first colony of white men ever settled in the west.

Two days after Columbus set forth upon his homeward voyage, he fell in again with the Pinta. The master had found no gold, so he determined to join

20

Columbus once more. He now came on board and tried to make his peace with Columbus, but the Admiral received him coldly, for he had little faith in his excuses. And now once more together, the two little vessels sailed homeward. But soon storms arose, the ships were battered by wind, tossed about hither and thither by waves, and at length separated again. More than once Columbus feared that his tiny vessel would be engulfed in the stormy seas, and the results of his great enterprise never be known. But at length the shores of Portugal were sighted, and on Friday, the 15th of March, 1493, he landed Again at Palos, in Spain, from whence he had set forth more than seven months before.

The people of Palos had hardly hoped to see again those who had sailed away on so desperate an adventure. Now, when they saw only one of the three vessels return their joy was mingled with grief. When, however, they learned that Columbus returned in triumph, and that India had been reached, their joy knew no bounds. Shops were closed, bells were rung, and all the people in holiday attire thronged to the harbour, and with shouts and cheers they bore Columbus in triumph to the church, there to give thanks to God for his safe and glorious return. And ere the shouts had died away, a second vessel was seen approaching. It was the Pinta which, though parted from the Nina, had also weathered the storms and now came safely to port.

At once on landing Columbus had sent a letter to the King and Queen telling them of his return. Now he received an answer; it was addressed to Don Christopher Columbus, our Admiral of the Ocean Sea, Viceroy and Governor of the Islands discovered in the Indies. It bade him to come at once to court. It told him that a new expedition would immediately be fitted out; so with a heart overflowing with joy and pride, Columbus set forth to Barcelona where the King and Queen then were.

The great news of his voyage and discovery had outsped him, and the people of Barcelona received him with every mark of respect and honour. As he passed through the streets, riding on a splendid horse and surrounded by the greatest nobles of Spain, they cheered him again and again. They gazed in wonder also at the dark-skinned savages, the gaily coloured parrots, and other strange things he had brought with him from out the Sea of Darkness.

Sitting on a throne of state beneath a canopy of cloth of gold, with the young Prince of Spain beside them , the King and Queen received Columbus. At his approach they rose, and standing they welcomed back to their realm as a mighty prince he who had gone forth a simple sailor. And as Columbus would have knelt to kiss their hands they raised him, and bade him be seated beside them as an equal. Seldom did the haughty rulers of Spain show such great honour even to the proudest nobles in the land.

And so while King, and Queen, and courtiers listened breathlessly Columbus told of all he had done, of all the marvels he had seen, of the richness and fairness of the lands he had found and claimed for Spain. And when he had finished the King and Queen fell upon their knees, and clasping their hands they raised eyes filled with tears of joy to heaven, giving thanks to God for His great mercies. The courtiers too fell upon their knees and joined their prayers to those of the King and Queen, while over all the triumphant notes of the Te Deum rang out.

So ended the great voyage of Columbus. He had shown the way across the Sea of Darkness; he had proved that all the stories of its monsters and other dangers were false. But even he had no idea of the greatness of his discovery. He never realised that he had shown the way to a new world; he believed to the day of his death that he had indeed found new islands, but that his greatest feat was that of finding a new way to the Old World. Yet now being made a noble, he took for his coat of arms a, group of golden islands in an azure sea, and for motto the words, "To Castile and Leon, Columbus gave a New World."

Now began a time of pomp and splendour for Columbus. He who had gone forth a penniless sailor now rode abroad in gorgeous array; often he might be seen with the Queen on one hand and John, the young Prince of Spain, on the other. Sometimes even the King himself would ride with him, and seeing him so high in royal favour all the greatest and proudest nobles of the land were eager to make much of him. So they feted him, flattered him, and spread banquets for him. But some were jealous of the great fame of Columbus, and they made light of his discoveries.

It is told how, one day at a banquet when every one talked of these wonderful deeds, one of the guests spoke slightingly of them. "It is all very well," he said to Columbus, "but in a great country like Spain, where there are such numbers of daring sailors and learned folk besides, many another man might have done the same as you. We should have found the Indies even if you had not."

To this speech Columbus answered nothing, but he asked for an egg to be brought to him. When it was brought he placed it on the table saying, "Sirs, I will lay a wager with any of you that you cannot make this egg stand up without anything at all to support it."

One after the other they tried, but no one could do it. At length it came round to Columbus again. And he, taking it in his hand, struck it sharply on the table so that one end was chipped a little, and it stood upright.

"That, my lord, is my answer, " he said, looking at the courtier who had scoffed. And all the company were silent. For they saw he was well answered. Columbus had shown that after a deed is once done it is simple, and every one knows how to do it. What he had done in sailing across the Sea of Darkness was only wonderful because no one ,else had thought of doing it.

Portugal was now very jealous of Spain's success, and King Ferdinand of Spain was fearful lest King John of Portugal should seize the new islands which Columbus had discovered. So he appealed to the Pope to settle the matter. And the Pope decided that all new lands discovered west of an imaginary line drawn through the Atlantic Ocean west of the Azores and from pole to pole should belong to Spain. All discoveries east of this line should belong to Portugal. If you will look at a map of the world you will see that this gave to Spain all the Americas with their islands (except a little bit of Brazil) and to Portugal the whole of Africa.

But almost before this matter was settled Columbus had set forth again on another voyage across the great ocean, now no longer the Sea of Darkness: this time he had no difficulty in getting a company. For every one was eager to go with him, even many of the sons of great nobles. This time too the passage was made without any doubts and fears, but with joyful expectations.

Columbus had hoped great things of the little colony that he had left behind him. But when he cast anchor one night before the fort his heart sank. All was dark and silent on shore. Yet still hoping, he ordered two cannon to be fired as a signal to the colonists. The cannon boomed through the still, warm darkness of the night, and slowly the echoes died away. But there was no answer save the sighing of the sea, and the scream of the startled birds. From the fort there came no sound or any sign of life, and with sad forebodings the Spaniards waited for the dawn.

Then it was seen that the fort was a ruin. It had been burned and sacked. Torn clothing and broken vessels were strewn around, but as the Spaniards wandered sadly among the ruins they found no trace of their companions save eleven graves with the grass growing above them.

At first no natives would come near the white men, for they feared their anger. But at length, tempted by the offer of gifts and other friendly signs, they came. They told how the Spaniards had quarreled amongst themselves, how the fort had been attacked by unfriendly Indians from another island, and how all the white men had been slain.

Thus ended the first white colony ever planted in Western lands. All traces of it have vanished, and upon the spot where La Navida stood there is now a little fishing village called Petit Anse.

Columbus founded other colonies, but they succeeded no better than the first one. In all he made four voyages across the Atlantic, and in the third he landed upon the coast of South America, near the mouth of the Orinoco. But Columbus did not know that at last he had discovered the great double Continent of America. He thought that he had merely discovered another island, and he named it La Isla Santa. Afterwards he was so delighted at the beauty of the land that he thought he must have found the Garden of Eden, so he became certain that he had landed on the eastern corner of Asia.

In 1506 Columbus died. And it is sad to think that he who, by his great faith and great daring, led the way across the Sea of Darkness, and gave a New World to the Old died in poverty and neglect. The men who had wept for joy at the news of his discovery shed no tear over his grave. He died "unwept, unhonoured and unsung." Years passed before men recognised what a great man had dwelt among them: years passed before any monument was raised to his memory. But indeed he had scarce need of any, for as has been well said, "The New World is his monument." And every child of the New World must surely honour that monument and seek never to deface it.

23

Chapter 5 - How America Was Named

"The New World is his monument." And yet the New World does not bear the name of Columbus. So in this chapter I am going to tell you how America was named.

As soon as Columbus had shown the way across the Sea of Darkness many were eager to follow in his footsteps. "There is not a man," he says himself, "down to the very tailors, who does not beg to be allowed to become a discoverer." Among the many who longed to sail the seas there was a man named Amerigo Vespucci.

Like Columbus, Amerigo Vespucci was an Italian. He was born in Florence and there for nearly forty years he lived quietly, earning his living as a clerk in the great merchant house of Medici. But although he was diligent at business his thoughts were not wholly taken up with it, and in his leisure hours he loved to read books of geography, and pore over maps and charts.

After a time business took Amerigo to Spain. He was there when Columbus returned from his famous first voyage, and very likely saw him pass through the streets of Barcelona on his day of triumph. Just when Amerigo and Columbus met we do not know. But very soon we find Amerigo in the service of the merchant who supplied Columbus with food and other necessaries for his second voyage. It has been thought by some that Vespucci went with Columbus on this voyage, but that is not very likely. It was about this time, however, that Vespucci went on his first voyage in which he explored the coast of Venezuela or of Central America. It is very doubtful which. Before going on this voyage he had been in Spain about four years, and not having succeeded very well as a merchant he decided to give up trading and take to a sea life.

No voyages perhaps have been more written about and fought over than those of Amerigo Vespucci. Some will have it that he went only two voyages, and say he was a braggart and a vainglorious fool if he said he went more. Others think that he went at least four voyages and probably six. And most people are now agreed that these last are right, and that he who gave his name to the great double Continent of America was no swaggering pretender but an honest and upright man.

In the first two voyages that he made Vespucci sailed under the flag of Spain. In the second two he sailed in the service of the King of Portugal. But after his fourth voyage he returned again to Spain. There he received a large salary and the rank of captain. Later he was made Pilot Major of Spain, and was held in high honour till his death.

Yet in all the voyages Vespucci went, whether under the flag of Portugal or of Spain, he was never leader. He went as astronomer, or as pilot, while other men captained the expeditions.

It is from Amerigo's letters alone that we gather the little we know about his voyages. For although he says in one of his letters that he has written a book called "The Four Voyages" it has never been found, and perhaps was never published. One long letter, however, which he wrote to an old schoolfellow was so interesting that it was published and read by many people all over Europe. It was, says an old English writer, "abrode in every mannes handes."

Amerigo's voyages led him chiefly to Central and South America and he became convinced that South America was a continent. So soon, what with the voyages of Vespucci and the voyages of other great men, it became at last quite certain that there was a vast continent beyond the Atlantic ocean. Map-makers, therefore, began to draw a huge island, large enough to form in itself a continent, south of the Equator. They called it the New World, or the land of the Holy Cross, but the Northern Continent was still represented on the maps by a few small islands, or as a part of Asia.

Thus years passed. Daring sailors still sailed the stormy seas in search of new lands, and learned men read the tales of their adventures and wrote new books of geography.

Then one day a professor who taught geography at the Monastery of St. Dié in Alsace published a little book on geography. In it he spoke of Europe, Asia and Africa, the three parts of the world as known to the ancients. Then he spoke of the fourth part which had been discovered by Amerigo Vespucci, by which he meant what we now call South America. "And," continues this professor, "I do not see what is rightly to hinder us calling this part Amerige or America, that is, the land of Americus after its discoverer Americus."

This is the first time the word America was ever used, and little did this old German professor, writing in his quiet Alsatian College, think that he was christening the great double continent of the New World. And as little did Amerigo think in writing his letter to his old school fellow that he was to be looked upon as the discoverer of the New World.

At first the new name came slowly into use and it appears for the first time on a map made about 1514. In this map America is shown as a great island continent lying chiefly south of the Equator.

All the voyages which Columbus had made had been north of the Equator. No man yet connected the land south of the Equator with him, and it was at first only to this south land that the name America was given.

Thirty years and more went by. Many voyages were made, and it became known for certain that Columbus had not reached the shores of India by sailing west, and that a great continent barred the way north as well as south of the Equator.

Then a famous map-maker gave the name of America to both continents.

But many Spaniards were jealous for the fame of Columbus, and they thought that the Northern Continent should be called Colonia or Columbiana. One, anxious that the part in the discovery taken by Ferdinand and Isabella should not be forgotten, even tried to make people call it Fer-Isabelica.

But all such efforts were in vain. America sounded well, people liked it, and soon every one used it.

Amerigo Vespucci himself had nothing to do with the choice, and yet because others gave his name to the New World many hard things have been said of him.

25

He has been called in scorn a "land lubber, " a beef and biscuit contractor," and other contemptuous names. Even one of the greatest American writers has poured scorn on him. "Strange," he says, "that broad America must wear the name of a thief. Amerigo Vespucci, the pickle dealer of Seville . . . whose highest naval rank was a boatswain's mate in an expedition that never sailed, managed in this lying world to supplant Columbus and baptise half the earth with his own dishonest name."

But it was the people of his day, and not Vespucci, who brought the new name into use. Vespucci himself had never any intention of being a thief or of robbing Columbus of his glory. He and Columbus had always been friends, and little more than a year before he died Columbus wrote a letter to his son Diego which Vespucci delivered. In this letter Columbus says, "Amerigo Vespucci, the bearer of this letter . . . has always been wishful to please me. He is a very honest man. . . . He is very anxious to do something for me, if it is in his power."

It was only accident which gave the name of America to the New World, and perhaps also the ingratitude of the great leader's own generation.

Later generations, however, have not been so unmindful of Columbus and his deeds; Americans have not allowed his great name to be wholly forgotten. The district in which the capital of the United States is situated is called Columbia. In Canada too there is the great province of British Columbia, and in South America the 'United States of Colombia, besides many towns all named in honour of the great discoverer.

Chapter 6 - How The Flag of England Was Planted on the Shores of the New World

Christopher Columbus showed the way across the Sea of Darkness; Amerigo Vespucci gave his name to the great double continent, but it was another Italian, John Cabot, who first landed on the Continent of North America.

Like Columbus, Cabot was born in Genoa. When, however, he left his own land he did not go to Spain like Columbus, but to England.

He had been living in England for some years when the news of the first great voyage of Columbus was brought there. Soon every one was talking about the wonderful discovery from the King and his court downward.

Cabot was a trader and a daring sailor, well used to sailing on the stormy seas. Yet even he was awed by what Columbus had done. To find that way never known before, and by sailing west to reach the east "where the spices grow" seemed to him " a thing more divine than human. "And he too longed to follow Columbus, and maybe discover new lands.

King Henry VII was eager to claim new lands as the Kings of Spain and Portugal were doing. So he listened to the persuasions of John Cabot. And in spite of the Pope - who had divided all the undiscovered world between the Kings of Spain and Portugal - gave him leave to sail forth to "the seas of the east and west and north" and to plant the banner of England upon any islands, countries or regions belonging to heathens or infidels which he might discover. He bade his "well-beloved John Cabot" take five ships and set forth on the adventure at his " own proper costs and charges." For Henry was a King "wise but not lavish," and although he wanted England to have the glory of new discoveries he was not eager to spend his gold on them.

But where could a poor sailor find money enough for so great an adventure?

So a year went past, and although Cabot had the King's leave to go he did not set out. But he did not let the King forget. And at length close-fisted Henry listened to "the busy request and supplication" of the eager sailor, and consented to fit out one small ship.

So at five o'clock one sweet May morning a frail little vessel called the Matthew, with a crew of but eighteen men, sailed out from Bristol harbour. Many people came to see the vessel sail. For they were nearly all Bristol men who were thus venturing forth on the unknown deep, and their friends crowded to the harbour to wish them godspeed.

It was a great occasion for Bristol, and indeed for all England, for it was the first voyage of discovery with which the English king and people had to do. So the tiny whitesailed ship put out to sea, followed by the prayers and wishes of those left behind. With tear-dimmed eyes they watched it till it faded from view. Then they turned homewards to pray for the return of their loved ones.

Round the coast of Ireland the vessel sped. But at last its green shores faded from sight and the little company of eighteen brave men were alone upon the trackless waves.

Westward and ever westward they sailed,

"Over the hazy distance, Beyond the sunset's rim"

Week after week went by. Six weeks and then seven, and still no land appeared. Those were days of anxiety and gloom. But still the hope of the golden west lured Cabot on, and at length one day in June he heard the glad cry of "Land! Land!"

So on St. John's Day, in 1497, John Cabot landed somewhere on the coast of America. He called the land Prima Tierra Vista or First Land Seen, and because of the day upon which it was found he called an island near to it St. John's Isle.

We cannot tell exactly where Cabot east anchor: it may have been at Cape Breton or somewhere on the coast of Labrador. But wherever it was that he landed he there set up a great cross and unfurled the flag of England, claiming the land for King Henry.

When Cabot set out he was full of the ideas of Columbus. He had hoped to find himself on the coast of Asia and in the land of gold and spices. Now he knew himself mistaken. He did not see any natives, but he knew the land was inhabited, for he found notched trees, snares for wild animals and other signs of habitation which he took home.

He had found no "golden cities," he had had speech with no stately potentate. Yet he was not utterly disappointed. For the country he had found seemed to him fair and fertile, and the quantities of fish which swarmed in the seas amazed both himself and his men. They had no need of lines or even of nets. They had but to let down a basket weighted with a stone and draw it up again to have all the fish they wanted.

Cabot stayed but a short time in the new-found land. He would fain have stayed longer and explored further, but he feared lest his provisions would give out, and so regretfully he turned homeward.

Great was the excitement in Bristol when the tiny ship came to anchor there once more, little more than three months after it had sailed away. And so strange were the tales Master Cabot had to tell that the folk of Bristol would hardly have believed him (for he was a poor man and a foreigner) had not his crew of honest Bristol men vouched for the truth of all he said. Every one was delighted. Even thrifty King Henry was so much pleased that he gave Cabot £10. It seems a small enough sum for one who had found "a new isle." But we must remember that it was worth more than £100 would be worth today.

Cabot at any rate found it enough with which to buy a suit of silk. And dressed in this new splendour he walked about the streets of Bristol followed by gaping crowds. He was now called the Great Admiral, and much honour was paid to him. Every one was eager to talk with him, eager to go with him on his next voyage: and that even although they knew that many of the crew would be thieves and evil-doers. For the King had promised to give Cabot for sailors all prisoners except those who were confined for high treason.

We know little more of John Cabot. Later King Henry gave him a pension of £20 a year. It seems likely that the following year he set out again across the broad Atlantic, taking his sons with him. "The rest is silence."

How John Cabot ended his life, where he lies taking his rest, we do not know.

"He sleeps somewhere in sod unknown, Without a slab, without a stone."

We remember him chiefly because he was the first to lead Englishmen across the Atlantic, the first to plant the flag of England upon the Continent of North America, which, in days to come, was to be the home of two great English speaking peoples.

Chapter 7 - How The Flag of France Was Planted in Florida

As years went on many voyages of discovery and exploration were made to the New World by both the Spaniards and the Portuguese, but chiefly by the Spaniards. America was the land of golden hopes, the land of splendid adventure, and the haughty knights of Spain, thirsting for gold and for fame, were lured thither. They sought the fabled seven cities of gold, they sought the fountain of eternal youth. Through the dark pathless forests, across the wide prairies they flashed in glittering array, awaking the vast silences with the clash of arms. They came in all the pomp and splendour of warfare; they brought also the Cross of Christ, threatening the heathen with death if they did not bow to Him and be baptised. And it seemed for a time as if they, and they only, would possess the vast continent. But expedition after expedition ended in disaster. The Spaniards found neither the far-famed seven cities nor the fountain of youth. And the Redmen, instead of accepting their religion, hated them and it with a deep hatred.

But the Spaniards were not long left in undisputed possession of America. The French King too desired to have new lands across the seas, and he saw no reason why Spain and Portugal should divide the New World between them.

"I would fain see Father Adam's will," he said, "in which he made you the sole heirs to so vast an inheritance. Until I do see that, I shall seize as mine whatever my good ships may find upon the ocean. "

From France, therefore, daring men sailed forth to the New World. And there they set up the arms of their country, claiming broad lands for their King.

And now came the time when all Christian lands were torn asunder by religious strife. The Reformation had begun, and everywhere there was discord between the people who followed the old religion and those who followed the new. In France those who followed the new religion were called Huguenots. They were often hardly used, and were denied freedom to worship God in their own way. Many of them therefore longed to get away from France, and go to some new country where they would have the freedom they desired.

So a few grave, stern men gathered together and determined to set out for some place in the New World where they might make a home.

Then one February day in 1562 two little ships sailed away from France. Westward they sailed until about two and a half months later they landed in what is now Florida.

It was May Day, the sun shone and all the world seemed gay and green, and these Protestant adventurers thought they had never seen so fair a land. It was, they said, the fairest, fruitfullest and pleasantest of all the world, "abounding in honey, venison and wildfowl." The natives were friendly and told the newcomers by signs that the seven golden cities were not far off. That rejoiced their hearts, for even those stern old Huguenots were not above following the quest for gold.

Here then in this far-off land the Huguenots set up a stone pillar carved with the arms of the King of France. And kneeling round it they gave thanks to God for having brought them to so fair a country. Then returning to their ships they sailed northward along the coast, For they had not come to settle, but merely to explore, and find out a good spot on which to found a colony.

But the land seemed so fair, the air so balmy, that they were ready to settle there at once, and never return to France.

At length after inspecting several places the adventurers reached a spot not far from what is now Beaufort in South Carolina. Here they landed, and knowing that many of the men were already eager to remain in this beautiful country, Jean Ribaut, their leader, resolved to found a colony. So he called them all together, and speaking wise and brave words to them asked who among them would remain.

"Declare your minds freely unto me," he said, "and remember that if you decide to remain you will for ever be famous, and be known as the first white men who inhabited this land."

Ribaut had scarcely finished speaking when nearly all the men replied with a shout, "We ask nothing better than to remain in this beautiful country."

Indeed so many were anxious to remain that Ribaut had enough to do to

29

persuade a sufficient number to man the ships to return with him.

In the end thirty men were chosen to remain. At once they set about building a fort which they called Charlesfort in honour of the boy King, Charles IX, who was then upon the throne.

The men worked so well that in a very few days the fort was so far finished that it was fit to live in. Food and ammunition were brought from the ships, and a man named Albert de la Pierria was chosen as Governor. Then for the last time Ribaut gathered all the men together and took leave of those to be left behind.

"Captain Albert," he said, "I have to ask you in the presence of all these men, to quit yourself so wisely in your charge, that I shall be able to commend you to your King.

"And you," he said, turning to the soldiers, "I beg you to esteem Captain Albert as if he were myself, and to yield to him that obedience that a true soldier owes to his general and captain. I pray you live as brethren together without discord. And in so doing God will assist you, and bless your enterprises."

Then farewells were said, and Ribaut sailed away, leaving the thirty white men alone in the wilderness.

From north to south, from east to west, in all the vast continent there were no white men save themselves. The little company was made up of young nobles, sailors, merchants and artisans. There were no farmers or peasants among them, and when they had finished their fort none of them thought of clearing the land and sowing corn. There was no need: Ribaut would soon return, they thought, bringing with him all they required. So they made friends with the Indians, and roamed the forest wilds in search of gold and of adventures, without care for the future.

But the days and weeks passed and Ribaut did not return. For when he arrived home he found that France was torn with civil war, and that it was impossible to get ships fitted out to sail to America.

Soon the little colony began to feel the pangs of hunger. Daily they scanned the pitiless blue sea for a glimpse of Ribaut's returning sail. No sail appeared, and daily their supplies dwindled away. Had it not been for the friendly Redmen they might all have perished. For the Indians were generous, and as long as they had food themselves they shared it with their white friends. But at length they could spare no more. Indeed they had already given the Pale-faces so much food that they themselves, they said, would be forced to roam the woods in search of roots and herbs to keep them from starving until harvest was ripe. They told the Frenchmen, however, of two rich and powerful chiefs who held sway over land which lay to the south, where they might obtain endless supplies of corn and vegetables.

This was indeed good news to the Frenchmen. And guided by their Indian friends they lost no time in setting out to beg food from those dusky potentates.

When the Frenchmen reached the wigwams of one of these chiefs they were received with great honour. They found that their Redskin friends had spoken truly. Here there was food in abundance; and after a great feast they returned joyfully to the fort, carrying with them a great supply of corn and beans, and - what was still better - a promise from the friendly chief that he would give them more food whenever they had need of it.

Once more the colonists rejoiced in plenty. But not for long. For the very night they arrived home their storehouse took fire, and all the food which they had brought with such joy was destroyed.

Again famine stared them in the face. In their plight they once more appealed to the savage chief who supplied their wants as generously as before; promising them that as long as his meal should last they should never want. So for the time being the colonists were saved from starvation.

But another danger now threatened them, for quarrels arose among the men. Albert de Pierria who had been set over them as captain proved to be cruel and despotic. He oppressed the men in many ways, hanging and imprisoning at will those who displeased him. Soon the men began to murmur under his tyranny. Black looks greeted Albert de Pierria: he answered them with blacker deeds. At length one day for some misdeed he banished a soldier to a lonely island, and left him there to die of hunger. This was more than the colonists could well bear. Their smouldering anger burst forth, and seizing the tyrant they put him to death. Then they chose one of their number called Nicolas Barre to be their captain.

They were rid of their tyrant, and that brought peace for a time to the little colony. But the men had grown to hate the place. The land which had once seemed to them so fair now seemed no better than a prison, and they longed to escape from it.

They had, however, no ship, and although all around them tall trees grew no one of them knew anything of ship building. Still, so strong was their desire to leave the hated spot that they resolved to build one.

They set to work with. a will. Soon the sound of saw and hammer awoke the silence of the forest. High and low, noble and peasant, all worked together, the Indians, even, lending a hand.

At length their labours were over and the rough little ship was afloat. It made but a sorry appearance. The planks were rough-hewn by the hatchet, and caulked with the moss which grew in long streamers on the trees. The cordage was Indian made, and the sails were patched together from shirts and bedclothes. Never before had men thought to dare the ocean waves in so crazy a craft. But the colonists were in such eagerness to be gone that they chose rather to risk almost certain death upon the ocean than remain longer in their vast prison house.

So they loaded the ship with as much food as they could collect, and saying farewell to their Indian friends, they spread their patchwork sails, and glided out to sea drunken with joy at the thought of returning to France.

At first the wind blew fair, and the little ship sped gaily homeward. Then came a calm. The sun burned overhead, no faintest breeze stirred the slack sails, and the ship lay as if at anchor upon the glassy waters. And as the ship lay motionless the slender stock of food grew less and less. Soon there was nothing left but maize, and little of that. At first a tiny handful was each man's daily portion; then it was counted by grains. But jealously hoarded although it was the maize at length gave out, and there was nothing left to eat but their leather shoes and jerkins.

Then to the pain of hunger was added the pain of thirst, for the water barrels were emptied to the last drop. Unable to endure the torture some drank the sea, water and so died in madness. Beneath the burning sun every timber of the crazy little ship warped and started, and on all sides the sea flowed in. Still through all their agony the men clung to life. And sick with hunger, maddened with thirst as they were they laboured unceasingly bailing out the water. But they laboured now with despair in their hearts, and they gave up hope of ever seeing their beloved France again. Then at length the pitiless sun was overcast, a wild wind arose, and the glassy sea, whipped to fury, became a waste of foam and angry billows. The tiny vessel was tossed about helplessly and buffeted this way and that.

"In the turning of a hand," says an old writer, "the waves filled their vessel half full of water, and bruised it upon one side."

The wretched men now gave themselves up for lost. They cared no longer to bail, but cast themselves down into the bottom of the boat, and let it drift where it would. Only one man among them did not utterly lose heart. He set himself now to encourage the others, telling them that if only the wind held, in three days they would see the shores of France.

This man was so full of hope that at length he aroused the others from their despair. Once more they began the weary work of bailing, and in spite of all the fury of the wind and waves the little vessel kept afloat.

At last the storm passed. Once more the fainting wanderers righted their vessel, and turned the prow towards the shores of France. But three days passed, and no land was seen, and they became more despairing than before.

For now the last grain of corn was eaten, the last drop of water drunk. Mad with thirst, sick with hunger, the men strained their weary eyes over the rolling waste of waters. No land was in sight. Then a terrible thought crept into one mind after another. In a low hoarse whisper one man and then another spoke out his thought-that one man should die for his fellows.

So deep were they sunk in woe that all were of one mind. So lots were cast, and the man upon whom the lot fell was killed.

These tortured wayfarers had become cannibals.

Kept alive in this terrible fashion the men sailed on, and at length a faint grey streak appeared on the horizon. It was the long-looked-for shore of France. But the joy was too great for their over-strained minds. The sight of land seemed to rob them of all power of thought or action. With salvation in sight they let the little vessel drift aimlessly this way and that.

While they thus drifted aimlessly a white sail hove in sight, and an English vessel bore down upon them. In the English vessel there happened to be a Frenchman who had sailed with Ribaut on his first voyage to Florida. He soon recognised his countrymen in spite of their sorry plight, and they were brought aboard the English vessel. And when they had been given food and drink, and were somewhat revived, they told their tale of misery.

32

The Englishmen were in doubt for some time as to what it was best to do. In the end they decided to set the most feeble on the shores of France, and to carry the others prisoners to the Queen of England, who at that time was about to send an expedition to Florida.

So ended the first attempt of the French to found a colony in North America.

Chapter 8 - How The French Founded a Colony in Florida

Two years after Ribaut's ill-fated expedition another company of Frenchmen set sail for America. This time Reté de Laudonnière was captain. He had been with Ribaut two years before, and now again he landed on the same spot where Ribaut had first landed, and set up the arms of France.

As they saw his ship come the Indians ran down to the beach welcoming him with cries of excitement and joy, and taking him by the hand the chief led him to the pillar which Jean Ribaut had set up. It was wreathed in flowers, and baskets of corn stood before it. For the Indians looked upon it as an idol, and made offerings to it. They kissed it with a great show of reverence, and begged the Frenchmen to do the same. "Which we would not deny them," says Laudonnière, who himself tells the story, "to the end we might draw them to be more in friendship with us."

Laudonnière was so delighted with the natives' friendly greeting that he resolved to found his colony among these kindly Indians. So a little way up the river which Ribaut had named the river of May, but which is now the St. John's, he built a fort.

It was late one evening in June when the Frenchmen reached the spot where they intended to build the fort; wearied with their long march through the forest they lay down upon the ground and were soon fast asleep.

But at day-break Laudonnière was astir. He commanded a trumpet to be sounded, and when all the men were aroused and stood together he bade them give thanks to God for their safe arrival. So standing beneath the waving palms, with the deep blue sky arching overhead, the men sang a psalm of thanksgiving and praise. Then kneeling they prayed long and earnestly.

The prayer ended, the men arose, and full of happy courage turned to their work. Every one took part with right good will. Some brought earth, some cut logs; there was not a man who had not a shovel or hatchet or some tool in his hand. The work went on merrily, and soon above the banks of the river the fort rose, secure and strong, fenced and entrenched on every side. In honour of their King Charles these new colonists called their fort Caroline, just as Ribaut had called his Charlesfort.

But as the native Chief Satouriona watched the fort grow he began to be uneasy. He wondered what these pale-faced strangers were about, and he feared lest they should mean evil towards him. So he gathered his warriors together, and one day the Frenchmen looked up from their labours to see the heights above them thick with savages in their war paint.

At once the Frenchmen dropped their tools and prepared to defend themselves. But Satouriona, making signs of peace, and leaving most of his warriors behind him, came down into the camp followed by a band of twenty musicians who blew ear-piercing blasts upon discordant pipes.

Having reached the camp Satouriona squatted on his haunches, showing that he wanted to take counsel with the Frenchmen. Then with many signs and gestures he told the Frenchmen that his great enemies the Thimagoes were near, and that if the Frenchmen wished to continue in friendship with him they must promise to help him against these powerful and hated foes.

Laudonnière feared to lose Satouriona's friendship. And thereupon with signs, helped out now and again with a word or two, a, treaty was made between the Indians and the Frenchmen, Laudonnière promising to help Satouriona against his enemies, the Thimagoes. With this treaty Satouriona was delighted, and he commanded his warriors to help the Frenchmen in building their fort, which they very readily did.

Then, mindful of his promise, as soon as the fort was finished, Laudonnière sent off some of his followers under one of his officers to find out who the Thimagoes really were of whom Satouriona spoke with such hate. Guided by some Indians, this officer soon came upon the Thimagoes. But instead of fighting with them he made friends with them, which greatly disgusted his Indian guides.

Meanwhile Satouriona, delighted at the idea of being able to crush his enemies with the Frenchmen's help, had gathered all his braves together and made ready for war.

Ten chiefs and five hundred warriors, fearful in war paint and feathers, gathered at the call. Then seeing that Laudonnière was not making any preparations for war, he sent messengers to him.

"Our chief has sent us," they said, "and he would know whether you will stand by your promise to show yourself a friend of his friends, an enemy of his enemies and go with him to war."

"Tell your chief, replied Laudonnière, " that I am not willing to purchase his friendship with the enmity of another. Notwithstanding I will go with him. But first I must gather food for my garrison, neither are my ships ready. An enterprise such as this needs time. Let your chief abide two months, then if he hold himself ready I will fulfil my promise to him."

The Indian carried this answer to the Chief who, when he heard it, was filled with wrath. He was not, however, to be stayed from war, and he determined to go alone.

With great ceremony he prepared to set out. In an open space near the river a huge fire was lit. In a wide circle round this the warriors gathered. Their faces were fearful with paint, and their hair was decorated with feathers, or the heads of wolves and bears and other fierce animals. Beside the fire was placed a large bowl of water, and near it Satouriona stood erect, while his braves squatted at his feet. Standing thus he turned his face, distorted with wrath and hatred, towards the enemy's country. First he muttered to himself, then he cried aloud to his god the

34

Sun. And when he had done this for half an hour he put his hand into the bowl of water, and sprinkled the heads of his braves. Then suddenly, as if in anger, he cast the rest of the water into the fire, putting it out. As he did so he cried aloud:

"So may the blood of our enemies be poured out and their lives extinguished."

In reply a hoarse yell went up from the savage host, and all the woods resounded with the fiendish noise.

Thus Satouriona and his braves set forth for battle. In a few days they returned singing praises to the Sun, and bringing with them twenty-four prisoners and many scalps.

And now Laudonnière made Satouriona more angry than ever with him. For he demanded two of these prisoners. Laudonnière wanted them so that he might send them back to the chief of the Thimagoes as a proof that he at least was still friendly, for he already regretted his unwise treaty. But when Satouriona heard Laudonnière's request he was very angry and treated it with scorn.

"Tell your chief," he said, "that he has broken his oath, and I will not give him any of my prisoners."

When Laudonnière heard this answer he in his turn was very angry, and he resolved to frighten Satouriona into obeying him. So taking twenty soldiers with him he went to the chief's village. Leaving some of the soldiers at the gate, and charging them to let no Indians go in or out, he went into Satouriona's hut with the others. In perfect silence he came in, in perfect silence he sat down and remained so for a long time which, says Laudonnèire, put the chief "deeply in the dumps."

At length when he thought that Satouriona was completely frightened, Laudonnière spoke.

"Where are your prisoners?" he said. "I command them to be brought before me." Thereupon the chief, "angry at the heart and astonied wonderfully," stood a long time without making any answer. But when at last he spoke it was boldly and without fear.

"I cannot give you my prisoners," he said. "For seeing you coming in such warlike guise they were afraid and fled to the woods. And not knowing what way they went we could not by any means find them again."

Laudonnière, however, pretended that he did not understand what the chief said, and again he asked for the prisoners.

The chief then commanded his son to go in search of them, and in about an hour he returned bringing them with him. As soon as they were brought before Laudonnière the prisoners greeted him humbly. They lifted up their hands to heaven, and then threw themselves at his feet. But Laudonnière raised them at once, and led them away to the fort, leaving Satouriona very angry.

Laudonnière now sent the prisoners back to the Thimagoes' chief, who was greatly delighted at the return of his braves. He was still more delighted when the Frenchmen marched with him against another tribe who were his enemies, and defeated them.

But while Laudonnière was thus making both friends and enemies among the

Indians all was not peace in the colony itself. Many of the adventurers had grown tired of the loneliness and sameness of the life. The food was bad, the work was hard, and there seemed little hope that things would ever be better. And for all their hardships it seemed to them the Governor was to blame. So they began to murmur and be discontented, gathering together in groups, whispering that it would be a good deed to put an end to Laudonnière and choose another captain.

And now when the discontent was at its height Laudonnière fell ill. Then one of the ringleaders of the discontent urged the doctor to put poison in his medicine. But the doctor refused. Next they formed a plot to hide a barrel of gunpowder under his bed and blow him up. But Laudonnière discovered that plot, and the ringleader fled to the forest.

About this time a ship arrived from France bringing food for the colony, so that for a time things went a little better. And when the ship sailed again for home Laudonnière sent the worst of the mutineers back in it. In their place the captain left behind some of his sailors. But this proved a bad exchange. For these sailors were little better than pirates, and very soon they became the ringleaders in revolt. They persuaded some of the older colonists to join them. And one day they stole a little ship belonging to the colony, and set off on a plundering expedition to the West Indies.

On the seas they led a wild and lawless life, taking and plundering Spanish ships. But after a time they ran short of food, and found themselves forced to put into a Spanish port. Here in order to make peace with the Spaniards they told all they knew about the French colony.

Thus it was that for the first time the Spaniards learned that the heretic Frenchmen had settled in their land, and speedily the news was sent home to Spain.

Meanwhile Laudonnière was greatly grieved for the loss of his ship. And as days passed, and there was no sign of the mutineers' return, he set his men to work to build two new ships.

For a time the work went well. But soon many of the men grew tired of it and they began to grumble. Why should men of noble birth, they asked, slave like carpenters? And day by day the discontent increased.

At last one Sunday morning the men sent a message to Laudonnière asking him to come out to the parade ground to meet them. Laudonnière went, and he found all the colony waiting for him with gloomy faces. At once one of them stepped forward, and asked leave to read a paper in the name of all the others. Laudonnière gave permission. The paper was read. It was full of complaints about the hard work, the want of food, and other grievances. It ended with a request that the men should be allowed to take the two ships which were being built and sail to Spanish possessions in search of food. In fact they wanted to become pirates like those mutineers who had already sailed away.

Laudonnière refused to listen to this request. But he promised that as soon as the two ships were finished they should be allowed to set out in search of gold mines.

The mutineers separated with gloomy faces; they were by no means satisfied with Laudonnière's answer, and the discontent was as deep as ever. Laudonnière now again became very ill and the malcontents had it all their own way. Soon nearly every one in the fort was on their side, and they resolved to put an end to Laudonnière's tyranny.

Late one night about twenty men all armed to the teeth gathered together and marched to Laudonnière's hut. Arrived there they beat loudly on the door demanding entrance. But Laudonnière and his few remaining friends knew well what this loud summons meant, and they refused to open the door. The mutineers, however, were not to be easily held back; they forced open the door, wounding one man who tried to hinder them, and in a few minutes with drawn swords in hand, and angry scowls on their faces, they crowded round the sick man's bed. Then holding a gun at his throat they commanded him to give them leave to set forth for Spanish waters. But the stern old Huguenot knew no fear. Even with the muzzle of the gun against his throat he refused to listen to the demands of the lawless crew.

His calmness drove them to fury. With terrible threats, and more terrible oaths, they dragged him from his bed. Loading him with fetters they carried him out of the fort, threw him into a boat and rowed him out to the ship which lay anchored in the river. All the loyal colonists had by this time been disarmed, and the fort was completely in the hands of the mutineers. Their leader then drew up a paper giving them leave to set forth to Spanish possessions. And this he commanded Laudonnière to sign.

Laudonnière was completely in the power of the mutineers. He was a prisoner and ill, but his spirit was unbroken, and he refused to sign. Then the mutineers sent him a message saying that if he did not sign they would come on board the ship and cut his throat. So, seeing no help for it, Laudonnière signed.

The mutineers were now greatly delighted at the success of their schemes. They made haste to finish the two little ships which they had been building, and on the 8th of December they set sail. As they went they flung taunts at those who stayed behind, calling them fools and dolts and other scornful names, and threatening them with all manner of punishments should they refuse them free entrance to the fort on their return.

As soon as the mutineers were gone Laudonnière's friends rowed out to him, set him free from his fetters, and brought him back to the colony.

They were now but a very small company, but they were at peace with each other, and there was plenty to do. So the weeks went quickly by. They finished the fort, and began to build two new ships to take the place of those which the mutineers had stolen. But they never thought of tilling the ground and sowing seed to provide bread for the future. Thus more than three months passed. Then one day an Indian brought the news that a strange ship was in sight. Laudonnière at once sent some men to find out what ship this might be, and whether it was friend or foe.

It proved to be a Spanish vessel which the mutineers had captured and which

37

was now manned by them. But the mutineers who had sailed away full of pride and insolence now returned in very humble mood. Their buccaneering had not succeeded as they had hoped. They were starving, and instead of boldly demanding entrance, and putting in force their haughty threats, they were eager to make terms. But Laudonnière was not sure whether they really came in peace or not. So he sent out a little boat to the mutineers' ship. On the deck of it there was an officer with one or two men only. But below, thirty men, all armed to the teeth, were hidden. Seeing only these one or two men in the boat the mutineers let her come alongside. But what was their astonishment when armed men suddenly sprang from the bottom of the boat and swarmed over the sides of their vessel. Many of the mutineers were stupid with drink, all of them were weak with hunger, and before they could seize their arms, or make any resistance, they were overpowered and carried ashore.

There a court-martial was held, and four of the ringleaders were condemned to death. But these bold bad men were loath to die.

"Comrades," said one, turning to the loyal soldiers near, "will you stand by and see us die thus shamefully?"

"These," replied Laudonnière, sharply, "are no comrades of mutineers and rebels."

All appeals for mercy were in vain. So the men were shot and their bodies hanged on gibbets near the mouth of the river as a lesson to rebels.

After this there was peace for a time in Fort Caroline. But it soon became peace with misery, for the colony began to starve. The long-expected ship from France did not come. Rich and fertile land spread all round them, but the colonists had neither ploughed nor sown it. They trusted to France for all their food. Now for months no ships had come, and their supplies were utterly at an end.

So in ever increasing misery the days passed. Some crawled about the meadows and forest, digging for roots and gathering herbs. Others haunted the river bed in search of shell-fish. One man even gathered up all the fish bones he could find and ground them to powder to make bread. But all that they scraped together with so much pain and care was hardly enough to keep body and soul together. They grew so thin that their bones started through the skin. Gaunt, hollow-eyed spectres they lay about the fort sunk in misery, or dragged themselves a little way into the forest in search of food. Unless help came from France they knew that they must all soon die a miserable death. And amid all their misery they clung to that last hope, that help would come from France. So, however feeble they were, however faint with hunger, they would crawl in turns to the top of the hill above the fort straining their dimming eyes seaward. But no sail appeared.

At length they gave up all hope, and determined to leave the hated spot. They had the Spanish ship which the mutineers had captured, and another little vessel besides which they had built. But these were not enough to carry them all to France, so gathering all their last energy they began to build another boat. The hope of getting back to France seemed for a time to put a little strength into their famine stricken bodies. And while they worked Laudonnière sailed up the river in search of food. But he returned empty-handed. Famishing men cannot work, and soon the colonists began to weary of their labours.

The neighbouring Indians, too, who might have given them food, were now their enemies. They indeed now and again brought scant supplies of fish to the starving men. But they demanded so much for it that soon the colonists were bare of everything they had possessed. They bartered the very shirts from their backs for food. And if they complained of the heavy price the Indians laughed at them.

"If thou makest so great account of thy merchandise," they jeered, "eat it and we will eat our fish."

But summer passed. The grain began to ripen, and although the Indians sold it grudgingly the colony was relieved from utter misery for the time being.

But now fresh troubles arose, for the Frenchmen quarreled with the chief of the Thimagoes for whose sake they had already made enemies of Satouriona and his Indians.

Thinking themselves treated in an unfriendly manner by the Thimagoes the Frenchmen seized their chief, and kept him prisoner until the Indians promised to pay a ransom of large quantities of grain.

The Indians agreed only because they saw no other means of freeing their chief. They were furiously angry with the Frenchmen and, seething with indignation against them, they refused to pay an ounce of grain until their chief had been set free: and even then they would not bring it to Fort Caroline, but forced the Frenchmen to come for it. The Frenchmen went, but they very quickly saw that they were in great danger. For the village swarmed with armed warriors who greeted the colonists with scowls of deepest hatred. After a few days, therefore, although only a small portion of the ransom had been paid, the Frenchmen decided to make for home as fast as possible.

It was a hot July morning on which they set off. Each man besides his gun carried a sack of grain, so the progress was slow. They had not gone far beyond the village when a wild war whoop was heard. It was immediately followed by a shower of arrows. The Frenchmen replied with a hot fire of bullets. Several of the Indians fell dead, and the rest fled howling into the forest.

Then the Frenchmen marched on again. But they had scarcely gone a quarter of a mile when another war whoop was heard in front. It was answered from behind, and the Frenchmen knew themselves surrounded. But they stood their ground bravely. Dropping their bags of corn they seized their guns. A sharp encounter followed, and soon the Indians fled again into the forest. But again and again they returned to the attack, and the Frenchmen had to fight every yard of the way. At nine o'clock the fight began, and the sun was setting when at length the Indians gave up the pursuit. When the Frenchmen reached their boats they counted their losses. Two had been killed, and twenty-two injured, some of them so badly that they had to be carried on board the boats. Of all the bags of grain with which they had started out only two remained. It was a miserable ending to the expedition.

The plight of the colony was now worse than ever. The two sacks of grain were soon consumed; the feeble efforts at building a ship had come to nothing. But rather than stay longer the colonists resolved to crowd into the two small vessels they had, and sail homeward if only they could gather food enough for the voyage. But where to get that food none knew.

One day full of troubled, anxious thoughts Laudonnière climbed the hill and looked seaward. Suddenly he saw something which made his heart beat fast, and brought the colour to his wasted cheeks. A great ship, its sails gleaming white in the sunlight was making for the mouth of the river. As he gazed another and still another ship hove in sight. Thrilling with excitement Laudonnière sent a messenger down to the fort with all speed to tell the news, and when they heard it the men who had seemed scarce able to crawl arose and danced for joy. They laughed, and wept, and cried aloud, till it seemed as if joy had bereft them of their wits.

But soon fear mingled with their joy. There was something not altogether familiar about the cut and rig of the ships. Were they really the long-looked-for ships from France, or did they belong to their deadly and hated enemies, the Spaniards? They were neither one nor the other. That little fleet was English, under command of the famous admiral, John Hawkins, in search of fresh water of which they stood much in need. The English Admiral at once showed himself friendly. To prove that he came with no evil intent he landed with many of his officers gaily clad, and wearing no arms. The famine-stricken colonists hailed him with delight, for it seemed to them that he came as a deliverer.

Gravely and kindly Hawkins listened to the tale of misery, yet he was glad enough when he heard that the Frenchmen had decided to leave Florida, for he wanted to claim it for Queen Elizabeth and England. When, however, he saw the ships in which they meant to sail homewards he shook his head. "It was not possible," he said, "for so many souls to cross the broad Atlantic in those tiny barques." So he offered to give all the Frenchmen a free passage to France in his own ships. This Laudonnière refused. Then Hawkins offered to lend him, or sell him, one of his ships. Even this kindness Laudonnière hesitated to accept.

Thereupon there arose a great uproar among the colonists, they crowded round him clamouring to be gone, threatening that if he refused the Englishman's offer they would accept it and sail without him.

So Laudonnière yielded. He told Hawkins that he would buy the ship he offered, but he had no money. The Englishman, however, was generous. Instead of money he took the cannon and other things now useless to the colonists. He provided them with food enough for the voyage, and seeing many of the men ragged and barefoot, added among other things fifty pairs of shoes.

Then with kindly good wishes Hawkins said farewell and sailed away, leaving behind him many grateful hearts. As soon as he was gone the Frenchmen began to prepare to depart also. In a few days all was ready, and they only waited for a fair wind in order to set sail. But as they waited, one day, the fort was again thrown into a state of excitement by the appearance of another fleet of ships. Again the question was asked, were they friends or foes, Spaniards or Frenchmen?

40

At length, after hours of sickening suspense, the question was answered, they were Frenchmen under the command of Ribaut.

The long-looked-for help had come at last. It had come when it was no longer looked for, when it was indeed unwelcome to many. For the colonists had grown utterly weary of that sunlit cruel land, and they only longed to go home. France with any amount of tyranny was to be preferred before the freedom and the misery of Florida.

But to abandon the colony was now impossible, for besides supplies of food the French ships had brought many new colonists. This time, too, the men had not come alone but had brought their wives and families with them. Soon the fort which had been so silent and mournful was filled with sounds of talk and laughter. Again, the noise of hatchet and hammer resounded through the woods, and the little forsaken corner of the world awoke once more to life.

Chapter 9 - How the Spaniards Drove the French Out of Florida

Scarcely a week had passed before the new peace and happiness of the French colony was brought to a cruel end.

Late one night the men on board the French ships saw a great black hulk loom silently up out of the darkness. It was followed by another and another. No word was spoken, and in eerie silence the strange ships crept stealthily onwards, and cast anchor beside the French. The stillness grew terrible. At length it was broken by a trumpet call from the deck of one of the silent new-comers.

Then a voice came through the darkness. "Gentlemen," it asked, "whence does this fleet come?"

"From France," was the reply.

"What are you doing here?" was the next question.

"We are bringing soldiers and supplies for a fort which the King of France has in this country, and for many which he soon will have."

"Are you Catholics or Lutherans?"

The question came sharply across the dark water. It was answered by many voices.

"We are Lutherans," cried the French, "we are of the new religion."

Then it was the Frenchmen's turn to ask questions.

"Who are you," I they cried, "and whence come ye?"

"I am Pedro Menendez," replied the voice out of the darkness. "I am Admiral of the fleet of the King of Spain. And I am come into this country to hang and behead all Lutherans whom I may find by land or by sea. And my King has given me such strict commands that I have power to pardon no man of them. And those commands I shall obey to the letter, as you will see. At dawn I shall come aboard your ship. And if there I find any Catholic he shall be well-treated, but every heretic shall die."

In reply to this speech a shout of wrath went up from the Frenchmen.

"If You are a brave man," they cried, "why wait for dawn? Come on now, and see what you will get."

Then in their anger they heaped insults upon the Spaniards, and poured forth torrents of scoffing words. Thereupon Menendez was so enraged that he swore to silence those Lutheran dogs once and for ever. So the order was given, and his great ship slowly moved towards the French.

The threats of the French had been but idle boasting; they could not withstand the Spaniards, for their leader was ashore with most of his soldiers. So cutting their cables they fled out to sea pursued by the foe.

There was a mad chase through the darkness. But the heretic devils, as the Spaniards called them, were skilful sailors. Menendez could not catch them, and when day dawned he gave up the chase and moodily turned back to Fort Caroline.

Here he found the French ready for him, and they seemed so strong that he would not attack, but sailed away southwards until he reached the river of Dolphins.

Here Menendez landed and took possession of the country in the name of the King of Spain. While cannon boomed and trumpets blew he stepped on shore followed by his officers and gentlemen. In all the gay trappings of knighthood, with many-coloured banners fluttering in the breeze, they marched. Then as they advanced another procession came toward them. At the head of it was a priest in all the pomp and splendour of his priestly robes. He carried a gilded crucifix in his hand, and as he marched he sang a Te Deum.

When the two processions met Menendez and all his company knelt, and baring their heads kissed the crucifix. So was the land claimed for Spain and the Catholic faith, and St. Augustine, the oldest town in the United States, was founded.

Meanwhile, the fleeing French ships had turned, followed the Spaniards, and seen them land. Then they went back to Fort Caroline with the news.

While these things had been happening Laudonnière had been very ill. He was still in bed when Ribaut, followed by several of his chief officers, came to his room to tell him the news which the returning ships had just brought. And beside his sickbed they held a council of war. It was decided to attack the Spaniards and drive them from the land. But how?

First one plan and then another was discussed, and to each some one objected. But at length it was decided to go by sea and attack the Spaniards suddenly in their newly-founded fort.

So almost every man who could hold a gun set forth with Ribaut, and Laudonnière was left in the fort with the feeble and sick, and scarcely a man besides who had ever drawn a sword or fired a shot. Their leader was as sick and feeble as any of them. But he dragged himself from his bed to review his forces. They were poor indeed, but Laudonnière made the best of them. He appointed each man to a certain duty, he set a, watch night and day, and he began to repair the broken-down walls of the fort, so that they would be able to make some show of resistance in ease of attack.

While Laudonnière was thus ordering his poor little garrison the ships carrying the rest of the colonists sailed on their way. The wind was fair, and in the night they crept close to where the

Spanish vessels lay.

But when day dawned and the Spaniards saw the French vessels close to them they fled to the shelter of their harbour. And a sudden storm arising the French were driven out to sea again.

As Menendez watched them from the shore he rejoiced. He knew by the number of the ships that most of the French colonists must be in them, and he hoped that they would all be lost in the storm.

Then as he watched a sudden thought came to him. While the Frenchmen were battling with wind and waves he resolved to move quickly over land and take Fort Caroline. For he knew that it must be almost, if not quite, unprotected.

One of the French mutineers who had deserted Laudonnière was now in the Spanish fort. He would show the way. Full of this splendid idea, eager to carry it out at once, he ordered Mass to be said, then he called a council and laid his plan before his officers. They, however, met his eagerness with coldness. It was a mad and hopeless plan, they thought, and they did their best to dissuade Menendez from it. But Menendez was determined to go.

"Comrades," he said, "it is now that we must show our courage and our zeal. This is God's war, and we must not turn our backs upon it. It is war against heretics, and we must wage it with blood and with fire."

But the Spanish leader's eager words awoke no response in the hearts of his hearers. They answered him only with mutterings. Still Menendez insisted. The debate grew stormy, and angry words were flung this way and that.

At length, however, Menendez had his way. The clamour was stilled, the officers gave a grudging consent, and preparations for the march were begun. In a few days all was ready, and the expedition set out. It was a simple matter. There was no great train of sumpter mules or baggage wagons. Each man carried his own food and ammunition, and twenty axemen marched in front of the little army to cleave a way through the forest.

The storm still raged. Rain fell in torrents, and the wind howled ceaselessly as on and on the men trudged. They plunged through seas of mud, and grass which grew waist high, and threaded their way along the narrow paths cloven for them by the axemen.

So for three days they toiled onward. Their food was gone, their ammunition soaked, they were drenched to the skin, footsore and famishing, when upon the third night they lay down upon the muddy ground, cursing their leader for having brought them forth to died thus miserably. But while the men cursed Menendez prayed. All night he prayed. And before day dawned he called his officers to a council. They were now within a mile of Fort Caroline, and he was eager to attack.

But his officers were sick of the whole business. The men were utterly disheartened; one and all they clamoured to return.

Yet once again Menendez bent them to his will. In the darkness of the forest he spoke to the wretched, shivering, rain-drenched men. He taunted, he persuaded, and at length wrung from them a sullen consent to follow him.

43

So once again the miserable march was begun, and when day dawned they stood on the hill above the fort .

No sound came from it, no watchman stood upon the ramparts. For towards morning, seeing that it rained harder than ever, the captain of the guard had sent his men to bed, for they were soaked to the skin and he was sorry for them. In such rain and wind what enemy would venture forth? he asked himself. It was folly to stay abroad on such a night he thought. So he dismissed the guard, and went off to bed.

Thus none heard or saw the approach of the Spaniards. Then suddenly the silence of the dawn was broken with fierce war cries.

"At them," shouted the Spaniards, "God is with us!"

The sleeping Frenchmen started from their beds in terror. Half naked they sprang to arms. On every side the Spaniards poured in. The dim light of dawn showed the dark cruel faces, and the gleam of drawn swords. Then clash of steel, screams of frightened women and children, curses, prayers, all mingled together in terrible confusion.

At the first alarm Laudonnière sprang from his bed, and seizing his sword called his men to follow him. But the Spaniards surrounded him, his men were slain and scattered, and he himself was forced back into the yard of his house. Here there was a tent. This stopped his pursuers, for they stumbled over the cordage and became entangled with it. The confusion gave Laudonnière a few minutes' respite in which he escaped through a breach in the ramparts, and took refuge in the forest. A few others fleeing this way and that escaped likewise. But some, the first moment of terror past, resolved to return and throw themselves on the mercy of the Spaniards rather than face starvation in the woods.

"They are men" said one; "it may be when their fury is spent they will spare our lives. Even if they slay us what of that? It is but a moment's pain. Better that than to starve here in the woods or be torn to pieces by wild beasts."

Still some held back, but most agreed to throw themselves upon the mercy of the Spaniards.

So unarmed and almost naked as they were, they turned back to give themselves up. But little did these simple Frenchmen understand the fury of the foe. When they neared the fort the Spaniards rushed out upon them and, unheeding their cries for mercy, slew them to a man. Those who had held back, when they saw the fate of their companions, fled through the forest. Some sought refuge among the Indians. But even from that refuge the Spaniards hunted them forth and slew them without pity. Thus the land was filled with bloodshed and ruin. Many were slain at once by the sword, others were hanged on trees round the fort, and over them Menendez wrote, "I do this not as to Frenchmen but as to Lutherans." Only a few miserable stragglers, after untold sufferings, reached the little ship which still lay at anchor in the river. Among these was Laudonnière.

Their one desire now was to flee homewards, and unfurling their sails they set out for France.

The colony of Fort Caroline was wiped out, and rejoicing at the success of his bold scheme, Menendez marched back to St. Augustine where a Te Deum was sung in honour of this victory over heretics.

Meanwhile the Frenchmen who had set forth to attack St. Augustine by sea had been driven hither and thither by the storm, and at length were wrecked. But although the ships were lost all, or nearly all, of the men succeeded in reaching the shore in safety. And not knowing what had happened at Fort Caroline they set out in two companies to try to reach the fort by land.

But they never reached the fort. For one morning scarcely ten days after the destruction of Fort Caroline some Indians came to Menendez with the news that they had seen a French ship wrecked a little to the south.

The news delighted Menendez, and he at once set out to capture the shipwrecked men. It was not long before he saw the lights of the French camp in the distance. But on coming nearer it was seen that they were on the other side of an arm of the sea, so that it was impossible to reach them. Hiding, therefore, in the bushes by the water's edge Menendez and his men watched the Frenchmen on the other side. The Spaniards soon saw that their enemies were in distress. They suspected that they were starving, for they could be seen walking up and down the shore seeking shellfish. But Menendez wanted to make sure of the state they were in, and he made up his mind to get nearer to the Frenchmen. So he put off his fine clothes, and dressing himself like a common sailor, got into a boat and rowed across the water.

Seeing him come one of the Frenchmen swam out to meet him. As he drew near Menendez called out to him: "Who are you, and whence come ye?"

"We are followers of Ribaut, Viceroy of the King of France," answered the Frenchman."

"Are you Catholics or Lutherans?" asked Menendez.

"We are Lutherans," answered the man.

Then after a little more talk Menendez told who he was.

With this news the man swam back to his companions. But he soon returned to the boat to say that five of the French leaders wished to speak with the Spanish leader, and begged for safe conduct to his camp.

To this Menendez readily agreed, and returning to his own side he sent the boat back to bring the Frenchmen over.

When they landed Menendez received them courteously. And after returning his ceremonious greetings the Frenchmen begged the Spaniards to lend them a boat so that they might cross the river which lay between them and Fort Caroline.

At this request Menendez smiled evilly. "Gentlemen," he said, "it were idle for you to go to your fort. It has been taken, and every man is slain."

But the Frenchmen could not at first believe that he spoke the truth. So in proof of his words the Spanish leader bade his men show the heretics the plunder which had been taken from their fort. As they looked upon it the hearts of the Frenchmen sank.

Then ordering breakfast to be sent to them Menendez left them, and went to breakfast with his own officers.

45

Breakfast over he came back to the Frenchmen, and as he looked at their gloomy faces his heart rejoiced. "Do you believe now," he asked, "that what I told you is true?"

"Yes," replied the Frenchmen, "we believe. It would be useless now to go to the fort. All we ask of you is to lend us ships so that we may return home."

"I would gladly do so," replied Menendez, "if you were Catholics, and if I had ships. But I have none."

Then seeing that he would give them no help to reach home, the Frenchmen begged Menendez at least to let them stay with his people until help came to them from France. It was little enough to ask, they thought, as France and Spain were at peace. But there was no pity or kindliness in the Spanish general's heart.

"All Catholics," he replied sternly, "I would defend and succour. But as for you, you are Lutherans, and I must hold you as enemies. I will wage war against you with blood and fire. I will wage it fiercely, both by land and sea, for I am Viceroy for my King in this country. I am here to plant the holy Gospel in this land , that the Indians may come to the light and knowledge of the Holy Catholic, faith of our Lord Jesus Christ, as taught by the Roman Church. Give up your banners and your arms, and throw yourselves on my mercy, and I will do with you as God gives me grace. In no other way can you have truce or friendship with me."

To this the Frenchmen knew not what to say. First they consulted together, then some of them went back across the water to take counsel with those who waited there. They talked long, and anxiously those on the Spanish side awaited their return. At length one of their messengers returned, and going to Menendez he offered him a large sum of money if he would swear to spare their lives.

But Menendez would promise nothing. The Frenchmen were helpless. They were starving and in his hands. And both he and they knew it. They saw no hope anywhere, so they yielded to the Spanish general's demands.

Once more the boat was sent across the water, and this time it came back laden with banners, arms and armour. Then guarded by Spanish soldiers the Frenchmen were brought across by tons. As each batch landed they found themselves prisoners; their arms were taken from them and their hands were tied behind their backs.

All day, hour after hour, the boat plied to and fro: and when all the Frenchmen had been brought over they were ordered to march forward. The Spanish general walked in front. But he did not go far, for the sun was already setting, and it was time to camp for the night. So but a little way from the shore he stopped, and drew a line in the sand. And when the wretched Frenchmen reached that line, weaponless and helpless as they were, they were one and all put to death. Then, glorying in his deed, Menendez returned to St. Augustine.

But he had not yet completely wiped out the French colony. For besides those he had so ruthlessly slain there was another large party under Ribaut, who, ignorant of all that had happened, were still slowly making their way to Fort Caroline. But again news of their whereabouts was brought to Menendez by

Indians, and again he set off to waylay them.

He found them on the same spot as he had found the first party. But this time the Frenchmen had made a raft, and upon this they were preparing to cross the water when the Spaniards came upon them. The Frenchmen were in such misery that many of them greeted the appearance of their enemies with joy. But others were filled with misgiving. Still they resolved to try to make terms with the Spaniards. So first one of his officers, and then Ribaut himself, rowed across the strip of water to parley with the Spanish leader. They found him as pitiless as their companions had found him. And seeing that they could make no terms with him many of the Frenchmen refused to give themselves up, and they marched away. But after much parleying, and many comings and goings across the river, Ribaut, believing that Menendez would spare their lives, yielded up himself and the rest of his company to the Spaniards.

He was soon undeceived. For he was led away among the bushes, and his hands were tied behind his back. As his followers came over they, too, were bound and led away. Then as trumpets blew and drums beat the Spaniards fell upon their helpless prisoners and slew them to a man.

When Ribaut saw that his hour was come he did not flinch. "We are but dust," he said, "and to dust we must return: twenty years more or less can matter little." So with the words of a psalm upon his lips he met the swordthrust.

Not till every man lay dead was the fury of the Spaniards sated. Then, his horrible labour ended, Menendez returned once more in triumph to his fort.

Those of the French who had refused to give themselves up to Menendez now wandered back to the shore where their ship had been wrecked. Out of the broken pieces they tried to build a ship in which they might sail homeward. But again news of their doings was brought to Menendez by the Indians. And again he set out to crush them. When the Frenchmen saw the Spaniards come they fled in terror. But Menendez sent a messenger after them promising that if they yielded to him he would spare their lives. Most Of them yielded. And Menendez kept his promise. He treated his prisoners well. But, when an opportunity arrived, he sent them home to end their lives as galley slaves.

Chapter 10 - How a Frenchman Avenged the Death of His Countrymen

When the news of these terrible massacres reached France it was greeted with a cry of horror. Even the boy King, Charles IX, Catholic though he was, demanded redress. But the King of Spain declared that the Frenchmen had been justly served. The land upon which they had settled was his, he said, and they had no right to be there. He was sorry that they were Frenchmen, but they were also pirates and robbers, and had received only the just reward of their misdeeds.

Neither Charles nor his mother, who was the real ruler in France at this time, wished to quarrel with the King of Spain. So finding that no persuasions would move him, and that instead of being punished Menendez was praised and rewarded, they let the matter drop.

But there was one man in France who would not thus tamely submit to the tyranny of Spain. His name was Dominique de Gourges. He hated the Spaniards with a deadly hatred. And when he heard of the Florida massacre he vowed to avenge the death of his countrymen. He sold all that he had, borrowed what money he could, and with three ships and a goodly company of soldiers and sailors set sail.

At first, however, he kept, his real object secret. Instead of steering straight for Florida he steered southward, making believe that he was going to Africa for slaves. But after encountering storms and contrary winds he turned westward, and when off the coast of Cuba he gathered all his men together and told them what he had set out to do.

In vivid, terrible words he recounted to them the horrible slaughter. "Shall we let such cruelty go unpunished?" he asked. "What fame for us if we avenge it! To this end I have given my fortune, and I counted on you to help me. Was I wrong?"

"No," they all cried, "we will go with you to avenge our countrymen!"

So with hearts filled with thoughts of vengeance they sailed onward to Fort Caroline.

The Spaniards had repaired the fort and now called it Fort Mateo. They had also built two small forts nearer the mouth of the river to guard the entrance to it. Now one afternoon the men in these forts saw three ships go sailing by. These were the French ships bringing Gourges and his companions. But the men in the forts thought that they were Spanish ships and therefore fired a salute. Gourges did not undeceive them. He fired a salute in reply and, sailing on as if he were going elsewhere, was soon lost to sight.

At length, having found a. convenient place out of sight of the forts, he drew to the shore. But when he would have landed he saw that the whole beach was crowded with savages armed with bows and arrows and ready for war. For the Indians, too, had taken the strange ships to be Spanish. And as they had grown to hate the Spaniards with a deadly hatred they were prepared to withstand their landing.

Fortunately, however, Gourges had on board a trumpeter who had been in Florida with Laudonnière. So now he sent him on shore to talk with the Indians. And as soon as they recognised him they greeted him with shouts of joy. Then they led him at once to their chief who was no other than Satouriona, Laudonnière's one-time friend.

So amid great rejoicings the Frenchmen landed. Then Satouriona. poured into their ears the tale of his wrongs. He told them how the Spaniards stole their corn, drove them from their huts and their hunting grounds, and generally ill-treated them. "Not one peaceful day," he said, "have the Indians known since the Frenchmen went away."

When Gourges heard this he was well pleased. "If you have been ill-treated by the Spaniards," he said, "the French will avenge you."

At this Satouriona, leaped for joy.

"What!" he cried, "will you fight the Spaniards?"

48

"Yes," replied Gourges, "but you must do your part also."

"We will die with you," cried Satouriona, "if need be."

"That is well," said Gourges. "How soon can you be ready? For if we fight we should fight at once."

"In three days we can be ready," said the Indian.

"See to it then," said Gourges, "that you are secret in the matter so that the Spaniards suspect nothing."

"Have no fear," replied Satouriona; "we wish them more ill than you do."

The third day came and, true to his word, Satouriona appeared surrounded by hundreds of warriors, fearful in paint and feathers. Then some by water, some by land, the French and Indians set forth, and after many hardships and much toil they reached one of the forts which the Spaniards had built near the river Is mouth. From the shelter of the surrounding trees they gazed upon it.

"There!" cried Gourges, "there at last are the thieves who have stolen this land from our King. There are the murderers who slew our countrymen."

At his words the men were hardly to be restrained. In eager whispers they begged to be led on. So the word was given, and the Frenchmen rushed upon the fort.

The Spaniards had just finished their mid-day meal when a cry was heard from the ramparts. "To arms! to arms! the French are coming!"

They were taken quite unawares, and with but short resistance they fled. The French and Indians pursued them and hemmed them in so that not one man escaped. In like manner the second fort was also taken, and every man slain or made prisoner.

The next day was Sunday, and Gourges spent it resting, and making preparations to attack Fort Mateo.

When the Spaniards in Fort Mateo saw the French and their great host of yelling, dancing Indians they were filled with fear. And in order to find out how strong the force really was one of them dressed himself as an Indian and crept within the French lines. But almost at once he was seen by a young Indian chief. And his disguise being thus discovered he was seized and questioned. He owned that there were scarce three hundred men in the fort and that, believing the French to number at least two-thousand, they were completely terror-stricken. This news delighted Gourges, and next morning he prepared to attack.

The fort was easily taken. When the Spaniards saw the French attack, panic seized them and they fled into the forest. But there the Indians, mad with the desire of blood and vengeance, met them. Many fell before the tomahawks; others turned back choosing rather to die at the hands of the French than of the Indians. But which way they turned there was no escape. Nearly all were slain, a few only were taken prisoner.

When the fight was over Gourges brought all the prisoners from the three forts together. He led them to the trees where Menendez had hanged the Frenchmen a few months before. There he spoke to them.

"Did you think that such foul treachery, such, abominable cruelty would go

49

unpunished?" he said. "Nay, I, one of the most lowly of my King's subjects, have taken upon myself to avenge it. There is no name shameful enough with which to brand your deeds, no punishment severe enough to repay them. But though you cannot be made to suffer as you deserve you shall suffer all that an enemy may honourably inflict. Thus your fate shall be an example to teach others to keep the peace and friendly alliance, which you have broken so wickedly."

And having spoken thus sternly to the trembling wretches Gourges ordered his men to hang them on the very same trees upon which Menendez had hanged the Frenchmen. And over their heads he nailed tablets of wood upon which were burned the words "Not as Spaniards or as Mariners, but as Traitors, Robbers and Murderers."

Then at length the vengeance of Gourges was satisfied. But indeed it was scarce complete, for Menendez the chief over and leader of the Spaniards was safe in Europe, and beyond the reach of any private man's vengeance. The Spaniards, too, were strongly entrenched at St. Augustine, so strongly indeed that Gourges knew he had not force enough to oust them. He had not even men enough to keep the three forts he had won. So he resolved to destroy them.

This delighted the Indians, and they worked with such vigour that in one day all three forts were made level with the ground. Then, having accomplished all that he had come to do, Gourges made ready to depart. Whereupon the Indians set up a wail of grief. With tears they begged the Frenchmen to stay, and when they refused they followed them all the way to the shore, praising them and giving them gifts, and praying them to return.

So leaving the savages weeping upon the shore the Frenchmen sailed away, and little more than a month later they reached home.

When they heard of what Gourges had done the Huguenots rejoiced, and they greeted him with honour and praise. But Philip of Spain was furiously angry. He demanded that Gourges should be punished, and offered a large sum of money for his head. King Charles, too, being in fear of the King of Spain, looked upon him coldly, so that for a time he was obliged to flee away and hide himself.

Gourges had used all his money to set forth on his expedition, so for a few years he lived in poverty. But Queen Elizabeth at length heard of him and his deeds. And as she, too, hated the Spaniards she was pleased at what he had done, and she asked him to enter her service. Thus at length he was restored to honour and favour. And in honour and favour he continued all the rest of his life.

Chapter 11 - The Adventures of Sir Humphrey Gilbert

The terrible disasters in Florida did not altogether stop French adventurers from going to the New World. But to avoid conflict with Spain they sailed henceforth more to the northern shores of erica, and endeavoured to found colonies there. This made. Englishmen angry. For by right of Cabot's voyages they claimed all America. from Florida to Newfoundland, which, says a writer in the time of Queen Elizabeth, "they bought and annexed unto the crowne of England." The English, therefore, looked upon the French as interlopers and usurpers. The

French, however, paid little attention to the English claims. They explored the country, named mountains, rivers, capes, and bays, and planted colonies where they liked. Thus began the long two hundred years' struggle between the French and English for possession of North America.

The French had already planted a colony on the St. Lawrence when an Englishman, Sir Humphrey Gilbert, determined also to plant one in North America.

He was the first Englishman ever to attempt to found a colony in America. Many Englishmen had indeed sailed there before him. But they had only gone in quest of gold and of adventures, and without any thought of founding a New England across the seas. This now, with Queen Elizabeth's permission, was what Sir Humphrey hoped to do.

He set out with a little fleet of five ships. One of these was called the Raleigh, and had been fitted out by the famous Sir Walter Raleigh who was Gilbert's step-brother. Walter Raleigh, no doubt, would gladly have gone with the company himself. But he was at the time in high favour with Good Queen Bess, and she forbade him to go on any such dangerous expedition. So he had to content himself with helping to fit out expeditions for other people.

The Raleigh was the largest ship of the little fleet, and Sir Walter spared no cost in fitting it Out. But before they had been two days at sea the Captain of the Raleigh and many of his men fell ill. This so greatly discouraged them that they turned back to Plymouth.

Sir Humphrey was sad indeed at the loss of the largest and best-fitted ship of his expedition, but he held on his way undaunted. They had a troublous passage. Contrary winds, fogs and icebergs delayed them. In a fog two of the ships named the Swallow and the Squirrel separated from the others. But still Sir Humphrey sailed on.

At length land came in sight. But it was a barren, unfriendly coast, "nothing but hideous rocks and mountains, bare of trees, and void of any green herbs," says one who went with the expedition. And seeing it so uninviting they sailed southward along the coast, looking for a fairer land.

And now to their great joy they fell in again with the Swallow. The men in the Swallow were glad, too, to see the Golden Hind and the Delight once more. They threw their caps into the air and shouted aloud for joy.

Soon after the re-appearance of the Swallow the Squirrel also turned up, so the four ships were together again. Together they sailed into the harbour of St. John's in Newfoundland. Here they found fishermen from all countries. For Newfoundland had by this time become famous as a fishing-ground, and every summer ships from all countries went there to fish.

Sir Humphrey, armed as he was with a commission from Queen Elizabeth, was received with all honour and courtesy by these people. And on Monday, August 5th, 1583, he landed and solemnly took possession of the country for two hundred leagues north, south, east and west, in the name of England's Queen.

First his commission was read aloud and interpreted to those of foreign lands

51

who were there. Then one of Sir Humphrey's followers brought him a twig of a hazel tree and a sod of earth, and put them into his hands, as a sign that he took possession of the land and all that was in it. Then proclamation was made that these lands belonged to her Majesty Queen Elizabeth of England by the Grace of God. "And if any person shall utter words sounding to the dishonour of her Majesty, he shall lose his ears, and have his ship and goods confiscated." The arms of England, engraved on lead and fixed to a pillar of wood, were then set up, and after prayer to God the ceremony came to an end. Thus Newfoundland became an English possession, and by right of Sir Humphrey Gilbert's claims it is the oldest colony of the British Empire.

Sir Humphrey Gilbert had taken possession of the land. But it soon became plain that it would be impossible to found a colony with the wild riff-raff of the sea of which his company was formed. Troubles began at once. A few indeed went about their business quietly, but others spent their time in plotting mischief. They had no desire to stay in that far country; so some hid in the woods waiting a chance to steal away in one or other of the ships which were daily sailing homeward laden with fish. Others more bold plotted to steal one of Sir Humphrey's ships and sail home without him. But their plot was discovered. They, however, succeeded in stealing a ship belonging to some other adventurers. It was laden with fish and ready to depart homeward. In this they sailed away leaving its owners behind.

The rest of Sir Humphrey's men now clamoured more than ever to be taken home. And at length he yielded to them. But the company was now much smaller than when he set out. For besides those who had stolen away, many had died and many more were sick. There were not enough men to man all four ships. So the Swallow was left with the sick and a few colonists who wished to remain, and in the other three Sir Humphrey put to sea with the rest of his company.

He did not, however, sail straight homeward. For he wanted to explore still further, and find, if he could, an island to the south which he had heard was very fertile. But the weather was stormy, and before they had gone far the Delight was wrecked, and nearly all on board were lost.

"This was a heavy and grievous event, to lose at one blow our chief ship freighted with great provision, gathered together with much travail, care, long time, and difficulty. But more was the loss of our men to the number almost of a hundred souls." So wrote Master Edward Hay who commanded the Golden Hind, and who afterwards wrote the story of the expedition.

After this "heavy chance" the two ships that remained beat up and down tacking with the wind, Sir Humphrey hoping always that the weather would clear up and allow him once more to get near land. But day by day passed. The wind and waves continued as stormy as ever, and no glimpse of land did the weary sailors catch.

It was bitterly cold, food was growing scarce, and day by day the men lost courage. At length they prayed Sir Humphrey to leave his search and return homeward. Sir Humphrey had no wish to go, but seeing his men shivering and hungry he felt sorry for them, and resolved to do as they wished.

"Be content," he said. "We have seen enough. If God send us safe home we will set forth again next spring."

So the course was changed, and the ships turned eastward. "The wind was large for England," says Hay, "but very high, and the sea, rough." It was so rough that the Squirrel in which Sir Humphrey sailed was almost swallowed up. For the Squirrel was only a tiny frigate of ten tons. And seeing it battered to and fro, and in danger of sinking every moment, the captain of the Golden Hind and many others prayed Sir Humphrey to leave it and come aboard their boat. But Sir Humphrey would not.

"I will not forsake my little company going homeward,' he said. "For I have passed through many storms and perils with them."

No persuasions could move him, so the captain of the Golden Hind was fain to let him have his way. One afternoon in September those in the Golden Hind watched the little Squirrel anxiously as it tossed up and down among the waves. But Sir Humphrey seemed not a whit disturbed. He sat in the stern calmly reading. And seeing the anxious faces of his friends he cheerfully waved his hand to them.

"We are as near to heaven by sea as by land," he called, through the roar of waves.

Then the sun went down. Darkness fell over the wild sea, and the ships could only know each other's whereabouts by the tossing lights.

Suddenly to the men on the Golden Hind it seemed as if the lights of the little frigate went out. Immediately the watch cried out that the frigate was lost.

"It was too true. For in that moment the frigate was devoured and swallowed up by the sea."

Yet the men on the Golden Hind would not give up hope. All that night they kept watch, straining their eyes through the stormy darkness in the hope of catching sight of the frigate or of some of its crew. But morning came and there was no sign of it on all the wide waste of waters. Still they hoped, and all the way to England they hailed every small sail which came in sight, trusting still that it might be the Squirrel. But it never appeared. Of the five ships which set forth only the Golden Hind returned to tell the tale. And thus ended the first attempt to found an English colony in the New World.

Chapter 12 - About Sir Walter Raleigh's Adventures in the Golden West

The first attempt to found an English colony in America had been an utter failure. But the idea of founding a New England across the seas had now taken hold of Sir Humphrey's young step-brother, Walter Raleigh. And a few months after the return of the Golden Hind he received from the Queen a charter very much the same as his brother's. But although he got the Charter Raleigh himself could not sail to America, for Queen Elizabeth would not let him go. So again he had to content himself with sending other people.

It was on April 27th, 1584, that his expedition set out in two small ships. Raleigh knew some of the great Frenchmen of the day, and had heard of their attempt to found a colony in Florida. And in spite of the terrible fate of the Frenchmen he thought Florida would be an excellent place to found an English colony.

So Raleigh's ships made their way to Florida, and landed on Roanoke Island off the coast of what is now North Carolina. In those days of course there was no Carolina, and the Spaniards called the whole coast Florida right up to the shores of Newfoundland.

The Englishmen were delighted with Roanoke. It seemed to them a fertile, pleasant land, "the most plentiful, sweete, fruitfull and wholesome of all the worlde." So they at once took possession of it "in the right of the Queen's most excellent Majesty as rightful Queen and Princess of the same."

The natives, too, seemed friendly "and in their behaviour as mannerly and civil as any man of Europe." But the Pale-faces and the Redskins found it difficult to understand each other.

"What do you call this country?" asked an Englishman.

"Win gan da coa," answered the Indian.

So the Englishmen went home to tell of the wonderful country of Wingandacoe. But what the Indian had really said was "What fine clothes you have!"

However, the mistake did not matter much. For the Englishmen now changed the name of the land from whatever it had been to Virginia in honour of their Queen.

This first expedition to Roanoke was only for exploring, and after a little the adventurers sailed home again to tell of all that they had seen. But Raleigh was so pleased with the report of Roanoke Island which they brought home, to him that he at once began to make plans for founding a colony there. And the following April his ships, were ready and the expedition set out under his cousin, Sir Richard Grenville.

But now almost as soon as they landed troubles began with the Indians. One of them stole a silver cup, and as it was not returned the Englishmen in anger set fire to the corn-fields and destroyed them. This was a bad beginning. But the Englishmen had no knowledge yet of how cruel and revengeful the Redman could be. So it was with no misgivings that Sir Richard left a colony of over a hundred men in the country. And promising to return with fresh supplies in the following spring he sailed homeward.

The Governor of this colony was named Ralph Lane. He was wise and able, but he was soon beset with difficulties. He found that the place chosen for a colony was not a good one, For the harbour was bad, the coast dangerous, and many of the Indians were now unfriendly. So he set about exploring the country, and decided as soon as fresh supplies came from England to move to a better spot.

Spring came and passed, and no ships from England appeared. The men began to starve. And seeing this the Indians who had feared them before, now began to be scornful and taunt them.

"Your God is not a true god," they said, "or he would not leave you to starve."

They refused to sell the colonists food no matter what price was offered. Their

54

hatred of the English was so great indeed that they resolved to sow no corn in order that there should be no harvest; being ready to suffer hunger themselves if they might destroy the colony utterly.

As the days passed the Englishmen daily felt the pinch of hunger more and more. Then Lane divided his company into three, and sent each in a different direction so that they might gather roots and herbs and catch fish for themselves, and also keep a lookout for ships.

But things went from bad to worse; the savages grew daily bolder and more insolent, and the colonists lived constantly in dread of an attack from them.

At length, although he had tried hard to avoid it, Lane was forced to fight them. They were easily overcome, and fled to the woods. But Lane knew well that his advantage was only for the moment. Should help not come the colony would be wiped out. Then one day, about a week after the fight with the Indians, news was brought to Lane that a great fleet of twenty-three ships had appeared in the distance.

Were they friends, or were they foes? That was the great question. The English knew the terrible story of Fort Caroline. Were these Spanish ships? Fearing that they might be Ralph Lane looked to his defenses, and made ready to withstand the enemy, if enemy they proved to be, as bravely as might be.

But soon it was seen that their fears were needless, the ships were English, and two days later Sir Francis Drake anchored in the wretched little harbour.

Drake had not come on purpose to relieve the colony. He had been out on one of his marauding expeditions against the Spaniards. He had taken and sacked St. Domingo, Cartagena, and Fort St. Augustine. And now, sailing home in triumph, chance had brought him to Raleigh's colony at Roanoke. And when he saw the miserable condition of the colonists, and heard the tale of their hardships, he offered to take them all home to England. Or, he said, if they chose to remain he would leave them a ship and food and everything that was necessary to keep them from want until help should come.

Both Lane and his chief officers who were men of spirit wanted to stay. So they accepted Drake's offer of the loan of a ship, agreeing that after they had found a good place for a colony and a better harbour, they would go home to England and return again the next year.

Thus the matter was settled. Drake began to put provisions on board one of his ships for the use of the colony. The colonists on their side began writing letters to send home with Drake's ships. All was business and excitement. But in the midst of it a great storm arose. It lasted for four days and was so violent that most of Drake's ships were forced to put out to sea lest they should be dashed to pieces upon the shore.

Among the ships thus driven out to sea was that which Drake had promised to give Ralph Lane. And when the storm was over it was nowhere to be seen.

So Drake offered another ship to Lane. It was a large one, too large to get into the little harbour, but the only one he could spare. Lane was now doubtful what was best to do. Did it not seem as if by driving away their ship God had stretched

55

out His hand to take them from thence? Was the storm not meant as a sign to them?

So not being able to decide by himself what was best to do, Lane called his officers and gentlemen together, and asked advice of them.

They all begged him to go home. No help had come from Sir Richard Grenville, nor was it likely to come, for Drake had brought the news that war between Spain and England had been declared. They knew that at such a time every Englishman would bend all his energies to the defeat of Spain, and that Raleigh would have neither thoughts nor Money to spare for that far-off colony.

At length it was settled that they should all go home. In haste then the Englishmen got on board, for Drake, was anxious to be gone from the dangerous anchorage "which caused him more peril of wreck," says Ralph Lane, "than all his former most honourable actions against the Spaniards."

So on the 19th of June 1586, the colonists set sail and arrived in England some six weeks later. They brought with them two things which afterward proved to be of wit great importance. The first was tobacco. The use of it had been known ever since the days of Columbus, but it was now for the first time brought to England. The second was the potato. This Raleigh planted on his estates in Ireland, and to this day Ireland is one of the great potato growing countries of the world.

But meanwhile Raleigh had not forgotten his colonists, and scarce a week after they had sailed away, a ship arrived laden "with all manner of things in most plentiful manner for the supply and relief of his colony."

For some time the ship beat up and down the coast searching vainly for the colony. And at length finding no sign of it, it returned to England. About a fortnight later Sir Richard Grenville also arrived with three ships. To his astonishment when he reached Roanoke he saw no sign of the ship which he knew had sailed shortly before him. And to his still greater astonishment he found the colony deserted. Yet he could not believe that it had been abandoned. So he searched the country up and down in the hope of finding some of the colonists. But finding no trace of them he at length gave up the search and returned to the forsaken huts. And being unwilling to lose possession of the country, he determined to leave some of his men there. So fifteen men were left behind, well provided with everything necessary to keep them for two years. Then Sir Richard sailed homeward.

In spite of all these mischances Raleigh would not give up his great idea. And the following year he fitted out another expedition. This time there were a few women among the colonists, and John White, who had already been out with Lane, was chosen as Governor.

It was now decided to give up Roanoke which had proved such an unfortunate spot, and the new company of colonists was bound for Chesapeake Bay. But before they settled there they were told to go to Roanoke to pick up the fifteen men left by Sir Richard Grenville and take them to Chesapeake also.

When, however, they reached Roanoke the Master of the vessels, who was by birth a Spaniard, and who was perhaps in league with the Spanish, said that it was too late in the year to go seeking another spot. So whether they would or not he landed the colonists, and sailed away, leaving only one small boat with them.

Thus perforce they had to take up their abode in the old spot. They found it deserted. The fort was razed to the ground, and although the huts were still standing they were choked with weeds and overgrown with wild vines, while deer wandered in and out of the open doors. It was plain that for many months no man had lived there. And although careful search was made, saving the bones of one, no sign was found of the fifteen men left there by Sir Richard. At length the new colonists learned from a few friendly Indians that they had been traitorously set upon by hostile Indians. Most of them were slain; the others escaped in their boat and went no man knew whither.

The Englishmen were very angry when they heard that, and wanted to punish the Indians. So they set out against them. But the Indians fled at their coming, and the Englishmen by mistake killed some of the friendly Indians instead of their enemies. Thus things were made worse instead of better.

And now amid all these troubles on the 18th of August, 1587, a little girl was born. Her father was Ananias Dare, and her mother was the daughter of John White, the Governor. The little baby was thus the grand-daughter of the Governor, and because she was the first English child to be born in Virginia she was called Virginia.

But matters were not going well in the colony. Day by day the men were finding out things which were lacking and which they felt they must have if they were not all to perish. So a few days after Virginia was christened all the chief men came to the Governor and begged him to go back to England to get fresh supplies, and other things necessary to the life of the colony. John White, however, refused to go. The next day not only the men but the women also came to him and again begged him to go back to England. They begged so hard that at last the Governor consented to go.

All were agreed that the place they were now in was by no means the best which might be chosen for a colony, and it had been determined that they should move some fifty miles further inland. Now it was arranged that if they moved while the Governor was away they should carve on the trees and posts of the door the name of the place to which they had gone, so that on his return he might be able easily to find them. And also it was arranged that if they were in any trouble or distress they should carve a cross over the name.

All these matters being settled John White set forth. And it was with great content that the colonists saw their Governor go. For they knew that they could send home no better man to look after their welfare, and they were sure he would bring back the food and other things which were needed.

But when White arrived in England he found that no man, not even Raleigh, had a thought to spare for Virginia. For Spain was making ready all her mighty sea power to crush England. And the English were straining every nerve to meet and break that power. So John White had to wait with what patience he could. Often his heart was sick when he thought of his daughter and his little granddaughter, Virginia Dare, far away in that great unknown land across the sea. Often he longed to be back beside them. But his longings were of no avail. He could but wait. For every ship was seized by Government and pressed into the service of the country. And while the Spaniards were at the gate it was accounted treason for any Englishman to sail to western lands.

So the summer of 1588 passed, the autumn came, and at length the great Armada sailed from Spain. It sailed across the narrow seas in pride and splendour, haughtily certain of crushing the insolent sea dogs of England. But "God blew with His breath and they were scattered." Before many days were over these proud ships were fleeing before the storm, their sails torn, their masts splintered. They were shattered upon the rocky shores of Scotland and Ireland. They were swallowed by the deep.

The sea power of Spain was broken, and the history of America truly began. For as has been said "the defeat of the Invincible Armada was the opening event in the history of the United States."

Free now from the dread of Spain, ships could come and go without hindrance. But another year and more passed before John White succeeded in getting ships and provisions and setting out once more for Virginia.

It was for him an anxious voyage, but as he neared the place where the colony had been, his heart rejoiced, for he saw smoke rising from the land. It was dark, however, before they reached the spot, and seeing no lights save that of a huge fire far in the woods the Governor sounded a trumpet call. The notes of the trumpet rang through the woods and died away to silence. There was no answer. So the men called and called again, but still no answer came. Then with sinking heart John White bade them sing some well-known English songs. For that, he thought, would surely bring an answer from the shore.

So through the still night air the musical sound of men's voices rang out. But still no answer came from the silent fort. With a heart heavy as lead the Governor waited for the dawn. As soon as it was light he went ashore. The fort was deserted. Grass and weeds grew in the ruined houses. But upon a post "in fair capital letters" was carved the word "Croatoan." This was the name of a neighbouring island inhabited by friendly Indians. There was no cross or sign of distress carved over the letters. And when the Governor saw that he was greatly comforted.

He spent some time searching about for other signs of the colonists. In one place he found some iron and lead thrown aside as if too heavy to carry away, and now overgrown with weeds. In another he found five chests which had evidently been buried by the colonists, and dug up again by the Indians.

They had been burst open and the contents lay scattered about the grass. Three of these chests John White saw were his own, and it grieved him greatly to see his things spoiled and broken. His books were torn from their covers, his pictures and maps were rotten with the rain, and his armour almost eaten through with rust.

58

At length, having searched in vain for any other signs of the colonists, the English returned to the ships and set sail for Croatoan.

But now they encountered terrible storms. Their ships were battered this way and that, their sails were torn, their anchors lost. And at length in spite of all entreaties, the captain resolved to make sail for England. So John White never saw Croatoan, never knew what had become of his dear ones. And what happened to little Virginia Dare, the first English girl to be born on the soil of the United States, will never be known. But years afterwards settlers were told by the Indians that the white people left at Roanoke had gone to live among the Indians. For some years it was said they lived in a friendly manner together. In time, however, the medicine men began to hate the Pale-faces, and caused them all to be slain, except four men, one young woman, and three boys. Was the young woman perhaps Virginia Dare? No one can tell.

All Raleigh's attempts at founding a colony had thus come to nothing. Still he did not despair. Once again he sent out an expedition. But that too failed and the leader returned having done nothing. Even this did not break Raleigh's faith in the future of Virginia. "I shall yet live to see it an English nation," he said.

But although Raleigh's faith was as firm as before, his money was gone. He had spent enormous sums on his fruitless efforts to found a colony. Now he had no more to spend.

And now great changes came. Good Queen Bess died and James of Scotland reigned in her stead. Raleigh fell into disgrace, was imprisoned in the Tower, and after a short release was beheaded there. Thus an end came to all his splendid schemes. Never before perhaps had such noble devotion to King and country been so basely requited. At the time it was said that "never before was English justice so injured or so disgraced" as by the sentence of death passed upon Raleigh. No man is perfect, nor was Raleigh perfect. But he was a great man, and although all his plans failed we remember him as the first great coloniser, the first Englishman to gain possession of any part of North America.

PART II STORIES OF VIRGINIA

Chapter 13 - The Adventures of Captain John Smith

Raleigh was the true father of England beyond the seas. He was a great statesman and patriot. But he was a dreamer too and all his schemes failed. Other men followed him who likewise failed. But it would take too long to tell of them all, of Bartholomew Gosnold who discovered and named Martha's Vineyard and Cape Cod; of Bartholomew Gilbert, brave Sir Humphrey's son, who was slain by Indians, and of many more besides.

Again and again men tried to plant a colony on the shores of America. Again and again they failed. But with British doggedness they went on trying, and at length succeeded.

Raleigh lay in the Tower of London, a prisoner accused of treason. All his lands were taken from him. Virginia, which had been granted to him by Queen Elizabeth was the King's once more to give to whom he would. So now two companies were formed, one of London merchants called the London Company, one of Plymouth merchants called the Plymouth Company. And both these companies prayed King James to grant them permission to found colonies in Virginia. Virginia therefore was divided into two parts; the right to found colonies in the southern half being given to the London Company, the right to found colonies in the northern half being given to the Plymouth Company upon condition that the colonies founded must be one hundred miles distant from each other.

These companies were formed by merchants. They were formed for trade, and in the hope of making money, in spite of the fact that up to this time no man had made money by trying to found colonies. in America, but on the contrary many had lost fortunes.

Of the two companies now formed it was only the London Company which really did anything. The Plymouth Company indeed sent out an expedition which reached Virginia. But the colony was a failure, and after a year of hardships the colonists set sail for England taking home with them such doleful accounts of their sufferings that none who heard them ever wished to help to found a colony.

The expedition of the London Company had a better fate. It was in December, 1606, that the little fleet of three ships, the Susan Constant, the Godspeed and the Discovery, put out from England, and turned westward towards the New World.

With the expedition sailed Captain John Smith. He was bronzed and bearded like a Turk, a swaggering, longheaded lovable sort of man, ambitious, too, and not given to submit his will to others. Since a boy of sixteen he had led a wandering adventurous life - a life cramful of heroic deeds, of hairbreadth escapes of which we have no space to tell here. But I hope some day you will read his own story of these days. For he was a writer as well as a warrior, and "what his sword did his pen wrote." Every American boy and girl should read his story, for he has been called the first American writer.

Now with this saucy, swaggering fellow on board, troubles were not far to seek. The voyage was long and tedious. For six weeks adverse winds kept the little fleet prisoner in the English Channel within sight of English shores, a thing trying to the tempers of men used to action, and burning with impatience to reach the land beyond the seas. They lay idle with nothing to do but talk. So they fell to discussing matters about the colony they were to found. And from discussing they fell to disputing until it ended at length in a bitter quarrel between Smith and another of the adventurers, Captain Edward Wingfield.

Captain Wingfield was twice John Smith's age, and deemed that he knew much better how a colony ought to be formed than this dictatorial youth of twenty-seven. He himself was just as dictatorial and narrow into the bargain. So between the two the voyage was by no means peaceful.

Good Master Hunt, the preacher who went with the expedition, in spite of the fact that he was so weak and ill that few thought he would live, did his best to still the angry passions.

To some extent he succeeded. And when a fair wind blew at length the ships spread their sails to it and were soon out of sight of England. Two months of storm and danger passed before the adventurers sighted the West Indies. Here they went ashore on the island of San Dominica. Delighted once more to see land and escape from the confinement of the ship, they stayed three weeks among the sunny islands. They hunted and fished, traded with the savages, boiled pork in hot natural springs, feasted on fresh food and vegetables, and generally enjoyed themselves.

But among all this merry-making Wingfield did not forget his anger against John Smith. Their quarrels became so bad that Wingfield decided to end both quarrels and John Smith. So he ordered a gallows to be set up and, having accused Smith of mutiny, made ready to hang him. But John Smith stoutly defended himself. Nothing could be proved against him. He laughed at the gallows, and as he quaintly puts it "could not be persuaded to use them."

Nevertheless, although nothing could be proved against him, there were many who quite agreed that Captain John Smith was a turbulent fellow. So to keep him quiet they clapped him in irons and kept him so until their arrival in Virginia. After leaving the West Indies the adventurers fell into more bad weather, and lost their course; but finally they arrived safely in Chesapeake Bay.

They named the capes on either side Henry and Charles, in honour of the two sons of their King. Upon Cape Henry they set up a brass cross upon which was carved "Jacobus Rex" and thus claimed the land for England. Then they sailed on up the river which they named James River, in honour of the King himself. Their settlement they named Jamestown, also in his honour. Jamestown has now disappeared, but the two capes and the river are still called by the names given them by these early settlers.

Before this expedition sailed the directors of the Company had arranged who among the colonists were to be the rulers. But for some quaint reason they were not told. Their names, together with many instructions as to what they were to do, were put into a sealed box, and orders were given that this box was not to be opened until Virginia was reached.

The box was now opened, and it was found that John Smith was named among the seven who were to form the council. The others were much disgusted at this, and in spite of all he could say, they refused to have him in the council. They did, however, set him free from his fetters. Of the council Wingfield was chosen President. All the others, except John Smith, took oath to do their best for the colony. Then at once the business of building houses was begun. While the council drew plans the men dug trenches and felled trees in order to clear space on which to pitch their tents, or otherwise busied themselves about the settlement.

The Indians appeared to be friendly, and often came to look on curiously at these strange doings. And Wingfield thought them so gentle and kindly that he would not allow the men to build any fortifications except a sort of screen of interwoven boughs.

61

Besides building houses one of the colonists' first cares was to provide themselves with a church. But indeed it was one of the quaintest churches ever known. An old sail was stretched beneath a group of trees to give shelter from the burning sun. And to make a pulpit a plank of wood was nailed between two trees which grew near together. And here good Master Hunt preached twice every Sunday while the men sat on felled trunks reverently listening to his long sermons.

While the houses were being built Smith, with some twenty others, was sent to explore the country. They sailed up the river and found the Indians to all appearance friendly. But they found no gold or precious stones, and could hear nothing of a passage to the Pacific Ocean which they had been told to seek. So they returned to Jamestown. Arriving here they found that the day before the Indians had attacked the settlement and that one Englishman lay slain and seventeen injured.

This was a bitter disappointment to Wingfield who had trusted in the friendliness of the Indians. But at length he was persuaded to allow fortifications to be built. Even then, however, the colonists were not secure, for as they went about their business felling trees or digging the ground the savages would shoot at them from the shelter of the surrounding forest. If a man strayed from the fort he was sure to return wounded if he returned at all; and in this sort of warfare the stolid English were no match for the wily Indians. "Our men," says Smith, "by their disorderly straggling were often hurt when the savages by the nimbleness of their heels well escaped."

So six months passed, and the ships which had brought out the colonists were ready to go back to England with a cargo of wood instead of the gold which the Company had hoped for. But before the ships sailed Smith, who was still considered in disgrace, and therefore kept out of the council, insisted on having a fair trial. For he would not have Captain Newport go home and spread evil stories about him.

Smith's enemies were unwilling to allow the trial. But Smith would take no denial. So at length his request was granted, the result being that he was proved innocent of every charge against him, and was at length admitted to the council.

Now at last something like peace was restored, and Captain Newport set sail for home. He promised to make all speed he could and to be back in five months' time. And indeed he had need to hasten. For the journey outward had been so long, the supply of food so scant, that already it was giving out. And when Captain Newport sailed it was plain that the colonists had not food enough to last fifteen weeks.

Such food it was too! It consisted chiefly of worm-eaten grain. A pint was served out daily for each man, and this boiled and made into a sort of porridge formed their chief food. Their drink was cold water. For tea and coffee were unknown in those days, and beer they had none. To men used to the beer and beef of England in plenty this indeed seemed meagre diet. "Had we been as free of all sins as gluttony and drunkenness," says Smith, "we might have been canonised as saints, our wheat having fried some twenty-six weeks in the ship's hold, contained as many worms as grains, so that we might truly call it rather so much bran than corn. Our drink was water, our lodging castles in the air."

There was fish enough in the river, game enough in the woods. But the birds and beasts were so wild, and the men so unskilful and ignorant in ways of shooting and trapping, that they succeeded in catching very little. Besides which there were few among the colonists who had any idea of what work meant. More than half the company were "gentlemen adventurers," dare devil, shiftless men who had joined the expedition in search of excitement with no idea of labouring with their hands.

Badly fed, unused to the heat of a Virginian summer the men soon fell ill. Their tents were rotten, their houses yet unbuilt. Trees remained unfelled, the land untilled, while the men lay on the bare ground about the fort groaning and in misery. Many died, and soon those who remained were so feeble that they had scarce strength to bury the dead or even to crawl to the "common kettle" for their daily measure of porridge.

In their misery the men became suspicious and jealous, and once more quarrels were rife. Wingfield had never been loved. Now many grew to hate him, for they believed that while they starved he kept back for his own use secret stores of oil and wine and other dainties. No explanations were of any avail, and he was deposed from his office of President and another chosen in his place.

As autumn drew on the misery began to lessen. For the Indians, whose corn was now ripe, began to bring it to the fort to barter it for chisels, and beads, and other trifles. Wild fowl too, such as ducks and geese, swarmed in the river.

So with good food and cooler weather the sick soon began to mend. Energy returned to them, and once more they found strength to build and thatch their houses. And led by Smith they made many expeditions among the Indians, bringing back great stores of venison, wild turkeys, bread, and grain in exchange for beads, hatchets, bells and other knick-knacks.

But all the misery through which the colonists had passed had taught them nothing. They took no thought for the time to come when food might again be scarce. They took no care of it, but feasted daily on good bread, fish and fowl and "wild beasts as fat as we could eat them," says Smith.

Now one December day Smith set out on an exploring expedition up the Chickahominy River. It was a hard journey, for the river was so overgrown with trees that the men had to hew a path for the little vessel. At length the barque could go no further, so Smith left it, and went on in a canoe with only two Englishmen, and two Indians as guides.

For a time all went well. But one day he and his companions went ashore to camp. While the others were preparing a meal, Smith, taking one of the Indians with him, went on to explore a little further. But he had not gone far when he heard the wild, blood-curdling war whoop of the Indians. Guessing at once that they had come against him he resolved to sell his life as dearly as might be. So seizing the Indian guide he tied his arm fast to his own with his garters. Then with pistol in his right hand, and holding the Indian in front of him as a shield, he

63

pushed as rapidly as he could in the direction of the camp.

Arrows flew round him thick and fast, but Smith's good buff coat turned them aside. The whole forest was alive with Indians, but although from the shelter of the trees they showered arrows upon Smith none dared approach him to take him. For they knew and dreaded the terrible fire stick which he held in his hand. Smith fired again and yet again as he retreated, and more than one Indian fell, never more to rise. He kept his eyes upon the bushes and trees trying to catch glimpses of the dusky figures as they skulked among them, and paid little heed to the path he was taking. So suddenly he found himself floundering in a quagmire.

Still he fought for dear life, and as long as he held his pistol no Redman dared come near to take him. But at length, chilled and wet, and half dead-with cold, unable to go further, he saw it was useless to resist longer. So he tossed away his pistol. At once the savages closed in upon and, dragging him out of the quagmire, led him to their chief.

Smith had given in because he knew that one man stuck in a quagmire could not hope to keep three hundred Indians long at bay. But he had sharp wits as well as a steady hand, and with them he still fought for his life. As soon as he was brought before the chief he whipped out his compass, and showing it to the chief, explained to him that it always pointed north, and thus the white men were able to find their way through the pathless desert.

To the Indians this seemed like magic; they marvelled greatly at the shining needle which they could see so plainly and yet not touch. Seeing their interest Smith went on to explain other marvels of the sun, and moon, and stars, and the roundness of the earth, until those who heard were quite sure he was a great "medicine man."

Thus Smith fought for his life. But at length utterly exhausted, he could say no more. So while the chief still held the little ivory compass, and watched the quivering needle, his followers led Smith away to his own camp fire. Here lay the other white men dead, thrust through with many arrows. And here the Indians warmed and chafed his benumbed body, and treated him with all the kindness they knew. But that brought Smith little comfort. For he knew it was the Indian way. A famous warrior might be sure of kindness at their hands if they meant in the end to slay him with awful torture.

And so, thoroughly warmed and restored, in less than an hour Smith found himself fast bound to a tree, while grim warriors, terribly painted, danced around him, bows and arrows in hand. They were about to slay him when the chief, holding up the compass, bade them lay down their weapons. Such a medicine man, he had decided, must not thus be slain. So Smith was unbound.

For some weeks Smith was marched hither and thither from village to village. He was kindly enough treated, but he never knew how long the kindness would last, and he constantly expected death. Yet he was quite calm. He kept a journal, and in this he set down accounts of many strange sights he saw, not knowing if indeed they would ever be read.

At length Smith was brought to the wigwam of the great Powhatan*, the chief

64

of chiefs, or Emperor, as these simple English folk called him. To receive the white prisoner the Powhatan put on his greatest bravery. Feathered and painted, and wearing a wide robe of raccoon skins he sat upon a broad couch beside a fire. On either side of him sat one of his wives and behind in grim array stood his warriors, row upon row. Behind them again stood the squaws. Their faces and shoulders were painted bright red, about their necks they wore chains of white beads, and on their heads the down of white birds.

It was a weird scene, and the flickering firelight added to its strangeness. Silent and still as statues the warriors stood. Then as John Smith was led before the chief they raised a wild shout. As that died away to silence one of the Powhatan's squaws rose and brought a basin of water to Smith. In this he washed his hands, and then another squaw brought him a bunch of feathers instead of a towel, with which to dry them.

After this the Indians feasted their prisoner with savage splendour. Then a long consultation took place. What was said Smith knew not. He only knew that his life hung in the balance. The end of the consultation he felt sure meant life or death for him.

At length the long talk came to an end. Two great stones were placed before the chief. Then as many as could lay hands on Smith seized him, and dragging him to the stones, they threw him on the ground, and laid his head upon them. Fiercely then they brandished their clubs and Smith knew that his last hour had come, and that the Indians were about to beat out his brains.

But the raised clubs never fell, for with a cry Pocahontas, the chief's young daughter, sprang through the circle of warriors. She stood beside the prisoner pleading for his life. But the Indians were in no mood to listen to prayers for mercy. So seeing that all her entreaties were in vain she threw herself upon her knees beside Smith, put her arms about his neck, and laid her head upon his, crying out that if they would beat out his brains they should beat hers out too.

Of all his many children the Powhatan loved this little daughter best. He could deny her nothing. So Smith's life was saved. He should live, said the Powhatan, to make hatchets for him, and bells and beads for his little daughter.

Having thus been saved, Smith was looked upon as one of the tribe. Two days later he was admitted as such with fearsome ceremony.

Having painted and decorated himself as frightfully as he could, the Powhatan caused Smith to be taken to a large wigwam in the forest. The wigwam was divided in two by a curtain and in one half a huge fire burned. Smith was placed upon a mat in front of the fire and left alone. He did not understand in the least what was going on, and marvelled greatly what this new ceremony might mean. But he had not sat long before the fire when he heard doleful sounds coming from the other side of the curtain. Then from behind it appeared the Powhatan with a hundred others as hideously painted as himself, and told Smith that now that they were brothers he might go back to his fort.

So with twelve guides Smith set out. Yet in spite of all their feasting and ceremonies Smith scarcely believed in the friendship of the Indians, and no one was more surprised than himself when he at length reached Jamestown in safety.

*This chief's name was Wahunsunakok, the name of the tribe Powhatan and the English called the chief the Powhatan.

Chapter 14 - More Adventures of Captain John Smith

Smith had been away from the settlement nearly a month, and he returned to find the colony in confusion and misery. Many had died, and those who remained were quarrelling among themselves. Indeed some were on the point of deserting and sneaking off to England in the one little ship they had. They were not in the least pleased to see Smith return, and they resolved once more to get rid of him. So they accused him of causing the death of the two men who had gone with him, and condemned him to death. Thus Smith had only escaped from the hands of the Indians to be murdered by his own people.

The order went forth. He was to be hanged next day.

But suddenly all was changed, for a man looking out to sea saw a white sail. "Ship ahoy!" he shouted, "ship ahoy!"

At the joyful sound the, men forgot their bickerings, and hurrying to the shore welcomed the new arrival. It was Captain Newport with his long promised help. He soon put a stop to the hanging business, and also set poor Captain Wingfield free. For he had been kept prisoner ever since he had been deposed.

Newport had brought food for the colony, but he had also brought many new settlers. Unfortunately, too, one day the storehouse was set on fire, and much of the grain was destroyed. So that in spite of the new supplies the colony would soon again have been in the old starving condition had it not been for Pocahontas. She was resolved that her beloved white chief should want for nothing, and now every four or five days she came to the fort laden with provisions. Smith also took Captain Newport to visit the Powhatan, and great barter was made of blue beads and tinsel ornaments for grain and foodstuffs.

After a time Captain Newport sailed home again, taking the deposed President Wingfield with him. He took home also great tales of the savage Emperor's might and splendour. And King James was so impressed with what he heard that he made up his mind that the Powhatan should be crowned. So in autumn Captain Newport returned again to Jamestown, bringing with him more settlers, among them two women. He also brought a crown and other presents to the Powhatan from King James, together with a command for his coronation. So Smith made a journey to the Powhatan's village and begged him to come to Jamestown to receive his presents. But the Powhatan refused to go for he was suspicious and stood upon his dignity.

"If your King has sent me presents," he said, "I also am a king, and this is my land. Eight days will I wait here to receive them. Your Father Newport must come to me, not I to him."

So with this answer Smith went back, and seeing nothing else for it Captain Newport set out for the Powhatan's village with the presents. He did not in the least want to go, but the King had commanded that the Powhatan was to be crowned. And the King had to be obeyed. He arrived safely at Weronocomoco, and the next day was appointed for the coronation.

First the presents were brought out and set in order. There was a great four-poster bed with hangings and curtains of damask, a basin and ewer and other costly novelties such as never before had been seen in these lands.

After the gifts had been presented the Englishmen tried to place a fine red cloak on the Powhatan's shoulders. But he would not have it. He resisted all their attempts until at last one of the other chiefs persuaded him that it would not hurt him, so at last he submitted.

Next the crown was produced. The Powhatan had never seen a crown, and had no idea of its use, nor could he be made to understand that he must kneel to have it put on.

"A foul trouble there was," says one of the settlers who writes about it. No persuasions or explanations were of any avail. The Englishmen knelt down in front of him to show him what he must do. They explained, they persuaded, until they were worn out. It was all in vain. The Powhatan remained as stolid as a mule. Kneel he would not.

So at length, seeing nothing else for it, three of them took the crown in their hands, and the others pressed with all their weight upon the Powhatan's shoulders so that they forced him to stoop a little, and thus, amid howls of laughter, the crown was hastily thrust on his head. As soon as it was done the soldiers fired a volley in honour of the occasion. At the sound the newly-crowned monarch started up in terror, casting aside the men who held him. But when he saw that no one was killed, and that those around him were laughing, he soon recovered from his fright. And thanking them gravely for their presents he pompously handed his old shoes and his raccoon cloak to Captain Newport as a present for King James. Thus this strangest of all coronations came to an end.

This senseless ceremony did no good, but rather harm. The Powhatan had resisted being crowned with all his might, but afterwards he was much puffed up about it, and began to think much more of himself, and much less of the white people.

Among others, Smith thought it was nothing but a piece of tomfoolery and likely to bring trouble ere long.

For some months now he had been President, and as President he wrote to the London Company, "For the coronation of Powhatan," he said, "by whose advice you sent him such presents I know not, but this give me leave to tell you, I fear they will be the confusion of us all, ere we hear from you again."

Smith told the Company other plain truths. They had been sending out all sorts of idle fine gentlemen who had never done a day's work in their lives. They could not fell a tree, and when they tried the axe blistered their tender fingers. Some of them worked indeed cheerfully enough, but it took ten of them to do as much work as one good workman. Others were simply stirrers up of mischief. One of these Smith now sent back to England "lest the company should cut his throat." And Smith begged the Company to keep those sort of people at home in the

67

future, and send him carpenters and gardeners, blacksmiths and masons, and people who could do something.

Captain Newport now sailed home, and Smith was left to govern the colony and find food for the many hungry mouths. He went as usual to trade with the Indians. But he found them no longer willing to barter their corn for a little copper or a handful of beads. They now wanted swords and guns. The Powhatan too grew weary of seeing the Pale-faces squatting on the land of which he was crowned king. He forgot his vows of friendship With Smith. All he wanted was to see the Palefaces leave his country. And the best way to get rid of them was to starve them.

But although the Powhatan had grown tired of seeing the Pale-faces stride like lords through his land, he yet greatly admired them. And now he wanted more than anything else to have a house, a palace as it seemed to him, with windows and fireplaces like those they built for themselves at Jamestown. For in the little native houses which his followers could build there was no room for the splendid furniture which had been sent to him for his coronation. So now he sent to Smith asking him to send white men to build a house. Smith at once sent some men to begin the work, and soon followed with others.

On their way to the Powhatan's town Smith and his companions stopped a night with another friendly chief who warned them to beware of the Powhatan.

"You will find him use you well," he said. "But trust him not. And be sure he hath no chance to seize your arms. For he hath sent for you only to cut your throats."

However in spite of this warning Smith decided to go on. So he thanked the friendly chief for his good counsel, and assuring him that he would love him always for it, he went on his way.

It was winter time now, and the rivers were half frozen over, the land was covered with snow, and icy winds blew over it. Indeed the weather was so bad that for a week Smith and his men could not go on, but had to take refuge with some friendly Indians. Here in the warm wigwams they were cosy and jolly. The savages treated them kindly, and fed them well on oysters, fish, game and wild-fowl. Christmas came and went while they were with these kindly savages, and at length, the weather becoming a little better, they decided to push on. After many adventures they reached the Powhatan's village. They were very weary from their long cold journey, and taking possession of the first houses they came to they sent a message to the Powhatan, telling him that they had come, and asking him to send food.

This the old chief immediately did, and soon they were dining royally on bread, venison and turkeys. The next day, too, the Powhatan sent them supplies of food. Then he calmly asked how long they were going to stay, and when they would be gone.

At this Smith was greatly astonished, for had not the Powhatan sent for him?

"I did not send for you," said the wily old savage, "and if you have come for corn I have none to give you, still less have my people. But," he added slyly, "if perchance you have forty swords I might find forty baskets of corn in exchange for them."

"You did not send for me?" said Smith in astonishment. "How can that be? For I have with me the messengers you sent to ask me to come, and they can vouch for the truth of it. I marvel that you can be so forgetful."

Then, seeing that he could not fool the Pale-faces the old chief laughed merrily, pretending that he had only been joking. But still he held to it that he would give no corn except in exchange for guns and swords.

"Powhatan," answered Smith, "believing your promises to satisfy my wants, and out of love to you I sent you my men for your building, thereby neglecting mine own needs. Now by these strange demands you think to undo us and bring us to want indeed. For you know well as I have told you long ago of guns and swords I have none to spare. Yet steal from you or wrong you I will not, nor yet break that friendship which we have promised each other, unless by bad usage you force me thereto."

When the Powhatan heard Smith speak thus firmly he pretended to give way and promised that within two days the English should have all the corn he and his people could spare. But he added, "My people fear to bring you corn seeing you are all armed, for they say you come not hither for trade, but to invade my country and take possession of it. Therefore to free us of this fear lay aside your weapons, for indeed here they are needless, we being all friends."

With such and many more cunning words the Powhatan sought to make Captain Smith and his men lay aside their arms. But to all his persuasions Smith turned a deaf ear.

"Nay," he said, "we have no thought of revenge or cruelty against you. When your people come to us at Jamestown we receive them with their bows and arrows. With you it must be the same. We wear our arms even as our clothes."

So seeing that he could not gain his end, the old chief gave in. Yet one more effort he made to soften the Englishman's heart.

"I have never honoured any chief as I have you," he said, with a sigh, "yet you show me less kindness than any one. You call me father, but you do just as you like."

Smith, however, would waste no more time parleying, and gave orders for his men to fetch the corn. But while he was busy with this the Powhatan slipped away and gathered his warriors. Then suddenly in the midst of their business Smith and one or two others found themselves cut off from their comrades, and surrounded by a yelling crowd of painted savages. Instantly the Englishmen drew their swords and, charging into the savages, put them to flight. Seeing how easily their warriors had been routed and how strong the Pale-faces were, the savage chiefs tried to make friends with them again, pretending that the attack upon them was a mistake, and that no evil against them had been intended.

The Englishmen, however, put no more trust in their words and sternly, with loaded guns and drawn swords in hand, bade them to talk no more, but make haste and load their boat with corn. And so thoroughly cowed were the savages by the fierce words and looks of the Pale-faces that they needed no second bidding. Hastily laying down their bows and arrows they bent their backs to the work, their one desire now being to get rid as soon as possible of these fierce and powerful intruders.

When the work was done, however, it was too late to sail that night, for the tide was low. So the Englishmen returned to the house in which they lodged, to rest till morning and wait for high water.

Meanwhile the Powhatan had by no means given up his desire for revenge, and while the Englishmen sat by their fire he plotted to slay them all. But as he talked with his braves Pocahontas listened. And when she heard that the great Pale-face Chief whom she loved so dearly was to be killed, her heart was filled with grief, and she resolved to save him. So silently she slipped out into the dark night and, trembling lest she should be discovered, was soon speeding through the wild lonesome forest towards the Englishmen's hut. Reaching it in safety she burst in upon them as they sat in the firelight waiting for the Powhatan to send their supper.

"You must not wait," she cried, "you must go at once. My father is gathering all his force against you. He will indeed send you a great feast, but those who bring it have orders to slay you, and any who escape them he is ready with his braves to slay. Oh, if you would live you must flee at once," and as she spoke the tears ran down her cheeks.

The Englishmen were truly grateful to Pocahontas for her warning. They thanked her warmly, and would have laden her with gifts of beads and coloured cloth, and such things as the Indians delighted in, but she would not take them.

"I dare not take such things," she said. "For if my father saw me with them he would know that I had come here to warn you, and he would kill me." So with eyes blinded with tears, and her heart filled with dread, she slipped out of the fire-lit hut, and vanished into the darkness of the forest as suddenly and silently as she had come.

Left alone, the Englishmen, cocking their guns and drawing their swords, awaited the coming of the foe. Presently eight or ten lusty fellows arrived, each bearing a great platter of food steaming hot and excellent to smell. They were very anxious that the Englishmen should at once lay aside their arms and sit down to supper. But Captain Smith would take no chances. Loaded gun in hand he stood over the messengers and made them taste each dish to be certain that none of them were poisoned. Having done this he sent the men away. "And bid your master make haste," he said, "for we are ready for him."

Then the Englishmen sat down to supper; but they had no thought of sleep and all night long they kept watch.

Powhatan too kept watch, and every now and again he would send messengers to find out what the Englishmen were about. But each time they came the savages found the Englishmen on guard, so they dared not attack. At last day dawned, and with the rising tide the Englishmen sailed away, still to all seeming on friendly terms with the wily Indians.

70

Smith had now food enough to keep the colony from starvation for a short time at least. But his troubles were by no means over. The Indians were still often unfriendly, and the colonists themselves lazy and unruly. Some indeed worked well and cheerfully, but many wandered about idly, doing nothing.

At length it came about that thirty or forty men did all the work, the others being simply idle loiterers. Seeing this, Smith called all the colonists together one day and told them that he would suffer the idleness no longer. "Every one must do his share," he said, "and he who will not work shall not eat." And so powerful had he grown that he was obeyed. The idle were forced to work, and soon houses were built and land cleared and tilled.

At length there seemed good hope that the colony would prosper. But now another misfortune befell it. For it was found that rats had got into the granaries and eaten nearly all the store of corn. So once again expeditions set forth to visit the Indians and gather more from them. But their supply, too, was running short; harvest was still a long way off, and all the colonists could collect was not enough to keep them from starvation. So seeing this Smith divided his men into companies, sending some down the river to fish, and others into the woods to gather roots and wild berries. But the lazy ones liked this little. They would have bartered away their tools and firearms to the savages for a few handfuls of meal rather than work so hard. They indeed became so mutinous that Smith hardly knew what to do with them. But at length he discovered the ringleader of these "gluttonous loiterers." Him he "worthily punished," and calling the others together, he told them very plainly that any man among them who did not do his share should be banished from the fort as a drone, till he mended his ways or starved.

To the idlers Smith seemed a cruel task-master; still they obeyed him. So the colony was held together, although in misery and hunger and without hope for the future.

At length one day to the men on the river there came a joyful sight. They saw a ship slowly sailing towards them. They could hardly believe their eyes, for no ship was expected; but they greeted it with all the more joy. It was a ship under Captain Samuel Argall, come, it is true, not to bring supplies, but to trade. Finding, however, that there was no hope of trade Captain Argall shared what food he had with the famished colonists, and so for a time rescued them from starvation. He also brought the news that more ships were setting out from home bringing both food and men.

In June, 1609, this fleet of nine ships really did set out. But one ship was wrecked on the way, another, the Sea Venture, was cast ashore on the Bermudas; only seven arrived at length at Jamestown, bringing many new colonists. Unfortunately among these new arrivals there were few likely to make good colonists. They were indeed for the most part wild, bad men whose friends had packed them off to that distant land in the hope of being rid of them forever. "They were," said one of the old colonists who wrote of them, "ten times more fit to spoil a Commonwealth than either to begin one or but help to maintain one."

Now with all these "unruly gallants" poured into his little commonwealth Smith found his position of President even more difficult than before. Still, for a time, if he could not keep them altogether in order he at least kept them in check.

Then one day by a terrible accident his rule was brought to a sudden end. He was returning from an expedition up the James River when, through some carelessness, a bag of gunpowder in his boat was exploded. Smith was not killed by it, but he was sorely hurt. In great pain, and no longer able to think and act for others, he was carried back to Jamestown.

Here there was no doctor of any kind, and seeing himself then only a useless hulk, and in danger of death, Smith gave up his post, and leaving the colony, for which during two and a half years he had worked and thought and fought so hard, he sailed homeward.

Many of the unruly sort were glad to see him go, but his old companions with whom he had shared so many dangers and privations were filled with grief. "He ever hated baseness, sloth, pride and indignity," said one of them. "He never allowed more for himself than for his soldiers with him. Upon no danger would he send them where he would not lead them himself. He would never see us want what he either had or could by any means get us. He loved action more than words, and hated falsehood and covetousness worse than death."

So, loved and hated, but having all unknown to himself made a name which would live forever in the history of his land, the first great Virginian sailed from its shores. He returned no more. Some twenty years later he died in London, and was buried in the church of St. Sepulchre there. Upon his tomb was carved a long epitaph telling of his valiant deeds. But in, the great Fire of London the tomb was destroyed, and now no tablet marks the resting-place of the brave old pioneer.

Chapter 15 - How the Colony was Saved

After Smith left, the colony of Jamestown fell into wild disorder. Every one wanted to go his own way. A new President named Percy had indeed been chosen. But although an honest gentleman he was sickly and weak, and quite unfit to rule these turbulent spirits. So twenty or more would-be presidents soon sprang up, and in the whole colony there was neither obedience nor discipline.

No work was done, food was recklessly wasted, and very quickly famine stared the wretched colonists in the face. The terrible time afterwards known as the Starving Time had begun. When their stores were gone the settlers tried to get more in the old way from the natives. But they, seeing the miserable plight of the Pale-faces, became insolent in their demands, and in return for niggardly supplies of food exacted guns and ammunition, swords and tools.

And now there was no man among the colonists who knew how to manage the Indians as Smith had managed them. There was no man among them who thought of the future. All they wanted was to stay for a time the awful pangs of hunger. So they bartered away their muskets and powder, their tools, and everything of value of which they were possessed. But even so the food the

Indians gave them in return was not enough to keep body and soul together.

The colony became a place of horror, where pale skeleton-like creatures roamed about eyeing each other suspiciously, ready to kill each other for a crust or a bone. They quarreled among themselves, and they quarreled with the natives. And the natives, now no longer filled with awe, lay in wait for them and killed them almost without resistance if they ventured to crawl beyond the walls of the fort. Many more died of hunger and of disease brought on by hunger.

So less than eight months after Smith had sailed away, of the five hundred men he had left behind him but sixty remained alive. The colony was being wiped out, and the little town itself was disappearing; for the starving wretches had no strength or energy to fell trees and hew wood, and as soon as a man died his house was pulled down by his comrades and used as firewood. Already, too, weeds and briers overgrew the land which had been cleared for corn. Greater misery and desolation it is hard to imagine. Yet the unhappy beings sank into a still deeper horror. Unable to relieve the pangs of hunger, they turned cannibal and fed upon each other. Thus the last depths of degradation were sounded, the last horrors of the Starving Time were reached.

Then at length one May day two ships came sailing up the James River and anchored in the harbour. From their decks bronzed men in patched and ragged garments looked with astonished eyes upon the desolate scene.

These were the men of the wrecked Sea Venture, who had been cast ashore upon the Bermudas. Their ship had gone down, but they had been able to save both themselves and nearly everything out of her. Some of the best men of the expedition had sailed in the Sea Venture. Their leaders were brave and energetic; so instead of bemoaning their fate they had set to work with right good will, and after ten months' labour had succeeded in building two little ships which they named the Patience and the Deliverance. Then, having filled them with such stores as they could muster, they set sail joyfully to join their comrades at Jamestown. But now what horror and astonishment was theirs! They had hoped to find a flourishing town, surrounded by well tilled fields. Instead they saw ruins and desolation. They had hoped to be greeted joyfully by stalwart, prosperous Englishmen. Instead a few gaunt, hollow-cheeked spectres, who scarce seemed men, crawled to meet them.

Lost in amazement the newcomers landed, and as they listened to the tragic tale pity filled their hearts. They gave the starving wretches food, and comforted them as best they could. They had no great stores themselves, and they saw at once that with such scant supplies as they had it would be impossible to settle at Jamestown.

Even if they could get through the summer, the autumn would bring no relief, for the fields, where the corn for the winter's use should already have been sprouting, lay neglected and overgrown with weeds and briers. The houses where the newcomers might have lodged had disappeared. The very palisading which surrounded the settlement as a bulwark against the Indians had been pulled down for firewood. All the tools and implements which might have been used to rebuild the place had been bartered away to the Indians. The Indians themselves were no longer friendly, but hostile. Whichever way they looked only misery and failure stared them in the face.

The Captains of the Patience and Deliverance talked long together, but even they could see no ray of hope. So with heavy hearts they resolved once more to abandon Virginia. They were loath indeed to come to this decision, loath indeed to own themselves defeated. But there seemed no other course left open to them.

So one day early in June the pitiful remnant of the Jamestown Colony went on board the two waiting ships. Sir Thomas Gates, the brave and wise captain of the expedition, was the last to leave the ruined town. With backward looks he left it, and ere he weighed anchor he fired a last salute to the lost colony. Then the sails were set, and the two little ships drifted down stream towards the open sea, carrying the beaten settlers back to old England.

Another attempt to plant a New England beyond the seas had failed.

But next day as the little ships dropped down stream the sailors on the lookout saw a boat being rowed towards them. Was it an Indian canoe? Did it come in peace or war? It drew nearer. Then it was seen that it was no Indian canoe, but an English tug boat manned by English sailors. With a shout they hailed each other, and news was exchanged. Wonderful news it was to which the brokenhearted colonists listened.

Lord Delaware, the new Governor of Virginia, had arrived. His three good ships, well stored with food and all things necessary for the colony, were but a little way down stream. There was no need for the settlers to flee home to escape starvation and death.

It may be that to some this news was heavy news. It may be that some would gladly have turned their backs forever upon the spot where they had endured so much misery. But for the most part the colonists were unwilling to own defeat, and they resolved at once to return. So the ships were put about, and three days after they had left Jamestown, as they believed forever, the colonists once more landed there.

As Lord Delaware stepped on shore he fell upon his knees giving thanks to God that he had come in time to save Virginia. After that the chaplain preached a sermon, then the new Governor, with all his company about him, read aloud the commission given to him by King James.

This was the first royal commission ever given to a governor of an English colony in America. In it Lord Delaware was given the power of life and death over "all and every person and persons now inhabiting, or which shall hereafter inhabit within the precincts of the said colony." The colonists were in fact to be his subjects. And having read aloud his commission, and having thus as it were shown his authority, Lord Delaware next spoke sternly to his new subjects. He warned them that he would no longer endure their sluggish idleness or haughty disobedience. And if they did not amend their ways they might look to it that the most severe punishment of the law would come upon them. Having thus spoken his mind plainly, to cheer them he told of the plentiful and good stores he had brought with him, of which all those who worked well and faithfully should have a share.

Now a new life began for the colony. All the settlers were made to work for some hours every day. Even the gentlemen among them, "whose breeding never knew what a day's labour meant," had to do their share. Soon the houses were rebuilt, the palisades stood again in place, two forts were erected to guard against attacks by the Indians, and at length the colony seemed to be on the fair way to success.

Of course this did not all happen at once. The idlers were not easily turned into diligent workers, or unruly brawlers into peaceful citizens. Indeed it was only through most stern, and what would seem to us now most cruel punishments, that the unruly were forced to keep the law.

The winter after Lord Delaware came out as Governor, although not so hard as that of the Starving Time, was yet severe, and many of the colonists died. Lord Delaware, too, became so ill that in the spring he sailed home to England, and after a little time Sir Thomas Dale took his place as Deputy Governor.

Sir Thomas Dale was both a soldier and a statesman. He was full of energy and courage. Far-seeing and dogged, he was merciless to the evildoers, yet kindly to those who tried to do well. Under his stern yet righteous rule the colony prospered.

At first only men settlers had come out, then one or two women joined them, and now many more women came, so that the men, instead of all living together, married and had homes of their own. Then, too, at first all a man's labour went into the common stock, and the men who worked little fared as well as those who worked a great deal. So the lazy fellow did as little as he could. "Glad when he could slip from his labour," says an old writer, "or slumber over his task he cared not how."

Thus most of the work of the colony was left to the few who were industrious and willing. Sir Thomas Dale changed that. In return for a small yearly payment in corn he gave three acres of land to every man who wished it, for his own use. So, suddenly, a little community of farmers sprang up. Now that the land was really their own, to make of it what they would, each man tilled it eagerly, and soon such fine crops of grain were raised that the colony was no longer in dread of starvation. The settlers, too, began to spread and no longer kept within the palisade round Jamestown, "more especially as Jamestown," says an old writer, "was scandalised for an unhealthy aire." And here and there further up the river little villages sprang up.

Since Smith had gone home the Indians had remained unfriendly, and a constant danger to the colonists. And now as they became thus scattered the danger from the Indians became ever greater. Old Powhatan and his men were constantly making raids upon the Pale-faces with whom he had once been so friendly. And in spite of the watch they kept he often succeeded in killing them or taking them prisoner. He had also by now quite a store of swords, guns and tools stolen from the English. And how to subdue him, or force him to live on friendly terms with them once more, none knew.

Pocahontas, who had been so friendly and who had more than once saved the Pale-faces from disaster, might have helped them. But she now never came near their settlement; indeed she seemed to have disappeared altogether. So the English could get no aid from her.

But now it happened one day that one of the adventurers, Samuel Argall, who was, it is written, "a good Marriner, and a very civil gentleman," went sailing up the Appomattox in search of corn for the settlement. He had to go warily because no one could tell how the Indians would behave, for they would be friends or foes just as it suited them. If they got the chance of killing the Pale-faces and stealing their goods they would do so. But if they were not strong enough to do that they would willingly trade for the coloured cloths, beads and hatchets they so much wanted.

Presently Argall came to the country of one of the chiefs with whom he had made friends. While here he was told that Pocahontas, the great Powhatan's daughter, was living with the tribe. As soon as he heard this Captain Argall saw at once that here was a means of forcing the Powhatan to make peace, and he resolved at all costs to get possession of Pocahontas. So sending for the chief he told him he must bring Pocahontas on board his ship.

But the chief was afraid and refused to do this.

"Then we are no longer brothers and friends," said Argall.

"My father," said the chief, "be not wroth. For if I do this thing the Powhatan will make war upon me and upon my people."

"My brother," said Argall," have no fear; if so be that the Powhatan shall make war upon you I will join with you against him to overthrow him utterly. I mean, moreover, no manner of hurt to Pocahontas, but will only keep her as hostage until peace be made between the Powhatan and the Pale-faces. If therefore you do my bidding I will give to you the copper kettle which you desire so much."

Now the chief longed greatly to possess the copper kettle. So he promised to do as Argall asked, and began to cast about for an excuse for getting Pocahontas on board. Soon he fell upon a plan. He bade his wife pretend that she was very anxious to see the Englishman's ship. But when she asked to be taken on board he refused to go with her. Again and again she asked. Again and again the chief refused. Then the poor lady wept with disappointment and at length the chief, pretending to be very angry, swore that he would beat her if she did not cease her asking and her tears. But as she still begged and wept he said he would take her if Pocahontas would go too.

To please the old woman Pocahontas went. Captain Argall received all three very courteously, and made a great feast for them in his cabin. The old chief, however, was so eager to get his promised kettle that he could little enjoy the feast, but kept kicking Captain Argall under the table as much as to say, "I have done my part, now you do yours."

At length Captain Argall told Pocahontas that she must stay with him until peace was made between her father and the white men. As soon as the old chief and his wife heard that they began to howl, and cry, and make a great noise, so as to pretend that they knew nothing about the plot. Pocahontas too began to cry. But Argall assured her that no harm was intended her, and that she need have no fear. So she was soon comforted and dried her eyes.

As for the wily old Indians they were made quite happy with the copper kettle and a few other trifles, and went merrily back to the shore.

A messenger was then sent to the Powhatan telling him that his daughter, whom he loved so dearly, was a prisoner, and that he could only ransom her by sending back all the Pale-faces he held prisoner, with all their guns, swords and tools which he had stolen.

When Powhatan got this news he was both angry and sorry. For he loved his daughter very dearly, but he loved the Englishmen's tools and weapons almost more. He did not know what to do, so for three months he did nothing. Then at last he sent back seven of his prisoners, each one carrying a useless gun.

"Tell your chieftain," he said, "that all the rest of the arms of the Pale-faces are lost, or have been stolen from me. But if the Pale-faces will give back my daughter I will give satisfaction for all the other things I have taken, together with five hundred bushels of corn, and will make peace forever."

But the Englishmen were not easily deceived. They returned a message to the chief saying, "Your daughter is well used. But we do not believe the rest of our arms are either lost or stolen, and therefore until you send them we will keep your daughter."

The Powhatan was so angry when he got this message that for a long time he would have no further dealings with the Pale-faces, but continued to vex and harass them as much as he could.

At length Sir Thomas Dale, seeking to put an end to this, took Pocahontas, and with a hundred and fifty men sailed up the river to the Powhatan's chief town.

As soon as the savages saw the white men they came down to the river's bank, jeering at them and insulting them, haughtily demanding why they had come.

"We have brought the Powhatan's daughter," replied the Englishmen. "For we are come to receive the ransom promised, and if you do not give it willingly we will take it by force."

But the savages were not in the least afraid at that threat. They jeered the more.

"If so be," they cried, "that you are come to fight you are right welcome, for we are ready for you. But we advise you, if you love your lives, to retire with haste. Else we will serve you as we have served others of your countrymen."

"Oh," answered the Englishmen, "we must have a better answer than that," and driving their ship nearer to the shore they made ready to land.

But as soon as they were within bow shot the savages let fly their arrows. Thick and fast they fell, rattling on the deck, glancing from the men's armour, wounding not a few. This reception made the Englishmen angry, so without more ado they launched their boats and made for the shore. The savages fled at their coming, and so enraged were the colonists against them that they burned their houses, and utterly destroyed their town. Then they sailed on up the river in pursuit of the Redmen.

Next day they came up again with the savages. They were now not so insolent and sent a messenger to ask why the Pale-faces had burned their town.

"Why did you fire upon us?" asked the Englishmen, sternly.

"Brothers," replied the Redmen, "we did not fire upon you. It was but some stray savages who did so. We intend you no hurt and are your friends."

With these and many other fair words they tried to pacify the Pale-faces. So the Englishmen, who had no wish to fight, made peace with them. Then the Indians sent a messenger to the Powhatan who was a day's journey off; and the Englishmen were told they must wait two days for his answer.

Meanwhile the Englishmen asked to see their comrades whom the Indians had taken prisoner.

"We cannot show them to you," replied the wily Redmen, "for they have all run away in fear lest you should hang them. But the Powhatan's men are pursuing after them, and will doubtless bring them back."

"Then where are the swords and guns which you have stolen from us?" demanded the Englishmen.

"These you shall have to-morrow," replied the Redmen.

But, as the Englishmen well knew, this was all idle talk and deceit, and next day no message came from the Powhatan, neither were any swords nor guns forthcoming. So once more the Englishmen set sail and went still further up the river.

Here quite close to another village belonging to the Powhatan they came upon four hundred Indians in war paint. When they saw the Englishmen the Indians yelled and danced, and dared them to come ashore. This the Englishmen, nothing daunted, accordingly did. The Redmen on their side showed no fear, but walked boldly up and down among the Englishmen, demanding to speak with their captain.

So the chiefs were brought to Sir Thomas.

"Why do you come against us thus?" they asked. "We are friends and brothers. Let us not fight until we have sent once again to our King to know his pleasure. Then if he sends not back the message of peace we will fight you and defend our own as best we may."

The Englishmen knew well that by all this talk of peace the Indians wanted but to gain time so that they might be able to carry away and hide their stores. Still they had no desire to fight if by any other means they might gain their end. So they promised a truce until noon the day following. "And if we then decide to fight you, you shall be warned of it by the sounding of our drums and trumpets," they said.

The truce being settled Pocahontas' two brothers came on board the Englishmen's ships to visit their sister. And when they saw that she was well cared for, and appeared to be quite happy they were very glad, for they had heard that she was ill treated and most miserable. But finding her happy they promised to persuade their father to ransom her, and make friends again with the Pale-faces.

Seeing them thus friendly Sir Thomas suggested that Pocahontas' two brothers should stay on board his vessel as hostages while he sent two of his company to parley with the Powhatan. This was accordingly done, and Master John Rolfe and Master Sparkes set off on their mission. When, however, they reached the village where the Powhatan was hiding they found him still in high dudgeon, and he refused to see them, or speak with them. So they had to be content with seeing his brother, who treated them with all courtesy and kindness and promised to do his best to pacify the Powhatan.

It was now April, and high time for the colonists to be back on their farms sowing their corn. So with this promise they were fain to be content in the meantime. And having agreed upon a truce until harvest time they set sail once more for Jamestown, taking Pocahontas with them.

One at least among the company of Englishmen was glad that the negotiations with the Powhatan had come to nothing, and that Pocahontas had not been ransomed. That was Master John Rolfe. For Pocahontas, although a savage, was beautiful and kind, and John Rolfe had fallen madly in love with her. So he had no desire that she should return to her own tribe, but rather that she should return to Jamestown and marry him.

Pocahontas, too, was quite fond of John Rolfe, although she had never forgotten her love for the great White Chief whose life she had saved. The Englishmen, however, told her that he had gone away never to come back any more, and that very likely he was dead. Pocahontas was then easily persuaded to marry John Rolfe. But he himself, although he loved her very much, had some misgivings. For was this beautiful savage not a heathen?

That difficulty was, however, soon overcome. For Pocahontas made no objection to becoming a Christian. So one day there was a great gathering in the little church at Jamestown when the heathen princess stood beside the fort, and the water of Christian baptism was sprinkled on her dark face, and she was given the Bible name of Rebecca.

And now when the Powhatan heard that his daughter was going to marry one of the Pale-faces he was quite pleased. He forgot all his anger and sulkiness, sent many of his braves to be present at the wedding, and swore to be the friend and brother of the Pale-faces forever more.

Sir Thomas Dale was delighted. So every one was pleased, and one morning early in April three hundred years ago all the inhabitants of the country round, both Redman and White, gathered to see the wedding. And from that day for eight years, as long as the Powhatan lived, there was peace between him and his brothers, the Pale-faces.

Chapter 16 - How Pocahontas Took a Journey Over the Seas

At peace with the Indians, the colonists could till their fields without fear of attack. And now, besides corn, they began to grow tobacco.

You remember that Columbus had noticed how the natives of his "India" smoked rolled-up dried leaves. But, no one paid much attention to it. Then the men of Raleigh's expedition again noticed it. They tried it themselves, found it comforting, and brought both tobacco and the habit home with them. And soon not only the seafaring adventurers but many a man who was never likely to see the ocean, or adventure beyond his native town, had taken to smoking. That, too, despite his king's disgust at it. For James thought smoking was "a custom loathsome to the eye, hateful to the nose, harmful to the brain, dangerous to the lungs, and in the black smoking fumes thereof nearest resembling the horrible Stygian smoke of the pit that is bottomless." He indeed wrote a little book against it, which he called "A Counterblaste to Tobacco." But no one paid much attention to him. The demand for tobacco became greater and greater, and soon the Virginian farmers found that there was a sale for as much tobacco as they could grow, and that a crop of it paid better than anything else.

Up till now the colony had. been a constant disappointment to the "adventurers" - that is, to the people who had given the money to fit out the expeditions - the shareholders we would now call them.

Most of them had adventured their money, not with any idea of founding a New England beyond the seas where men should settle down as farmers and tillers of the soil. They had adventured it rather for the finding of gold and pearls, jewels and spices, so that it might be repaid quickly, and a hundredfold. But year by year passed, and all these glittering hopes were doomed to disappointment. No gold was found. The adventurers saw their money being swallowed up for nought. They grew discontented and grumbled, some of them refused to pay any more, refused to throw more away on an empty dream. They little knew that they were helping to found a new State which in time was to become one of the world's greatest powers. They little knew that in days to come their money should produce a harvest a thousand, thousandfold, and that from the broad land, of which they had helped to settle a tiny corner, was to come wealth such as in their wildest imaginings, they had never dreamt.

Meanwhile, anything a Virginian wanted he could buy with tobacco. Indeed, after a time the Virginians threw themselves with such complete enthusiasm into the growing of tobacco that they were reproached for neglecting everything else because of it.

The English were not the only people who had set forth to find golden wealth and broad lands beyond the seas. Both the French and the Dutch had carried their standard across the ocean, and planted it upon the further shores. Already, too, the struggle for possession began.

Captain Argall, in one of his many expeditions, sailing northward to the Bay of Fundy, found a French colony settled there. Argall swooped down upon them, and claiming the whole continent by right of Cabot's discovery, he utterly destroyed the colony, burning the houses to the ground, and carrying off the cattle.

Argall next found a Dutch colony on the Hudson River. Here he contented himself with ordering the Governor to pull down the Dutch flag and run up the English one. To save his colony the Dutchman did as he was commanded. But as soon as the arrogant Englishman was out of sight he calmly ran up his own flag once more.

Meanwhile under Sir Thomas Dale Virginia continued to prosper. Then after five years' rule Sir Thomas went home and the colony was left to a new ruler. With him went John Rolfe and his wife Pocahontas, together with their little baby son.

Now began a wonderful new life for the beautiful Indian. Only a few years before she had been a merry, little, half naked savage, turning cart wheels all over the Jamestown fort, and larking with the boys. Now she found herself treated as a great lady.

In those days the people in England had very little idea of the life out in the wilds. The Powhatan, they had heard, was a king, a sort of emperor, indeed, and they doubtless pictured him as living in a stately palace, wearing a golden crown and velvet robes. That a "king" should be a half-naked savage, living in a mud hut, wearing a crown of feathers on his head, and a string of beads about his neck, they could not imagine. As the Powhatan was a king then his daughter was a princess, and as such must be treated with all respect.

It is even said that John Rolfe was roundly scolded by King James for daring to marry a princess without first asking leave.

"For," he gravely pointed out, "if the Powhatan was a king and Pocahontas his daughter, when the Powhatan died Rolfe or his baby son might become King of Virginia. It was not meet or right that a commoner should thus lightly take upon himself to marry the daughter of a brother sovereign."

Every one, then, was ready to treat Pocahontas with deference. Besides this John Smith wrote to the Queen relating all that she had done for the Colony of Virginia and begging her to be kind to the Indian girl who had done so much for England. For that or some other reason the Queen took an interest in the little dusky Princess. Pocahontas was presented to her, and was often seen at the theatre or other entertainment with her. The ladies of the court were made to treat Pocahontas with great ceremony. They addressed her as "Princess" or "Lady," remained standing before her, and walked backwards when they left her presence; famous artists painted her portrait; poets wrote of her, and in one of his plays Ben Johnson calls her

The Blessed Pokahontas, as the historian calls her And great King's daughter of Virginia.

In fact she became the rage. She was the talk of the town. Even coffee-houses and taverns were named after her,-La Belle Sauvage (the beautiful savage). And it is interesting to remember that a great publishing house in London takes its name from one of these old taverns. Books go out to all the world from the sign of La Belle Sauvage, thus forming a link between the present and that half-forgotten American "princess" of so long ago.

In spite of all the homage and flattery poured upon her, Pocahontas yet remained modest and simple, enchanting all who met her. And among all the new delights of England she had the joy of seeing once again the great White Chief she had loved and called her father in days gone by.

81

Her joy was all the greater because she had believed him to be dead. When Smith first came to see her her feelings were so deep that at first she could not speak. She greeted him in silence, then suddenly turning away she hid her face and wept. But after a little she recovered herself, and began to speak of the old days, and of how she had thought he was dead. "I knew no other," she said, "until I came to Plymouth."

In many ways Pocahontas showed her joy at again recovering her old friend. But when she found that Smith was not going to treat her as an old friend, but as if she were a great lady, and call her Princess like all the others round her, she was hurt.

"You did promise the Powhatan that what was yours should be his, and he did promise the like to you," she said. "A stranger in his land you called him father, and I shall do the same by you."

"Lady," replied Smith, "I dare not allow that title, for you are a King's daughter."

But from the man who had known her in those strange, wild days in far-off Virginia, from the man she had looked upon as a great and powerful chief, Pocahontas would have no such nonsense. She laughed at him.

"You were not afraid," she said defiantly, "to come into my father's country, and cause fear in him, and in all his people save me. And fear you here that I should call you father? I tell you then I will. And you shall call me child. And so I will be forever and ever your countryman."

Pocahontas took all the strangeness of her new surroundings very simply. But some of her attendants were utterly overwhelmed with wonder and awe at the things they saw. One man in particular, who was accounted a very clever man among his own people, had been sent by the Powhatan to take particular note of everything in England. Among other things he had been charged to count the people! So on landing at Plymouth he provided himself with a long stick and proceeded to make a notch in it for every man he met. But he met so many people that he could not make notches fast enough; so in a very short time he grew weary of that and threw his stick away.

Coming to London he was more amazed than ever. Never had he seen so great a city nor so many folk all gathered together, and among them not one familiar face. So he welcomed Captain John Smith like an old friend, and eagerly questioned him as to the wonders of this strange country. More especially he asked to see God, the King and Queen, and the Prince.

Captain Smith tried as best he could to explain to the poor heathen about God, telling him He could not be seen. As, to the King, he added, "you have seen him."

"No," said the Indian, "I have not seen your great King."

Then when Captain Smith explained that the little man with a jeweled feather in his cap and sword by his side, who had one day spoken to him was the King, the Indian was much disappointed.

"You gave Powhatan a white dog," he said, "which Powhatan fed as himself. But your King gave me nothing."

However if the old Indian was disappointed with the manner in which the King had received him he was much made of by others. For every one was eager to see this wild savage. And often to please these new friends he would sing to them and make their blood creep by his wild dances.

Pocahontas loved England where she was so kindly treated. She took to the new life so well that it is said she soon "became very formal and civil after our English manner." But she who had been used to roam the wild woods could not live in the confinement of towns, and soon she became very ill. So she made up her mind at length, sorely against her will, to go back to Virginia with her husband. Captain Argall was about to return there as Deputy Governor. So Pocahontas and her husband took passages in his boat.

But Pocahontas was never again to see her native shore. She went on board Captain Argall's boat, the George, and indeed set sail from London, but before she reached Gravesend she became so ill that she had to be taken ashore, and there she died. She was buried in the chancel of the Parish Church. Later the Church was burned down, but it was rebuilt, and as a memorial to Pocahontas American ladies have placed a stained glass window there, and also a pulpit made of Virginian wood.

John Rolfe returned alone to Virginia, leaving his little son Thomas behind him in the care of an uncle. He remained in England until he was grown up, and then went to his native land. There he married, and had a daughter, and became the ancestor of several Virginian families who are to this day proud to trace their descent from beautiful Pocahontas and her English husband.

Chapter 17 - How the Redmen Fought Against Their White Brothers

The Colony of Virginia which had prospered so greatly under Sir Thomas Dale had fallen again on evil days. For Samuel Argall, who now governed, proved a tyrant. Dale had been autocratic, but he had been autocratic for the good of the colony. Argall was autocratic for his own gains. He extorted money and tribute from the colonists to make himself rich, and profits which should have gone to the company went into his pocket. Again and again the colonists sent home complaints of Argall's doings. At length these complaints became so loud and long that the company once more sent Lord Delaware out as Governor.

But on the way Lord Delaware died, and the party of settlers he was bringing out arrived without him. On their arrival Argall at once took possession of Lord Delaware's private papers, and much to his disgust he found among them one telling Lord Delaware to arrest Argall and send him back to England.

This made Argall very angry; it also made him more despotic and cruel than ever. In consequence still more bitter complaints reached home from the colonists.

At this time the company at home were quarrelling among themselves. But in the end they sent out a new Governor called Sir George Yeardley. He, too, had orders to arrest Argall and send him home. But Argall somehow came to know of it, and he made up his mind not to go home a prisoner. So before the new Governor could arrive he packed up his goods, and leaving the colony to take care of itself, sailed gaily off to England.

The Virginians now were heartily tired of despots, and thought that it was time that they had some say in the matter of governing themselves. At the head of the company at home there was at this time a wise man named Sandys. He also thought that it would be best for the colony to be self-governing.

And so on July 30th, 1619, the first General Election was held in Virginia, and the first Parliament of Englishmen in America met. There were by this time about two thousand people living in the colony, and the settlements were scattered about on both sides of the river for sixty miles or so above Jamestown. So the colony was divided into eleven parts or constituencies, each constituency sending two members to the little parliament. These members were called burgesses, and the parliament was called the House of Burgesses. But there was no special building in which the burgesses could gather, so the meetings were held in the little wooden church at Jamestown. And thus with such small beginnings were the first foundations of a free and independent nation laid. And because of the founding of this House of Burgesses 1619 stands out as the year most to be remembered in all the early days of Virginia.

But 1619 has to be remembered for another, and this time a sad reason: for it saw not only the beginnings of freedom, but the beginnings of slavery.

Just a month after the opening of the House of Burgesses a Dutch vessel anchored at Jamestown. The captain had been on a raiding expedition off the coast of Africa, and he had on board a cargo of negroes, whom he had stolen from their homes. Twenty of these he sold to the farmers. And thus slavery was first introduced upon the Virginian plantations.

In 1619, too, there arrived the first ship-load of women colonists. Nearly all the settlers were men. A few indeed had brought their wives and daughters with them, but for the most part the colony was a community of men. Among these there were many who were young, and as they grew rich and prosperous they wanted to marry and have homes of their own. But there was no one for them to marry. So at length some one at home fell upon the plan of persuading young women to go out to Virginia to settle there, and in 1619 a ship-load of ninety came out. As soon as they arrived they found many young men eager to marry them, and sometimes they must have found it difficult to make a choice. But as soon as a young man was accepted he had to pay the Company 120 Ibs., afterwards raised to 150 Ibs., of tobacco as the price of his bride's passage across the seas. Then they were free to marry as soon as they pleased.

After this from time to time women went out to the colony. Sometimes we read of "a widow and eleven maids," or again of "fifty maids for wives." And always there came with them a letter from the company at home to the old men of the colony reminding them that these young women did not come to be servants. "We pray you therefore to be fathers to them in their business, not enforcing them to marry against their wills, neither send them to be servants," they wrote. And if the girls did not marry at once they were to be treated as guests and "put to several householders that have wives till they can be provided of husbands."

Helped in this quaint fashion and in others the colony prospered and grew ever larger. It would have prospered even more had it not been for the outbreak of a kind of plague, which the colonists simply called "the sickness." It attacked chiefly the new settlers, and was so deadly that in one year a thousand of them died. Doctors were not very skilful in those days, and although they did their best, all their efforts were of little use, till at length the dread disease wore itself out.

But in spite of all difficulties the colony grew, the settlements extended farther and farther in a long line up and down both banks of the James from Chesapeake Bay to what is now Richmond. Had the Indians been unfriendly, the colony could not have stretched out in this fashion without great danger to the settlers. But for eight years the Redmen had been at peace with their white brothers, and the settlers had lost all fear of attack from them. The Indians, indeed, might be seen wandering freely about the towns and farms. They came into the houses, and even shared the meals of the farmer and his household. Nothing, to all outward seeming, could be more friendly than the relations between the Redmen and the settlers.

Then after eight years, old Powhatan, the father of Pocahontas, died, and his brother became chief of the tribe. It may be that this new chief was known not to be so friendly to the Pale-faces as his brother had been. In any case the Governor took the precaution of sending a messenger to him with renewed expressions of friendship.

Opekankano received the messenger kindly and sent him back to his master. "Tell the Pale-faces," he said, "that I hold the peace so sure that the skies shall fall sooner than it should be broken."

But at this very time he and his people were plotting utterly to destroy the settlers. Yet they gave no hint of it. They had planned a general massacre, yet two days before the 22nd of March, the day fixed for it, some settlers were safely guided through the woods by the Indians. They came as usual, quite unarmed, into the settlers' houses, selling game, fish and furs in exchange for glass beads and such trifles. Even on the night of the 21st of March they borrowed the settlers' boats so that many of their tribe could get quickly across the river. Next morning in many places the Indians were sitting at breakfast with the settlers and their families when suddenly, as at a given signal, they sprang up, and, seizing the settlers own weapons, killed them all, sparing neither men, women nor children. So sudden was the onslaught that many a man fell dead without a cry, seeing not the hand which smote him. In the workshops, in the fields, in the gardens, wherever they were, wherever their daily work took them, they were thus suddenly and awfully struck down.

For days and weeks the Indians had watched the habits of the settlers until they knew the daily haunts of every man. Then they had planned one swift and deadly blow which was to wipe out the whole colony. And so cunning was their plot, so complete and perfect their treachery, that they might have succeeded but for the love of one faithful Indian. This Indian, named Chanco, lived with one of the settlers named Pace, and had become his servant. But Pace treated him more as a son than as a servant, and the Indian had become very devoted to him. When, then, this Indian was told that his chief commanded him to murder his master he felt that he could not do it. Instead, he went at once to Pace and told him of the plot. Pace then made ready to defend himself, and sent warnings to all the other settlers within reach. Thus a great many of the colonists were saved from death, but three hundred and fifty were cruelly slain.

This sudden and treacherous attack, after so many years of peace, enraged the white men, and they followed the Redmen with a terrible vengeance. They hunted them like wild beasts, tracking them down with bloodhounds, driving them mercilessly from place to place, until, their corn destroyed, their houses burned, their canoes smashed to splinters, the Indians were fain to sue for mercy, and peace once more was restored for more than twenty years.

Chapter 18 - How Englishmen Fought a Duel With Tyranny

At last Virginia prospered. But while it prospered the man who had first conceived the idea of this New England beyond the seas had fallen on evil days. Sir Walter Raleigh had been thrown into prison by King James. There for twelve long years he languished, only to be set free at length on condition that he should find a gold-mine for his King. He failed to find the mine, and by his efforts only succeeded in rousing to greater heights than before the Spanish hatred against him. For Spain claimed the land and gold of which Raleigh had gone in search. And now the King of Spain demanded that he should be punished. And James, weakly yielding to his outcry, condemned Sir Walter to death. So on 29th of October, 1618, this great pioneer laid his head upon the block, meeting death as gallantly as ever man died.

"I shall yet live to see it (Virginia) an English nation," he had said, after his own fifth failure to found a colony, and his words had come true. But long ere his death Raleigh had ceased to have any connection with Virginia. And perhaps there was scarce a man among those who had made their homes there who remembered that it was Raleigh who had prepared the way, that but for Raleigh a new Spain and not a New England might have been planted on the American shores.

So the death of Raleigh made no difference to the fortunes of Virginia. But the same stupidity, that same "wonderful instinct for the wrong side of every question" which made James kill his great subject, also made him try to stifle the infant colony. So while in spite of sickness and massacre the colony prospered, the company at home was passing through strenuous times. The head or treasurer of the company was still that Sir Edwin Sandys who had been the chief mover in giving the colony self-government. King James, who was full of great ideas about the divine right of kings, had never forgiven him that. He was as eager as any of his people to build up a colonial Empire, but he desired that it should be one which should be dependent on himself. He had no intention of allowing colonies to set themselves up against him.

Now the time came to elect a new treasurer, and the company being very pleased with Sandys, decided to elect him again. But when King James heard that, he was very angry. He called the company a school of treason and Sandys his greatest enemy. Then, flinging himself out of the room in a terrible passion, he shouted "Choose the Devil if you will, but not Sir Edwin Sandys."

Still in spite of the King's anger the company decided to go its own way. They had their charter sealed with the King's seal, signed with the King's name, which gave them the right of freely electing their own officers, and not even the King should be allowed to interfere with that right.

On the day of the election nearly five hundred of the "adventurers" gathered together. Three names were put up for election, Sir Edwin's heading the list. But just as the voting was to begin a messenger from the King arrived.

"It is not the King's pleasure that Sir Edward Sandys should be chosen," he said, "so he has sent to you a list of four, one of which you may choose."

At this, dead silence fell upon the company, every man lost in amazement at this breach of their charter. For minutes the heavy silence lasted. Then there arose murmurs which grew ever louder until amid cries of anger it was proposed to turn the King's messengers out.

"No," said the Earl of Southampton, "let the noble gentlemen keep their places. Let them stay and see that we do everything in a manner which is fair and above board. For this business is of so great concernment that it can never be too solemnly, too thoroughly or too publicly examined."

Others agreed that this was right. So the messengers stayed. Then there came impatient cries from every part of the hall, "The Charter! The Charter! God save the King!"

So the charter was brought and solemnly read.

Then the secretary stood up. "I pray you, gentlemen," he said, "to observe well the words of the charter on the point of electing a Governor. You see it is thereby left to your own free choice. This I take it is so very plain that we shall not need to say anything more about it. And no doubt these gentlemen when they depart will give his Majesty a just information of the case."

This speech was received with great noise and cheering. In the midst of it a friend of Sir Edwin's stood up and begged for silence. And when the noise had abated a little he said, "Sir Edwin asks me to say that he withdraws his name for election. I therefore propose that the King's messengers choose two names and that we choose a third. Then let all these three names be set upon the balloting box. And so go to the election in God's name. And let His will be done."

Thereupon with one voice the whole assembly cried out, "Southampton! Southampton!"

The King's messengers then pretended that they were quite pleased. "The King," they said, "had no desire to infringe their rights. He desired no more than that Sir Edwin Sandys should not be chosen."

Then they named two from the King's list, and the ballot was immediately taken; the result being that one of the King's men had two votes, the other but one, and the Earl of Southampton all the rest.

When the King heard of this result he was a little anxious and apologetic. The messengers, he said, had mistaken his intention. He had only meant to recommend his friends, and not to forbid the company to elect any other. But once again Englishmen had fought a duel with tyranny, and won.

From this day, however, the King's hatred of the company became deadly. He harassed it in every way and at last in 1624 took its charter away, and made Virginia a Crown Colony. Henceforth in theory at least self-government was taken away from Virginia, and to the King alone belonged the right of appointing the Governor and Council. But in fact the change made little difference to the colony. For in the spring of 1625 King James died, and his son Charles I, who succeeded him upon the throne, had so much else to trouble him that he paid little heed to Virginia.

Chapter 19 - The Coming of the Cavaliers

With a new King on the throne life in Virginia went on much as it had done. Governors came and went, were good or bad, strong or weak. There were troubles with the Indians, and troubles at home about the sale of tobacco; still the colony lived and prospered. The early days of struggle were over.

Virginia now was no longer looked upon as a place of exile where with luck one could make a fortune and return home to England to enjoy it. Men now began to find Virginia a pleasant place, and look upon it as their home. The great woods were full of game, the streams were full of fish, so that the Englishman could shoot and angle to his heart's content. The land was so fertile that he did not need to work half so hard to earn a living as he had to do at home; while the climate was far kindlier.

So the colony prospered. And it was to this prosperous colony that in 1642 Sir William Berkeley was appointed Governor. He was a courtly, hot-tempered, imperious gentleman, a thorough cavalier who dressed in satin and lace and ruled like a tyrant. He did not believe in freedom of thought, and he spent a good deal of time persecuting the Puritans who had found refuge in Virginia.

For just about the time of Berkeley's appointment a fierce religious war between Cavalier and Puritan was beginning in England, and already some Puritans had fled to Virginia to escape persecution at home. But Berkeley soon showed them that they had come to the wrong place and bade them "depart the Colony with all convenience."

Berkeley did not believe in freedom of thought, and he disapproved just as much of education, for that had encouraged freedom of thought. "I thank God," he said some years later, "there are no free schools in Virginia or printing, and I hope we shall not have them these hundred years. For learning has brought disobedience and heresy, and sects into the world, and printing has divulged them, and libels against the best government. God keep us from both."

In England the quarrel between King and people grew ever fiercer and more bitter. Virginia so far away heard the echo of it, and there, as in England, men took sides. The men in Virginia were ready enough to stand up to the King and speak their mind when he threatened their liberties. But when they heard that the people in England had taken the King prisoner and were talking of beheading him they were horrified. To lay hands upon his person, to lead him to the block, to take his life! That seemed to them very terrible. And when at length the news of the King's death reached Virginia the Virginians forgot their grievances, they became King's men. And Berkeley, a fervent Royalist, wrote to his brother Royalists at home asking them to come out to Virginia, there to find new homes far from the rule of the hated "usurper" Cromwell.

Many came, fleeing from their native land "in horror and despairs at the bloody and bitter stroke." Before the year was out at least a thousand Cavaliers had found a home in Virginia. They were kindly, even affectionately, received. Every house was open to them, every hand stretched out to help.

In October the House of Burgesses met and at once declared that the beheading of "the late most excellent and now undoubtedly sainted King" was treason. And if any one in Virginia dared to defend "the late traitorous proceedings against the aforesaid King of most happy memory" they too would be found guilty of treason and worthy of death. Worthy of death too should be any one who seemed by word or deed to doubt the right of "his Majesty that now is" to the Colony of Virginia. Thus Charles II, a homeless wanderer, was acknowledged King of Virginia.

In this manner did little Virginia fling down the gauntlet to Great Britain. It was a daring deed, and one not likely to go unheeded by the watchful Cromwell. Yet two years and more passed. Then British ships appeared off Jamestown. At once the Virginians made ready to resist; cannon were mounted; the gay Cavaliers turned out in force, sword by side, gun in hand. Then a little boat flying a white flag was seen to put off for the shore. It was a messenger from the British captain.

It would be much better for them, he said, to yield peacefully than to fight and be beaten. For hold out against the great strength of Britain they could not. His words had weight with the Virginians. Yet long and seriously they debated. Some would have held out, but others saw only misery and destruction in such a course. So at length they surrendered to the might of Cromwell.

The conditions were not severe. They had to submit, and take the oath of allegiance to the British Parliament. Those who refused were given a year's time in which to leave the colony. And as for their love of the King? Why, they might pray for him, and drink his health in private, and no man would hinder them. Only in public such things would not be tolerated.

In bitterness of heart the Cavalier Governor gave up his post, sold his house in Jamestown, and went away to live in his great country house at Green Spring. Here amid his apple-trees and orchards he lived in a sort of rural state, riding forth in his great coach, and welcoming with open arms the Cavaliers who came to him for aid and comfort in those evil times.

These Cavaliers were men and women of good family. They came from the great houses of England, and in their new homes they continued to lead much the same life as they had done at home. So in Virginia. there grew up a Cavalier society, a society of men and women accustomed to command, accustomed to be waited upon; who drove about in gilded coaches, and dressed in silks and velvets. Thus the plain Virginian farmer became a country squire. From these Cavalier families were descended George Washington, James Madison and other great men who helped to make America.

The years of the Commonwealth passed quietly in Virginia. Having made the colonists submit, the Parliament left them to themselves, and Virginia for the first time was absolutely self-governing. But the great Protector died, the Restoration followed, when the careless, pleasure-loving King, Charles II was set upon the throne.

In Virginia too there was a little Restoration. When the news was brought the Cavaliers flung up their caps and shouted for joy. Bonfires were lit, bells were rung and guns fired, and to the sound of drum and trumpet Charles by the Grace of God King of England, Scotland, France, Ireland and Virginia was proclaimed to all the winds of heaven. A new seal was made upon which were the words "En dat Virginia quintum" meaning "Behold Virginia gives the fifth (dominion)." Henceforth Virginia was often called by the name of the "Old Dominion."

Nor was that all. For with the Restoration of the Stuarts Berkeley too was restored. The haughty Cavalier left his country manor house and came back to rule at Jamestown once more, as Governor and Captain General of Virginia.

During the Commonwealth there had been little change made in the government of Virginia, except that the right of voting for the Burgesses had been given to a much larger number of people.

That did not please Sir William Berkeley at all. He took away the right from a good many people. When he came back to power too he found the House of Burgesses much to his liking. So instead of having it re-elected every year he kept the same members for fourteen years lest the people should elect others who would not do his bidding.

This made the people discontented. But they soon had greater causes for discontent. First there was the Navigation Law. This Law had been passed ten years before, but had never really been put in force in America. By this Law it was ordered that no goods should be exported from the colonies in America except in British ships. Further it was ordered that the colonies should not trade with any country save England and Ireland or "some other of His Majesty's said plantations." It was a foolish law, meant to hurt the Dutch, and put gold into the pockets of British merchants. Instead it drove the colonies to rebellion.

Virginia had yet another grievance. Virginia, which for eight years had been self-governing, Virginia which had begun to feel that she had a life of her own, a place of her own among the nations, suddenly found herself given away like some worthless chattel to two of the King's favourites -the Earl of Arlington and Lord Culpeper.

The careless, laughter-loving King owed much to his friends who had rescued him from beggary, and set him upon his father's throne. Here was an easy way of repaying two of them. If they really desired that wild land beyond the seas, where only savages lived, and where the weed which his pompous grandfather had disliked so much grew, why they should have it! So he carelessly signed his royal name and for a yearly rent of forty shillings "all that dominion of land and water commonly called Virginia" was theirs for the space of thirty-one years.

It was but a scratch of the pen to the King. It was everything to the Virginians, and when news of it reached them all Virginia was ablaze. They who had clung to the King in his evil days, they who had been the last people belonging to England to submit to the Commonwealth to be thus tossed to his favourites like some useless toy, without so much as a by your leave! They would not suffer it. And they sent a messenger to England to lay their case before the King.

As to Charles, he was lazily astonished to find that any one objected to such a little trifle. And with his usual idle good nature he promised that it should be altered. But he had no intention of hurrying. Meanwhile out in Virginia events were hastening.

Chapter 20 - Bacon's Rebellion

For some time now the Indians had been an increasing terror to the white men. They had grown restless and uneasy at the constantly widening borders of the settlements. Day by day the forest was cleared, the cornfields stretched farther and farther inland, and the Redman saw himself driven farther and farther from his hunting-ground.

So anger arose in the Redman's heart. He lurked in the forests which girded the lonely farms and, watching his opportunity, crept stealthily forth to slay and burn. Settler after settler was slain in cold blood, or done to death with awful tortures, and his pleasant homestead was given to the flames. Day by day the tale of horror grew, till it seemed at length that no farm along the borders of the colony was safe from destruction. Yet the Governor did nothing.

Helplessly the Virginians raged against his sloth and tyranny. He was a traitor to his trust, they declared, and feared to wage war on the Indians lest it should spoil his fur trade with them. But that was not so. A deadlier fear than that kept Berkeley idle. He knew how his tyranny had made the people hate him, and he feared to arm them and lead them against the Indians, lest having subdued these foes they should turn their arms against him.

But the men of Virginia were seething with discontent and ripe for rebellion. All they wanted was a leader, and soon they found one. This leader was Nathaniel Bacon, a young Englishman who had but lately come to the colony. He was dashing and handsome, had winning ways and a persuasive tongue. He was the very man for a popular leader, and soon at his back he had an army of three hundred armed settlers, "one and all at his devotion."

Bacon then sent to the Governor asking for a commission to go against the Indians. But Berkeley put him off with one excuse after another; until at length goaded into rebellion Bacon and his men determined to set out, commission or no commission.

91

But they had not gone far when a messenger came spurring behind them in hot haste. He came with a proclamation from the Governor denouncing them all as rebels, and bidding them disperse at once on pain of forfeiting their lands and goods. Some obeyed, but the rest went on with Bacon, and only returned after having routed the Indians. Their defeat was so severe that the battle is known as the Battle of Bloody Run, because it was said the blood of the Indians made red the stream which flowed near the battlefield.

The Indians for the time were cowed, and Bacon marched slowly home with his men.

Meanwhile Berkeley had gathered horses and men and had ridden out to crush this turbulent youth. But hearing suddenly that the people had risen in revolt, he hastened back to Jamestown with all speed. He saw he must do something to appease the people. So he dissolved the House of Burgesses which for fourteen years had done his bidding, and ordered a new election. This pacified the people somewhat. But they actually elected the rebel Bacon as one of the members of the House.

Bacon was not, however, altogether to escape the consequences of his bold deeds. As soon as he returned he was taken prisoner and led before the Governor. The stern old Cavalier received this rebel with cool civility.

"Mr. Bacon," he said, "have you forgot to be a gentleman?"

"No, may it please your honour," answered Bacon,

"Then," said the Governor, "I will take your parole."

So Bacon was set free until the House of Burgesses should meet. Meantime he was given to understand that if he made open confession of his misdeeds in having marched against the Indians without a commission, he would be forgiven, receive his commission, and be allowed to fight the Indians. It was not easy to make this proud young man bend his knee. But to gain his end Bacon consented to beg forgiveness for what he deemed no offence. The Governor meant it to be a solemn occasion, one not lightly to be forgotten. So when the burgesses and council were gathered the Governor stood up.

"If there be joy in the presence of the angels over one sinner that repenteth," he said, "there is joy now, for we have a penitent sinner come before us. Call Mr. Bacon."

The doors were thrown wide open and in marched Bacon, tall and proud, looking grave indeed but little like a repentant sinner. At the bar of the House he knelt on one knee, and reading from a paper written out for him confessed his crimes, begging pardon from God, the King, and the Governor.

When his clear young voice ceased the old Governor spoke.

"God forgive you," he said, solemnly. "I forgive you." Three times he repeated the words and was silent.

"And all that were with him?" asked one of the council.

"Yea," said the Governor, "and all that were with him."

Thus the matter seemed ended. There was peace again and the House could now proceed to further business.

92

Part of that business was to settle what was to be done about the Indian war. Some of the people hoped that they might get help from friendly Indians. So the Indian Queen, Pamunky, had been asked to come to the Assembly and say what help she would give. Her tribe was the same as that over which the Powhatan had ruled so long ago. And although it was now but a shadow of its former self she had still about a hundred and fifty braves at command whose help the Englishmen were anxious to gain.

Queen Pamunky entered the Assembly with great dignity, and with an air of majesty walked slowly up the long room. Her walk was so graceful, her gestures so courtly, that every one looked at her in admiration. Upon her head she wore a crown of black and white wampum. Her robe was made of deer skin and covered her from shoulders to feet, the, edges of it being slit into fringes six inches deep. At her right hand walked an English interpreter, at her left her son, a youth of twenty.

When Queen Pamunky reached the table she stood still looking at the members coldly and gravely, and only at their urgent request did she sit down. Beside her, as they had entered the room, stood her son and interpreter on either hand.

When she was seated the chairman asked her how many men she would send to help them against the enemy Indians. All those present were quite sure that she understood English, but she would not speak to the chairman direct, and answered him through her interpreter, bidding him speak to her son.

The young Indian chieftain however also refused to reply. So again the Queen was urged to say how many men she could send.

For some minutes she sat still, as if in deep thought. Then in a shrill high voice full of passionate fervour, and trembling as if with tears, she spoke in her own tongue, and ever and anon amid the tragic torrent of sound the words "Tatapatamoi chepiack, Tatapatamoi chepiack" could be heard.

Few present understood her. But one of the members did, and shook his head sadly.

"What she says is too true, to our shame be it said," he sighed. "My father was general in that battle of which she speaks. Tatapatamoi was her husband, and he led a hundred men against our enemies, and was there slain with most of his company. And from that day to this no recompense has been given to her. Therefore she upbraids us, and cries, 'Tatapatamoi is dead.'"

When they heard the reason for the Indian Queen's anger many were filled with sympathy for her.

The chairman however was a crusty old fellow, and he was quite unmoved by the poor Queen's passion of grief and anger. Never a word did he say to comfort her distress, not a sign of sympathy did he give. He rudely brushed aside her vehement appeal, and repeated his question.

"What men will you give to help against the enemy Indians?"

With quivering nostrils, and flashing eyes, the Indian Queen drew herself up scornfully, she looked at him, then turned her face away, and sat mute.

Three times he repeated his question.

93

Then in a low disdainful voice, her head still turned away, she muttered in her own language "Six."

This would never do. The lumbering old chairman argued and persuaded, while the dusky Queen sat sullenly silent. At length she uttered one word as scornfully as the last. "Twelve," she said. Then rising, she walked proudly and gravely from the hall.

Thus did the blundering old fellow of a chairman, for the lack of a few kindly words, turn away the hearts of the Indians, and lose their help at a moment when it was sorely needed.

The new House had many other things to discuss besides the Indian wars, and the people, who had been kept out of their rights for so long, now made up for lost time. They passed laws with feverish haste. They restored manhood suffrage, did away with many class privileges, and in various ways instituted reforms. Afterwards these laws were known as Bacon's Laws.

But meanwhile Bacon was preparing a new surprise for every one.

One morning the town was agog with news. "Bacon has fled, Bacon has fled!" cried every one.

It was true. Bacon had grown tired of waiting for the commission which never came. So he was off to raise the country. A few days later he marched back again at the head of six hundred men.

At two o'clock one bright June day the sounds of drum and trumpet were heard mingled with the tramp of feet and the clatter of horses' hoofs; and General Bacon, as folk began to call him now, drew up his men not an arrow's flight from the State House.

The people of Jamestown rushed to the spot. Every window and balcony was crowded with eager excited people. Men, women and children jostled each other on the green, as Bacon, with a file of soldiers on either hand, marched to the State House.

The white-haired old Governor, shaking with anger, came out to meet the insolent young rebel. With trembling fingers he tore at the fine lace ruffles of his shirt, baring his breast.

"Here I am!" He cried. "Shoot me! 'Fore God 'tis a fair mark. Shoot me! Shoot me!" he repeated in a frenzy.

But Bacon answered peaceably enough. "No, may it please your honour," he said, "we will not hurt a hair of your head, nor of any other man's. We are come for a commission to save our lives from the Indians which you have so often promised. And now we will have it before we go."

But when the stern old Cavalier refused to listen to him, Bacon too lost his temper, and laying his hand on his sword, swore he would kill the Governor, Council, Assembly and all, rather than forego his commission. His men, too, grew impatient and filled the air with their shouts.

"We will have it, we will have it!" they cried, at the same time pointing their loaded guns at the windows of the State House.

Minute by minute the uproar increased, till at length one of the Burgesses, going

94

to a window, waved his handkerchief ("a pacifeck handkercher" a quaint old record calls it) and shouted, "You shall have it, you shall have it."

So the tumult was quieted. A commission was drawn up making Bacon Commander-in-Chief of the army against the Indians, and a letter was written to the King praising him for what he had done against them. But the stern old Governor was still unbending, and not till next day was he browbeaten into signing both papers.

The young rebel had triumphed. But Berkeley was not yet done with him, for the same ship which carried the letter of the Burgesses to the King also carried a private letter from Berkeley in which he gave his own account of the business. "I have for above thirty years governed the most flourishing country the sun ever shone over," he wrote, "but am now encompassed with rebellion like waters."

And as soon as Bacon was safely away, and at grips once more with the Indians, the Governor again proclaimed him and his followers to be rebels and traitors.

Bacon had well-nigh crushed the Indian foe when this news was brought to him. He was cut to the quick by the injustice.

"I am vexed to the heart," he said, "for to think that while I am hunting Indian wolves, tigers, and foxes which daily destroy our harmless sheep and lambs, that I, and those with me, should be pursued with a full cry, as a more savage and no less ravenous beast."

So now in dangerous mood he marched back to Jamestown. Things were looking black for him, but his men were with him heart and soul. When one of them, a Scotsman named Drummond, was warned that this was rebellion he replied recklessly, "I am in over shoes, I will be in over boots."

His wife was even more bold. "This is dangerous work," said some one, "and England will have something to say to it."

Then Sarah Drummond picked up a twig, and snapping it in two, threw it down again. "I fear the power of England no more than that broken straw," she cried.

Bacon now issued a manifesto in reply to Berkeley's proclamation, declaring that he and his followers could not find in their hearts one single spot of rebellion or treason. "Let Truth be bold," he cried, "and let all the world know the real facts of this matter." He appealed to the King against Sir William, who had levied unjust taxes, who had failed to protect the people against the Indians, who had traded unjustly with them, and done much evil to his Majesty's true subjects.

So far there had only been bitter words between the old Governor and the young rebel, and Bacon had never drawn his sword save against the Indians. Now he turned it against the Governor, and, marching on Jamestown, burned it to the ground, and Berkeley, defeated, fled to Accomac.

Everywhere Bacon seemed successful, and from Jamestown he marched northward to settle affairs there also "after his own measures." But a grim and all-conquering captain had now taken up arms against this victorious rebel-Captain Death, whom even the greatest soldier must obey. And on October 1st, 1676, Bacon laid down his sword for ever. He had been the heart and soul of the rebellion, and with his death it collapsed swiftly and completely.

95

Bacon was now beyond the Governor's wrath, but he wreaked his vengeance on those who had followed him. For long months the rebels were hunted and hounded, and when caught they were hanged without mercy. The first to suffer was Colonel Thomas Hansford. He was a brave man and a gentleman, and all he asked was that he might be shot like a soldier, and not hanged like a dog. But the wrathful Governor would not listen to his appeal, and he was hanged. On the scaffold he spoke to those around, praying them to remember that he died a loyal subject of the King, and a lover of his country. He has been called the first martyr to American liberty.

Another young Major named Cheesman was condemned to death, but died in prison, some say by poison.

The Governor, when he was brought before him, asked fiercely: "What reason had you for rebellion?"

But before the Major could reply his young wife stepped from the surrounding crowd, and threw herself upon her knees before the Governor. "It was my doing," she cried. " I persuaded him, and but for me he would never have done it. I am guilty, not he. I pray you therefore let me be hanged, and he be pardoned."

But the old Cavalier's heart was filled to overflowing with a frenzy of hate. He was utterly untouched by the poor lady's brave and sad appeal, and answered her only with bitter, insulting words.

Drummond too was taken. He was indeed "in over boots" and fearless to the last. The Governor was overjoyed at his capture, and with mocking ceremony swept his hat from his head, and, bowing low, cried exultantly, "Mr. Drummond, you are very welcome. I am more glad to see you than any man in Virginia. Mr. Drummond, you shall be hanged in half an hour."

"What your honour pleases," calmly replied Drummond. And so he died.

It seemed as if the Governor's vengeance would never be satisfied. But at length the House met, and petitioned him to spill no more blood. "For," said one of the members, "had we let him alone he would have hanged half the country."

News of his wild doings, too, were carried home, and reached even the King's ears. "The old fool," cried he, "has hanged more men in that naked country than I did for the murder of my father." So Berkeley was recalled.

At his going the whole colony rejoiced. Guns were fired and bonfires lit to celebrate the passing of the tyrant.

Berkeley did not live long after his downfall. He had hoped that when he saw the King, and explained to him his cause, that he would be again received into favour. But his hopes were vain. The King refused to see him, and he who had given up everything, even good name and fame, in his King's cause died broken-hearted, a few months later.

Chapter 21 - The Story of the Knights of the Golden Horseshoe

Bacon was driven into rebellion by evil government and tyranny. But the rising did little good. Bacon's Laws were done away with and Lord Culpeper, one of the two nobles to whom Charles II had given Virginia, came out as Governor. He soon showed himself a greedy tyrant, caring nothing for the happiness of his people, and bent only on making money for himself.

Other governors followed him, many of them worthless, some never taking the trouble to come to Virginia at all. They stayed at home, accepting large sums of money, and letting other people do the work. But they were not all worthless and careless. Some were good, and one of the best was a Scotsman, Alexander Spotswood. He was a lieutenant governor. That is, the Governor in name was the Earl of Orkney, who was given the post as a reward for his great services as a soldier. But he never crossed the Atlantic to visit his noble province. Instead he sent others to rule for him. They were in fact the real governors, although they were called lieutenant governors.

Spotswood loved Virginia, and he did all he could to make the colony prosperous. He saw that the land was rich in minerals, and that much could be done with iron ore. So he built smelting furnaces, and altogether was so eager over it that he was called the Tubal Cain of Virginia. For Tubal Cain, you remember, "was an instructor of every artificer in brass and iron."

Spotswood also planted vines, and brought over a colony of Germans to teach the people how to grow them properly, and make wine. It was he, too, who first explored "the West."

Virginia up till now had lain between the sea and the blue range of mountains which cut it off from the land behind. To the English that was a land utterly unknown. All they knew was that the French were claiming it. But Governor Spotswood wanted to know more. So one August he gathered a company of friends, and set forth on an exploring expedition. With servants and Indian guides they made a party of about fifty or so, and a jolly company they were. They hunted by the way, and camped beneath the stars. There was no lack of food and drink, and it was more like a prolonged picnic than an exploring expedition.

The explorers reached the Blue Ridge, and, climbing to the top of a pass, looked down upon the beautiful wild valley beyond, through which wound a shining river. Spotswood called the river the Euphrates. But fortunately the name did not stick, and it is still called by its beautiful Indian name of Shenandoah.

Spotswood named the highest peak he saw Mount George in honour of the King, and his companions gave the next highest peak the name of Mount Alexander in honour of the Governor whose Christian name was Alexander. Then they went down into the valley below, and on the banks of the river they buried a bottle, inside which they had put a paper declaring that the whole valley belonged to George I, King by the Grace of God of Great Britain, France, Ireland and Virginia.

After that the merry party turned homewards. They climbed to the top of the gap, took a last look at the fair valley of the unknown West, and then went down once more into the familiar plains of Virginia.

For this expedition all the horses were shod with iron, a thing very unusual in Virginia where there were no hard or stony roads. So as a remembrance of their

97

pleasant time together Spotswood gave each of his companions a gold horseshoe set with precious stones for nails. Graven upon them were the Latin words, Sic juvat transcendere montes which mean, "Thus it is a pleasure to cross the mountains." Later all those who took part in the expedition were called Knights of the Golden Horseshoe.

Up to about this time the people in Virginia had been altogether English. Now a change came.

In France Louis XIV was persecuting the Protestants, or Huguenots, as they were called. He ordered them all to become Catholics or die, and he forbade them to leave the country. But thousands of them refused to give up their religion, and in spite of the King's commands they stole away from the country by secret ways. Many of them found a refuge in America.

In the north of Ireland, which had been settled chiefly by Scotsmen, the Presbyterians were being persecuted by the Church of England; at the same time the English Parliament was hampering their trade with unfair laws. So to escape from this double persecution many Scotch-Irish fled to America.

In Germany too the Protestants were being persecuted by the Catholic Princes. They too fled to America.

All these widely varying refugees found new homes in other colonies as well as in Virginia, as we shall presently hear. In Virginia it was chiefly to the Shenandoah Valley that they came, that valley which Spotswood and his knights of the Golden Horseshoe had seen and claimed for King George. The coming of these new people changed Virginia a good deal.

After the death of King Charles the coming of the Cavaliers had made Virginia Royalist and aristocratic, so now the coming of those persecuted Protestants and Presbyterians tended to make it democratic. That is, the coming of the Cavaliers increased the number of those who believed in the government of the many by the few. The coming of the European Protestants increased the number of those who believed in the government of the people by the people.

So in the House of Burgesses there were scenes of excitement. But these were no longer in Jamestown, for the capital had been removed to Williamsburg. Jamestown, you remember, had been burned by Bacon. Lord Culpeper however rebuilt it. But a few years later it was again burned down by accident. It had never been a healthy spot; no one seemed very anxious to build it again, so it was forsaken, and Williamsburg became and remained the capital for nearly a hundred years.

Today all that is left of Jamestown, the first home of Englishmen in America, is the ivy-grown ruin of the church.

PART III STORIES OF NEW ENGLAND

Chapter 22 - The Story of the Pilgrim Fathers

While the Colony of Virginia was fighting for life, and struggling against tyranny, other colonies were taking root upon the wide shores of America.

You will remember that in 1606 a sort of double company of adventurers was formed in England, one branch of which - the London Company - founded Jamestown. The other branch - the Plymouth Company - also sent out an, expedition, and tried to found a colony at the mouth of the Kennebec River. But it was a failure. Some of the adventurers were so discouraged with the cold and bleak appearance of the land that they sailed home again in the ship which had brought them out. Only about forty-five or so stayed on. The winter was long and cold, and they were so weary of it, so homesick and miserable, that when in the spring a ship came out with provisions they all sailed home again. They had nothing good to say of Virginia, as the whole land was then called by the English. It was far too cold, and no place for Englishmen, they said.

Still some of the adventurers of the Plymouth Company did not give up hope of founding a colony. And nine years after this first attempt, our old friend Captain John Smith, recovered from his wounds received in Virginia and as vigorous as ever, sailed out to North Virginia. In the first place be went "to take whales, and also to make trials of a mine of gold and of copper" and in the long run he hoped to found a colony.

It was he who changed the name from North Virginia to New England, by which name it has ever since been known. He also named the great river which he found there Charles River after Prince Charles, who later became King Charles I, and all along the coast he marked places with the names of English towns, one of which he named Plymouth.

But Smith did not succeed in founding a colony in New England; and several adventurers who followed him had no better success. The difficulties to be overcome were great, and in order to found a colony on that inhospitable coast men of tremendous purpose and endurance were needed. At length these men appeared.

Nowadays a man may believe what he likes either in the way of politics or religion. He may belong to any political party he pleases, or he may belong to none. He may write and make speeches about his opinions. Probably no one will listen to him; certainly he will not be imprisoned for mere opinions. It is the same with religion. A man may go to any church he likes, or go to none. He may write books or preach sermons, and no one will hinder him.

But in the days of King James things were very different. In those days there was little freedom either in thought or action, in religion or politics. As we have seen King James could not endure the thought that his colony should be self-governing and free to make laws for itself. Consequently he took its charter away. In religion it was just the same. In England at the Reformation the King had been made head of the Church. And if people did not believe what the King and Clergy told them to believe they were sure, sooner or later, to be punished for it.

Now in England more and more people began to think for themselves on matters of religion. More and more people found it difficult to believe as King and Clergy wished them to believe. Some found the Church of England far too like the old Church of Rome. They wanted to do away with all pomp and ceremony and have things quite simple. They did not wish to separate from the

Church; they only wanted to make the Church clean and pure of all its errors. So they got the name of Puritans. Others however quite despaired of making the Church pure. They desired to leave it altogether and set up a Church of their own. They were called Separatists, or sometimes, from the name of a man who was one of their chief leaders, Brownists.

These Brownists did not want to have bishops and priests, and they would not own the King as head of the Church. Instead of going to church they used to meet together in private houses, there to pray to God in the manner in which their own hearts told them was right. This of course was considered treason and foul wickedness. So on all hands the Brownists were persecuted. They were fined and imprisoned, some were even hanged. But all this persecution was in vain, and the number of Separatists instead of decreasing increased as years went on.

Now at Scrooby, a tiny village in Nottinghamshire, England, and in other villages round, both in Nottinghamshire and Lincolnshire, there were a number of Separatists. Every Sunday these people would walk long distances to some appointed place, very likely to Scrooby, or to Babworth, where there was a grave and reverent preacher, to hold their meetings.

But they were never left long in peace. They were hunted and persecuted on every side, till at length they decided to go to Holland where they heard there was freedom of religion for all men.

To many of them this was a desperate adventure. In those days few men traveled. For the most part people lived and died without once leaving their native villages. To go into a new country, to learn a new language, to get their living they know not how, seemed to some a misery almost worse than death. Still they determined to go, such was their eagerness to serve God aright.

The going was not easy. They were harassed and hindered in every fashion. Again and again evil men cheated them, and robbed them of almost all they possessed, leaving them starving and penniless upon the sea shore. But at length, overcoming all difficulties, in one way or another, they all reached Amsterdam.

Even here however they did not find the full freedom and peace which they desired, and they next moved to Leyden.

They found it "a beautiful city and of a sweet situation." Here they settled down and for some years lived in comfort, earning their living by weaving and such employments, and worshipping God at peace in their own fashion.

But after about eleven or twelve years they began once more to think of moving. They had many reasons for this, one being that if they stayed longer in Holland their children and grandchildren would forget how to speak English, and in a few generations they would no longer be English, but Dutch. So they determined to go to some place where they could still remain English, and yet worship God as they thought right.

And the place their thoughts turned to was the vast and unpeopled country of America. But which part of America they could not at first decide. After much talk however they at length decided to ask the Virginian Company to allow them to settle in their land, but as a separate colony, so that they might still have religious freedom.

Two messengers were therefore despatched to London to arrange matters with the company. The Virginian Company was quite willing to have these Separatists as settlers. But do what they would they could not get the King to promise them freedom to worship God. All that they could wring from him was a promise that he would take no notice of them so long as they behaved peaceably. To allow or tolerate them by his public authority, under his broad seal, was not to be thought of.

That was the best the Virginian Company or any of their friends could do for the Separatists. And with this answer the messengers were obliged to return to Leyden. When the English men and women there heard it they were much disturbed. Some felt that without better assurance of peace they would be foolish to leave their safe refuge. But the greater part decided that poor though the assurance was they would be well to go, trusting in God to bring them safely out of all their troubles. And after all they reflected "a seal as broad as the house floor would not serve the turn" if James did not wish to keep his promise, so little trust did they put in princes and their oaths.

So it was decided to go to the New World, and after much trouble everything was got ready. A little ship called the Speedwell was bought and fitted up. Then those who had determined to go went down to the sea shore accompanied by all their friends.

Their hearts were heavy as they left the beautiful city which had been their home for the last twelve years. But they knew that they were pilgrims and strangers upon the earth, and they looked only to find in heaven an abiding place. So steadfastly they set their faces towards the sea. They went on board, their friends following sorrowfully. Then came the sad parting. They clung to each other with tears, their words of farewell and prayers broken by sobs. It was so pitiful a sight that even among the Dutchmen who looked on there was scarce a dry eye.

At length the time came when the last farewell had to be said. Then their pastor fell upon his knees on the deck, and as they knelt round him he lifted his hands to heaven, and with tears running down his cheeks prayed God to bless them all.

So the sails were hoisted and the Speedwell sailed away to Southampton. Here she found the Mayflower awaiting her, and the two set forth together. But they had not gone far before the captain of the Speedwell complained that his ship was leaking so badly that he dared not go on. So both ships put in to Dartmouth, and here the Speedwell was thoroughly overhauled and mended, and again they set out.

But still the captain declared that the Speedwell was leaking. So once more the pilgrims put back, this time to Plymouth. And here it was decided that the Speedwell was unseaworthy, and unfit to venture across the great ocean. That she was a rotten little boat is fairly certain, but it is also fairly certain that the Captain did not want to sail to America, and therefore he made the worst, instead of the best, of his ship.

If it is true that he did not want to cross the ocean he now had his way. For the Speedwell was sent back to London with all those who had already grown tired of the venture, or who had grown fearful because of the many mishaps. And the Mayflower, taking the rest of the passengers from the Speedwell, and as many of the stores as she could find room for, proceeded upon her voyage alone.

Among those who sailed in her were Captain Miles Standish and Master Mullins with his fair young daughter Priscilla. I daresay you have read the story Longfellow made about them and John Alden. At the first John Alden did not go as a Pilgrim. He was hired at Southampton as a cooper, merely for the voyage, and was free to go home again if he wished. But he stayed, and as we know from Longfellow's poem he married Priscilla.

Now at length these Pilgrim Fathers as we have learned to call them were really on their way. But all the trouble about the Speedwell had meant a terrible loss of time, and although the Pilgrims bad left Holland in July it was September before they finally set sail from Plymouth, and their voyage was really begun.

And now instead of having fair they had foul weather. For days and nights, with every sail reefed, they were driven hither and thither by the wind, were battered and beaten by cruel waves, and tossed helplessly from side to side. At length after two months of terror and hardships they sighted the shores of America.

They had however been driven far out of their course, and instead of being near the mouth of the Hudson River, and within the area granted to the Virginian Company, they were much further north, near Cape Cod, and within the area granted to the Plymouth Company, where they had really no legal right to land. So although they were joyful indeed to see land, they decided to sail southward to the mouth of the Hudson, more especially as the weather was now better.

Soon however as they sailed south they found themselves among dangerous shoals and roaring breakers, and, being in terror of shipwreck, they turned back again. And when they once more reached the shelter of Cape Cod harbour they fell on their knees and most heartily thanked God, Who had brought them safely over the furious ocean, and delivered them from all its perils and miseries.

They vowed no more to risk the fury of the tempest, but to settle where they were in the hope of being able to make things right with the Plymouth Company later on. So in the little cabin of the Mayflower the Pilgrims held a meeting, at which they chose a Governor and drew up rules, which they all promised to obey, for the government of the colony. But this done they found it difficult to decide just what would be the best place for their little town, and they spent a month or more exploring the coast round about. At length they settled upon a spot.

On Captain John Smith's map it was already marked Plymouth, and so the Pilgrims decided to call the town Plymouth because of this, and also because Plymouth was the last town in England at which they had touched. So here they all went ashore, choosing as a landing place a flat rock which may be seen to this day, and which is now known as the Plymouth Rock.

"Which had been to their feet as a doorstep, Into a world unknown-the corner-stone of a nation!"

The Pilgrim Fathers had now safely passed the perils of the sea. But many more troubles and miseries were in store for them. For hundreds of miles the country lay barren and untilled, inhabited only by wild Redmen, the nearest British settlement being five hundred miles away. There was no one upon the shore to greet them, no friendly lights, no smoke arising from cheerful cottage fires, no sign of habitation far or near. It was a silent frost-bound coast upon which they had set foot.

The weather was bitterly cold and the frost so keen that even their clothes were frozen stiff. And ere these Pilgrims could find a shelter from the winter blasts, trees had to be felled and hewn for the building of their houses. It was enough to make the stoutest heart quake. Yet not one among this little band of Pilgrims flinched or thought of turning back. They were made of sterner stuff than that, and they put all their trust in God.

"May not and ought not the children of those fathers rightly say," writes William Bradford, who was their Governor for thirty-one years, "our fathers were Englishmen which came over this great ocean and were ready to perish in the wilderness? But they cried unto the Lord and He heard their voice." The winter was an unusually severe one. And so, having no homes to shelter them or comfort of any kind, many of the Pilgrims died. Many more became seriously ill. Indeed at one time there were not more than six or seven out of a hundred and more who were well and able to work. And had it not been for the wonderful devotion and loving kindness of these few the whole colony might have perished miserably. But these few worked with a will, felling trees, cooking meals, caring for the sick both day and night.

The first winter the Pilgrim Fathers, it was said, "endured a wonderful deal of misery with infinite patience." But at length spring came, and with the coming of warmth and sunshine the sickness disappeared. The sun seemed to put new life into every one. So when in April the Mayflower, which had been in harbour all winter, sailed homeward not one of the Pilgrims sailed with her.

The little white-winged ship was the last link with home. They had but to step on board to be wafted back to the green hedgerows and meadows gay with daisies and buttercups in dear old England. It was a terrible temptation. Yet not one yielded to it. With tears streaming down their faces, the Pilgrims knelt upon the shore and saw the Mayflower go, following her with prayers and blessings until she was out of sight. Then they went back to their daily labours. Only when they looked out to sea the harbour seemed very empty with no friendly little vessel lying there.

Meanwhile among all the miseries of the winter there had been one bright spot. The Pilgrims had made friends with the Indians. They had often noticed with fear Redmen skulking about at the forest's edge, watching them. Once or twice when they had left tools lying about they had been stolen. But whenever they tried to get speech with the Indians they fled away.

What was their surprise then when one morning an Indian walked boldly into the camp and spoke to them in broken English!

103

He told them that his name was Samoset, and that he was the Englishmen's friend. He also said he could tell them of another Indian called Squanto who could speak better English than he could. This Squanto had been stolen away from his home by a wicked captain who intended to sell him as a slave to Spain. But he had escaped to England, and later by the help of Englishmen had been brought back to his home. All his tribe however had meantime been swept away by a plague, and now only he remained.

Samoset also said that his great chief named Massasoit or Yellow Feather wished to make friends with the Palefaces. The settlers were well pleased to find the Indian ready to be friendly and, giving him presents of a few beads and bits of coloured cloth, they sent him away happy. But very soon he returned, bringing Squanto and the chief, Yellow Feather, with him. Then there was a very solemn pow-wow; the savages gorgeous in paint and feathers sat beside the sad-faced Englishmen in their tall black hats and sober clothes, and together they swore friendship and peace. And so long as Yellow Feather lived this peace lasted.

After the meeting Yellow Feather went home to his own wigwams, which were about forty miles away. But Squanto stayed with the Englishmen. He taught them how to plant corn; he showed them where to fish and hunt; he was their guide through the pathless forests. He was their staunch and faithful friend, and never left them till he died. Even then he feared to be parted from his white friends, and he begged them to pray God that he too might be allowed to go to the Englishmen's heaven.

Besides Yellow Feather and his tribe there were other Indians who lived to the east of the settlement, and they were by no means so friendly. At harvest time they used to steal the corn from the fields and otherwise harass the workers. As they went unpunished they grew ever bolder until at length one day their chief, Canonicus, sent a messenger to the Governor with a bundle of arrows tied about with a large snakeskin. This was meant as a challenge. But the Governor was not to be frightened by such threats. He sent back the snakeskin stuffed with bullets and gunpowder, and with it a bold message.

"If you would rather have war than peace," he said, "you can begin when you like. But we have done you no wrong and we do not fear you."

When the chief heard the message and saw the gunpowder and bullets he was far too much afraid to go to war. He was too frightened to touch the snakeskin or even allow it to remain in his country, but sent it back again at once.

This warlike message however made the settlers more careful, and they built a strong fence around their little town, with gates in it, which were shut and guarded at night. Thus the Pilgrims had peace with the Redmen. They had also set matters right with the Plymouth Company, and had received from them a patent or charter allowing them to settle in New England. Other Pilgrims came out from home from time to time, and the little colony prospered and grew, though slowly.

They were a grave and stern little company, obeying their Governor, fearing God, keeping the Sabbath and regarding all other feast days as Popish and of the evil one.

104

It is told how one Christmas Day the Governor called every one out to work as usual. But some of the newcomers to the colony objected that it was against their conscience to work on Christmas Day.

The Governor looked gravely at them. "If you make it a matter of conscience," he said, "I will release you from work upon this day until you are better taught upon the matter." Then he led the others away to fell trees and saw wood. But when at noon he returned he found those, whose tender consciences had not allowed them to work, playing at ball and other games in the streets. So he went to them, and took away their balls and other toys. "For," said he, "it is against my conscience that you should play while others work."

And such was the power of the Governor that he was quietly obeyed, "and," we are told, "since that time nothing hath been attempted that way, at least openly."

They were stern, these old settlers, and perhaps to our way of thinking narrow, and they denied themselves much that is lovely in life and quite innocent. Yet we must look back at them with admiration. No people ever left their homes to go into exile for nobler ends, no colony was ever founded in a braver fashion. And it is with some regret we remember that these brave Pilgrim Fathers have given a name to no state in the great union. For the Colony of Plymouth, having held on its simple, severe way for many years, was at length swallowed up by one of its great neighbours, and became part of the State of Massachusetts. But that was not till 1692. Meanwhile, because it was the first of the New England colonies to be founded, it was often called the Old Colony.

Chapter 23 - The Founding of Massachusetts

For ten years after the coming of the Pilgrim Fathers charters were constantly granted to "adventurers" of one kind or another for the founding of colonies in New England. And, driven by the tyranny of King James and of his son Charles I, small companies of Puritans began to follow the example of the Pilgrim Fathers and go out to New England, there to seek freedom to worship God. For King James, although brought up as a Presbyterian himself, was bitter against the Puritans. "I shall make them conform themselves," he had said, "or I will harry them out of the land."

And as he could not make them conform he "harried" them so that many were glad to leave the land to escape tyranny. King James has been called the British Solomon, but he did some amazingly foolish things. This narrow-minded persecution of the Puritans was one. Yet by it he helped to form a great nation. So perhaps he was not so foolish after all.

As has been said many companies were formed, many land charters granted for Northern Virginia, or New England, as it was now called. At length a company of Puritans under the name of the Massachusetts Bay Company got a charter from Charles I, granting them a large tract of land from three miles south of the Charles River to three miles north of the Merrimac, and as far west as the Pacific. Of course no one in those days realised what a huge tract that would be. For no man yet guessed how great a continent America was, or by what thousands of miles the Pacific was separated from the Atlantic. This charter was not unlike that given to Virginia. But there was one important difference. Nowhere in the charter did it say that the seat of government must be in England.

So when Charles dismissed his Parliament, vowing that if the members would not do as he wished he would rule without them, a great many Puritans decided to leave the country. They decided also to take their charter with them and remove the Company of Massachusetts Bay, bag and baggage, to New England.

Charles did nothing to stop them. Perhaps at the time he was pleased to see so many powerful Puritans leave the country, for without them he was all the freer to go his own way. So in the spring of 1630 more than a thousand set sail, taking with them their cattle and household goods.

Many of these were cultured gentlemen who were thus giving up money, ease and position in order to gain freedom of religion. They were not poor labourers or artisans, not even for the most part traders and merchants. They chose as Governor for the first year a Suffolk gentleman named John Winthrop. A new Governor was chosen every year, but John Winthrop held the post many times, twice being elected three years in succession. Although we may think that he was narrow in some things, he was a man of calm judgment and even temper, and was in many ways a good Governor. From the day he set forth from England to the end of his life he kept a diary, and it is from this diary that we learn nearly all we know of the early days of the colony.

It was in June of 1630 that Winthrop and his company landed at Salem, and although there were already little settlements at Salem and elsewhere this may be taken as the real founding of Massachusetts. Almost at once Winthrop decided that Salem would not be a good centre for the colony, and he moved southward to the Charles River, where he finally settled on a little hilly peninsula. There a township was founded and given the name of Boston, after the town of Boston in Lincolnshire, from which many of the settlers had come.

Although these settlers had more money and more knowledge of trading, the colony did not altogether escape the miseries which every other colony had so far suffered. And, less stout-hearted than the founders of Plymouth, some fled back again to England. But they were only a few, and for the most part the new settlers remained and prospered.

These newcomers were not Separatists like the Pilgrim Fathers but Puritans. When they left England they had no intention of separating themselves from the Church of England. They had only desired a simpler service. But when they landed in America they did in fact separate from the Church of England. England was so far away; the great ocean was between them and all the laws of Church and King. It seemed easy to cast them off, and they did.

So bishops were done away with, great parts of the Common Prayer Book were rejected, and the service as a whole made much more simple. And as they wished to keep their colony free of people who did not think as they did the founders of Massachusetts made a law that only Church members might have a vote.

With the Plymouth Pilgrims, however, Separatists though they were, these

Puritans were on friendly terms. The Governors of the two colonies visited each other to discuss matters of religion and trade, and each treated the other with great respect and ceremony.

We read how when Governor Winthrop went to visit Governor Bradford the chief people of Plymouth came forth to meet him without the town, and led him to the Governor's house. There he and his companions were entertained in goodly fashion, feasting every day and holding pious disputations. Then when he departed again, the Governor of Plymouth with the pastor and elders accompanied him half a mile out of the town in the dark.

But although the Puritans of Massachusetts were friendly enough with dissenters beyond their borders they soon showed that within their borders there was to be no other Church than that which they had set up.

Two brothers for instance who wanted to have the Prayer Book used in full were calmly told that New England was no place for them, and they were shipped home again. Later a minister named Roger Williams was banished from Massachusetts, for he preached that there ought to be no connection between Church and State; that a man was responsible to God alone for his opinions; and that no man had a right to take from or give to another a vote because of the Church to which he belonged.

It seemed to him a deadly sin to have had anything whatever to do with the Church of England, a sin for which every one ought to do public penance. He also said that the land of America belonged to the natives, and not to the King of England. Therefore the King of England could not possibly give it to the settlers, and they ought to bargain for it with the natives. Otherwise they could have no right to it.

This idea seemed perfectly preposterous to those old settlers, for, said they, "he chargeth King James to have told a solemn, public lie, because in his patent he blessed God that he was the first Christian prince that had discovered this land." They might think little enough of their King in their hearts, but it was not for a mere nobody to start such a ridiculous theory as this.

We, looking back, can see that Williams was a good and pious man, a man before his time, right in many of his ideas, though not very wise perhaps in his way of pressing them.

upon others who did not understand them. But to his fellow colonists he seemed nothing but a firebrand and a dangerous heretic. So they bade him be gone out of their borders. He went southward to what is now Rhode Island, made friends with the Indians there, bought from them some land, and founded the town of Providence.

Chapter 24 - The Story of Harry Vane

About this time there came to Massachusetts a handsome young adventurer named Sir Harry Vane. His face "was comely and fair," and his thick brown hair curly and long, so that he looked more like a Cavalier than a Puritan. He was in fact the eldest son of a Cavalier, one of the King's chosen councilors. But in spite of his birth and upbringing, in spite even of his looks, Harry Vane was a Puritan. And he gave up all the splendour of life at court, he left father and mother and fortune, and came to New England for conscience' sake.

"Sir Henry Vane hath as good as lost his eldest son who is gone to New England for conscience' sake," wrote a friend. "He likes not the discipline of the Church of England. None of our ministers would give him the Sacrament standing: no persuasions of our Bishops nor authority of his parents could prevail with him. Let him go."

As soon as Harry Vane arrived in Massachusetts he began to take an interest in the affairs of the colony. And perhaps because of his great name as much as his fair face, grey-haired men who had far more experience listened to, his youthful advice and bowed to his judgment. And before six months were passed he, although a mere lad of twenty-three, was chosen as Governor. A new Governor, you remember, was chosen every year.

At home Harry Vane had been accustomed to the pomp and splendour of courts and now he began to keep far greater state as Governor than any one had done before him. Because he was son and heir to a Privy Councilor in England the ships in the harbour fired a salute when he was elected, and when he went to church or court of justice a bodyguard of four soldiers marched before him wearing steel corslet and cap, and carrying halberds. He made, too, a sort of royal progress through his little domain, visiting all the settlements.

But although begun with such pomp Vane's year of office was by no means a peaceful one. He was young and inexperienced, and he was not strong enough to deal with questions which even the oldest among the settlers found hard to settle. Yet with boyish presumption he set himself to the task. And although he failed, he left his mark on the life of the colony. His was one more voice raised in the cause of freedom. His was one more hand pointing the way to toleration. But he was too tempestuous, too careless of tact, too eager to hurry to the good end. So instead of keeping the colony with him he created dissension. People took sides, some eagerly supporting the young Governor, but a far larger party as eagerly opposing him.

So after nine months of office Harry Vane saw that where he had meant to create fair order his hand created only disorder. And utterly disheartened he begged the Council to relieve him of the governorship and allow him to go home to England.

But when one of his friends stood up and spoke in moving terms of the great loss he would be, Harry Vane burst into tears and declared he would stay, only he could not bear all the squabbling that had been going on, nor to hear it constantly said that he was the cause of it.

Then, when the Council declared that if that was the only reason he had for going they could not give him leave, he repented of what he had said, and declared he must go for reasons of private business, and that anything else he had said was only said in temper. Whereupon the court consented in silence to his going.

All this was not very dignified for the Governor of a state, but hardly surprising from a passionate youth who had undertaken a task too difficult for him, and felt himself a failure. However Vane did not go. He stayed on to the end of his time, and even sought to be re-elected.

But feeling against him was by this time far too keen. He was rejected as Governor, and not even chosen as one of the Council. This hurt him deeply, he sulked in a somewhat undignified manner, and at length in August sailed home, never to return.

He had flashed like a brilliant meteor across the dull life of the colony. He made strife at the time, but afterwards there was no bitterness. When the colonists were in difficulties they were ever ready to ask help from Harry Vane, and he as readily gave it. Even his enemies had to acknowledge his uprightness and generosity. "At all times," wrote his great-hearted adversary, Winthrop, "he showed himself a true friend to New England, and a man of noble and generous mind."

He took a great part in the troublous times which now came upon England, and more than twenty years later he died bravely on the scaffold for the cause to which he had given his life.

Chapter 25 - The Story of Anne Hutchinson and the Founding of Rhode Island

About a year before Harry Vane came to Massachusetts another interesting and brilliant colonist arrived. This was a woman named Anne Hutchinson. She was clever, "a woman of a ready wit and bold spirit." Like Williams she was in advance of her times, and like him she soon became a religious leader. She was able, she was deeply interested in religion, and she saw no reason why women should not speak their minds on such matters.

Men used to hold meetings to discuss questions of religion and politics to which women were not allowed to go. Anne Hutchinson thought this was insulting; and she began to hold meetings for women in her own home. These meetings became so popular that often as many as a hundred women would be present. They discussed matters of religion, and as Mrs. Hutchinson held "dangerous errors" about "grace and works" and justification and sanctification, this set the whole colony agog.

By the time that Harry Vane was chosen Governor the matter had become serious. All the colony took sides for or against. Harry Vane, who stood for toleration and freedom, sided with Mrs. Hutchinson, while Winthrop, his great rival, sided against her. Mrs. Hutchinson was supported and encouraged in her wickedness by her brother-in-law John Wheelright, a "silenced minister sometimes in England." She also led away many other godly hearts.

The quarrel affected the whole colony, and was a stumbling-block in the way of all progress. But so long as Harry Vane was Governor, Mrs. Hutchinson continued her preaching and teaching. When he sailed home, however, and Winthrop was Governor once more, the elders of the community decided that Mrs. Hutchinson was a danger to the colony, and must be silenced. So all the elders and leaders met together in assembly, and condemned her opinions, some as being "blasphemous, some erroneous, and all unsafe."

A few women, they decided, might without serious wrong meet together to pray and edify one another. But that a large number of sixty or more should do so every week was agreed to be "disorderly and without rule." And as Mrs. Hutchinson would not cease her preaching and teaching, but obstinately continued in her gross errors, she was excommunicated and exiled from the colony.

Like Williams, Mrs. Hutchinson went to Rhode Island. To the sorrow of the godly, her husband went with her. And when they tried to bring him back he refused. "For," he said, "I am more dearly tied to my wife than to the Church. And I do think her a dear saint and servant of God."

In Rhode Island Mrs. Hutchinson and her friends founded the towns of Portsmouth and Newport. Others who had been driven out of one colony or another followed them, and other towns were founded; and for a time Rhode Island seems to have been a sort of Ishmael's land, and the most unruly of all the New England colonies. At length however all these little settlements joined together under one Governor.

At first the colony had no charter, and occupied the land only by right of agreement with the Indians. But after some time Roger Williams got a charter from Charles II. In this charter it was set down that no one should be persecuted "for any difference in opinion on matters of religion." Thus another new state was founded, and in Rhode Island there was more real freedom than in almost any other colony in New England.

Massachusetts was at this time, as we can see, not exactly an easy place to live in for any one whose opinions differed in the slightest from those laid down by law. Those same people who had left their homes to seek freedom of conscience denied it to others. But they were so very, very sure that their way was the only right way, that they could not understand how any one could think otherwise. They were good and honest men. And if they were severe with their fellows who strayed from the narrow path, it was only in the hope that by punishing them in this life, they might save them from much more terrible punishment in the life to come.

Chapter 26 - The Founding of Harvard

One very good thing we have to remember about the first settlers of Massachusetts is that early in the life of the colony they founded schools and colleges. A good many of the settlers were Oxford and Cambridge men, though more indeed came from Cambridge than from Oxford, as Cambridge was much the more Puritan of the two. But whether from Oxford or from Cambridge they were eager that their children born in this New England should have as good an education as their fathers had had in Old England. So when Harry Vane was Governor the colonists voted £400 with which to build a school. This is the first time known to history that the people themselves voted their own money to found a school.

It was decided to build the school at "Newtown." But the Cambridge men did not like the name, so they got it changed to Cambridge, "to tell their posterity whence they came."

Shortly before this a young Cambridge man named John Harvard had come out to Massachusetts. Very little is known of him save that he came of simple folk, and was good and learned. "A godly gentleman and lover of learning," old writers call him. "A scholar and pious in his life, and enlarged towards the country and the good of it, in life and in death."

Soon after he came to Boston this godly gentleman was made minister of the church at Charlestown. But he was very delicate and in a few months he died. As a scholar and a Cambridge man he had been greatly interested in the building of the college at Cambridge. So when he died he left half his money and all his books to it. The settlers were very grateful for this bequest, and to show their gratitude they decided to name the college after John Harvard.

Thus the first University in America was founded. From the beginning the college was a pleasant place, "more like a bowling green than a wilderness," said one man. "The buildings were thought by some to be too gorgeous for a wilderness, and yet too mean in others' apprehensions for a college. "

"The edifice," says another, "is very faire and comely within and without, having in it a spacious hall, and a large library with some bookes to it."

Of Harvard's own books there were nearly three hundred, a very good beginning for a library in those far-off days. But unfortunately they were all burnt about a hundred years later when the library accidentally took fire. Only one book was saved, as it was not in the library at the time.

Harvard's books are gone, nor does anything now remain of the first buildings "so faire and comely within and without." But the memory of the old founders and their wonderful purpose and energy is still kept green, and over the chief entrance of the present buildings are carved some words taken from a writer of those times. "After God had carried us safe to New England, and we had builded our houses, provided necessaries for our livelihood, rear'd convenient places for God's worship, and settled the Civil Government, one of the next things we longed for and looked after was to advance learning and perpetuate it to Posterity, dreading to leave an illiterate ministry to the Churches when our present ministers shall be in the Dust."

John Harvard was a good and simple man. In giving his money to found a college he had no thought of making himself famous. But "he builded better than he knew," for he reared for himself an eternal monument, and made his name famous to all the ends of the earth. And when kings and emperors are forgotten the name of Harvard will be remembered.

Chapter 27 - How Quakers First Came to New England

It was about the middle of the seventeenth century when a new kind of religion arose. This was the religion of the Quakers. George Fox was the founder of this sect, and they called themselves the Friends of Truth. The name Quaker was given to them by their enemies in derision because they "trembled before the Lord."

The Quakers were a peace-loving people; they tried to be kind and charitable; they refused to go to law; and they refused to fight. They also gave up using titles of all kinds. For, "my Lord Peter and my Lord Paul are not to be found in the Bible." They refused to take off their hats to any man, believing that that was a sign of worship which belonged to God only. They refused also to take oath of any kind, even the oath of allegiance to the King, because Christ had said, "Swear not at all." They used "thee" and "thou" instead of "you" in speaking to a single person (because they thought it more simple and truthful), and they refused to say "goodnight" or "goodmorrow," "for they knew night was good and day was good without wishing either." There was a great deal that was good in their religion and very little, it would seem, that was harmful, but they were pronounced to be "mischievous and dangerous people."

Men did not understand the Quakers. And, as often happens when men do not understand, they became afraid of them. Because they wore black clothes and broad-brimmed hats they thought they must be Jesuits in disguise. So ignorance bred fear, and fear brought forth persecution, and on all sides the Quakers were hunted and reviled. They were fined and imprisoned scourged and exiled and sold into slavery. Then, like other persecuted people, they sought a refuge in New England across the seas. But the people there were just as ignorant as the people at home, and the Quakers found no kindly welcome.

The first Quakers to arrive in New England were two women. But before they were allowed to land officers were sent on board the ship to search their boxes. They found a great many books, which they carried ashore, and while the women were kept prisoner on board the ship the books were burned in the market place by the common hangman. Then the women were brought ashore and sent to prison, for no other reason than that they were Quakers.

No one was allowed to speak to them on pain of a fine of £5, and lest any should attempt it even the windows of the prison were boarded up. They were allowed no candle, and their pens, ink, and paper were taken from them. They might have starved but that one good old man named Nicholas Upshal, whose heart was grieved for them, paid the gaoler to give them food. Thus they were kept until a ship was ready to sail for England. Then they were put on board, and the captain was made to swear that he would put them ashore nowhere but in England.

"Such," says an old writer, "was the entertainment the Quakers first met with at Boston, and that from a people who pretended that for conscience' sake they had chosen the wilderness of America before the well-cultivated Old England."

The next Quakers who arrived were treated much in the same fashion and sent back to England; and a law was made forbidding Quakers to come to the colony. At this time the same good old man who had already befriended them was grieved. "Take heed," he said, "that you be not found fighting against God, and so draw down a judgment upon the land." But the men of Boston were seized with a frenzy of hate and fear, and they banished this old man because he had dared to speak kindly of the accursed sect."

It is true the men of New England had some excuse for trying to keep the Quakers out of their colony. For some of them were foolish, and tried to force their opinions noisily upon others. They interrupted the Church services, mocked the magistrates and the clergy, and some, carried away by religious fervour, behaved more like mad folk than the disciples of a religion of love and charity.

Yet in spite of the law forbidding them to come, Quakers kept on coming to the colony, and all who came were imprisoned, beaten, and then thrust forth with orders never to return. But still they came. So a law was made that any Quaker coming into the colony should have one of his ears cut off; if he came again he should have a second ear cut off; if he came a third time he should have his tongue bored through with a hot iron.

But even this cruel law had no effect upon the Quakers. They heeded it not, and came in as great or even greater numbers than before.

The people of Boston were in despair. They had no wise to be cruel; indeed, many hated, and were thoroughly ashamed of, the cruel laws, made against these strange people. But they were nevertheless determined that Quakers should not come into their land. So now they made a law that any Quaker who came to the colony and refused to go away again when ordered should be hanged. This, they thought, would certainly keep these pernicious folk away. But it did not.

For the Quakers were determined to prove to all the world that they were free to go where they would, and that if they chose to come to Boston no man-made laws should keep them out. So they kept on coming. The magistrates knew not what to do. They had never meant to hang any of them, but only to frighten them away. But having made the law, they were determined to fulfil it, and five Quakers were hanged, one of them a woman. But while the fifth was being tried another Quaker named Christison, who had already been banished, calmly walked into the court.

When they saw him the magistrates were struck dumb. For they saw that against determination like this no punishment, however severe, might avail. On their ears Christison's words fell heavily.

"I am come here to warn you, he cried, "that you should shed no more innocent blood. For the blood that you have shed already cries to the Lord God for vengeance to come upon you."

Nevertheless he too was seized and tried. But he defended himself well. By what law will you put me to death?" he asked.

"We have a law," replied the magistrates, "and by our law you are to die."

"So said the Jews to Christ," replied Christison: " 'We have a law, and by our law you ought to die.' Who empowered you to make that law? How! Have you power to make laws different from the laws of England?"

"No," said the Governor.

"Then," said Christison, "you are gone beyond your bounds. Are you subjects to the King? Yea or nay?"

"Yea, we are so."

"Well," said Christison, "so am I. Therefore, seeing that you and I are subjects to the King, I demand to be tried by the laws of my own nation. For I never heard, nor read, of any law that was in England to hang Quakers."

Yet in spite of his brave defence Christison was condemned to death. But the sentence was never carried out. For the people had grown weary of these cruelties; even the magistrates, who for a time had been carried away by blind hate, saw that they were wrong. Christison and many of his friends who had lain in prison awaiting trial were set free.

The Quakers, too, now found a strange friend in King Charles. For the doings of the New Englanders in this matter reached even his careless ears, and he wrote to his "Trusty and well-beloved" subjects bidding them cease their persecutions, and send the Quakers back to England to be tried. This the people of Massachusetts never did. But henceforth the persecutions died down. And although from time to time the Quakers were still beaten and imprisoned no more were put to death. At length the persecution died away altogether and the Quakers, allowed to live in peace, became quiet, hard-working citizens.

Chapter 28 - How Maine and New Hampshire Were Founded

North of Massachusetts two more colonies, New Hampshire and Maine, were founded. But they were not founded by men who fled from tyranny, but by statesmen and traders who realised the worth of America, not by Puritans, but by Churchmen and Royalists. The two men who were chiefly concerned in the founding of these colonies were Sir Ferdinando Gorges and Captain John Mason. They were both eager colonists, and they both got several charters and patents from the King, and from the New England Company.

It would be too confusing to follow all these grants and charters, or all the attempts at settlements made by Mason and Gorges and others. The land granted to them was often very vaguely outlined, the fact being that the people who applied for the land, and those who drew up the charters, had only the vaguest ideas concerning the land in question. So the grants often overlapped each other, and the same land was frequently claimed by two people, and of course confusion and quarrels followed.

In 1629 Mason and Gorges, being friends, agreed to divide the province of Maine between them, and Mason called his part New Hampshire, after the county of Hampshire in England, of which he was fond. Mason and Gorges each now had an enormous tract of land, but they wanted still more.

The French, as you know, had already made settlements in Canada, But just at this time that buccaneering sea captain, David Kirke, besieged Quebec, took it and carried its brave governor, Champlain, away prisoner. Now, as soon as they heard of this Gorges and Mason asked the King to give them a grant of part of the conquered land, for it was known to be a fine country for fur trade, and was also believed to be rich in gold and silver mines. In answer to this petition the King granted a great tract of land to Gorges and Mason. This they called Laconia, because it was supposed to contain many lakes. They never did much with it however, and in a few years when peace was made with France it had all to be given back to the French.

Both Mason and Gorges spent a great deal of money trying to encourage colonists to settle on their land, and the people of Massachusetts were not at all pleased to have such powerful Churchmen for their neighbours.

As has been said, land grants often overlapped, and part of the land granted to Gorges and Mason was also claimed by Massachusetts. The Massachusetts colonists insisted on their rights. Both Gorges and Mason therefore became their enemies, and did their best to have their charter taken away. To this end Gorges got himself made Governor General of the whole of New England, with power to do almost as he liked, and he made ready to set out for his new domain with a thousand soldiers to enforce his authority.

When this news reached Massachusetts the whole colony was thrown into a state of excitement. For in this appointment the settlers saw the end of freedom, the beginning of tyranny. Both Gorges and his friend Mason were zealous Churchmen and the Puritans felt sure would try to force them all to become Churchmen also.

This the settlers determined to resist with all their might. So they built forts round Boston Harbour and mounted cannon ready to sink any hostile vessel which might put into port. In every village the young men trained as soldiers, and a beacon was set up on the highest point of the triple hill upon which Boston is built. And daily these young men turned their eyes to the hill, for when a light appeared there they knew it would be time to put on their steel caps and corslets and march to defend their liberties. Ever since the hill has been called Beacon Hill.

But the danger passed. The new ship which was being built for Ferdinando Gorges mysteriously fell to pieces on the very launching of it, and Captain Mason died. "He was the chief mover in all the attempts against us," says Winthrop. "But the Lord, in His mercy, taking him away, all the business fell on sleep."

But still Gorges did not give up his plans. He did not now go out to New England himself as he had meant to do, but sent first his nephew and then his cousin instead. They, however, did not trouble Massachusetts much.

Over the Province of Maine, Sir Ferdinando ruled supreme. He could raise troops, make war, give people titles, levy taxes. No one might settle down or trade in his province without his permission, and all must look upon him as the lord of the soil and pay him tribute. It was the feudal system come again, and Sir Ferdinando Gorges was as near being a king as any ruler of America ever has been. He drew up a most elaborate constitution, too, for his kingdom, making almost more offices than there were citizens to fill them. For, after all, his kingdom was a mere wilderness containing two fishing villages and here and there a few scattered settlements. And when the deputy governor arrived to rule this

115

kingdom he found his "palace" merely a broken-down store house with "nothing of household stuff remaining but an old pot, a pair of tongs and a couple of irons."

Thus side by side with the Puritan colonies of New England, colonies which were almost republics, there was planted a feudal state which was almost a monarchy. Of all the New England colonies, New Hampshire and Maine were the only two which were not founded for the sake of religion. For although the English Church was established in both as the state religion that was merely because the proprietors were of that Church. The colonies were founded for the sake of trade and profit. But they grew very slowly.

In 1647 Sir Ferdinando Gorges died, and Maine was left much to itself. For his son John took little interest in his father's great estate. Thirty years later his grandson, another Ferdinando, sold his rights to Massachusetts. From that time till 1820, when it was admitted to the Union as a separate state, Maine was a part of Massachusetts.

Neither did the heirs of Mason pay much attention to their estates at first. And when they did there was a good deal of quarrelling and a good deal of trouble, and at length they sold their rights to twelve men, who were afterwards known as the Masonian Proprietors.

There was a great deal of trouble, too, before New Hampshire was finally recognised as a separate colony. It was joined to Massachusetts and separated again more than once. But at last, after many changes, New Hampshire finally became a recognised separate colony. And although Captain John Mason died long before this happened he has been called the founder of New Hampshire.

"If the highest moral honour," it has been said, "belongs to founders of states, as Bacon has declared, then Mason deserved it. To seize on a tract of the American wilderness, to define its limits, to give it a name, to plant it with an English colony, and to die giving it his last thoughts among worldly concerns, are acts as lofty and noble as any recorded in the history of colonisation."

Chapter 29 - The Founding of Connecticut and War with the Indians

Many of the people who founded Massachusetts Colony were well-to-do people, people of good family, aristocrats in fact. They were men accustomed to rule, accustomed to unquestioning obedience from their servants and those under them. They believed that the few were meant to rule, and the many meant to obey. The idea that every grown-up person should have a share in the government never entered their heads. Their Governor, Winthrop, was an aristocrat to the backbone. He believed heartily in the government of the many by the few, and made it as difficult as possible for citizens to obtain the right of voting.

But there were many people who were discontented with this aristocratic rule. Among them was a minister named Thomas Hooker, like John Harvard a graduate of Emmanuel College, Cambridge.

So, being dissatisfied, he and his congregation decided to move away and found a new colony. They were the more ready to do this, as the land round Boston was

116

not fertile, and so many new settlers had come, and their cattle and flocks had increased so rapidly, that it was already difficult to find food and fodder for man and beast. Adventurers who had traveled far afield had brought back glowing reports of the beauty and fertility of the Connecticut Valley, and there Hooker decided to settle.

But for several reasons many of the people of Massachusetts objected to his going. He and his people, they said, would be in danger from the Dutch, who already had a settlement there, and who claimed the whole valley. They would also be in danger from the Indians, who were known to be hostile, and lastly, they would be in danger from the British Government because they had no charter permitting them to settle in this land. The people at home, they said, "would not endure they should sit down without a patent on any place which our King lays claim unto."

The people of Massachusetts were keeping quiet and going along steadily in their own way, without paying any heed to the British Government. They wanted to be left alone, and they did not want any one else to do things which might call attention to them. And besides all this they were greatly troubled at the thought of losing an eloquent preacher like Hooker. Every church was like a candlestick giving light to the world. "And the removing of a candlestick," they said, "is a great judgment, which is to be avoided."

But in spite of all arguments Hooker determined to go. So one June morning he and his congregation set forth. They sent their furniture by water and they themselves, both men and women, started to walk the hundred miles, driving their cattle before them; only Mrs. Hooker, who was ill, being carried in a litter.

They went slowly, allowing the cattle to graze by the wayside, living chiefly on the milk of the cows and the wild fruits they found. It was no easy journey, for their way led through the pathless wilderness, their only guides being the compass and the sun. For in those days we must remember that beyond the settlements the whole of America was untrodden ground. Save the Indian trails there were no roads. Here they had to fell trees and make a rough bridge to cross a stream; there they hewed their way through bushy undergrowth. Again they climbed steep hillsides or picked their way painfully through swamps, suffering many discomforts and fatigues.

But there were delights, too, for the sky was blue above them: birds sang to them night and morning, and wild flowers starred the ground and scented the air. All day they marched beneath the sunny blue sky, every evening they lit their watch-fires as a protection against wild beasts and lay down to rest beneath the stars, for "they had no cover but the heavens, nor any lodgings but those which simple nature afforded them."

For a fortnight they journeyed thus through the wilderness. Then they reached the Connecticut River and their journey's end. And here they built a little town which they called Hartford.

Other communities followed the example of Hooker and his flock, and Wethersfield and Windsor were built. At first all these towns remained a part of

117

Massachusetts in name at least. But after a time the settlers met together at Hartford and, agreeing to form a little republic of their own, they drew up a set of rules for themselves; the chief difference from those of Massachusetts being that the religious tests were done away with, and a man need no longer be a member of a church in order to have the right to vote. It is also interesting to remember that in these Fundamental Orders, as they called their Constitution, there is no mention of the British King or Government. These colonists had settled new land without a charter, and they made laws without recognising any authority but their own. Thus the Colony of Connecticut was founded.

Besides these towns, John Winthrop, the son of the Governor of Massachusetts, founded a fort at the mouth of the Connecticut River. For he saw it was a good place for trade with the Indians. This fort was called SayeBrook after Lord Saye and Sele and Lord Brook, two Puritan lords who had obtained a grant of land along the Connecticut River.

But this new colony was very nearly wiped out as soon as begun. For one of the dangers which the people of Massachusetts foretold proved a very real one. This was the danger from the Indians. The Indians are divided into several families, such as the Algonquins, the Hurons, the Iroquois, each of these families again containing many tribes. All the Indians in New England belonged to the Algonquin family, but were, of course, divided into many tribes. One of these tribes was called the Pequots. They were very powerful, and they tyrannised over the other tribes round about. They hated the white men, and whenever they had the opportunity they slew them.

The new Colony of Connecticut was far nearer their hunting-ground than Massachusetts. It was a far easier prey, and from the very beginning the Pequots harassed the settlers. They made no open attack, but skulked about, murdering men and women, now here, now there, appearing suddenly and vanishing again as swiftly.

This sort of thing could not be endured, and the English determined to put a stop to it. So messengers were sent to the Indians to demand that the murderers should be given up to the English. When the Indians saw the English boats appear they did not seem in the least afraid, but came running along the water-side shouting, "What cheer, Englishmen, what cheer? What do you come for?"

But the Englishmen would not answer.

And the Pequots, never thinking that the Englishmen meant war, kept running on beside the boats as they sailed up the river.

"What cheer, Englishmen, what cheer?" they kept repeating. "Are you angry? Will you kill us? Do you come to fight?"

But still the Englishmen would not answer.

Then the Indians began to be afraid. And that night they built great fires on either side of the river, fearing lest the Englishmen might land in the darkness. All night long, too, they kept up a most doleful howling, calling to each other and passing the word on from place to place to gather the braves together.

Next morning early they sent an ambassador to the English captain. He was a big, splendid-looking man, very grave and majestic. "Why do you come here?" he asked.

"I have come," answered the captain, "to demand the heads of those who have slain our comrades. It is not the habit of the English to suffer murderers to live. So if you desire peace and welfare give us the heads of the murderers."

"We knew not," answered the wily Indian, "that any of our braves had slain any of yours. It is true we have slain some white men. But we took them to be Dutch. It is hard for us to know the difference between Dutch and English."

"You know the difference between Dutch and English quite well," answered the captain sternly. "And therefore seeing you have slain the King of England's subjects, we come to demand vengeance for their blood."

"We knew no difference between the Dutch and English," declared the Indian. "They are both strangers to us, and we took them to be all one. Therefore we crave pardon. We have not wilfully wronged the English."

"That excuse will not do," insisted the captain. "We have proof that you know the English from the Dutch. We must have the heads of those persons who have slain our men, or else we will fight you."

Then, seeing that he could not move the English captain from his determination, the ambassador asked leave to go back to his chief, promising to return speedily with his answer. He was allowed to go; but as he did not return very soon the Englishmen followed. Seeing this, the ambassador hurried to them, begging them not to come nearer, and saying that his chief could not be found, as he had gone to Long Island.

"That is not true," replied the English. "We know he is here. So find him speedily or we will march through the country and spoil your corn."

Hour after hour went past; the Englishmen always patiently waiting; the wily Indian always inventing some new excuse for delay. But at length the patience of the English was exhausted, and, beating their drums, they charged the savages. Some were killed, and, the rest fleeing, the English burned their wigwams and destroyed their corn, and carried off their mats and baskets as booty.

But the Pequots were not in the least subdued, and more than ever they harassed the colonists of Connecticut. So the men of Connecticut sent to Massachusetts and to Plymouth asking for help. The people of Plymouth, however, said the quarrel was none of theirs and sent no help, but from Massachusetts about twenty men were sent. Besides this, a few friendly Indians, glad at the chance of punishing their old tyrants, joined with the white men.

So one moonlight night the little company embarked, and, sailing along the coast, landed at a spot about two days' journey from the Pequot fort. As they got near to it most of the Indians who had come with the English took fright and ran away. So less than a hundred Englishmen were left to attack seven hundred Indians.

A little before dawn they reached the fort. The Indians were all sleeping and keeping no guard, so the Englishmen quietly took possession of both entrances to the fort.

119

Then suddenly through the still morning air the sharp sound of a volley of musketry rang out "as though the finger of God had touched both match and flint." Affrighted, the Indians sprang from their sleep yelling in terror. They scarce had time to seize their bows and arrows when, sword in hand, the Englishmen stormed into the fort. A fierce fight followed, showers of arrows fell upon the Englishmen, but they did little hurt, and glanced off for the most part harmless from their thick buff coats and steel corslets.

During the fight some of the huts were set on fire, and soon the whole village was a roaring mass of flames. Many perished miserably in the fire, others who fled from it were cut down by the Englishmen, or escaping them, fell into the hands of their own countrymen. They found no mercy, for they had given none; and, remembering the awful tortures which their fellow-countrymen had suffered, the Englishmen had no compassion on their murderers.

Ere an hour had passed the fight was over. Out of four hundred Indians not more than five escaped. The Pequots were utterly wiped out and their village a heap of smoking ruins. Never before had such terrible vengeance overtaken any Indian tribe. And all the other tribes were so frightened and amazed that for forty years there was peace in New England. For no Redmen dare attack these terrible conquerors.

Chapter 30 - The Founding of New Haven

In spite of the menace of the Redmen, Englishmen continued to settle in the land they claimed. Even while the Pequot war was going on a new colony had been founded, still further south upon the shores of New England. This colony was founded by a minister named John Davenport.

John Davenport had fled from persecution in England, and, followed by his congregation, including many wealthy people, had sought,—like so many other Puritans,—a refuge in New England. The newcomers however, would not join the other Puritans, but decided to found a colony all to themselves which should be ruled only by laws found in the Bible. They called their settlement New Haven, and here the law that none but church members should vote was very strictly enforced.

Each of the towns was governed by seven men known as the Pillars of the Church. These men served as judges, but no juries were allowed, because no mention of them is found in the Bible. The laws were very strict, but the famous pretended "Blue Laws" of New Haven, which people used to make fun of, never existed. In these it was pretended that there were such absurd laws as, "No one shall cook, make beds, sweep house, cut hair or shave on the Sabbath. No woman shall kiss her child on the Sabbath or fasting day. No one shall keep Christmas, make minced pies, dance, play cards or play on any instrument of music except the drum, trumpet or jew's-harp." Some of the old Puritan laws seem to us indeed quaint enough, but there are none quite so absurd as these. They were invented by an early "tourist," who sought to make fun of these earnest, God-fearing colonists.

The New Haven colonists, like those of Connecticut, had no charter from the King of England. They settled the land not by agreement with him, but by agreement with the Indians.

Davenport and his followers bought the land upon which they settled from the Indians. To one chief they gave "twelve coats of English trucking cloth, twelve alchemy spoons, twelve hatchets, twelve hoes, two dozen of knives, twelve porringers, and four cases of French knives and scissors." To another, "eleven coats of trucking cloth, and one coat of English cloth."

The agreement was all duly and properly written out and signed by the chiefs, but, of course, as the chiefs could not write they made their marks. The first agreement was signed not only by the chief and his council, but also by the chief's sister.

We have now heard of seven New England colonies being founded. But later on, as we shall see, Plymouth joined with Massachusetts, and New Haven with Connecticut, thus making only five New England colonies as we know them today. And of those five, one (Maine) was not recognised as a separate colony but as part of Massachusetts after 1677. It remained part of Massachusetts until 1820, when it entered the Union as a state.

Meanwhile Massachusetts, New Hampshire, Plymouth, Connecticut, and New Haven all joined together, promising to help each other in case of war with the Indians, Dutch, or French, who were constant dangers to them all alike. They called themselves the United Colonies of New England. This union, however, was only for defence. Each colony was still quite independent of the others and managed its own affairs as before. It was only the first shadow of the great Union which was to come many years later. It was also one more proof that the colonies were growing up and thinking for themselves for they asked no one's leave to form this union. They thought it was necessary to their safety, so they entered into it. Only Rhode Island was not asked to join; there was still too much bitterness over religious matters between the settlers there and in the other colonies.

There were no more Puritan colonies founded, for Puritans ceased now to come to New England in large numbers. The reason was that the great fight between King and People, between Cavalier and Puritan had begun in old England. And when the Puritans won, and could have their own way at home, they were no longer so eager to set forth to seek a New England beyond the seas. So the Puritans ceased to cross the seas, and as we have seen, in their place many Cavaliers came to Virginia.

Chapter 31 - The Hunt for the Regicides

The Commonwealth of England did not last long. In 1660 King Charles II was restored. England then became an unsafe abode for all those who had helped to condemn Charles I to death, and two of those men, General Edward Whalley and William Goffe, fled to America. They were kindly received by the Puritans of Boston, and after a time they moved on to New Haven. But even in America they were not safe, and Royalist messengers were sent from England to arrest them, and take them home to be tried.

The Governor of Massachusetts pretended to be very eager to help these messengers. In reality he did nothing to help, but hindered them, rather. News of the search for the fugitives soon reached New Haven, and at once the people there helped them to hide. For their minister, John Davenport, had bidden them to "hide the outcasts and betray not him that wandereth."

Goffe and Whalley knew that the people of New Haven would not betray them. But lest their enemies should gain any inkling of their being there they left the town and, going to another, showed themselves openly. Then secretly by night they returned to New Haven.

For a whole month they lay hid there in the cellars of the minister's house. But soon that refuge became no longer safe, for the men in search of them had, in spite of their strategy, traced them to New Haven and set out to arrest them.

One Saturday the Royalists reached Guilford, not sixteen miles away. Here they demanded horses from the Governor to take them on to New Haven. But the Governor had little desire to help them. So with one excuse after another he put them off until it was too late to start that night. The next day was Sunday, and it was strictly against the laws of Puritan New England to ride or drive on Sunday save to church. So the Royalist messengers, chafing with impatience, might bribe and command as much as they liked; not a man would stir a hand to help them till Monday morning.

Meanwhile a messenger was speeding on his way to New Haven to warn the Parliamentarians. And while their pursuers were kicking their heels in enforced idleness they slipped away, and found a new hiding place in a mill some miles off. But even this was thought not to be safe, and they fled once more, and at length found refuge in a cave deep in the forest.

So on Monday when at length the Royalists arrived, the birds had flown. The minister owned that they had been there, but declared that they had vanished away, no man knowing when or whither.

The Royalists scoured the country far and wide in search of the fugitives. But their efforts were in vain. They were very much in earnest, but they were strangers, and they did not know the country. No one would help them in their search, and at length, very angry with the people of New Haven, they gave it up and returned to Boston.

Then, having spent several months in their cave, the Parliamentarians crept forth again. For two years they lived hidden in a friendly house. The King, however, was not satisfied, and after two years messengers again came out from England, and the search was again begun, more eagerly than before. Again, however, Goffe and Whalley were warned, and again they fled to the cave.

Here they lived in safety while the Royalists swept the country round in search of them. But they had many narrow escapes.

Once when they had left the shelter of their cave they were almost caught. Their pursuers were upon their heels, and to reach the cave without being taken prisoner seemed impossible. As the two men fled before their foes they came to a little river crossed by a wooden bridge. It was their last hope. Instead of crossing the bridge they crept beneath it, and crouched close to the water. On came the pursuers. They made no pause. Their horses thundered across the bridge and galloped away and away, while beneath the fugitives waited breathlessly. Then when all was quiet again they crept back to the shelter of their cave.

But at length the cave became a safe retreat no longer, for it was discovered by the Indians. And the fugitives, afraid lest the Indians, tempted by the large reward offered, might betray their hiding-place, resolved to seek another.

By this time the fury of the search for them had somewhat abated and another minister, John Russell, offered them a refuge in his house. This minister lived at a place called Hadley. Hadley was many miles from New Haven. It was a lonely settlement on the edge of the wilderness, and to reach it about a hundred miles of pathless forest had to be crossed. But with stout hearts the hunted men set out. By day they lay hidden in some friendly house, or in some lonely cave or other refuge. By night they journeyed onward. At length they reached their new hiding-place.

It was wonderfully contrived. The minister had lately made some alterations in his house, and in doing so he had made a safe retreat. In the attic there was a large cupboard with doors opening into rooms on either side. In the floor of the cupboard there was a trap door which led down into another dark cupboard below, and from there a passage led to the cellar. So that, should the house be searched, any one in the upper rooms could slip into the cupboard, from there reach the cellar, and thus escape. Here the regicides now took up their abode. And so well was their secret kept that they lived there for ten or fifteen years, their presence being unsuspected even by the inhabitants of the little town.

Henceforth the world was dead to them, and they were dead to the world. They were both soldiers. On many a field of battle,-Gainsborough, Marston, Naseby, Worcester, and Dunbar,-they had led their men to victory. They had been Members of Parliament, friends of the Great Protector, and had taken part in all the doings of these stirring times.

Now all that was over. Now no command, no power was left to them. The years went by, dragging their slow length of days, and bringing no change or brightness to the lives of these two men who lived in secret and alone. It was a melancholy life, the monotony only broken by visits from the minister, or a few other friends, who brought them all the gossip and news of the town. These were but small matters. But to the two men shut off from all other human beings they seemed of rare interest.

After ten years Whalley died. It is believed that he was buried in the cellar of the house in which for so long he had found a hiding-place. Then, for five years or so more, Goffe dragged out his life alone.

As one might imagine, the King was not at all pleased with Massachusetts and New Haven for thus sheltering the regicides; and in 1665 he suppressed New Haven as a separate colony and joined it to Connecticut.

The New Haven people did not like this at all, and they fought against it with all their might. But at length they gave way and joined Connecticut.

The King was angry with Massachusetts, too, not only for protecting the regicides, but also because of what is known as the Declaration of Rights. In this the people of Massachusetts acknowledged the King as their ruler. But they also made it plain that so long as they did not make laws which ran counter to English laws they expected to be let alone. This made King Charles angry, and if it had not been that he was busy fighting with Holland very likely the people of Massachusetts would have had to suffer for their boldness at once. As it was they were left in peace a little longer.

Chapter 32 - King Philip's War

Meanwhile the people of New England had another foe to fight.

You remember that the Pilgrim Fathers had made a treaty with the Indians when they first arrived. As long as the old Chief Massasoit lived he kept that treaty. But now he was dead, and his son Philip ruled.

You will wonder, perhaps, why an Indian chief should have a name like Philip. But Philip's real name was Metacomet. He, however, wanted to have an English name, and to please him the English called him Philip. And by that name he is best known.

For a time all went well. But very soon Philip and his tribe grew restless and dissatisfied. When they saw the white men coming in always greater and greater numbers, and building towns and villages further and further into the land, they began to fear them and long to drive them away. And at length all their thoughts turned to war.

Friendly Indians and "praying Indians," as those who had become Christians were called, came now to warn the Pale-faces and tell them that Philip was gathering his braves, and that he had held a war dance lasting for several weeks. In the night, too, people in lonely farms awoke to hear the wild sound of drums and gun shots. But still the English hoped to pacify Philip. So they sent him a friendly letter telling him to send away his braves, for no white man wished him ill.

But Philip returned no answer.

Then one Sunday while the people were at church and the houses were all deserted Indians attacked the little town of Swansea, burning and plundering. The next day and the next they returned, tomahawk and firebrand in hand, and so the war began.

Other tribes joined with King Philip, and soon New England was filled with terror and bloodshed. The men of New England gathered in force to fight the Indians. But they were a hard foe to fight, for they never came out to meet the Pale-faces in open field.

At first when the British began to settle in America they had made it a rule never to sell firearms to the Indians. But that rule had long ago been broken through. Now the Indians not only had guns, but many of them were as good shots as the British. Yet they kept to their old ways of fighting, and, stealthily as wild animals, they skulked behind trees, or lurked in the long grass, seeking their

124

enemies. They knew all the secret forest ways, they were swift of foot, untiring, and mad with the lust of blood. So from one lonely village to another they sped swiftly a the eagle, secretly as the fox. And where they passed they left a trail of blood and ashes.

At night around some lonely homestead all would seem quiet. Far as the eye could see there would be no slightest sign of any Redman, and the tired labourer would go to rest feeling safe, with his wife and children beside him. But ere the first red streaks of dawn shivered across the sky he would be awakened by fiendish yells. Ere he could seize his gun the savages would be upon him. And the sun when it rose would show only blackened, blood-stained ruins where but a few hours before a happy home had been.

Yet with this red terror on every side the people went on quietly with their daily life. On week days they tilled their fields and minded their herds, on Sundays they went, as usual, to church, leaving their homes deserted. But even to church they went armed, and while they knelt in prayer or listened to the words of their pastor their guns were ever within reach of their hands.

One Sunday, while in the village of Hadley the people were all at church, the Indians crept up in their usual stealthy fashion. Suddenly the alarm was given, and, seizing their guns which stood by their sides, the men rushed out of the meeting-house. But they were all in confusion: the attack was sudden, they were none of them soldiers, but merely brave men ready to die for their homes and their dear ones, and they had and they had no leader.

Then suddenly a stranger appeared amongst them. He was dressed in quaint old-fashioned clothes. His hair and beard were long and streaked with grey. He was tall and soldierly, and his eyes shone with the joy of battle.

At once he took command. Sharply his orders rang out. Unquestioningly the villagers obeyed, for he spoke as one used to command. They were no longer an armed crowd, but a company of soldiers, and, fired by the courage and skill of their leader, they soon put the Indians to flight.

When the fight was over the men turned to thank their deliverer. But he was nowhere to be found. He had vanished as quickly and mysteriously as he had come.

"What did it mean?" they asked. "Who was the strange leader? Had God in His mercy sent an angel from heaven to their rescue ?"

No one could answer their questions, and many decided that indeed a miracle had happened, and that God had sent an angel to deliver them.

This strange leader was no other than the regicide, Colonel Goffe, who, as we know, had for many years lived hidden in the minister's house. From his attic window he had seen the Indians creeping stealthily upon the village. And when he saw the people standing leaderless and bewildered, he had been seized with his old fighting spirit, and had rushed forth to lead them. Then, the danger being over, he had slipped quietly back to his hiding-place. There he remained hidden from all the world as before, until he died and was buried beside his friend.

Autumn passed and winter came, and the Indians gathered to their forts, for the

125

bare forests gave too little protection to them in their kind of warfare. When spring came they promised themselves to come forth again and make an end of the Pale-faces. But the Pale-faces did not wait for spring.

The Indians had gathered to the number of over three thousand into a strong fortress. It was surrounded by a marsh and the only entrance was over a bridge made by a fallen tree.

This fortress the New Englanders decided to attack and take. So, a thousand strong, they set out one morning before dawn and, after hours of weary marching through the snow, they reached the fort. Across the narrow bridge they rushed, and although many of their leaders fell dead, the men came on, nothing daunted. A fierce fight followed, for each side knew that they must win or die. Shut in on all sides by impassable swamps there was no escape. But not till dark was falling did the white men gain the victory. The ground was strewn with dead and dying, and in the gathering darkness the remaining Indians stole quietly away, and vanished like shadows. Then the New Englanders set fire to the wigwams, and, taking their wounded, marched back to their headquarters.

This was a sad blow to the Indians, but it did not by any means end the war which, as spring came on, broke out again in full fury. But gradually the white men got the upper hand. Instead of attacking, the Redmen fled before them. They lost heart and began to blame King Philip for having led them into war, and at length he was slain by one of his own followers.

Soon after this the war came to an end. But whole tracts of New England were a desert, a thousand of the bravest and best of the young men were killed. Many women and children, too, had been slain, and there was hardly a fireside in the whole of Massachusetts where there was not a vacant place. Numbers of people were utterly ruined and the colonies were burdened with a great debt.

As to the Indians their power was utterly broken, and their tribes were almost wiped out. Except the Mohegans, who had remained friendly throughout the war, there were few Indians left in south New England, where there was never again a war between white men and Indians.

Chapter 33 - How The Charter of Connecticut Was Saved

Meanwhile King Charles had not forgotten his anger against the people of Massachusetts. Besides the fact that they had harboured the regicides, he had many other reasons for being angry with them. For they refused to obey the Navigation Laws, and they refused to allow the Church of England to be established within the colony. They had coined money of their own, never made their officials swear allegiance to the throne, and had done many things just as they liked.

In fact Massachusetts seemed to Charles like a badly brought-up child, who, having come to manhood, wants to go his own way and cares nothing for the wishes or commands of his parents. He made up his mind not to have any more of this disobedience, and he took away the charter and made Massachusetts a Crown Colony. Thus after fifty-five years of practical freedom Massachusetts once more belonged to the King of England, by right of the discovery of John and Sebastian Cabot. Of course, the people of Massachusetts fought against this as hard as they could, but their struggle was useless, and a royal Governor was appointed to rule the colony.

Almost immediately, however, Charles died, and it was not until his brother, James II, was on the throne that Sir Edmund Andros came out as royal Governor. He came not only as Governor of Massachusetts but as Governor of all the New England Colonies. For the King wanted to make an end of all these separate colonies and unite them into one great province.

Andros soon made himself very much disliked, for he tried to rule New England too much as his master tried to rule Great Britain. He levied taxes as he pleased, he imprisoned innocent men if he chose, he allowed nothing to be printed without his permission, he seized lands and goods at will.

All New England felt the weight of the Governor's hand. He demanded Rhode Island's charter. But the Governor of Rhode Island replied that the weather was so bad he really could not send it. So Sir Edmund went to Rhode Island, dissolved its government and smashed its seal.

To Connecticut also Sir Edmund wrote in vain, demanding its charter. The men of Connecticut were, it seemed to him, an unruly lot. So one October day in 1687 he set out to visit this rebellious state and subdue it to his will.

He arrived in Hartford with a great train of gentlemen and soldiers. They made a mighty stir in the little town as they rode, jingling and clanking through the quiet streets, and drew rein before the state house. Into the chamber where the Council sat strode Andros looking pompous and grand in lace, and velvet, and a great flowing wig. Up to the table he strode, and in tones of haughty command, demanded the charter.

But the men of Connecticut would not lightly give up the sign of their beloved liberty. They talked and argued and persuaded. They spoke of the hardships they had endured, of the blood they had poured forth to keep their freedom in their new found homes, upon the edge of the wilderness.

But with such a man as Andros all appeals, all persuasions were in vain. To every argument he had but one answer,-he must and would have the charter.

Long and long the argument lasted. The day drew to a close and twilight fell. Through the dusky gloom men could hardly see each other's flushed, excited faces. Lights were called for, and candles were brought. Some were placed upon the table beside the metal box in which lay the charter. Still the debate went on, either side as unbending as before. Now many citizens, anxious to know how things went, slipped into the room and stood behind the members, listening as the debate was flung this way and that. Outside the night was dark, within the woodpanelled room the flickering candles shed but a dim, uncertain light.

They made strange dancing shadows, shining fitfully on the stern, eager faces of the men who sat round the table, but scarcely revealing against the gloom the crowd of anxious citizens behind.

Sir Edmund was weary of the talk. He would have no more of it, and, suddenly rising, he stretched out his hand to seize the charter. Then, swiftly from out the shadowy circle of listeners, a cloak was flung upon the table. It fell upon the candles and put them out. In a moment the room was in total darkness.

There was an outcry and a scuffling of feet, the sound of an opening window, a call for lights. But lights were no such speedy matters in those days when matches had not been invented. When at length the scratching of the tinder boxes was done and the candles relit, every one looked eagerly at the table. Behold, the charter was gone!

Sir Edmund stormed, and citizens and councilors looked blankly at each other. But meanwhile through the darkness a man sped. In his hand he held a parchment, and he never halted in his run till he reached a great oak tree. This oak he knew was hollow. Reaching it he thrust the parchment deep into the hole and carefully covered it up with dried leaves and bark. Thus was the charter of Connecticut saved.

The man who saved it was Captain Wadsworth. Ever afterwards the tree was called the Charter Oak, and until about sixty years ago it stood a memorial of his deed. But some wise folk say this story of the Charter Oak is all a fairy tale. That may be so. But it deserves to be true.

Yet though the men of Connecticut may have succeeded in saving the sign and symbol of their freedom, they could not save the reality. For whether Sir Edmund Andros was in possession of their charter or not he stamped upon their liberties just the same. In the public record the secretary wrote: "His Excellency Sir Edmund Andros, Knight Captain General and Governor of His Majesty's Territory and Dominion in New England, by order from his Majesty, King of England, Scotland and Ireland, the 31st of October, 1687, took into his hands the government of this Colony, of Connecticut, it being by his Majesty annexed to the Massachusetts and other Colonies under his Excellency's Government.

"Finis."

"Finis, " as you know, means "the end." And one cannot but feel sorry for that stern, old, freedom loving Puritan gentleman who wrote the words. For indeed to him the loss of freedom must have seemed the end of all things.

Sir Edmund's rule, however, did not last long. For the British soon grew tired of James II and his tyrannous ways, and they asked Prince William of Orange to come and be their King. William came, the people received him with delight, King James fled away to France, and the "glorious Revolution," as it was called, was accomplished.

When the news reached New England there, too, was a little revolution. One spring morning there was a great commotion among the people of Boston. There was beating of drums, noise and shouting, and much running to and fro of young men carrying clubs. Soon it was seen that the city was in arms. The men marched to the castle, and demanded its surrender. And Andros, knowing himself to be helpless, yielded, though not without some "stomachful reluctances." The proud Governor's rule was at an end. He was taken prisoner, and through the streets where he had ridden in splendour he was now led a captive. Then the colonies set about restoring their governments as they had been before Sir Edmund Andros came.

But Andros had no mind to remain a prisoner. He and his friends who were imprisoned with him had a good deal of freedom. They were locked into their rooms at night, but during the day they were allowed to walk about anywhere within sight of the sentries, and their friends were allowed to come to see them quite freely. It would not be difficult to escape, thought Andros, and he resolved to do it. So he bribed one of his jailers, and, having procured woman's clothes, he dressed himself in them and calmly walked out of his prison.

He passed two sentries safely. But the third looked sharply at the tall woman who strode along so manfully. He looked at her boots. At once the sentry's suspicions were aroused; for Sir Edmund had not thought of changing them. No woman ever wore such boots as these, thought the sentry, and he challenged and stopped her. Then, peering beneath the rim of her bonnet, he saw no bashful woman's face, but the well-known features of the Governor.

So back to prison Andros went. After this he was not allowed so much freedom. But again he tried to escape, and this time he was more successful. He got not only out of Boston, but out of the colony. Once more, however, he was recognised and brought back.

The whole of New England had been agog with excitement, but at length things began to calm down, and "the world moved on in its old orderly pace," says a writer of the times.

In the midst of this calm two ships arrived from England with an order to those in power to proclaim William and Mary King and Queen. Then the colonies went mad with joy. From far and near the people flocked to Boston. Bells were rung, bonfires blazed, and after a great procession through the streets there was feasting at the Townhall. Thus "with joy, splendour, appearance and unanimity, as had never before been seen in these territories," were William and Mary proclaimed.

Sir Edmund Andros was now sent home to England a prisoner. But King William was not altogether pleased with all the colonists had done, and he was set free without any trial. He was not really a bad man, but he was dogged and pig-headed, without sympathy or imagination, and altogether the wrong man in the wrong place. Later on he came back to America as Governor of Virginia, and this time he did much better.

Meanwhile several changes were made in New England. Rhode Island and Connecticut kept their old charters, to which they had clung so lovingly. New Hampshire, too, remained a separate colony. But Plymouth, sad to say, that gallant little colony founded by the Pilgrim Fathers lost separate existence and became part of Massachusetts. Maine and even Nova Scotia, lately won from the French, were for the meantime also joined to Massachusetts.

Massachusetts was now a great colony and received a new charter. But things were not the same. The colony was now a royal province, and the Governor was no longer appointed by the people, but by the King. This chafed the people greatly, for they felt that their old freedom was gone. So for a time the history of

129

Massachusetts was hardly more than a dreary chronicle of quarrels and misunderstandings between Governor and people.

Chapter 34 - The Witches of Salem

We have all read stories about witches, but we do not really believe in them. They are exciting enough to read about, but we know they are merely bad-fairy sort of folk who are only to be met with in books, and not in real life. We should be very much astonished, and rather frightened perhaps, if we thought that witches were real, and that we might some day meet one.

But in those far-off days more than two hundred years ago very many people believed in witches. Although not always so, it was generally very old people, people who had grown ugly and witless with age who were accused of being witches. In almost any village might be seen poor old creatures, toothless, hollow cheeked, wrinkled, with nose and chin almost meeting. Bent almost double, they walked about with a crutch, shaking and mumbling as they went. If any one had an ache or a pain it was easily accounted for. For why, they were bewitched! The poor old crone was the witch who had "cast the evil eye" upon them. And sometimes these poor creatures were put to death for their so-called deeds of witchcraft.

People believed that these witches sold themselves to the Evil One, and that he gave them power to harm other people. And what made them more dangerous was the fact that they did not need to go near people to harm them, but could do evil at a distance by thinking wicked thoughts, or saying wicked words. Some even of the most saintly and most learned people, believed in witches and witchcraft. So there is nothing surprising in the fact that suddenly, in 1692, whole towns and villages of New England were thrown into a ferment of terror by stories of witchcraft.

It came about quite simply. Two little girls of nine and eleven, the niece and daughter of a minister named Samuel Parris, who lived in Salem village, began suddenly to behave in a most curious manner. They would creep into holes, hide under chairs and benches, twist themselves into queer positions, make curious gestures and weird noises, and talk arrant nonsense. Their parents knew not what to make of it, and so they called in the doctors. Nowadays a clever doctor would have found out pretty soon that the children were merely pretending and playing a foolish trick upon their elders. But in those days doctors were not very wise, and they knew not what to make of this new and strange disease. One of them, however, said he thought that the children must be bewitched.

That was a terrible thought, and at once the minister called in all the other ministers from round about and they spent a day fasting and praying that the children might be released from the evil enchantment. All the neighbours, too, came crowding to the house, eager to hear about the dreadful happenings. And the children, finding themselves all at once people of the first importance, and no doubt enjoying the fuss which was being made, went on more than ever with their mad antics.

It was quite plain to every one that the children were bewitched. But who had done it? Every day the children were asked this question, and at length they accused a poor old Indian woman, who was a servant in the family. And the poor old creature was beaten and terrified until she actually confessed that she was a witch, and in league with the Evil One.

Perhaps the children had a spite against the old woman, perhaps they did not realise at first how wicked and cruel they were. Certainly when they found what excitement they caused, and how interesting they had become to every one they forgot all else. They became bolder now and accused other old women. Soon more and older girls joined them, and many innocent people, both men and women, were accused by them of witchcraft.

They did all sorts of things to make people believe in these accusations. As soon as an old woman was brought in they would fall down on the ground screaming. If she moved they would cry out that she was crushing them to death; if she bit her lip they would declare that she was biting them and so on. They told strange tales, too, of how they had been made to write in a long, thick, red book, —the book of the Evil One. They talked a jumble of nonsense about a Black Man, a black dog and a yellow bird. They would seem to fall down in fits or to be struck dumb. And they so worked upon the superstitious fears of those present that at length both judges and jury, carried away by mysterious terror, would condemn the old woman to death.

Soon a kind of madness took possession of the people. Person after person was accused; wrongs and misfortunes ten or even twenty years old were remembered, and charged to this person or that. No man or woman was safe. Neither age nor youth, beauty, learning nor goodness were any safeguard. Not only the good name, but the very life of every Man was at the mercy of every other man. Terror and mistrust stalked abroad, and entered every home. Parents accused their children, children their parents, husbands and wives turned against each other until the prisons were filled to overflowing.

It was quite useless for the prisoners to declare that they were innocent. Few believed them. If any did they hardly dare say so, lest they should find themselves accused in their turn and lodged in prison. Yet at length some were brave enough to stand by their loved ones.

One determined young man with great difficulty succeeded in rescuing his mother from prison. In getting out the poor woman broke her leg, but her son lifted her on to his horse and carried her away to a swamp near by. Here he built her a hut and brought her food and kept her safe until all danger was passed.

One or two other men escaped with their wives and fled beyond the borders of the colony. Twenty, however, were put to death by hanging, among them a minister. All these twenty to the last declared their innocence. Many others, strange to say, confessed to being witches. They confessed because they were terrified into it. Many confessed because they saw that by so doing they might save their lives. But some, having confessed, were so distressed at having lied that they took back their confession. Then they were hanged without mercy.

131

For a year this terrible madness lasted. Then it passed as suddenly as it had come. The people awoke again to their right senses. The prison doors were opened and the poor innocent people were set free. The wicked children who had accused them were never punished unless their own hearts punished them. One of them at least repented bitterly, and years later openly acknowledged her sorrow for her share in the sad business.

The minister in whose house the persecution began was punished. For the people were so angry with him and the part he had taken that they would have no more to do with him, and he was obliged to leave Salem village.

Some others who had taken as great a part as he in hounding guiltless people to death remained impenitent and unpunished. But the jury and some of the judges made some amends. They did a hard thing, for they publicly acknowledged that they had been wrong. The jury wrote and signed a paper in which they said, "We do hereby declare that we justly fear that we were sadly deluded and mistaken, for which we are much disquieted and distressed in our minds. And do therefore humbly beg forgiveness."

One of the judges, Judge Sewall, was bitterly grieved at the part he had played. And on a day of general intercession he stood up before the whole congregation, acknowledging his guilt and praying God to forgive him. And throughout all his life he kept one day a year upon which he prayed and fasted in repentance.

Perhaps you may think that there is nothing in this story to make you proud of your ancestors. But think again. Think of the courage of those men and women who cheerfully went to death rather than save their lives by lying and making false confessions. Truth to those brave men and women was worth more than life. And is there nothing to be proud of in the fact that the judge and jury, when they found themselves in the wrong, had the manliness to own it publicly and without reserve?

To some of us nothing in all the world seems so hard as to own ourselves in the wrong.

Part IV STORIES OF THE MIDDLE AND SOUTHERN COLONIES

Chapter 35 - The Founding of Maryland

About the same time as Gorges was making laws for his little kingdom of New Hampshire another English gentleman was doing much the same somewhat farther south. This was Lord Baltimore.

The first Lord Baltimore was a Yorkshire gentleman named Calvert; he was a favourite of James I, who made him a baron, and he took his title from a tiny village in Ireland.

Like so many other men of his time Lord Baltimore was interested in America, and wanted to found a colony there. First he tried to found one in Newfoundland. There he received a large grant of land which he called Avalon after the fabled land in the story of King Arthur, and he had a kind of fairy vision of the warmth and sunny delights which were to be found in his new land.

But instead of being warm and sunny he found that Newfoundland was bleak and cold, so his fairy vision shriveled and died, and be came home and asked for a grant of land on the Potomac instead. In 1632 King James gave Lord Baltimore what he asked and called the land Maryland in honour of his wife, Queen Henrietta Maria.

But before the grant was sealed "with the King's broad seal" Lord Baltimore died. Not he, therefore, but his son, Cecilius, was the first "Lord Proprietary" of Maryland, and for his broad lands all he had to pay to King James was two Indian arrows, to be delivered at Windsor Castle every year on Tuesday in Easter week. He had also to pay one-fifth part of all the gold and silver which might be found within his borders. But no gold or silver was found in the colony, so there was nothing to pay.

Lord Baltimore did not himself go to America, but sent his brother, Leonard Calvert, as Governor. Maryland was not founded like the Puritan colonies for religious purposes, but like New Hampshire, merely for trade and profit. But in those days religion and religious strife entered into everything. So it did into the founding of Maryland.

For Lord Baltimore was a Catholic, and in England Roman Catholics in their turn, as well as dissenters, were persecuted, and Lord Baltimore hoped to found a refuge for them in his new possessions in America. So although, in the charter given by a Protestant King the Church of England was recognised as the state religion, in reality there was great religious freedom in Maryland, and for a time it was there only that Catholics found freedom in America.

But in order to secure toleration for the Catholic religion Lord Baltimore found himself obliged to tolerate all others. So men of all creeds came to settle in Maryland and find freedom.

The people of Virginia were very far from pleased when they heard of the new colony about to be planted so near them. For part of the land which had been given to Lord Baltimore they claimed as their own, and they looked upon the newcomers as intruders on their territory and resolved to maintain their rights. They did all they could to prevent the new settlers coming. Nevertheless, in spite of everything, Leonard Calvert set sail with his colonists, many of whom were well-to-do people, in two ships called the Ark and the Dove.

They had a prosperous voyage and landed in Virginia full of doubt lest the inhabitants, who were very angry at their coming, should be plotting something against them. But the letters which they carried from the King seemed to appease the anger of the Virginians for a little, and the newcomers sailed on again to their own destination in Chesapeake Bay.

So at length they reached the "wished-for country" and Calvert landed with solemn state to take possession of the land in the name of God and the King of England.

As he stepped ashore a salute was fired from the boats. Then, reverently kneeling, the colonists listened while Mass was said for the first time in English America. Mass being over, they formed a procession at the head of which a rough wooden cross was carried. Then when they reached a spot chosen beforehand

133

they planted the cross, and, kneeling round it, chanted the Litany of the Sacred Cross with great fervour.

And thus a new colony was begun.

With the Indians Calvert made friends, for he was both just and kind to them, paying them for their land in hoes, hatchets, coloured cloths and the beads and gew-gaws they loved. So in those early days there were no Indian wars and massacres in Maryland.

But although at peace with the Redmen the Marylanders were not at peace with their fellow white men. For the Virginians could not forget that Lord Baltimore had taken land which they had looked upon as their own. They had done their best to hinder him coming at all. And now that he had come they did their best to drive him away again. They tried to stir up mischief between the newcomers and the Indians by telling the Indians that these newcomers were Spaniards, and enemies of the English nation. They complained to the people in power at home, and did everything they could to make Maryland an uncomfortable dwelling place for those they looked upon as interlopers.

The chief enemy of the Marylanders among the Virginians was a man named William Clayborne. Before the coming of these new colonists he had settled himself upon the Isle of Kent, which was within their bounds, and now he absolutely refused either to move or to recognise the authority of Calvert as Governor; for he claimed the Isle of Kent as part of Virginia.

Calvert on his side insisted on his rights, and as neither would give way it came at length to fighting. There was bloodshed on both sides, now one, now the other getting the upper hand. Each appealed in turn to King, Parliament, or Protector, and so for more than twenty years the quarrel went on. But when the great Cromwell came to power he took Lord Baltimore's part, Catholic though he was. And at length in 1657, weary perhaps of the struggle, each side gave way a little and there was peace between the two colonies.

But in spite of the constant trouble with Clayborne the colony grew and prospered, for there was greater religious freedom to be found there than anywhere else either in England or America. And in the seventeenth century religion bulked more largely in an Englishman's thoughts than almost anything else. Then in 1649 the Governor issued an Act called the Toleration Act, which has made him famous. It gave freedom to every one to follow his own religion save Jews and Unitarians, and for those days it was a wonderfully liberal and broad-minded Act. It threatened with a fine of ten shillings any one who should in scorn or reproach call any man such names as popish priest, Roundhead, heretic. It declared that no person whatsoever within the Province professing to believe in Jesus Christ should be in any way troubled or molested for his or her religion.

This was the first law of its kind ever brought into force in America, and although suspended once or twice for short periods it remained almost continuously in force for many years.

Maryland becomes a royal province, 1691 Time went on and the great estate of

134

Maryland passed from one Lord Baltimore to another. Although founded as a refuge for Catholics there were far more Protestants than Catholics within the colony. And when William III, the Protestant King, came to the throne he deprived Baltimore of his rights, and made Maryland a royal province. The Church of England was then established, and Catholics forbidden to hold services. Thus Lord Baltimore's dream of providing a refuge for the oppressed was at an end.

But in 1715 Benedict, the fourth Lord Baltimore, became a Protestant, and Maryland was given back to him. It remained in possession of his family until the Revolution.

Chapter 36 - How New Amsterdam Became New York

All the colonies which we have so far talked about were founded by Englishmen. Now we come to one which was founded by another people who, like the English, were great sea rovers and adventurer's-the Dutch. Even before the landing of the Pilgrim Fathers the Dutch laid claim to the valleys of the Hudson and the Delaware.

In those days people still knew very little about the continent of North America. They knew it was a continent, but they did not believe it to be very wide, as is proved by charters like that of Virginia which made the colony extend from sea to sea. Nor did people know how long the continent was. They had no idea that the great double continent stretched from north to south all across the hemisphere, and they were continually seeking for that North-West passage which would lead them to India by way of the west.

Now in 1609 Henry Hudson, an English sailor in the pay of the Dutch, came seeking the North-West passage. He did not find it, but sailed into Delaware Bay and up the beautiful river which is now known by his name as far as where the town of Albany now stands. It was autumn when Hudson sailed up the river; the sky was gloriously blue, and the woods aflame with red and yellow, and he went home to tell the Dutch that he had found "as pleasant a land with grass and flowers and goodly trees as ever he had seen," "a very good land to fall with, and a pleasant land to see."

By right of Hudson's discoveries the Dutch claimed all the land between Cape Cod and Chesapeake Bay, and, tempted by his glowing descriptions, they very soon established trading ports upon the Hudson which they called the North River. The Delaware they called the South River.

The English too claimed the same land, and it was not until some years after the landing of the Pilgrim Fathers that the Dutch settled in the country. Then they formed a company and bought the Island of Manhattan where New York now stands from the Indians for about five pounds' worth of glass beads and other trifles.

Here they built a little fort which they called New Amsterdam in 1626.

The colony grew slowly. For the life was by no means an easy one, and the people of Holland lived in freedom and religious peace at home, so they had no need to cross the Atlantic to seek them. But the company wanted settlers. They therefore offered to give an estate with eighteen miles' bay or river frontage to every man who would bring, or send, fifty colonists. Many people at once became eager to win such a prize, and very soon there were little settlements all along the shores of the Hudson.

The men who received these huge estates were called patroons, which is the same word as our English patron, and they had power not unlike the feudal lords of old time. They were bound to supply each of their settlers with a farm, and also to provide a minister and a schoolmaster for every settlement. But on the other hand they had full power over the settlers. They were the rulers and judges, while the settlers were almost serfs, and were bound to stay for ten years with their patroon, to grind their corn at his mills, and pay him tribute.

Over the whole colony there was a Governor who was as a rule autocratic and sometimes dishonest, and there was a good deal of unrest in the colony. The patroons were soon at loggerheads with each other and with the Governor. There were quarrels with the Swedes, who had settled on the Delaware, and there was terrible fighting with the Indians.

At length the state of the colony became so bad that the settlers wrote home to Holland complaining of their Governor and blaming him for all their troubles. The people in Holland listened to this complaint and a new Governor was sent out. This was Peter Stuyvesant, the last and most famous of the Governors of New Amsterdam.

Peter Stuyvesant, Governor from 1647-1664; He was a fiery old fellow, with a great love of pomp, and a tremendous opinion of his own importance. He had lost a leg in the Spanish Wars, and now he stamped about with a wooden one. But as no plain wooden leg would please his taste for grandeur he had it bound with silver.

The people were heartily tired of their old Governor, so they hailed the coming of Stuyvesant with joy. But no sooner had their new Governor arrived than they began to wonder if after all the change was a happy one. For Stuyvesant seemed to look down upon them all. He landed with great state and pomp, and some of the chief inhabitants who had come to meet him were left standing bareheaded for several hours while he kept his hat on, as if he were Tsar of all the Russias.

When he took over the direction of affairs from the late Governor, he did it with great ceremony in presence of all the colonists. And the late Governor, thinking to make a good impression before he left, made a speech thanking the people for their faithfulness to him. But the stolid Dutchmen were not going to have any such farce. So they up and told him boldly that they would not thank him, for they had no reason to do so.

Stuyvesant, however, would not have any wrangling; he loudly and proudly declared that every one should have justice done to him, and that he would be to them as a father to his children. But his bearing was so haughty that some of them went away shaking their heads, and fearing that he would be but a harsh father.

136

And so it proved. If the settlers' lot had been hard under the rule of other governors, it was still harder under that of Stuyvesant. He was autocratic and hectoring. He stumped about with his wooden leg, and shouted every one else down, and no one dared oppose him. Some indeed, more brave than others, declared that they would write home to Holland to complain of his tyranny. But when Stuyvesant heard it he got so angry that he foamed at the mouth. "If any one appeals from my judgments," he shouted, "I shall make him a foot shorter and send the pieces to Holland. Let him appeal in that way."

But Stuyvesant with all his faults was a far better Governor than those who had gone before him. And he had no easy post, for on every side he found himself surrounded by other States, the inhabitants of which were constantly encroaching on the borders of New Netherland.

The English, both from Massachusetts and Connecticut, seemed to think that the Dutch had no rights at all. Where they found good land they settled, scoffing at the Dutch remonstrances.

Stuyvesant too was soon at loggerheads with the Swedes who had settled on the Delaware. The Dutch claimed both sides of the river and the Swedes laughed at their claims. They would sail up the river past the Dutch fort without stopping and displaying their colours, and when challenged, and asked for their reason, replied boldly that they would certainly do it again.

Then the Dutch began to build a new fort on land which the Swedes claimed, and the Swedes came and destroyed it. So things went from bad to worse, until at length Stuyvesant decided to put an end to it. He gathered an army of six hundred men, the largest army that had ever been gathered in North America, and with seven ships entered the Delaware.

Against a force like this the Swedes could not defend themselves, so they yielded on condition that they should march out of their forts with all the honours of war. This was granted to them and with colours flying, drums beating and trumpets playing the Swedes marched out and the Dutch marched in. Thus without a blow, after seventeen years of occupation, New Sweden became part of New Netherland. Later on this land captured from the Swedes was to become the State of Delaware.

From his triumph over the Swedes Stuyvesant was recalled by the news that there was war with the Indians. He soon brought that to an end also. But he was not always to be victorious, and at length the time came when the power of the Dutch was to be swept away before a still greater power.

Stuyvesant had ruled New Netherland for seventeen years. The colony had prospered, and the number of new settlers had steadily increased. During these same years Great Britain had been passing through stormy times. King Charles had been beheaded, the kingdom had been declared a Commonwealth with Cromwell at its head, but he was now dead, the Stuarts once more ruled, and King Charles II sat upon the throne. He cast a greedy eye upon New Netherland, for he wanted it for his brother, the Duke of York.

There was peace between Holland and Britain, but Charles II cared little about that. So in 1664 he secretly granted all the land lying between the Delaware and Connecticut rivers to his brother, and sent a fleet of four ships and about four hundred soldiers under Colonel Richard Nicolls to take possession of the country.

When Stuyvesant heard of it he made ready to resist. He gathered in what powder and shot be could from the surrounding settlements; he mounted cannon, he ordered every able-bodied man to take his turn at strengthening the fortifications and keeping guard. And having done all he could he sent a messenger to Nicolls asking why he had come.

Nicolls' reply was a summons to surrender the town. At the same time he promised that any one who would submit quietly should be protected by "his Majesty's laws and justice." "Any people from the Netherlands may freely come and plant here," he wrote, "vessels of their own country may freely come hither, and any of them may as freely return home in vessels of their own country."

But Peter Stuyvesant was hot to fight. So lest the easy terms should make any of the settlers willing to give in he tried to keep them secret. But the Council would not have it so.

"All that regards the public welfare must be made public," they said, and held to it.

Then, seeing he could not move them from their determination, in a fit of passion Stuyvesant tore Nicolls' letter in pieces, swearing that he would not be answerable for the consequences.

The people were growing impatient, and leaving their work upon the fortifications they stormed into the Council Chamber. In vain Stuyvesant tried to persuade them to return to their work. They would not listen to him. They replied to him only with curses and groans. Then from all sides came cries of, "The letter, the letter, we will have the letter."

So at last Stuyvesant yielded; the torn fragments were gathered together and a copy made. And when the people heard the terms they bade him yield. Still he would not, and he sent another message to Nicolls.

But Nicolls would not listen. "To-morrow," he said, "I will speak with you at Manhattan."

"Friends will be welcome," replied the messenger, "if they come, in friendly fashion."

"I shall come with my ships and my soldiers," answered Nicolls. "Hoist the white flag of peace on the fort, and then something may be considered."

When this answer was known terror seized the town. Women and children came to implore the Governor with tears to submit.

He would not listen to them. Like the fierce old lion he was he knit his brows and stamped with his wooden leg. "I would rather be carried a corpse to my grave than give in," he cried.

But he alone had any desire to fight. For in the whole fort there was not enough powder to last one day, from the river front there was absolutely no protection, and on the north there was only a rickety fence three or four feet high. There was little food within the fort, and not a single well. So all the chief inhabitants wrote

138

a letter to the Governor begging him to give in.

"You know, in your own conscience," they said, "that your fortress is incapable of making head three days against so powerful an enemy. And (God help us) whether we turn us for assistance to the north, or to the south, to the east or to the west 'tis all in vain! On all sides are we encompassed and hemmed in by our enemies. Therefore we humbly and in bitterness of heart, implore your Honour not to reject the conditions of so generous a foe."

This letter was signed by all the most important people of the town, even by Stuyvesant's own son. With every one against him he could hold out no longer. So he yielded and at eight o'clock on Monday morning, the 8th of September, 1664, he marched out of Fort Amsterdam at the head of his soldiers. With colours flying and drums beating they marched down to the riverside where a ship awaited them, and getting on board they set sail for Holland.

Then the Dutch flag was hauled down, the British flag was hoisted in its place, and New Amsterdam became New York, a name given it in honour of the King's brother, the Duke of York.

A few weeks later every other Dutch settlement had yielded to the British. Fort Orange became Fort Albany, so named for the Duke of York's second title, and Dutch dominion in North America was at an end.

As to Stuyvesant, he sailed home and was severely scolded by the West India Company for his "scandalous surrender." He was, however, able to defend himself, and prove to the directors that he had done his best. Then he returned to America and spent the rest of his life quietly on his farm, or "bowery" as it was called in Dutch.

Those of you who are familiar with New York know that there is still a part of it called The Bowery, and it may interest you to learn that it is so called in memory of the farm where this arrogant old lion of a Dutchman spent his last days. He spent them peacefully and happily. Now that he was no longer a ruler he lost much of his overbearing pride, and all that was kindly in his nature showed itself. Many who had feared and hated him came to love and admire him. Among others he made friends with the Englishman who had ousted him, and many a jolly evening he and Nicolls spent together cracking jokes and listening to each other's stories of the brave days gone by.

Peter Stuyvesant died at the age of eighty, and was buried in what is now St. Mark's Church, where a tablet on the wall marks the spot where he lies.

New York was now a proprietary colony like Maryland, its overlord being the Duke of York, and when in 1685 he became King of England New York became a Crown Colony.

The Dutch rule had been autocratic, the people having little say in the government. They had chafed against it and had hoped that the change of ruler would bring a change of government, and that they would be allowed freedom like the New England Colonies. But James was not the sort of man to allow freedom to people when he could prevent it. So the government of New York

139

continued as autocratic as before.

Meanwhile New York once more changed hands. In a time of peace the British had calmly and without a shadow of right taken the colony from the Dutch. Nine years later when the two countries were at war the Dutch took it back again.

It was just the same nine-year-old story over again. Only this time it was the Dutch who marched in and hoisted the Dutch flag over the fort.

Once more the names were changed; New York became New Orange, and the province was once more New Amsterdam.

But this was only for a month or two. The following year Holland and Britain made peace, and by the Treaty of Westminster all Dutch possessions in North America were given back to Britain, and Dutch rule in North America was at an end for ever.

Chapter 37 - How a German Ruled New York

When Sir Edmund Andros came to America, he had been made Governor of New York as well as of all New England. And while Massachusetts was having its revolution upon the accession of William and Mary there were exciting times in New York also. When the news of the imprisonment of Andros reached New York there was great agitation. Almost at the same time came the news that the French had declared war on England, which added to the people's excitement. For they suspected Nicholson, whom Andros had left in charge as Lieutenant-Governor, of being a Catholic; and a quite groundless idea got about that he meant to betray the colony into the hands of the French, or burn it to the ground.

There were very few Catholics in New York, and the Protestants had little need to fear them. But many of the Protestants were filled with a burning zeal for their faith, and of these Jacob Leisler, an honest, ignorant German, now became the leader. He refused to pay a tax because the tax collector was a "Papist," and therefore no fit person to receive the money. Other people followed his example, and day by day excitement grew.

At length Leisler was at the head of a great following. He got command of the fort, and drew up a declaration which he forced the captain of the militia and others to sign. In this he declared that the city was in danger, and that he would take possession of it until King William should appoint a Governor. Nicholson had no grit. He could not stand against a bold blusterer like Leisler, so he ran away. He went home "to render an account of the present deplorable state of affairs" to King William. But in order that Nicholson should not have it all his own way at home Leisler on his side sent an innkeeper, Joost Stoll, as his ambassador to King William to explain matters from his point of view.

Leisler now became very autocratic. He called himself Lieutenant-Governor, he disarmed and arrested all the "Papists," and every one was a "Papist" who did not yield readily to him. He had enormous power in his hands for good or evil, but he was far too ignorant and vain to use it well. Indeed he used it so badly that even some of the men who had hailed him with delight turned against him.

Leisler by many signs knew his popularity was failing. Then his friend, the innkeeper, returned from England with the doleful news that King William had taken not the slightest notice of him. The King indeed would not deign to recognise the existence of the upstart German "governor," and had appointed a new Governor who would shortly arrive in New York.

This was bad news for Leisler, and it seemed to drive him crazy. He grew more and more tyrannical. At length his tyranny became so bad that many of the chief people of New York wrote a letter to the King and Queen complaining of it.

In this letter they told the King and Queen that they were sore oppressed by "ill men" who ruled in New York "by the sword, at the sole will of an insolent alien, assisted by some few, whom we can give no better name than a rabble." From other parts of the colony too letters were written calling Leisler a bold usurper, and begging the King to do something "to break this heavy yoke of worse than Egyptian bondage."

Nor did the people confine themselves to writing letters. Leisler found himself insulted at every turn. He was mobbed, and stoned, and called "Dog Driver," "General Hog" and other ugly names.

Meanwhile on the stormy seas the ships bringing out the new Governor and Lieutenant-Governor were being tossed hither and thither. The waves dashed high, the wind drove the ships helplessly before it, and the Archangel, which bore the Governor was separated from the others, and driven far out of its course. Thus it happened that Ingoldsby, the Lieutenant-Governor, arrived in New York without the Governor. However he sent to Leisler asking him to allow the soldiers he had brought to enter the fort. This request made Leisler very angry. He refused to allow the soldiers to enter the fort unless Ingoldsby showed him orders in writing either from the King or Governor.

This Ingoldsby could not do, for all the orders were in the Governor's ship, and where that was he could not tell. And finding that Leisler would yield to no reasoning, after four days he landed his men with as much care as if he had been making a descent into an enemy's country, and lodged them in the town hall.

So six weeks passed. Ingoldsby was determined to stay, Leisler just as determined that he should go. At length Leisler sent Ingoldsby a notice to disband his force in two hours, or take the consequences. Ingoldsby refused to disband his force. So from the fort Leisler fired upon the soldiers in the town hall, and several were killed. More trouble seemed likely to follow, but some of Leisler's soldiers had already had enough, so they laid down their arms and went home.

Next day Governor Sloughter arrived. Hearing of all the commotion he landed hastily, and going to the town hall ordered the bell to be rung, and his commission to be read to the people.

Then he sent Ingoldsby to demand the surrender of the fort.

But Leisler was by this time crazy with the idea of his own importance. He refused to give up the fort until he received orders from the King direct, addressed to his very own self. This was absurd, for the King was hardly conscious of Leisler's existence. The Governor therefore paid no attention to these proud demands, and sent Ingoldsby again to demand possession of the fort.

141

Again Leisler refused. It could not be done so easily as all that, he said.

Still a third time the Governor demanded the fort. And again with scorn Leisler refused.

It was now nearly midnight, and the Governor decided to do nothing more till morning.

With morning reason seemed to return to Leisler. He wrote a letter to the Governor begging him to take the fort. But the Governor took no notice of the letter. He simply sent Ingoldsby to command the garrison to give up their arms and march out, promising at the same time free pardon to every one except Leisler and his Council. The men obeyed at once. They marched out and Leisler found himself a prisoner.

For two years he had lorded it in New York. Now his day was done. After a short trial he and his friend and son-in-law Milborne were condemned to death, and hanged as traitors.

At the time many applauded this severity, but afterwards most people were sorry. For after all Leisler had meant well, and in spite of his arrogance he had still many friends left. He was now looked upon as a martyr, and for many a long day New York was torn asunder with bitter strife over his tragic ending.

Chapter 38 - Pirates!

Colonel Sloughter whose rule began in such stormy times proved no good Governor. Indeed he was a bad man as well as a bad ruler. Others followed who were not a bit better, one at least being accused of being in league with the pirates who were now the terror of the seas.

The seventeenth century has been called "The Golden Age of Piracy." Never before or since have pirates had such a splendid time. After the discovery of America, the number of ships sailing the seas increased rapidly, until all the chief countries of Europe had far more ships afloat than they could possibly protect with their navies. So they readily became a prey to pirates.

Then, as they could not protect their merchantmen with their warships, most countries allowed private people in time of war to fit out ships armed with guns to capture the merchant shipping of the enemy. These ships were simply private men of war, and were called privateers. They always carried "letters of marque and reprisal" Which gave them the legal right to commit against enemy ships acts which, without those letters of marque, would have been considered acts of piracy. In the long run these privateers often became little better than pirates, and it has been said "privateers in time of war were a nursery for pirates against a peace."

The pirates' life was one of reckless daring. They were idle, swaggering, brutal. All the summer they sailed the seas, a terror to peaceful merchantmen, and when winter came, or when they were tired of plundering, they would retire to the West India Islands or Madagascar. Here, hidden in the depths of forests, they built for themselves strong castles surrounded by moats and walls. The paths leading to these castles were made with the greatest cunning. They were so narrow that people could only go in single file. They crossed and re-crossed in every direction, so that the castle was surrounded by a maze, and any one not knowing the secret might wander for hours without being able to find the dwelling which could not be seen until one was close upon it.

In these savage fastnesses the pirates lived in squalid splendour. They had numbers of slaves to wait upon them, the finest wines and foods, the richest dress and jewels, spoils of their travels. And when they had drunk and rioted in idleness to their heart's content they would once more set sail, and roam the seas in search of fresh adventure.

All sorts of people took to piracy, and scampish sons of noble houses might be found side by side with the lowest of scoundrels and vagabonds. In fact in those days any man who had a grudge against the world might turn pirate. Even women were found among them.

A jovial, brutal crew, they swaggered and swore their way through life. And if the gallows at the end always loomed over them what then? There was always plenty of rum in which to drown the thought.

Some of the pirates became very famous. The very sight of the Jolly Roger, as the pirates' black flag was called, struck terror to the hearts of merchantmen, and it is said that one pirate captured and sunk as many as four hundred ships before he was caught. Yet these ruffians often had dealings with seemingly respectable tradesmen. Having captured a few ships, and taken all the booty on board his own, the pirate would sail for some port. There he would show some old letters of marque, swear that he was a privateer, and had captured the goods lawfully from the enemy, for the world was always at war in those days. And as the goods were going cheap, too many questions would not be asked. Thus a profitable trade was done.

The Navigation Laws too helped pirates to thrive on the coasts of America. For they seemed so unjust and burdensome that people thought it no wrong to evade them. So, often, piracy and smuggling went hand in hand.

At length piracy grew so bad that people felt that something must be done to stop it. And when an Irishman named Lord Bellomont came out as Governor in 1696 he set about doing it. It was decided that the best way to do it was to send a swift and well-armed frigate under a captain who knew their haunts and ways, to catch these sea-robbers. For this, Captain Kidd, a tried sailor, was chosen, and he set sail with a somewhat ruffianly crew in the ship Adventure. But Captain Kidd was unlucky. Though he roamed the seas and sought the pirates in the haunts he knew so well he found never a one.

Nor could he find even enemy ships which, as a privateer, he might have attacked. Dutch ships, ships of the Great Mogul he met. But Britain was at peace with Holland and on most friendly terms with the heathen potentate. Pirates and ships of France he could not find.

Food and money were nearly gone, the crew grew mutinous. They had come forth for adventure, and not to sail the seas thus tamely and on short rations to boot. So there was angry talk between the crew and captain. Plainly they told him

143

that the next ship which came in sight, be it friend or foe, should be their prey. Kidd grew furious, and, seizing a hatchet, he hit one of the men on the head so that he fell senseless on the deck and died. Alone he stood against his mutinous crew. But in the end he gave way to them. He turned pirate, and any ship which came his way was treated as a lawful prize.

For two years after Captain Kidd left New York nothing was heard of him. Then strange and disquieting rumours came home. It was said that he who had been sent to hunt pirates had turned pirate himself; that he who had been sent as a protection had become a terror to honest traders. So orders were accordingly sent to Lord Bellomont to arrest Captain Kidd. A royal proclamation was also issued offering free pardon to all pirates save two, one of whom was William Kidd.

This was the news which greeted the new-made pirate when he arrived one day at a port in the West Indies. But those were lawless days. Captain Kidd's ship was laden with great treasure-treasure enough, he thought, to win forgiveness. At least he decided to brazen it out, and he set sail for New York.

His ship was no longer the Adventure but the Quedah Merchant. For the Adventure, being much battered after two years' seafaring, he had sunk her, and taken one of his many prizes instead. But on the way home he left the Quedah Merchant at San Domingo with all her rich cargo and, taking only the gold and jewels, he set sail again in a small sloop.

As he neared New York his heart failed him, and he began to think that after all forgiveness might not be won so easily. Cautiously he crept up to New York, only to learn that the Governor was at Boston. So he sent a messenger to the Governor confessing that acts of piracy had been committed, but without his authority. They were done, he said, when the men were in a state of mutiny, and had locked him up in his cabin.

Lord Bellomont was broad-minded and just, and had no desire to condemn a man unheard; so he sent back a message to Captain Kidd saying, "If you can prove your story true you can rely on me to protect you."

But Captain Kidd's story did not satisfy Lord Bellomont; so he was put into prison, and later sent home to England to be tried. There he was condemned to death and hanged as a pirate in 1701. Some people, however, never believed in his guilt. Whether he was guilty or not there is little doubt that he did not have a fair trial, and that he was by no means the shameless ruffian he was made out to be.

What became of the Quedah Merchant and all her rich cargo was never known. Indeed the most of Kidd's ill-gotten gains entirely disappeared. For when his sloop was searched very little treasure was found. So then it was said that Captain Kidd must have buried his treasure somewhere before he reached Boston. And for a hundred years and more afterwards all along the shore of Long Island Sound people now and again would start a search of buried treasure. But none was ever found.

Before his pirate friend met his end Lord Bellomont died. He was one of the few Governors the people had loved, and they sorrowed truly at his death. He was followed by Lord Cornby, a very bad man. Nevertheless in spite of Governors good and bad New York prospered. Every fresh tyranny in Europe which sent freedom-seekers to America added to the population. And as the first settlers were Dutch, New York had a more un-English population than almost any other of the colonies.

Chapter 39 - The Founding of New Jersey

Out of New York another state had been carved. For before New York had been taken from the Dutch, before Nicholls had so much as reached the shores of America, James, Duke of York, had already given part of the land which he did not yet possess to two of his friends, Lord Berkeley and Sir George Carteret. Sir George had been Governor of the Island of Jersey in the English Channel. When the Revolution broke out in England he had defended the island stoutly against the soldiers of the Parliament, and had kept the King's flag flying on British soil longer than any other man. So now that the Stuarts were restored King Charles remembered Carteret's loyalty, and he called this tract of land New Jersey in his honour. For this great estate Sir George and Lord Berkeley had to pay only ten shillings a year and a peppercorn.

Nicholls of course knew nothing about these grants, and when he heard of them he was grieved that the Duke should have given away so much valuable land. He had besides allowed some Puritans from New England and others to settle on the land after making agreements with the natives. And this led to trouble later on.

Meanwhile Sir George lost no time in settling his land in his own way. He at once sent out some colonists and Philip Carteret, a cousin of his own, as Governor.

On a summer day in 1665 Philip Carteret landed. He set up no crosses, and made no prayers, but with a hoe over his shoulder he marched at the head of his men, as a sign that he meant to live and work among them. A little way inland he chose a spot on which to build his town and called it Elizabeth, in honour of Sir George Carteret's Wife.

Things went well enough until the time came for rents to be paid. Then many of the settlers, who had been there before Carteret came, refused to pay. For they said they had bought their land from the Indians, and owed nothing to Sir George. But as the Governor insisted on his right they rose in rebellion. They held a meeting at Elizabethtown, deposed Philip Carteret, and chose James Carteret a weak and bad son of Sir George, as their Governor. Seeing nothing else for it Philip went home and laid his case before Sir George and the Duke. They both supported him, so the rebels submitted, James Carteret went off to New York, and Philip again became Governor of New Jersey.

Meanwhile Lord Berkeley had grown tired of all the trouble, and he sold his part of New Jersey to some Quakers. So henceforth New Jersey was divided into two, East Jersey and West Jersey, East Jersey belonging to Carteret, West Jersey to the Quakers.

In 1680 Sir George Carteret died, and his part of New Jersey was also sold to

Quakers, one of whom was William Penn, afterwards to become famous in American history. Soon after this New Jersey fell on very troublous times, of which it would take too long to tell. But at length the two Jerseys were again made into one, and in the time of Anne the colony became a Royal Province. Then for thirty-six years it was united to New York, but in 1738 was again divided and has remained a separate state ever since.

Chapter 40 - The Founding of Pennsylvania

Like other persecuted people, the Quakers sought a refuge in America. But even there they were not welcomed. The Puritans of Massachusetts who had fled from persecution, themselves turned persecutors as we have seen. The Quakers discovered that for them there was no Paradise of Peace in the lands beyond the sea. But when George Carteret sold his part of New Jersey Quakers bought it, a young man named William Penn being one of these Quakers.

This William Penn was the son of Sir William Penn, an admiral in the British Navy, and a friend of King Charles I. He was a Royalist and a Churchman, and when his handsome young son turned Quaker he was greatly grieved. At first indeed he was so angry that he turned young William out of the house. Later, however, seeing that his son was quite determined to be a Quaker, the Admiral forgave him, and before he died he asked the Duke of York to be kind to him. The Duke of York promised he would. And then there began a strange friendship between the Catholic Prince and the Quaker.

After the Quakers bought New Jersey a great many went there. They found not only a large amount of freedom, but a kindly government, for William Penn framed the laws.

The Quaker colony of New Jersey was to a certain extent a success, but there were troubles with neighbouring states, and troubles with other claimants of the land. So at length (exactly when we do not know), the idea of founding a real Quaker colony came into Penn's mind.

When Admiral Penn died the King owed him £16,000 and William Penn inherited that claim. So he asked the King to pay the debt not in money but in land in America. The extent of the land asked for was exceedingly vague, but it was at least as big as the whole of England. Charles however was always in want of money. So in 1681 he was pleased enough to give away this great tract of land, which after all was his more by imagination than anything else, and get rid of his debt; and acquire also the possibility of getting some gold as well. For in return for his land Penn agreed to pay two beaver skins a year, and a fifth of all the gold or silver which might be mined within his territory.

Charles not only gave Penn the land, but named it too. Penn meant to call his new country New Wales, but a Welshman who hated the Quakers objected to the name of his land being given to a Quaker colony, so Penn changed it to Sylvania, meaning Woodland, because of the magnificent forests which were there. But the King added Penn to Sylvania thus calling it Penn's Woodlands.

William Penn, however, was afraid that people would think that this was vanity on his part, and that he had called his province after himself; so he tried to have the name changed. He even bribed the King's secretary to do it, but in vain. As some one has said, if he had bribed the King himself he might have succeeded better. As it was he did not succeed, for King Charles was very pleased with the name.

"No," laughed the merry monarch, when Penn asked him to change it, "we will keep the name, but you need not flatter yourself that it is called after you. It is so called after your gallant father."

So as the King insisted Penn had to submit, and he consoled himself by thinking that as Penn means "hill" the name might be taken to mean Wooded Hills.

The tract of land of which Penn now became possessed was smiling and fertile and altogether desirable. It had only one fault, and that was that it had no sea coast.

In a new country where there were no roads, and where communication inland was difficult that was a great drawback. So Penn persuaded the Duke of York to give him that part of his province on which the Swedes had settled and which the Dutch had taken from the Swedes, on the west shores of Delaware Bay. Later this formed the State of Delaware, but in the meantime it was governed as a part of Pennsylvania.

Everything thus being settled, and the charter being granted, Penn drew up a form of government for his colony, chose his cousin, William Markham, as Governor, and sent him off in the autumn of 1681 with three shiploads of settlers.

With Markham, Penn sent a kindly letter to the Swedes of Delaware, telling them that he was now their Governor. "I hope you will not be troubled at the change," he said, "for you are now fixed at the mercy of no Governor who comes to make his fortune. You shall be governed by laws of your own making, and live a free and, if you will, a sober and industrious people. I shall not usurp the right of any, or oppress his person."

Penn also sent a letter to the Indians.

"There is a great God," he said, "that hath made the world and all things therein, to Whom you, and I, and all people, owe their being. This great God hath written His law in our hearts, by which we are taught and commanded to love and help, and do good to one another. Now this great God hath been pleased to make me concerned in your part of the world, and the King of the country where I live hath given me a great province therein. But I desire to enjoy it with your love and consent, that we may always live together as neighbours, and friends, else what would the great God do to us?"

With this letter Penn sent presents to the Indian chiefs and told them that he would soon come to see them himself, and make arrangements about the land.

But it was not till the following year that Penn set out for his colony. When he landed the Dutch and Swedes greeted him with joy. And to show that they acknowledged him as their Governor they presented him, as in old feudal times,

147

with a sod of earth, a bowl of water, and a branch of a tree. Penn then passed on to the spot which he had chosen for his capital. And as showing forth the spirit in which his colony was founded, he called his city Philadelphia or the city of brotherly love.

It was near this town that Penn met the Indian chiefs and made a treaty with them as he had promised to do. In the Indian language the spot was called the Place of Kings, and had been used as a meeting place by the surrounding tribes for long ages. Here there grew a splendid elm, a hoary giant of the forest which for a hundred years and more had withstood the tempests.

Beneath the spreading branches of this tree Penn took his stand. He was young and handsome, and although he wore the simple garb of the Quakers he had not yet perhaps quite forgotten the "modish" ways of his younger days, for about his waist he had knotted a pale blue scarf. Beside him stood his cousin, the deputy governor, and a few more soberly clad Quakers. In front of them, in a great half circle were ranged the Indians, the old men in front, the middle-aged behind, and last of all the young men. They were gorgeous in paint and feathers, and armed with hatchets, bows and arrows, but the Quakers carried no weapons of any kind.

Greetings being over, an ancient warrior advanced, and amid deep silence, tied a horn upon his forehead. This was the sign of his greatness, and also a sign that the spot was sacred. Immediately all the braves threw down their weapons, and seated themselves upon the grass. Then the old warrior announced that they were ready to hear the words of the White Chief.

Then Penn spoke to the gathered Indians reminding them that the Great Spirit wished all men to live in love and brotherhood, and as the Redman listened his heart went out in love to this White Chief who had friendship in his eyes, and kindliness in his voice. And there under the spreading branches of the great elm tree they swore to live in peace and brotherly love "as long as the rivers shall run, and while the sun, moon and stars endure."

These Indians never broke their word and for the next seventy years there was peace in Pennsylvania between the Redman and the White.

The Indians gave Penn the name of Onas which is the Algonquin word for Feather. Ever afterwards too they called the Governor of Pennsylvania Onas, and whoever and whatever he was, for them he was great and good.

But Penn was not only the great Chief Onas, he was also Father Penn. For he roamed the woods with the Indians, talking with them, and sharing their simple food like one of themselves. This greatly delighted the Indians, and to show their pleasure they would perform some of their wild dances. Then up Penn would spring and dance with the best of them. So he won their hearts. They loved him so much that the highest praise they could give any man was to say "he is like the great Onas," and it was said that any one dressed like a Quaker was far safer among the Indians than one who carried a gun.

Life seemed so easy in Pennsylvania that in the first years thousands of colonists came flocking to the new colony. It grew faster than any other colony, so fast indeed that houses could not be built quickly enough. So for a time many of

148

the new settlers had to live in caves dug out of the banks of the Delaware River. It was in one of these caves that the first baby citizen of the city of brotherly love was born.

Pennsylvania prospered and grew fast, but there were constant troubles with Lord Baltimore about the border line between his province and Penn's. The British Kings in those days gave land charters in the most reckless fashion and over and over again the boundaries of one province overlapped those of the others. Then of course there was trouble. This had happened with Virginia and Maryland. Now it happened with Maryland and Pennsylvania.

The quarrel at length became so bad that Penn went home to England to have the matter settled; after that for a time things were better, but the quarrel was not really settled. It was not settled until many years after both Penn and Lord Baltimore were dead. Then, in 1767, two English astronomers, Charles Mason and Jeremiah Dixon, surveyed and fixed the boundary which ever since has been known as the Mason and Dixon Line. Every mile a small stone was placed with B on one side and P on the other. Along the eastern part, too, every five miles a larger stone was placed with the arms of Penn on one side and those of Baltimore on the other. But further west these were discontinued. For in those days when there were few roads it was difficult to get these heavy stones carried to the proper places.

When Penn went back to England he had meant to return to his colony very soon. But fifteen years passed before be was able to do so. During this time King Charles II, who had given him the charter for his great Possessions, died, and his brother James, who as Duke of York had been Penn's friend, was driven from the throne. Then for a time Penn's great province was taken from him, because he was suspected of helping his old friend, the dethroned king. The colony was then placed under the control of the Governor of New York.

Two years later, however, Penn was cleared from the charge of treason and his right to Pennsylvania was again recognised. Then once more he crossed the seas to visit his possessions in the New World.

He found that in fifteen years great changes had been wrought. The two or three thousand inhabitants had now increased to twenty thousand. Many of the new settlers were not Quakers but Protestants from Germany, Holland and Sweden, and Presbyterians from Scotland and Ireland. Penn welcomed them all, but they on their side had grown apart from him. They were no longer his children. He was no longer Father Penn, but the Governor and proprietor.

From this Governor the settlers demanded greater liberties than they had. Penn was grieved, but he met the clamour in the most generous spirit. "Friends," he said, "if in the constitution there be anything that jars, alter it." So it was altered until practically the colonists became a self-governing people.

Now for a second time Penn felt himself obliged to return to England. He did not want to go, but longed to live out the rest of his life in his colony which, in spite of all troubles and difficulties, be loved dearly.

"I cannot think of such a voyage without great reluctance," he said. "For I promised myself that I might stay so long, at least, with you, as to render everybody entirely easy and safe. For my heart is among you, as well as my body, whatever some people may please to think. And no unkindness or disappointment shall ever be able to alter my love to the country."

So with just a little soreness in his heart Penn sailed away never to return. At home trouble and misfortune awaited him. And in the midst of his troubles sickness fell upon him. For six years a helpless invalid with failing mind, he lingered on. Then in 1718 he died. He was seventy-four. Only four years of his long life had been spent in America. Yet he left his stamp upon the continent far more than any other man of his time. He was the greatest, most broad-minded of all the colony builders. As he said himself he had sailed against wind and tide all his life. But the buffetings of fortune left him sweet and true to the end.

Chapter 41 - How Benjamin Franklin Came to Philadelphia

After Penn left his colony there was frequent trouble between the Governors and the people. Some of the Governors were untrustworthy, some were weak, none was truly great. But about ten years after Penn's death a truly great man came to Philadelphia. This was Benjamin Franklin. Of all the men of colonial times Franklin was the greatest.

Benjamin was the fifteenth child of his father, a sturdy English Nonconformist who some years before had emigrated from Banbury in England to Boston in America. As the family was so large the children had to begin early to earn their own living. So at the age of ten Benjamin was apprenticed to his own father, who was a tallow chandler, and the little chap spent his days helping to make soap and "dips" and generally making himself useful.

But he did not like it at all. So after a time he was apprenticed to his elder brother James, who had a printing press, and published a little newspaper called the Courant. Benjamin liked that much better. He soon became a good printer, he was able to get hold of books easily, and he spent his spare time reading such books as the "Pilgrim's Progress" and the "Spectator." Very soon too he took to writing, and became anxious to have an article printed in his brother's paper.

But as he was only a boy he was afraid that if his brother knew he had written the article he would never print it. So he disguised his handwriting, and slipped his paper under the door of the printing house at night. It was found next morning, and to Benjamin's delight was thought good enough to be printed in the paper. After that Benjamin wrote often for the little paper. In time however he and his brother began to quarrel, and when he was seventeen Benjamin decided to go to New York to seek his fortune there.

He took ship to New York in 1723 and arrived there one October day with very little money in his pocket and not a friend in the town. He did not find work in New York, but an old printer advised him to go to Philadelphia where he knew his son was in need of a printer.

Benjamin was already three hundred miles from home, and Philadelphia was another hundred miles farther, but he resolved to go.

Fifty miles of the way he trudged on foot, the rest he went by boat, and after nearly a week of most uncomfortable traveling he arrived one Sunday morning at Philadelphia. He was soaked to the skin, dirty and untidy, hungry and tired. His pockets bulged out with shirts and stockings, but save for one Dutch dollar they were empty of money.

Benjamin was tired and dirty, but before everything he was hungry; so he went to a baker's shop and bought three big rolls. As his pockets were full he tucked two of the rolls under his arm and strolled down the street devouring the third, while the clean tidy folk all ready to go to meeting stared at him in wonder.

Such was the first entry of one of America's greatest statesmen into the town which was henceforth to be his home and where he was to become famous; and as a clever Frenchman said "invent the Republic."

In Philadelphia Benjamin found work, and although after a year he left his new home and sailed for England, he soon returned. In ten years' time he was one of the fore most men of Philadelphia and took an interest in everything which concerned the life of the people. He established a circulating library; he was chosen Clerk of the General Assembly; he was appointed postmaster; he established a police force and fire brigade, and helped to found the University of Pennsylvania and the Philadelphia Hospital.

In fact he took an interest in everything connected with the welfare of his adopted city, and of Pennsylvania. And when troubles arose with the British Government Franklin was chosen to go to England to try to put matters right. Later on other colonies too asked for his help, and he went to England as the agent, not only of Pennsylvania but of Massachusetts, New Jersey and Georgia.

He was a philosopher and scientist as well as a diplomatist, and he was the first American whose fame spread all over the world.

Chapter 42 - The Founding of North and South Carolina

It was in the part of the United States which we now call North Carolina, you remember, that Sir Walter Raleigh tried to found a colony. That colony came to nothing, and the land which the white men had reclaimed from the wilderness returned once more to the wilderness.

Nearly a hundred years went past before white men again appeared in that part of the country. In 1629 King Charles I granted all this region to Sir Robert Heath, but he made no attempt to colonise it. Then a few settlers from Virginia and New England and the Barbados, finding the land vacant and neglected, settled there.

Meanwhile Charles II had come to the throne, and, wanting to reward eight of his friends who had been staunch to him during the Commonwealth, in 1663 he gave them all the land between latitude 30° and 36° and from sea to sea. If you look on the map you will see that this takes in nearly the whole of the Southern States.

Sir Robert Heath was by this time dead, and his heirs had done nothing with his great territory in America, but as soon as it was given to others they began to make a fuss. Charles II, however, said as Sir Robert had failed to plant a colony his claim no longer held good. So the eight new proprietors took possession of it. This tract of land had already been named Carolina by the Frenchman Ribaut in honour of Charles IX of France, and now the Englishmen who took possession of it kept the old name in honour of Charles II.

The Lords Proprietary then set about drawing up laws for their new country. After an old English title they called the oldest among them the Palatine. Palatine originally meant a person who held some office about a king's palace. It has come to mean one who has royal privileges. So a Prince Palatine is really a little king. When the Palatine died it was arranged that the next in age should take his place. As to the other seven proprietors they all had grand sounding titles, such as Chamberlain, Chancellor, Constable, High Steward, and so on.

Having settled all these grand sounding titles the proprietors went on to frame a system of laws. They called it the Grand Model or Fundamental Constitutions, but it was more like some old English feudal system than anything else. It might have done for the ancient Saxons of the ninth century; it was quite unsuitable for rough colonists in a new and almost uninhabited country. It was quite unsuited for men who had left Europe because they wanted to get away from old conventions and be more free.

Yet the Lords Proprietors said that the Grand Model was to be the law of Carolina for ever and ever. The settlers however, would have nothing to do with the Grand Model, for it was altogether too fanciful for them. The proprietors on their side persisted. But when they found it impossible to force the settlers to obey their laws they changed their Grand Model and tried again. Still it was of no use. The colonists would not have it. So at length, having altered their unalterable rules five times, they gave them up altogether and took to something more simple.

But among much that was foolish and unsuitable in the Grand Model there was one good thing. That was that every one was free to worship God in the way he thought right. If only seven men agreed together, said the Grand Model, they were enough to form a church. All it insisted upon was that people must acknowledge a God, and that they must worship Him openly. Nevertheless, in spite of this they made no provision for worship. No clergymen went with the settlers, and indeed for many years no clergymen settled among them.

But because there was religious freedom people of all religions came to Carolina. Quakers and dissenters of every description sought a refuge there. They came not only from England, but from the other colonies and from foreign countries.

You remember that the Protestants of France were called Huguenots, and that they had had to suffer many things at the hands of Catholic rulers until the good King Henry of Navarre protected them by the Edict of Nantes. Now Louis XIV, who was at this time on the throne of France, revoked that edict. He forbade the Huguenots to worship God in their own way, and he also forbade them to leave the country on pain of death.

But thousands braved death rather than remain and be false to their religion. Some were caught and cruelly punished, but many succeeded in escaping to

Holland, England and even to America. So many Huguenots now settled in Carolina. They were hard-working, high-minded people and they brought a sturdiness and grit to the colony which it might otherwise have lacked. Germans too came from the Palatinate, driven thence also by religious persecutions. Irish Presbyterians came fleeing from persecution in Ulster. Jacobites who, having fought for the Stuarts, found Scotland no longer a safe dwelling-place came seeking a new home.

These were all hardy industrious people. But besides these there came many worthless idlers who came to be known as "poor whites." These came because in the early days when the colony was but sparsely peopled, and more settlers were wanted, a law was passed that a new settler need not pay any debts he had made before he came to the colony; and for a year after he came he need pay no taxes. These laws of course brought many shiftless folk who, having got hopelessly into debt somewhere else, ran away to Carolina to get free of it. Indeed so many of these undesirables came that the Virginians called Carolina the Rogues' Harbour.

Besides all these white people there were a great many negroes especially in South Carolina. This came about naturally. The climate of Carolina is hot; there is also a lot of marshy ground good for growing rice. But the work in these rice fields was very unhealthy, and white men could not stand it for long. So a trade in slaves sprang up. Already men had begun to kidnap negroes from the West Coast of Africa and sell them to the tobacco planters of Virginia.

In those days no one saw anything wrong in it. And now that the rice fields of South Carolina constantly required more workers the trade in slaves increased. Whole shiploads were brought at a time. They were bought and sold like cattle, and if they died at their unhealthy work it mattered little, for they were cheap, and there were plenty more where they came from.

Chapter 43 - War With the Indians in North and South Carolina

At first there had been no intention of making two provinces of Carolina. But the country was so large and the settlements made so far apart that very soon it became divided into North and South Carolina. The first settlements made in North Carolina were made round Albemarle Sound, and those of South Carolina at Charleston. One Governor was supposed to rule both states, but sometimes each had a governor. And in all the early years there was trouble between the governors and the people. Sometimes the governors were good men, but more often they were rascals who cared for nothing but their own pockets. So we hear of revolutions, of governors being deposed and imprisoned, of colonists going to England to complain of their governors, of governors going to complain of the colonists.

But far worse than the quarrel between people and governor were the troubles with the Indians. Many thousands of white people had by this time settled in the Carolinas, and the Redman saw himself year by year being driven further and further from his old hunting grounds; so year by year his anger grew. At first he had been friendly to the white man because he brought with him beads and copper ornaments and "fire water." But now he began to hate him.

At length the Indians in North Carolina plotted to kill all the white people. Many tribes of Indians dwelt round the settlements, but the chief among them were the Tuscaroras. These Tuscaroras now arranged with all the other tribes that early on the morning before the new moon they should all with one accord, tomahawk and firebrand in hand, fall upon the Pale-faces and wipe them utterly from the face of the earth.

From tribe to tribe the word was passed till hundreds knew the secret. But the Redman is silent and crafty, and neither by sign nor word did he betray it to the Palefaces.

Suspecting nothing, with perfect faith in their friendship, the white people allowed the Indians to come and go freely in their settlements. Then one night in 1711 a great many appeared, asking for food. Still the white people had no suspicion of evil, and many Indians were allowed even to spend the night in their houses.

The Pale-faces slept peacefully, but for the Redmen there was little rest. They waited impatiently for the dawn. At length the first streaks of light shivered across the sky, and from the woods came a loud fierce war whoop. It was answered by the Indians within the settlements, and with tomahawk in one hand and firebrand in the other they fell upon the still sleeping settlers.

They spared neither man nor woman, neither the old nor the young; and when they could find no more to slay they set fire to the houses. Then those who had hidden themselves were forced to flee from the flames, only to fall beneath the tomahawk. The Swiss and Germans round New Berne and the Huguenots of Bath were the chief sufferers.

But the wonder is that any white men escaped. For their cruel work at an end, and the settlements nought but flaming ruins, the Indians marched through the woods seeking any who had escaped, gathering at length to a spot arranged beforehand. Here they drank "fire water," rejoicing savagely over their victory. Then drunk with brandy and with blood they staggered forth again to continue their horrible labours. For three days the slaughter lasted, for three days the forests rang with terrifying war cries, and village after village was laid in ashes. Then too weary and too drunk for further effort, the Indians ceased their awful work.

At first the white people had been utterly stunned by the suddenness and horror of the uprising, and they were quite incapable of suppressing it by themselves. But soon help came, both from South Carolina and Virginia. Friendly Indians too, who wished to prove to the Pale-faces that they had had no part in the massacre, joined the forces.

Hundreds of the Indians were slain in battle, others were driven from fort to fort. But not for two years were they thoroughly subdued. Then at length, finding themselves no match for the white men, those who were left fled from the province and joined the Five Nations in New York, making from this time forward Six Nations.

154

In South Carolina too there was war with the Indians. The Yamassees had been among the Indians who marched from South Carolina to fight against their brothers, the Tuscaroras. Yet a little later they too rose against the Pale-faces.

Several causes led to the war, but it was chiefly brought about by the Spaniards who had a settlement at St. Augustine to the south of Carolina. They hated the British, and although the two countries were now at peace the Spaniards did all they could to injure the British colonies in America and elsewhere. So now they sympathised with the Yamassees, both with their real and imaginary grievances, and encouraged them to rise against the British.

Secretly and silently then the Redmen laid their plans. But this time the war did not burst forth entirely without warning. For when the Redman has truly given his faith and love nothing makes him false.

Now there was a chieftain named Sanute who had given his friendship to a Scotsman named Fraser, and he could not bear to think of his friend being slaughtered. So one day Sanute came to Fraser's wife to warn her.

"The British are all bad," he said, "they will all go to an evil place. The Yamassees also will go there if they allow these Pale-faces to remain longer in the land. So we will slay them all. We only wait for the sign of a bloody stick which the Creeks will send. Then the Creeks, the Yamassees, and many other nations will join with the Spaniards to slay the British. So fly in all haste to Charleston. And if your own boat is not large enough I will lend you my canoe."

Mrs. Fraser was very much frightened when she heard Sanute speak like this. But when she told her husband he laughed at her fears. The idea that the Spaniards should join with the Indians against the British seemed to him quite absurd.

"How can the Spaniards go to war with us," he said, "while they are at peace with Great Britain?"

"I know not," replied Sanute." But the Spanish Governor has said that soon there will be a great war between the British and the Spaniards, and while we attack on land he will send great ships to block up the harbours, so that neither man nor woman may escape."

Then laying his hand upon his heart Sanute implored his white friends to flee with all haste. "But if you are determined to stay," he added, "then I will take on myself one last office of friendship, and so that you may not be tortured I will slay you with my own hand."

Still Fraser doubted. But his wife was so terrified that he yielded to her entreaties. And gathering his goods together he got into his canoe with his wife and child, and paddled away to Charleston.

Unfortunately in the hurry of departure Fraser either forgot to warn his friends in the plantation near him, or they, being warned, disregarded it; and a few days later the slaughter began. At daybreak the signal was given, and at the sound of the war whoop the seemingly peaceful Indians were turned suddenly into raging demons who, with tomahawk and torch in hand, sowed destruction and death around. So the land was filled with blood and wailing, pleasant homesteads were

155

laid in ruins, and only heaps of smouldering ashes marked where they had been.

But Governor Craven was one of the best governors of his time. He was a man of action and courage as well as a wise ruler, and he quickly gathered an army with which to march against the savages. The North Carolinians too, remembering gratefully the help which South Carolina had given to them in their need, sent men. Soon the Yamassees, and their friends were defeated and driven from the province. They fled across the border and took refuge in Spanish territory, where they were received with great rejoicing. They might indeed have been heroes returning from a victorious campaign, for the church bells were rung and salutes were fired in their honour.

The Yamassees were crushed, but they were not utterly conquered, from henceforth their hearts were filled with hatred against all the Carolinians. This hatred the Spaniards did their best to keep alive. They supplied the Indians with weapons, and made them valiant with "fire water." Thus encouraged they broke across the borders in small scalping parties, seizing and slaying, often with unspeakable tortures, all those who dwelt in lonely places. These frays were so unceasing, and so deadly, that at length hardly any one dared live in all the border region.

Meanwhile the war against the Indians had cost a great deal of money. And as the Lords Proprietor made a good deal of money out of the colony, the settlers thought they might as well bear some of the expense also. So they sent messengers home to arrange this matter. But the Lords Proprietor seemed to care little about their possessions except as a means of making money. And they refused to pay any of the cost of the war. This made the settlers angry.

The settlers revolt and Carolina becomes a royal province, 1719 They had never liked the rule of the Lords Proprietor; now they were heartily tired of it and they refused to stand it longer. King William III was now upon the throne, and the settlers asked him to make South Carolina a Crown Colony. To this King William agreed. Ten years later North Carolina also became a Crown Colony, and the two Carolinas from henceforth continued to be separate states.

Chapter 44 - The Founding of Georgia

South Carolina extended as far as the River Savannah, and between that river and the Spanish settlement at St. Augustine there stretched a great waste of country inhabited only by the Redmen who ever and anon made raids into Carolina. Southward from this the Spaniards claimed the land and called it Florida; but they made no effort to colonise the wilderness which stretched between Florida and the borders of South Carolina. So at length the idea of founding a British colony there occurred to an Englishman named James Oglethorpe.

He was a truly great man, and in an age when men were cruel to each other out of mere thoughtlessness he tried to make people kinder to their fellows.

In those days in England people could be imprisoned for debt. And if they could not pay they remained in prison often for years, and sometimes till they

156

died. They were starved and tortured, loaded with fetters, locked up in filthy dungeons, herded together with thieves and murderers, or those suffering from smallpox and other loathsome diseases. It was horrible, but no one troubled about it. There had always been misery in the world, there always would be, men thought, and no one had pity for prisoners.

But now young Oglethorpe had a friend who was imprisoned for debt, and, being treated in this horrible fashion, he died of smallpox. Oglethorpe's generous heart was grieved at the death of his friend, and he began to enquire into the causes of it. The things he discovered were so awful that he stood aghast with horror at the misery of the imprisoned debtors. And what was more he did not rest until he had made other people see the horror of it also. Soon there was an outcry all over England, and some of the worst evils were done away with.

Then the idea came to Oglethorpe that he would found a colony in America, where poor debtors who had regained their freedom might find a refuge and make a new start in life. He decided to found this colony to the south of South Carolina, so that it might not only be a refuge for the oppressed, but also form a buffer state between the Carolinas and Spanish Florida. So from George II Oglethorpe got a charter for the land lying between the Savannah and the Altamaha rivers, and in honour of the King the colony was called Georgia.

Many well-to-do people were by this time interested in his scheme. They gave him money for it, and he also got a large grant from Parliament. This was the first time that Parliament ever voted money to found a colony in America. Of all the thirteen colonies now founded Georgia alone received aid from the State.

Trustees were appointed to frame the laws, and a kind of proprietory government was created. The colonists were to be granted all the liberties of Englishmen, but they were not to be allowed to frame the laws or take any part in the government. After twenty-one years the rule of the trustees was to come to an end, and Georgia was to become a Crown Colony.

All these matters being arranged, men were sent round to visit the jails, and choose from among the prisoners those who were really good men and who through misfortune, rather than roguery, found themselves in prison. The Commissioners refused to take lazy or bad men, or those who, in going to Georgia, would leave wife or children in want at home. Besides poor debtors those who were being persecuted because of their religion in any European State were invited to come and find a refuge in Georgia. No slavery was to be allowed, and the sale of rum was forbidden throughout the whole colony. For Oglethorpe knew how the Redman loved "fire-water" and how bad it was for him, and he wanted the settlement of Georgia to be a blessing and not a curse to the Redman, as well as to the white man.

Soon far more people wanted to go than Oglethorpe could take. So crowds of poor wretches had to be turned away, bitterly disappointed that they could not go to this new land which, after their terrible sufferings, seemed to them a very paradise.

The preparations took some time, and it was about the middle of November,

1732, when at length the Anne hoisted her sails and turned her prow towards the west. There were about a hundred and twenty colonists on board with Oglethorpe as Governor, and it was nearly the end of January when the colonists landed on the southern shores of the Savannah and founded the town of the same name.

One of the first things Oglethorpe did was to make a treaty with the Indians, for he knew how greatly the peace and safety of the little colony depended on their friendship.

There were eight tribes of Creeks who claimed the land upon which Oglethorpe had settled. But before he allowed the colonists to land he himself went ashore and sought out the chieftain whose village was close to the spot he had chosen for his town. This chieftain was an old man of over ninety years, and at first he did not seem at all pleased at the idea of white men settling on his land. But Oglethorpe was kindly and friendly, he spoke gently to the old chief, and soon won his consent to the settlement, and a promise of friendship.

When then the colonists landed, instead of being greeted with a flight of arrows they were received with solemn ceremony, the braves coming down to the water's edge to greet them. First came the Medicine Man carrying in either hand a fan made of white feathers as signs of peace and friendship. Behind him followed the chieftain and his squaw, with twenty or thirty braves, who filled the air with wild yells of welcome.

When the Medicine Man reached Oglethorpe he paused, and dancing round him he swept him on every side with the white feather fans, chanting the while a tale of brave deeds. This done the chieftain next drew near, and in flowery words bade the White Chief and his followers welcome. Thus peacefully the settlement was begun.

But Oglethorpe wanted to be friends with the other tribes round, so he asked Tomo-chi-chi, the old chieftain, to invite them to a conference. And a few months later they all came. Oglethorpe received them in one of the new houses built by the settlers, and when they were all solemnly seated an old and very tall man stood up and made a long speech. He claimed for the Creeks all the land south of the Savannah.

"We are poor and ignorant," he said, "but the Great Spirit who gave the Pale-faces breath gave the Redmen breath also. But the Great Spirit who made us both has given more wisdom to the Pale-faces."

Then he spread his arms abroad and lengthened the sound of his words. "So we feel sure," he cried, "that the Great Spirit who lives in heaven and all around has sent you to teach us and our wives and children. Therefore we give you freely the land we do not use. That is my thought and not mine alone but the thought of all the eight nations of the Creeks. And in token thereof we bring you gifts of skins which is our wealth."

Then one by one the chief men of each nation rose up and laid a bundle of buck skins at Oglethorpe's feet.

In return Oglethorpe gave each of the chiefs a coat and hat trimmed with gold lace. Each of the braves likewise received some present. So a treaty of peace was signed, the Redmen promising to keep the good talk in their hearts as long as the sun shone, or water ran in the rivers. And so just and wise was Oglethorpe in all his dealings with the natives that in the early days of the settlement there were no wars with the natives.

Oglethorpe worked unceasingly for the good of the colony. He kept no state, but slept in a tent and ate the plainest of food, his every thought being given to the happiness of his people. And in return they loved him and called him father. If any one were sick he visited him, and when they quarreled they came to him to settle their disputes. Yet he kept strict discipline and allowed neither drinking nor swearing.

The work of the colony went on apace. About six weeks after the settlers landed some of the settlers from Charleston came to visit Oglethorpe, and they were astonished to find how quickly things had got on.

"It is surprising," one wrote, "to see how cheerfully the men work, considering they have not been bred to it. There are no idlers there. Even the boys and girls do their parts. There are four houses already up, but none finished. . . . He has ploughed up some land, part of which he has sowed with wheat. . . . He has two or three gardens, which he has sowed with divers sort of seeds. . . . He was palisading the town round. . . . In short he has done a vast deal of work for the time, and I think his name justly deserves to be immortalised."

But if Georgia had peace with the Indians it was far otherwise with the Spaniards. For the Spaniards were very angry with the British for daring to settle south of the Savannah. They vowed to root them out of America, and they set out to attack the little colony.

But Oglethorpe was a daring soldier as well as a wise statesman, and he succeeded in beating the Spaniards. It was at Frederica where the greatest battle took place. This town had been founded after Savannah and named Frederica, in honour of Frederick, Prince of Wales. It was built on an island off the coast called St. Simon, and, being near the Spanish border, it was well fortified. At the little village of St. Simon which was at the south end of the island, there were barricades and a high watch-tower where a constant watch was kept for ships. As soon as they were sighted a gun was fired, and a horseman sped off to the barracks with the news.

they attack the settlements, 1742 Here one day in July, 1742, a great fleet of Spanish vessels came sailing. They made a brave show with their high painted prows and shining sails, and they brought five thousand men who vowed to give no quarter.

Oglethorpe had but eight hundred men. Some were regular soldiers, some were fierce Highlanders glad to have a chance of a shot at the Spaniards, and not a few were friendly Indians. But small though his force was Oglethorpe did not despair. He had sent to Carolina for help which he was sure would come if he could but hold out for a few days. He thought, however, that the position at St. Simon was too dangerous. So he spiked his guns, destroyed all stores, and retreated to Frederica.

159

The Spaniards soon landed and, taking possession of St. Simon, set out to attack Frederica. But they found it no easy matter, for the town was surrounded by dense and pathless woods. And struggling through them the Spaniards stumbled into marshes, or got entangled in the dense undergrowth until in their weariness they declared that not the Evil One himself could force a passage through. Added to their other difficulties they were constantly harassed by scouting parties of wild Indians, and almost as wild Highlanders, sent out from Frederica by Oglethorpe.

But meanwhile no help appeared, and at length Oglethorpe, having discovered that the Spanish force was divided, decided to make a sortie and surprise one part of it. So with three hundred chosen men he marched out one dark night, and stole silently through the woods until he had almost reached the enemy's camp.

Then suddenly a Frenchman who was with the little British force discharged his musket, and fled towards the Spanish camp.

All hope of a surprise was at an end, and Oglethorpe returned hastily to the fort. But that the surprise had failed was not the worst. It was certain that the deserter would tell the Spaniards how weak the British were, and that thus heartened they would soon attack in force. Something, Oglethorpe decided, must be done to prevent that.

So he wrote a letter in French addressing it to the French deserter. This letter was written as if coming from a friend. It begged the Frenchman to tell the Spaniards that Frederica was in an utterly defenseless state, and to bring them on to an attack. Or if he could not persuade them to attack at least he must persuade them to remain three days longer at Fort Simon. For within that time two thousand men would arrive from Carolina and six British ships of war "which he doubted not would be able to give a good account of themselves to the Spanish invaders." Above all things the writer bade the Frenchman beware of saying anything about Admiral Vernon, the British admiral who was coming against St. Augustine. He ended by assuring him that the British King would not forget such good services, and that he should be richly rewarded.

This letter Oglethorpe gave to one of the Spanish prisoners they had taken, who for a small sum of money and his liberty, promised to deliver it to the French deserter. But instead of doing that he gave it, as Oglethorpe had expected he would, to the leader of the Spanish army.

The French deserter at once denied all knowledge of the letter or its writer, but all the same he was fettered and kept a prisoner while the Spanish leaders held a council of war. They knew not what to do. Some thought that the letter was a ruse (as indeed it was) merely meant to deceive them. But others thought that the British really had them in a trap. And while they were thus debating by good luck some British vessels appeared off the coast. And thinking them to be the men-of-war mentioned in the letter the Spaniards fled in such haste that although they had time to set fire to the barracks at St. Simon they left behind them a great cannon and large stores of food and ammunition.

Thus was the little colony saved from destruction.

By his brave stand and clever ruse Oglethorpe had saved not only Georgia but Carolina too. Yet South Carolina had cause for shame, for her Governor had paid no heed to Oglethorpe's call for help, and so far as he was concerned Georgia might have been wiped out. He indeed cared so little about it that when the governors of the other more northerly colonies wrote to Oglethorpe thanking and praising him he did not join with them. But much to his disgust, seeing their Governor so lax, some of the people of South Carolina themselves wrote to Oglethorpe to thank him.

"It was very certain," they wrote, "had the Spaniards succeeded in those attempts against your Excellency they would also have entirely destroyed us, laid our province waste and desolate, and filled our habitation with waste and slaughter. We are very sensible of the great protection and safety we have long enjoyed, by your Excellency being to the southwards of us, and keeping your armed sloops cruising on the coasts, which has secured our trade and fortunes more than all the ships of war ever stationed at Charleston. But more by your late resolution against the Spaniards when nothing could have saved us from utter ruin, next to the Providence of Almighty God, but your Excellency's singular conduct, and the bravery of the troops under your command. We think it our duty to pray God to protect your Excellency and send you success in all your undertakings."

But, although Oglethorpe had many friends, he had also enemies, some even within the colony he had done so much to serve. There were those within the colony who wanted rum and wanted slavery and said that it would never prosper until they were allowed. Oglethorpe, with all his might, opposed them, so they hated him. Others were discontented for far better reasons: because they had no share in the government, and because the land laws were bad.

Oglethorpe, too, had his own troubles, for he had spent so much on the colony that he was deeply in debt. So, having ruled for twelve years, he went home, and although be lived to a great old age, he never returned again to Georgia. At the age of fifty-five he married; then he settled down to the quiet life of an English gentleman. Learned men and fine ladies called him friend, poets sang of his deeds, and the great Samuel Johnson wanted to write his life.

"Heroic, romantic, and full of the old gallantry" to the end, he lived out his last days in the great manor house of an English village, and was laid to rest in the peaceful village church in 1785.

"But the Savannah repeats to the Altamaha the story of his virtues and of his valor, and the Atlantic publishes to the mountains the greatness of his fame, for all Georgia is his living, speaking monument."

Oglethorpe was the only one of all the founders of British colonies in America who lived to see their separation from the mother-country. But long ere that he had to see many changes in the settlement. For the colonists would not be contented without rum and slaves, and in 1749 both were allowed. A few years later the trustees gave up their claims and Georgia became a Crown Colony, and the people were given the right to vote and help to frame the laws under which they had to live.

PART V STORIES OF THE FRENCH IN AMERICA

Chapter 45 - How the Mississippi was Discovered

While the shores of the Atlantic from Nova Scotia to Georgia were being claimed and peopled by the British another and very different nation laid claim also to the mighty continent. Before Jamestown was founded the French had already set foot upon the St. Lawrence. Long before the Pilgrim Fathers sailed from Plymouth the flag of France was floating from the citadel of Quebec; and the French laid claim to the whole of Canada.

But the French and the British claimed these new lands in very different ways. The Englishmen came seeking freedom and a new home. The Frenchmen came seeking adventure. The Englishman painfully felled trees and cleared land, toiling by the sweat of his brow for the comfort of a home. The Frenchman set up crosses on the edge of pathless forests, claiming unknown lands for God and his King. He came as missionary, trader and adventurer rather than as farmer. And, led on by zeal for religion or desire for adventure, he pushed his settlements far into the wilderness.

So, long years went by. All along the Atlantic coasts spread fertile fields and fair homesteads. The British were content to live on the lands which they had cleared and tilled, and no adventurer sought to know what lay beyond the blue mountain range which shut him from the West.

Far otherwise was it with the French. Priests and traders were both full of a desire for conquest and adventure. Many of them indeed were so driven by the roving spirit that they left the towns altogether and lived alone among the forests, tracking the wild animals, and only coming to towns to sell the skins and get provisions.

These trappers brought back with them many strange tales of the forests and unknown wilds. They spoke of the Mississippi or "great water" of which the Indians told marvelous tales. And at length it seemed to their hearers that this great water could be no other than the long sought passage to India and the East.

Many people, fired by these tales, went in search of this great water. In 1673 two priests named Marquette and Joliet were the first to discover it. For many miles they floated down the Mississippi. On either side stretched endless forests and plains of waving grass, haunts of wild animals and of the Indians, - almost as wild. On they went, past the mouth of the yellow Missouri, on still till they came to the river Arkansas. At last, sure that the great river went southward and not westward as they had supposed, they decided to return.

It had been easy enough floating down, but now they had to battle against the stream, and it was only after weeks of toil that they at length reached Canada again with their news.

When he heard their story another adventurer named René Robert Cavelier Sieur de la Salle became eager to make certain of their discovery, and follow the river all the way to its mouth.

162

With great care and trouble he made his arrangements. He thought it would be impossible to compass so great a journey by canoes, so he built a little ship which he called the Griffin. It was the first ship which had been seen by the Indians round Lake Erie, and in amazement and fear they came to stare at it. In their ignorant terror they would have destroyed it had not careful watch been kept.

From the very beginning of his expedition La Salle found many difficulties. But at length they all seemed to be overcome, and he set out with his friend, Henri de Tonty, and about forty men.

Tonty was a man of courage, as bold and enterprising as La Salle himself. He was, too, much feared by the Indians, who thought him a great Medicine Man. For while fighting in Europe he had had one hand shot off. But he had replaced it with an iron hand, which he always wore covered with a glove. The Indians did not know this, and once or twice when they had been troublesome he had brought them to order by knocking them down with this hand. Not knowing the secret of it they marvelled greatly at his strength, and, fearing him accordingly, called him Iron Hand.

One of La Salle's great difficulties was lack of money. So before leaving the great lakes he collected a quantity of furs. Then he sent back the Griffin and half his men, with orders to sell these furs, and return with supplies for the expedition as quickly as possible. With the rest of his men La Salle journeyed on to the head of Lake Michigan in canoes.

It was no easy journey, for storms swept the lake. The waves tossed their frail canoes hither and thither so that they were often in danger of drowning. They were harassed, too, by unfriendly Indians. At length, worn out by fatigue, starving with cold and hunger, they reached the appointed place to await the return of the Griffin.

But the Griffin never came. In vain La Salle scanned the grey waters. Day after day passed, and no white sail flecked the dreary expanse. The Griffin was never heard of more.

With a heavy heart La Salle at length gave up the weary watch, and decided to go on with such men and supplies as he had. But with every step fresh difficulties arose. La Salle had many enemies, and they did their best to hinder and hamper him. His own men were discontented and mutinous. They had no love for their leader, no enthusiasm for the expedition, and the hardships and dangers of the way made them sullen.

They were half starved and worn out with fatigue; all they wanted was to get back to a comfortable life. They were sick of the wilderness and its hardships. Added to this the Indians told them bloodcurdling tales of the terrors of the "Father of Waters." It was a raging torrent of whirlpools, they said, full of poisonous serpents and loathly monsters. Those who ventured on it would never return.

This was more than the men could face. They chose rather the possibility of death among the Indians and the wilderness to its certainty among such horrors, and some of them ran away.

Depressed by this desertion La Salle resolved to camp for the rest of the winter. So on the banks of the river Illinois he built a fort which he called Creve-Coeur, or Heart-break.

But La Salle's brave heart was not yet broken. And here he began to build a new ship in which to sail down the Mississippi. There was wood in plenty around, and the work was begun. But many things, such as sails and rigging, which were necessary for the ship, the wilderness could not supply. And, seeing no other way, La Salle resolved to go back to Fort Frontenac to get them, leaving Tonty meanwhile to look after the building of the ship.

It was March when La Salle set out on his tremendous walk of a thousand miles. With him he took a faithful Indians guide and four Frenchmen. And seldom have men endured a journey more terrible.

The spring sun was just beginning to thaw the ice and snow of winter, so that the prairies were turned to marshes into which the travelers sank knee deep. The forests were pathless thickets through which they had to force a way with axe and hatchet. As a pathway the rivers were useless to them, for the ice was so thin that it would not bear their weight. And later when it thawed and broke up they still could not use their canoes lest they should be shattered by the floating masses of ice.

All day long they toiled knee deep in mud and half-melted snow, laden with baggage, guns and ammunition. At night they lay down without shelter of any kind. They were often hungry, they suffered constantly both from cold and heat. For at noon the sun beat down upon them fiercely, and at night the frost was so bitter that the blankets in which they lay wrapped were frozen stiff.

The hardships of the journey were so tremendous that the marvel is that any one lived to tell of them. Indeed, one by one the men fell ill, and when at length after three months of pain and peril they arrived at their journey's end only La Salle had strength or courage left.

Here more bad news greeted La Salle, for he now heard that a ship sent out from France laden with supplies for him had been wrecked. But even this cruel stroke of fortune could not break his spirit. Once more he set about gathering supplies, and made ready to return to Fort Heart-break.

But worse was yet to come. La Salle was about to start when he received a letter from Tonty. From this he learned that soon after he had left nearly all his men had mutinied. They had rifled the stores and demolished the fort; then, throwing into the river everything they could not carry, had made off. Only three or four had remained faithful. With these Tony was now alone in the wilderness.

This staggering news only made La Salle more eager to set out, for he could not leave his brave friend thus helpless. So once more the toilsome journey was begun. But when Heart-break was reached, La Salle found no friend to welcome him. All around there was nothing but silence and desolation, and ghastly ash-strewn ruins. The unfinished ship, like some vast skeleton, huge and gaunt, alone bore witness that white men had once been there.

Still La Salle would not despair. He spent the winter making friends with the

Indians and searching earnestly for some trace of Tonty. The winter was unusually severe, the whole land was covered with snow and both La Salle and some of his men became snow-blind for days. But at last with the melting of the snows light and joy came to him. The blindness passed, Tonty was found.

Once again the friends met. Each had a tale to tell, a tale of bitter disappointments and defeats. Yet in spite of all the blows of fortune Le Salle would not give in. Once more he set about making preparations for the expedition. But now he gave up the idea of building a ship, and decided to trust to canoes alone.

It was mid-winter when all was ready. The rivers were frozen hard. So, placing their canoes on sledges, the men dragged them over the ice. As they went southward and spring came on, the ice melted and would no longer bear them. The stream was soon filled with floating masses of broken ice, so they were obliged to land and wait until it had melted.

Then once more they set out. Every day now they drifted farther and farther into the heat of summer. The sun shone softly through the overhanging trees, the river banks were gay with flowers, and bright plumaged birds flashed through the sunlight. After the tortures of the past winters this green and fertile land seemed a very paradise. So on the adventurers passed where never white man had passed before; and at length they reached the mouth of the mighty river and stood upon the shore of the Gulf of Mexico.

And here, in 1682, while wondering savages looked on, this mere handful of white men claimed all the land through which they had passed for their King. The long silence of the wilderness was awakened for the first time by the sound of Latin chants. Guns were fired, and to the shouts of "God save the King," a pillar was set up.

Chapter 46 - King William's War and Queen Anne's War

At this time in Europe France and Britain were at war. When King William came to take possession of Britain, James II ran away to France. The King of France received him kindly, and soon declared war upon William. The war was fought not only in Europe but in America also, and it is known in America as King William's War, because William was King of Great Britain at the time. It was the beginning of a fierce struggle between British and French for possession of the vast continent of America - a struggle which was to last for seventy years; a struggle in which not only the white people but the Indians also took part, some fighting for the British, some for the French.

King William's War, 1690-1697 At this time Frontenac was Governor of Canada. He was one of the greatest nobles of France and lived surrounded with state and splendour. Proud and haughty and of a fiery temper, with white men he quarreled often, but he knew better than any other how to manage the Indians, and they feared him as they feared no white ruler who came before or after him. He would not allow the chiefs to call him brother as other governors had done. They were his children; to them he was the Great Father. Yet if need be he would paint his face, dress himself in Indian clothes, and, tomahawk in his hand, lead the war dance, yelling and leaping with the best of them.

King Louis now gave Frontenac orders to seize New York so that the French might have access to the Hudson River, and a port open all the year round and not frozen up for months at a time like Quebec.

So Frontenac made ready his forces. He gathered three armies and sent them by different ways to attack the British. But few of these forces were regular soldiers. Many of them were Indians, still more were coureurs de bois, wild bush-rangers who dressed and lived more like Indians than white men, and were as fearless, and lawless, and learned in the secrets of the forest as the Indians.

These armies set out in the depth of winter. French and Indian alike were smeared with war-paint and decked with feathers. Shod with snow shoes they sped over the snow, dragging light sledges behind them laden with food. For twenty-two days they journeyed over plains, through forest, across rivers, but at length one of the armies reached the village of Schenectady, the very farthest outpost of New York.

The people had been warned of their danger, but they paid no heed. They did not believe that the danger was real. So secure indeed did they feel that the gates were left wide open, and on either side for sentinels stood two snow men.

In all the village there was no sound, no light. Every one was sleeping peacefully. Then suddenly through the stillness there rang the awful Indian war whoop.

In terror the villagers leaped from their beds, but before they could seize their weapons they were struck down. Neither man, woman nor child was spared, and before the sun was high Schenectady was a smoking, blood-stained ruin.

The other parties which Frontenac had sent out also caused terrible havoc. They surprised and burned many villages and farms, slaughtering and carrying prisoner the inhabitants. Thus all New England was filled with bloodshed and terror.

But these horrors instead of making the British give in made them determined to attack Canada. New York and the colonies of New England joined together and decided to make an attack by land and by sea. The British determined to attack Canada

But what, with mismanagement, sickness, and bickerings among the various colonies, the land attack came to nothing. It was left for the fleet to conquer Canada.

The little New England fleet was commanded by Sir William Phips, a bluff, short-tempered sailor. He sailed up the St. Lawrence and anchored a little below Quebec.

Then the watching Frenchmen saw a small boat put off, flying a white flag. As it neared the shore some canoes went out to meet it and found that it was bringing a young British officer with a letter for Count Frontenac.

The officer was allowed to land, but first his eyes were blindfolded. Then as he stepped on shore a sailor seized each arm, and thus he was led through the streets.

Quebec is built on a height, and the streets are steep and narrow, sometimes being nothing more than flights of steps. And now, instead of being taken directly

166

to the Governor, the young officer was dragged up and down these steep and stony streets. Now here, now there, he was led, stumbling blindly over stones and steps, and followed by a laughing, jeering crowd, who told him it was a game of blind man's bluff.

At last, thoroughly bewildered and exhausted, he was led into the castle, and the bandage was suddenly taken from his eyes. Confused and dazzled by the bright light he stood for a moment gazing stupidly about him.

Before him, haughty and defiant, stood Frontenac surrounded by his officers. Their splendid uniforms glittered with gold and silver lace, their wigs were curled and powdered, their hats were decked with feathers, as if for a ball rather than for war.

For a moment the young Englishman stood abashed before them. Then, recovering himself, he handed his commander's letters to Frontenac.

The letter was written in English, but an interpreter read it aloud, translating it into French. In haughty language it demanded the surrender of Quebec, in the name of William and Mary, within an hour.

When the reading was finished the officer pulled his watch out of his pocket, and held it towards Frontenac.

"I cannot see the time," said he.

"It is ten o'clock," replied the Englishman. "By eleven I must have your answer."

Frontenac's brow grew dark with anger. Hitherto he had held himself in check, but now his wrath burst forth.

"By heaven," he cried, "I will not keep you waiting so long. Tell your General that I do not acknowledge King William. The Prince of Orange who calls himself so is a usurper. I know of no king of England save King James."

The Englishman was quite taken aback by Frontenac's vehemence. He felt he could not go back to his leader with such an answer.

"Will you give me your answer in writing?" he said.

"No," thundered Frontenac, "I will answer your general with the mouths of my cannon only. Let him do his best, and I will do mine."

And with this answer the Englishman was forced to be content. Once more his eyes were blindfolded, and again he was jostled and hustled through the streets until he reached his boat.

When Phips received Frontenac's proud answer he prepared to attack. But he was no match for the fierce old lion of a Frenchman. The New Englanders were brave enough, but they had little discipline, and, worse still, they had no leader worthy of the name. They spent shot and shell uselessly battering the solid rock upon which Quebec is built. Their aim was bad, and their guns so small that even when the balls hit the mark they did little damage.

At length, having wasted most of their ammunition in a useless cannonade, the British sailed away. The men were dejected and gloomy at their failure. Many of their ships had been sorely disabled by the French guns, and on the way home several were wrecked. As the others struggled homeward with their tale of disaster, New England was filled with sadness and dismay.

167

The attack on Canada had been an utter failure. Yet, had Phips but known it, Quebec was almost in his grasp. For although there were men enough within the fortress there was little food. And even before he sailed away the pangs of hunger had made themselves felt.

For seven years more the war lingered on, but now it chiefly consisted of border raids and skirmishes, and the New Englanders formed no more designs of conquering Canada. And at length in 1697, with the Treaty of Ryswick, King William's War came to an end.

In 1701 James, the exiled King of Britain, died; and Louis of France recognised his son James as the rightful King of Britain. This made King William angry. Louis also placed his grandson, the Duke of Anjou, on the throne of Spain. This made King William and the British people still more angry. For with a French King on the throne of Spain they thought it very likely that France and Spain might one day be joined together and become too powerful. So King William again declared war on France, but before the war began he died.

Queen Mary's sister Anne now became Queen; she carried on the war already declared. This war brought fighting in America as well as in Europe. In America it is called Queen Anne's War, and in Europe the War of the Spanish Succession.

Queen Anne's War, 1702-1713 This war was carried on in much the same manner as the last. There were Indian massacres, sudden sallies, attacks by land and sea. But this time the British were more determined. And although another attack on Quebec failed, just as the attack made by Phips had failed, one on Nova Scotia succeeded.

In the South, too, the Spaniards were defeated at Charleston. Taken altogether the British had the best of the fighting. And when at length peace was made by the Treaty of Utrect in 1713 Nova Scotia, Newfoundland, and the Hudson Bay Territory were given up to the British. Thus both in west and north the British enclosed the French possessions.

Chapter 47 - The Mississippi Bubble

Being thus encroached upon by the British the French became more determined to shut them out from the south. Already twelve years after La Salle's death another attempt had been made to found a town at the mouth of the Mississippi, and this time the attempt was successful.

This time the expedition was led by Pierre Le Moyne, Sieur d'Iberville. In 1698 with two ships he sailed out from France and, after some trouble, found the mouth of the Mississippi. He did not, however, build his fort here, but on the coast of what is now the State of Mississippi. Then, leaving one of his officers and his brother in command, he sailed home again to France.

While d'Iberville was away, his brother Bienville started on an expedition to explore the Mississippi. And he soon discovered that the French had taken possession none too soon, for not far from where New Orleans now stands, he fell in with a British ship. On board were a lot of French Huguenot families who had come to found a settlement on the Mississippi. Bienville talked to the captain, who told him that this was one of three ships sent out from England by a company formed of Huguenots and Englishmen who intended to found a colony on the Mississippi. They were not sure, however, whether they were on the Mississippi or not.

Bienville at once assured them that they were not, but were instead on a river which belonged to Louis of France, where already the French had several settlements. The British captain believed what he was told and, much to the Frenchmen's delight, turned back. Just at the spot where this took place the river makes a bed, and because of this it was given the name of English Bend, by which name it is known to this day.

D'Iberville only stayed long enough in France to gather more colonists and returned at once to Louisiana, where he founded two more towns along the coast. But the colonists sent out by Louis were of the lowest. Many of them were little more than rogues and vagabonds. The mere off-scourings of the towns, they were idle and extravagant, and the colony did not prosper.

Instead of putting gold into Louis' pockets, as he had hoped, he had constantly to pour it out to maintain the colony. Of that Louis soon grew tired. Besides this he wanted all the money he could gather to carry on the war (Queen Anne's War), which was still raging. So, in 1712, he handed Louisiana over to a wealthy merchant named Crozat to make what he could out of it.

Such great power was given to this merchant that he was little less than a king. He had every monopoly. Nobody in the colony could buy or sell the smallest thing without his permission, and every one had to work for him and not for themselves. But the people were by no means willing workers. They were, said one of their priests, "nearly all drunkards, gamblers, blasphemers and foes of everything that was good," and when they found that they are expected to work merely to put money into the proprietor's pocket they would not work at all.

So very soon Crozat found he could make nothing out of the colony. And after some vain efforts to make it pay he gave up his charter, and Louisiana once more became a royal possession.

Meanwhile France itself was in sore straits for money. Louis XIV, that magnificent and extravagant monarch, had died and left his country beggared and in want. The Duke of Orleans now ruled as Regent for little Louis XV. He was at his wit's end to know where to find money, when a clever Scots adventurer names John Law came to him with a new and splendid idea. this was to use paper money instead of gold and silver. The Regent was greatly taken with the idea, and he gave Law leave to issue the paper money. It was quite a good idea had it been kept within bounds. But it was not kept within bounds. All France went mad with eagerness to get some of the paper money which was, they thought, going to make them rich forever.

Besides issuing paper money, Law started what was known as the Mississippi Scheme or Company of the Indies in 1717. Louisiana, which had been received back from Crozat, was handed over to John Law, who undertook to settle the country, and work the gold and silver mines which were supposed to be there.

Law began at once to fill all France with stories of Louisiana and its delights. Gold and silver mines, he said, had been discovered there which were so rich that they could never be used up. Lumps of gold lay about everywhere, and one might have them for the picking up. As for silver, it was so common that it had little value except to be used for paving the streets. In proof of these stories lumps of gold said to have come from Louisiana were shown in the shops of Paris.

As to the climate, it was the most perfect on earth. It was never too hot, and never too cold, but always warm and sunny. The soil was so fertile that one had but to scratch it to produce the finest crops. Delicious fruits grew everywhere, and might be gathered all the year round. The meadows were made beautiful, and the air scented, with the loveliest of flowers. In fact Louisiana was painted as an earthly paradise, where nothing the heart could desire was lacking.

People believed these stories. And, believing them, it was not wonderful that they desired to possess for themselves some of these delights. So, rich and poor, high and low, rushed to buy shares in the Company. The street in Paris where the offices of the Company were was choked from end to end with a struggling crowd. The rich brought their hundreds, the poor their scanty savings. Great lords and ladies sold their lands and houses in order to have money to buy more shares. The poor went ragged and hungry in order to scrape together a few pence. Peers and merchants, soldiers, priests, fine ladies, servants, statesmen, labourers, all jostled together, and fought to buy the magic paper which would make them rich and happy beyond belief. Fortunes were made and lost in a day. Some who had been rich found themselves penniless; others who had always lived in poverty found themselves suddenly rolling in wealth which they did not know how to use. And John Law was the wizard whose magic wand had created all these riches. He was flattered and courted by every one. The greatest princes in the land came to beg favours of him. They came to him to beg, and he treated them haughtily as beggars, and bade them wait.

Day by day, and month by month, the madness increased, and the gigantic bubble grew larger and larger. Bienville, meanwhile, who had been deprived of his governorship, was once more made Governor of Louisiana. With a company of settlers, he returned again to the colony in 1718, and he at once set about building a capital, which, in honour of the Regent, he called New Orleans. The place he chose for a capital was covered with forest. So before any building could be done fifty men were set to fell the trees and clear a space. And then the first foundations of the new great city of New Orleans were laid.

But still the colony did not prosper. For the colonists were for the most part rogues and vagabonds, sent there by force, and kept there equally by force. They looked upon Louisiana as a prison, and tried constantly to escape from it.

Meanwhile no ships laden with gold and gems reached France, for no gold mines had ever been discovered. Then people began to grow tired of waiting. Some of them began to suspect that all the stories of the splendours of Louisiana were not true, and they tried to sell their paper money and paper shares, and get back the gold which they had given for them. Soon every one wanted to sell, and no one wanted to buy. The value of the paper money fell and fell, until it was worth less than nothing. People who had thought themselves millionaires found themselves beggars. Law, who had been flattered and courted, was now hated and cursed. And in terror of his life he fled from France in 1790 to die miserably in Italy a few years later.

As to Louisiana, a new set of stories were told of it. Now it was no longer described as a sort of earthly paradise, but as a place of horror and misery. It was a land of noisome marsh and gloomy forest, where prowled every imaginable evil beast. At certain times of the year the river flooded the whole land, so that the people were obliged to take refuge in the trees. There they lived more like monkeys than men, springing from tree to tree in search of food. The sun was so hot that it could strike a man dead as if with a pistol. This was called sunstroke. Luscious fruits indeed grew around, but they were all poisonous and those who ate of them died in agonies. In fact Louisiana was now pictured as a place to be shunned, as a place of punishment. "Be good or I will send you to the Mississippi" was a threat terrible enough to make the naughtiest child obedient.

The Mississippi bubble burst, - but still France clung to Louisiana. Once again it became a royal province, and at length after long years of struggle it began to prosper. The French had thus two great centres of power in America, one at Quebec amid the pine trees and snows of the North, and one at New Orleans amid the palm trees and sunshine of the South. And between the two fort after fort was built, until gradually north and south were united. Thus La Salle's dream came true.

It was during the time of peace after the end of Queen Anne's War that the French had thus strengthened their hold on America and joined Canada and Louisiana. They had also built a strong fortress on the Island of Cape Breton which commanded the mouth of the St. Lawrence. This fortress was called Louisburg in honour of King Louis, and it was the strongest and best fortified in the whole of New France. The walls were solid and high, and bristled with more than a hundred cannon. The moat was both wide and deep. Indeed the French believe that this fort was so strong that no power on earth could take it.

But the days of peace sped fast. Soon once more Europe was ablaze with war, France and Britain again taking opposite sides. In Europe this war is called the War of the Austrian Succession, because it was brought on by a quarrel among the nations of Europe as to who should succeed to the throne of Austria. In America it is called King George's War, as King George II was King of Britain at the time.

Like the other wars before it, it was fought in America as well as in Europe. The chief event in America was the capture of Louisburg in 1745. That redoubtable fortress which it was thought would hold off any attack, yielded after six weeks to an army chiefly composed of New England farmers and fishermen, and led by Maine merchant who had no knowledge of war.

When the news that Louisburg was taken reached New England the people rejoiced. Bells were rung, cannons were fired and bonfires blazed in all the chief

171

towns. In England itself the news was received with surprise and delight, and Pepperell, the merchant-soldier, was made a baronet and could henceforth call himself Sir William Pepperell.

But when the French heard that they had lost their splendid American fortress they were filled with dismay. One after another, three expeditions were sent to recapture it, but one after another they miscarried. And when at length, in 1748, peace was agreed upon, Louisburg was still in the hands of the New Englanders. The peace which was now signed is called the Peace of Aix-la-Chapelle. By it, it was agreed that each side should give back all its conquests, so that after all the terrible loss and bloodshed neither side was one whit the better.

The New Englanders had been greatly delighted at their conquest of Louisburg. The French, on the other hand, were greatly grieved, and when terms of peace were discussed Louis XV insisted that Louisburg should be restored. "That cannot be," said King George. "It is not mine to give, for it was taken by the people of Boston."

The French, however, were firm. So King George gave way, and Louisburg was restored to France, and Madras in India, which the French had taken, was in exchange restored to Britain. When the New Englanders heard of it, they were very angry. Madras was nothing to them; it was but a "petty factory" on the other side of the globe; while Louisburg was at their very doors, and of vast importance to their security. They had to obey and give it back. But they did so with bitterness in their hearts against a King who cared so little for their welfare.

Chapter 48 - How a Terrible Disaster Befell the British Army

We have now seen something of the great struggle between French and British for the continent of America. War after war broke out, peace after peace was signed. But each peace was no more than a truce, and even when the noise of cannon ceased there was nearly always war with the Redman, for he took sides and fought for French or British. And as years went past the struggle grew ever more and more bitter. If the French had their way, the British would have been hemmed in between the Alleghenies and the sea. If the British had had their way the French would have been confined to a little strip of land north of the St. Lawrence. It became plain at length to every one that in all the wide continent there was no room for both. One must go. But which?

The Peace at Aix-la-Chapelle was not a year old before the last, great struggle began. Both French and British had now cast their eyes on the valley of the Ohio, and the spot where Pittsburgh now stands became known as the Gateway of the West. The British determined to possess that gateway, but the French were just as determined to prevent them ever getting through it. So the French began to build a line of forts from Lake Erie southward to the gate of the west. Now, Virginia claimed all this land, and when two French forts had been built the Governor of Virginia began to be both alarmed and angry. He decided, therefore, to send a messenger to the French to tell them that they were on British ground, and bid them to be gone.

It was not an easy task, and one which had to be done with courtesy and firmness. Therefore Dinwiddie resolved to send a "person of distinction." So as his messenger he chose a young man named George Washington. He was a straightforward, tall young man, well used to a woodland life, but withal a gentleman, the descendant of one of the old Royalist families who had come to Virginia in the time of Cromwell, and just the very man for the Governor's purpose.

It was a long and toilsome journey through pathless forest, over hills, deep snows and frozen rivers, a journey which none but one skilled in forest lore could endure.

But at length after weeks of weary marching Washington arrived at Fort le Boeuf. The Frenchmen greeted him courteously, and entertained him in the most friendly fashion during the three days which the commander took to make up his answer. The answer was not very satisfactory. The commander promised to send Dinwiddie's letter to the Governor of Canada. "But meanwhile," he added, "my men and I will stay where we are. I have been commanded to take possession of the country, and I mean to do it to the best of my ability."

With this answer Washington set out again, and after many adventures and dangers arrived safely once more at Williamsburg.

In the spring the Frenchmen marched south to the Gateway of the West. Here they found a party of British, who had begun to build a fort. The French, who were in far greater numbers, surrounded them and bade them surrender. This the British did, being utterly unable to defend themselves. The French then seized the fort, leveled it to the ground, and began to build one of their own, which they called Fort Duquesne.

Upon this, Dinwiddie resolved to dislodge the French, and he sent a small force and when its leader died he took command. But he was not able to dislodge the French. So after some fighting he was obliged to make terms with the enemy and march home discomfited.

Up to this time the war was purely an American one. France and Britain were at peace, and neither country sent soldiers to help their colonies. It was the settlers, the farmers, fishermen and fur traders of New England and New France who fought each other.

And in this the French had one great advantage over the British. The French were united, the British were not. New France was like one great colony in which every man was ready to answer the call to battle.

The British were divided into thirteen colonies. Each one of the thirteen colonies was jealous of all the others; each was selfishly concerned with its own welfare and quite careless of the welfare of the others. But already the feelings of patriotism had been born. Among the many who cared nothing for union there were a few who did. There were some who were neither Virginians nor New Englanders, neither Georgians nor Carolinians, but Americans. These now felt that if they were not to become the vassals of France they must stand shoulder to shoulder.

A Congress of all the Northern Colonies was now called at Albany to discuss some means of defense. And at this Congress Benjamin Franklin proposed a plan of union. But the colonies would have nothing to say to it. Some took no notice of it at all, others treated it with scorn, or said it put too much power into the hands of the King. As to the King, when he heard of it he rejected it also, for, said he, it gave too much power to the colonies. So for the time being nothing came of it. Meanwhile the Governors of the various colonies wrote home to England, and, seeing how serious the matter was becoming, the British Government sent out two regiments of soldiers to help the colonies. They were about a thousand men in all, and were under the leadership of Major-General Edward Braddock.

As so as the French heard this they, too, sent soldiers to Canada. It was just like a game of "Catch who catch can." For as soon as the British knew that French troops were sailing to America they sent a squadron to stop them. But the French had got a start, and most of them got away. The British ships, however, overtook some which had lagged behind the others.

As soon as they were within hailing distance a red flag was suddenly run up to the masthead of the British flagship.

"Is this peace or war?" shouted the French captain.

"I don't know," answered the British, "But you had better prepare for war." He, however, gave the Frenchman little time to prepare, for the words were hardly out of his mouth before the thunder of cannon was heard.

The Frenchmen fought pluckily. But they were far outnumbered, and were soon forced to surrender.

Thus both on land and sea fighting had begun. Yet war had not been declared and King George and King Louis were still calling each other "dear cousin" or "dear brother," and making believe that there was no thought of war.

But the little success on sea was followed up by a bitter disaster on land.

General Braddock now commanded the whole army both home and colonial. He was a brave and honest man, but obstinate, fiery-tempered and narrow. He had a tremendous idea of what his own soldiers could do, and he was very scornful of the colonials. He was still more scornful of the Indians. "These savages," he said to Franklin, "may indeed be a formidable enemy to your raw American militia. But upon the King's regular and disciplined troops, sir, it is impossible that they should make any impression."

The haughty savages were quick to see that he looked down upon them. "He looks upon us as dogs," they said, and drawing their ragged blankets about them they stalked off deeply offended. With the same narrow pride Braddock turned away another useful ally.

This was Captain Jack, the Black Hunter. He was a white man, but he roamed the woods dressed like an Indian, followed be a band of men as reckless and lawless as himself. The Black Hunter, however, although he dressed like an Indian, was the white man's friend, the Redman's deadly foe.

He had been at one time, it was said, a peaceful settler living happily with his

174

wife and children. But one day he returned from hunting to find his cottage in ashes, and his wife and children dead among the ruins. In his grief and rage he vowed eternal vengeance on the Indians who had done the evil deed, robbing him for ever of home and happiness. Henceforth he roamed the woods a terror to the Redmen. For his aim was unerring, he could steal through the forest as silently and swiftly as they, and was as learned in all the woodland lore. His very name indeed struck terror to the hearts of all his foes.

Black Hunter now with his wild band of followers offered his help to Braddock. They were well armed, they cared neither for heat nor cold. they required no tents nor shelter for the night; not did they ask for any pay.

General Braddock looked at the gaunt weather-beaten man of the woods, clad in hunting shirt and moccasins, painted and bedecked with feathers like an Indian. Truly a strange ally, he thought. "I have experienced troops," he said, "on whom I can depend."

And finding that he could get no other answer Black Hunter and his men drew off, and disappeared into the woods whence they had come.

On the other hand Braddock had much to put up with. The whole success of the expedition depended on swiftness. The British must strike a blow before the French had time to arm. But when Braddock landed nothing was ready; there were no stores, no horses, no wagons. And it seemed impossible to gather them. Nobody seemed to care greatly whether the expedition set out or not. So, goaded to fury Braddock stamped and swore, and declared that nearly every one he had to do with was stupid or dishonest.

But at length the preparations were complete, and in June the expedition set out.

From the first things went wrong. Had Braddock gone through Pennsylvania he would have found a great part of his road cleared for him. But he went through Virginia, and had to hew his way through pathless forest.

In front of the army went three hundred axemen to cut down trees and clear a passage. Behind them the long baggage train jolted slowly onwards, now floundering axle deep through mud, now rocking perilously over stumps or stones. On either side threading in and out among the trees marched the soldiers. So day after day the many-coloured cavalcade wound along, bugle call and sound of drum awakening the forest silences.

The march was toilsome, and many of the men, unused to the hardships of the wilderness, fell ill, and the slow progress became slower still. At length Braddock decided to divide his force, and leaving the sick men and the heaviest baggage behind, press on more rapidly with the others. It was George Washington who went with him as an aide-de-camp who advised this.

So the sick and all baggage that could be done without were left behind with Colonel Dunbar. But even after this the progress was very slow.

Meanwhile news of the coming of the British army had been carried to the French at Fort Duquesne. And when they heard how great the force was, they were much alarmed. But a gallant Frenchman named Beaujeu offered to go out

175

and meet the British, lie in wait for them and take them unawares. But to do this he had need of Indian help. So council fires were lit and Beaujeu flung down the war hatchet. But the Indians refused it, for they were afraid of the great British force.

"Do you want to die, our father?" they asked, "and sacrifice us also?"

"I am determined to go," said Beaujeu. "What! Will you let your father go alone? I know we shall win."

Seeing him so confident the Indians forgot their fears, and the war dance was danced. Then, smeared with paint and led by Beaujeu himself dressed like a savage, they marched to meet the British.

There were about six hundred Indians and half as many Frenchmen. Stealthily they crept through the forest, flitting like shadows from tree to tree, closing ever nearer and nearer upon the British.

They, meanwhile, had reached the river Monongahela. They crossed it gaily, for they knew now that Fort Duquesne was near; their toilsome march was at an end, and victory was sure.

It was a glorious summer morning; the bands played, the men laughed and shouted joyously. The long line swept onward, a glittering pageant of scarlet and blue, of shining steel and fluttering banners.

Then suddenly out of the forest darted a man dressed like an Indian. When he saw the advancing column he stopped. Then turning, he waved to some one behind him. It was Beaujeu, and at his signal the air was rent with the terrible Indian war cry, and a hail of bullets swept the British ranks.

Shouting "God save the King" the British returned to fire. But it availed little, for they could not see the enemy. From the shelter of the forest, hidden behind trees, the French and Indians fired upon the British. They were an easy mark, for they stood solidly, shoulder to shoulder, their scarlet coats showing clearly against the green background. Still the British stood their ground firing volley after volley. It was quite useless, for they could see no enemy. The puffs of smoke were their only guides. To aim at the points where the smoke came from was all they could do. But for the most part their bullets crashed through the branches, or were buried in tree trunks, while the pitiless rain of lead mowed down the redcoats.

The American soldiers fared better. For as soon as they were attacked they scattered, and from behind the shelter of trees fought the Indians in their own fashion. Some of the British tried to do the same. But Braddock had no knowledge of savage warfare. To fight in such a manner seemed to him shocking. It was unsoldierly; it was cowardly. So he swore savagely at his men, calling them cowards, and beat them back into line with the flat of his sword. And thus huddled together they stood a brilliant, living target for the bullets of the savages.

Braddock himself fought with fury. He dashed here and there, swearing, commanding, threatening. Four horses were shot under him, and at last he himself fell wounded to death.

Washington too fought with fearless bravery, trying to carry out Braddock's frenzied orders. And although he escaped unhurt his clothes were riddled with holes, and twice his horse was shot under him.

For nearly three hours the terrible carnage lasted. Then flesh and blood could stand no more, and the men broke rank and fled. All night they fled in utter rout, bearing with them their wounded leader.

At length they reached Dunbar's camp. But even them they did not pause. For the news of the disaster had thrown the whole camp into confusion. Frantic orders were given, and obeyed with frenzied haste. Wagon loads of stores were burned, barrels of gunpowder were staved in, and the contents poured into the river; shells and bullets were buried. The, the work of destruction complete, the whole army moved on again in utter rout.

And now Braddock's dark, last hour had come. Brooding and silent he lay in his litter. This awful defeat was something he could not grasp. "Who would have thought it?" he murmured. "Who would have thought it?" But his stubborn spirit was yet unbroken. "We will know better how to do it another time," he sighed. A few minutes later he died.

His men buried him in the middle of the road, Washington reading over him the prayers for the dead. Then lest the Indians should find and desecrate his last resting-place the whole army passed over his grave.

Chapter 49 - The End of the French Rule in America

Braddock's campaign was a complete disaster. The French had triumphed, and even those Indians who up till now had been willing to side with the British were anxious to make friends with the French. For were they not the stronger? Surely it seemed to them the White Father of the St. Lawrence was more powerful than the White Father of the Hudson.

"If the English will not suffer the branches of the Great Tree of Peace to hide us from the French," they said, "we will go farther off. We will lie down and warm ourselves by the war fires of the French. We love to hear the sound of the war whoop. We delight in the war yell. It flies from hill to hill, from heart to heart. It makes the old heart young, it makes the young heart dance. Our young braves run to battle with the swiftness of the fawn. If you will not fight, the French will drive us from our hunting grounds. The English King does not aid us, we must join the strong. Who is strong? Who is strong? The French! The English have become weak."

War was now really declared between France and Britain and fighting took place in Europe as well as in America. And in America things went ill for the British. Defeats and disasters followed each other, things were muddled and went wrong continually. For truth to tell the British had no great leader either in England or in America, while the French had the Marquess Montcalm, one of the best soldiers in the French army, as their commander-in-chief.

At length, however, a great man came to power in England. This was William Pitt, known as the Great Commoner. He was, it has been said, the first Englishman of his time, and he made England the first country in the world. He was a great judge of men, and he had a happy way of choosing the right man for the right place. So now instead of defeats came victories, not only in America, but all over the world. "We are forced to ask every morning," said a witty man of the time, "what victory there has been for fear of missing one."

In America Louisburg fell once more into the hands of the British. Fort Duquesne too was taken, and the misery of Braddock's disaster was wiped out. Then in honour of the great statesman the name of the fort was changed to Pittsburg. It is still called by that name and is now one of the world's greatest manufacturing cities; and where Braddock fought and fell stretches a network of streets.

But although the British had many successes the key of Canada defied all efforts to take it. Quebec still frowned upon her rock, invulnerable as in the days of old lion-hearted Frontenac.

Among the men Pitt had chosen to lead the armies in America was Major-General James Wolfe. He was a long-legged, red-haired Englishman. There was nothing of the hero about his appearance except his bright and flashing eyes. It was this man who was sent to capture Quebec. Many people were astonished at Pitt's choice. "He is mad," said one stupid old man.

"Mad is he?" said King George. "Then I wish he would bite some others of my generals."

Led by a daring old sea captain the British war ships passed safely up the St. Lawrence and anchored off the Isle of Orleans a little below Quebec.

Once more British guns thundered against the high rock fortress. The town was laid in ruins, the country round was but a barren waste. Yet the fortress of Quebec was no nearer being taken than before. Weeks and months went past, the fleet rocked idly at anchor, the troops lay almost as idle in their tents. Only the gunners had work to do. And although they shattered the walls of Quebec the Frenchmen were undaunted.

"You may ruin the town," they said, "but you will never get inside."

"I will have Quebec if I stay here till the end of November," replied Wolfe.

But Montcalm smiled grimly. Winter, he knew, would be his ally. For then the St. Lawrence would be frozen from bank to bank and before that the British must sail away or be caught fast in its icy jaws.

Wolfe, who was frail and sickly by nature, now broke down beneath the strain and the constant disappointments. Helpless and in agony he lay on his sickbed, his mind still busy with plans of how to take Quebec.

"Doctor," he said, "I know you can't cure me but patch me up till I see this business through."

Soon he was about again, and making plans for his last desperate attempt to take Quebec.

Seeking to find a means of reaching the fortress he had himself examined all the north shores of the St. Lawrence. And just a little above the town he had found one spot where a narrow pathway led up the steep cliffs. It was so steep and narrow that the French never dreamed of any one making an attack that way, and it was carelessly guarded. But dangerous though it was it seemed to Wolfe the only way, and he determined to attempt it.

Soon his preparations were made, and one dark moonless night in September a long procession of boats floated silently down the river. In one of the boats sat Wolfe, and as they drifted slowly along in the starlight in a low voice he repeated Gray's poem called an Elegy in a Country Churchyard:

"The boast of heraldry, the pomp of power, And all that beauty, all that wealth e'er gave, Awaits alike th' inevitable hour, The paths of glory lead but to the grave."

"Gentlemen," said Wolfe when he finished, "I would rather have written those lines than take Quebec."

In dead silence now the boats drifted on. Then suddenly out of the darkness rang a sharp challenge.

"Who goes there?" was asked in French.

"France," replied a Highland officer who spoke good French.

"What regiment?" shouted the sentry.

"The Queen's," answered the officer glibly, for luckily he had learned from French prisoners that boats with provisions were expected by the enemy, and that very likely the Queen's regiment would convoy them.

The sentry was satisfied and let the boats pass. But they were not safe yet. A little further on they were challenged again.

The same officer replied.

"Speak louder!" cried the sentry.

"Hush!" replied the Highlander, "provision boats, I say. Do not make a noise; the British will hear us."

The sentry was quite deceived. He let the boats pass, and very soon the men were safely landed.

Then the climb began. Like wild mountain cats the men dashed at it. They swung themselves up by branches of trees, gripping projecting stones and roots with hand and knee. It was hot, breathless work, but soon they were near the top. But they had been heard. Once more the challenge rang out, "Who goes there?"

"France," panted a voice from below. But this time the sentry was not deceived. He could see nothing, but he fired at a venture down into the darkness.

It was too late. The first men had reached the top, and the guard was overpowered. So hour by hour up the steep cliff the red coats swarmed unhindered. When morning dawned four thousand British stood upon the plains of Abraham.

"This is a very serious business," said Montcalm when he heard of it, "but it can only be a small party."

Soon, however, more news was brought to him. It was no small party.

"Then we must crush them," he said, and with pale set face he rode forth to battle.

It was ten o'clock when the fight began. The French attacked first. The British awaited them calmly as they dashed on over the plain. On they came nearer and nearer. Then suddenly the order was given,

179

and , cheering wildly, the British charged.

A shot struck Wolfe in the wrist. Without pausing he tied a handkerchief about it. Again he was hit. Still he went on. Then a third shot struck his breast, and he fell. Hastily he was carried to the rear, and laid upon the ground.

"It is all over with me," he sighed. Then he lay still in a sort of stupor.

Suddenly one of the officers beside him cried out, "They run! They run!"

"Who run?" said Wolfe, rousing himself.

"The enemy, sir," answered the officer, "they give way everywhere."

"Now God be praised," murmured Wolfe. "I die happy." Then turning on his side he died.

Everywhere the French fled, and in their mad rush they carried along with them their gallant leader, Montcalm. He was sorely wounded, but still sat his horse as he rode within the gates of Quebec. Here an excited, eager crowd was gathered, waiting for news. And when they saw Montcalm's well-known figure on his black horse they were seized with dismay. For his face was white and drawn and blood flowed from his breast.

"Alas! Alas!" cried a woman in a piercing voice of despair, "the Marquess is killed!"

"It is nothing, it is nothing, good friends," he replied. "Do not trouble about me." So saying he fell from his horse into the arms of one of his officers.

That night he died.

He was glad to go. "It is better for me," he said, "for I shall not live to see Quebec surrender."

With him died the last hope of New France. The story of New France was done. The Story of Canada was about to begin as well as that of her mighty neighbour. For as a great English historian has said, "With the triumph of Wolfe on the Heights of Abraham began the history of the United States."

Meanwhile, however, the war still dragged on for another year. Then the following summer Montreal surrendered to the British, and French rule in America was completely at an end.

Fighting in America was over. But the war still went on in other parts of the world. Spain had also joined in the struggle, and from them the British took Cuba and the Philippine Islands. But at length in 1763 peace was made by the Treaty of Paris.

By this treaty Britain was confirmed in her claim to nearly the whole of French possessions in America. So that from the Atlantic to the Mississippi and from the Gulf of Mexico to Hudson Bay was now declared British except the peninsula forming Florida. That the Spaniards claimed. So in exchange for it the British gave back Cuba and the Philippines. And to make up to Spain for the loss of Florida France gave them New Orleans and resigned to Spain all claims to the land which La Salle had called Louisiana.

Thus nothing remained to France of all her great possessions in America, and the vast continent was divided between Spain and Britain. Never in all known history had a single treaty transferred such enormous tracts of land from one

180

nation to another.

Chapter 50 - The Rebellion of Pontiac

"Do you not know the difference between the King of France and the King of Britain?" a Frenchman once asked an Indian. "Go, look at the forts which our King has built, you will see that you can still hunt under their very walls. They have been built for your good in the places where you go. The British on the other hand are no sooner in possession of a place than they drive the game away, the trees fall before them, the earth is laid bare, so that you can scarcely find a few branches with which to make a shelter for the night."

The Frenchman spoke truth. The British settlers were, for the most part, grave and earnest men who had come to seek new homes. They felled trees and built their houses, and ploughed the land, turning wilderness into cornfields and meadow.

The Frenchmen came for the sake of religion or for adventure, they set up crosses and claimed the land for God and the King. They scattered churches and hamlets far in the wilderness, but left the wilderness and the forest still the Redman's hunting ground. The Frenchmen treated the Indians with an easy, careless sort of friendliness, while most of the British looked down upon them as savages.

So very soon after the British took possession of Canada the Indians became very discontented. For now they got no more presents, they were no longer treated as brothers, and they were hurt both in their pockets and their pride. "The English mean to make slaves of us," they said, in haughty indignation, and soon a plot to murder all the British was formed.

The French who still lived in Canada encouraged the Indians in their discontent, telling them that the English meant thoroughly to root them out. Then a great Medicine Man arose among them who preached war.

"The Great Spirit himself appeared unto me," he said. "Thus he spake. 'I am the Lord of Life. It is I who made all men. I work for their safety, therefore I give you warning. Suffer not the English to dwell in your midst, lest their poisons and their sickness destroy you utterly.'"

When they heard the Medicine Man speak thus, the Indians were greatly stirred. "The Lord of Life himself," they said, "moves our hearts to war." They became ever more and more eager to fight. They only wanted a leader, and found one in Pontiac, chief of the Ottawas.

He was subtle and fierce, haughty and ambitious, and by far the most clever and powerful chief who ever took up arms against the white man.

Now he sent messengers to all the Indian villages both far and near. With them these messengers carried a hatchet, stained with blood, and a war belt of scarlet wampum. When they came to a village they called the braves together. Then in their midst their spokesman flung down the blood stained hatchet, and holding the belt in his hand he made a passionate speech, reminding the Redmen of their wrongs, and calling upon them to be avenged upon their foes. And wherever the

181

messengers went the blood stained hatchet was seized, and the war dance danced.

At length all was arranged and upon a certain day in May the Indians were to rise in a body, and slay the British to a man. Only the French were to be spared.

Pontiac himself was to attack Fort Detroit, and so quietly and secretly were the preparations made that no one had the slightest suspicion of what was going forward. But the day before the attack a farmer's wife rowed across the river, and went to the Indian village to buy some maple sugar. While she was there she was much astonished to see some of the Indian braves filing off the barrels of their guns. The sight made her uneasy. "I wonder what they are up to?" she said.

When she got home she told her friends what she had seen.

"I believe they are up to some mischief," she repeated.

"I think so too," said a blacksmith, "they have been asking me to lend them files and saws."

As the settlers talked the matter over they became at length so uneasy that they sent to tell Major Gladwin, the commander of the fort, of what they had seen. He, however, thought nothing of it.

But later in the day a young Indian girl came to see him, to bring him a pair of moccasins which he had asked her to make. She seemed very sad and downcast, and after she had given the Major the moccasins she still loitered about.

"What's the matter?" asked a young officer.

The Indian girl did not answer, she only looked at him gravely with sorrowful brown eyes.

Still she lingered about, it was nearly dark, time almost to close the gates. At last the young officer watching her, became certain that something was the matter, and he urged his commander to see the girl again.

Major Gladwin at once called the girl to him. "What is the matter?" he asked. "Why are you so sad?"

Still she would not speak. Then the Major talked to her kindly, promising that whatever her secret was, it would be safe with him, and that he would never betray her. So at length the Indian girl spoke.

"The Indians mean to kill you all," she whispered; "the braves have filed off the ends of their gun barrels so that the guns can be hidden beneath their blankets. Tomorrow Pontiac will come with many warriors, and will ask to hold a Council within the fort. He will make a speech, and offer you a peace belt of wampum. At the end of the speech he will turn the belt round - that will be the signal. The chiefs will then spring up, draw the guns from their hiding places, and kill you all. Indians outside will kill all your soldiers. Not one of you will escape."

So saying the girl went sadly away.

Gladwin at once called his officers and told them what he had heard. They were convinced now that evil was afoot, and all night they kept watch lest the Indians should change their minds, and make their attack during the night.

But the night passed peacefully. When morning came a great many Indians were seen to be gathered about the fort, and at ten o'clock Pontiac, followed by his chiefs, entered the gateway.

They stalked in proudly, garbed in all the glory of savage splendours. They were cloaked in bright coloured blankets, and hung about with beads and hawk-bells. Their heads were decorated with eagle feathers, and their faces hideously painted.

Pontiac came first, and as he passed beneath the gateway, he started, and drew a sharp, deep breath. For both sides of the narrow street were lined with soldiers gun in hand. He had been betrayed! Yet the haughty chiefs made no sign. In silence they stalked on, not a muscle of their faces moving. Here and there as they passed on they saw traders standing about in groups, every man fully armed. Not a woman or child was to be seen.

At length the Indians reached the Council Hall. Here they found the commander seated awaiting them, surrounded by his officers. They, too, were armed, for every man of them wore a sword by his side and a brace of pistols in his belt.

Ill at ease now, the Indians gazed at each other in doubt what to do.

Then Pontiac spoke, "why," he asked, "do I see so many of my father's braves standing in the street with their guns?"

"Because I exercise my soldiers," replied Gladwin calmly, "for the good of their health, and also to keep discipline."

This answer made the Indians still more uneasy, but after some hesitation they all sat down on the floor. Then with due ceremony Pontiac rose, and holding the belt of peace in his hand began to speak. His words were fair. They had come, he said, to tell of their love for the English, "to smoke the pipe of peace, and make the bonds of friendship closer."

As he spoke his false and cunning words, the officers kept a watchful eye upon him. Would he give the signal or not, they asked themselves.

He raised the belt. At that moment Gladwin made a quick, slight signal. Immediately from the passage with out came the sound of grounding arms, and the rat-tat of a drum. Pontiac stood rigid, as one turned to stone. Then after a moment's deathly silence he sat down.

In the silence Gladwin sat looking steadily and fearlessly at the Indians. Then he replied shortly to Pontiac's fine speech, "The friendship of the British should be theirs," he said, "so long as they deserved it."

The Council was at an end. The gates of the fort which had been closed were now thrown open again, and the savages, balked in their treachery, stalked back to their wigwams.

But Pontiac was not yet beaten, and again he tried to master the fort by treachery. And when he found the gates of the fort shut against him, his rage was terrible. Then seeing they could not win Fort Detroit by treachery, the Indians attacked it in force. But in spite of all his horde of warriors, in spite of all his wiles, Pontiac could not take the fort although he besieged it for a whole year.

Meanwhile the savages over-ran the whole country, and every other fort, save Fort Pitt and Fort Niagara, fell into their hands. More often than not, they won their way into the forts by treachery, and having entered they slew, without mercy, men, women and children.

183

At Michilimackinac the Redskins invited the officers and soldiers to watch a game of ball. The invitation was accepted, and nearly all the soldiers stood about watching while the Indians with piercing yells dashed madly hither and thither after the ball. Crowds of Indians also looked on, among them many squaws wrapped in coloured blankets. The game was played just outside the fort, the gates stood open, and most of the soldiers had strolled out without their weapons to watch.

Suddenly the ball flew through the air and landed close to the gate of the fort. There was a mad rush after it. As they ran the Indians snatched the hatchets and knives which till now the squaws had hidden beneath their blankets. Screams of delight were changed to war cries. The two officers who stood by the gate were seized and carried away prisoner, while the rabble stormed into the fort slaying and robbing at will. Every one of the British was either killed or taken prisoner, but the French were left alone.

Thus all the land was filled with bloodshed and horror. There was no safety anywhere. In every bush an Indian might lurk, and night was made terrible with bloodcurdling war cries.

For nearly three years the war lasted. But by degrees Pontiac saw that his cause was lost. The French did not help him as he had expected they would. Some of his followers deserted, and other tribes refused to join him, and at last he saw himself forced to make peace. So there were flowery speeches, and the exchange of wampum belts, and peace was made.

Then Pontiac's army melted away like snow in summer, and the great Chief himself retired to the forest to live among his children and his squaws. A few years later he was traitorously slain by one of his own people.

PART VI: STORIES OF THE STRUGGLE FOR LIBERTY

Chapter 51 - The Boston Tea party

All these wars which had been fought on American soil had cost a great deal of money and many lives. Now it seemed to the British Government that the best way to be sure of peace in the future was to keep an army in America. They decided to do this. They also decided that America should pay for the army. And in order to raise the money a stamp tax was to be introduced. Newspapers, marriage licenses, wills, and all sorts of legal papers were henceforth to be printed on stamped paper, the price of stamps varying according to the importance of the paper from a few pence to as many pounds.

But when the Americans heard that this Act had been passed without their consent they were angry.

"No," they said to the British Government, "you cannot tax us without our consent. It is one of the foundations of British freedom that those who pay the tax must also consent to it. We are not represented in the British Parliament, our consent has not been asked, and we deny your right to tax us."

The whole country was filled with clamour. In every colony young men banded themselves together, calling themselves Sons of Liberty, and determined to resist the tax. "No taxation without representation" was the cry.

When the first boxes of stamps arrived they were seized and destroyed. Newspapers appeared with a skull and crossbones printed where the stamp should have been. There were riots and mass meetings everywhere.

The Americans did not merely resist, they resisted in a body. Nothing but the idea that their liberty was in danger made them act together. Over everything else they had been divided. Over that they were united. "There ought to be no New England men, no New Yorkers, known on the continent," said one man; "but all of us Americans."

Even in Britain there were people who thought this Stamp Act was a mistake. The great Pitt had been ill when it was passed into law, but when he returned to Parliament he spoke strongly against it.

"I was ill in bed," he said, "but if I could have been carried here in my bed I would have asked some kind friend to lay my on this floor, so that I might have spoken against it. It is a subject of greater importance than ever engaged the attention of this House; that subject always excepted, when nearly a century ago it was the question whether you yourselves were to be bond or free."

Pitt was thinking of the time when Englishmen strove with Charles I. He gloried in British liberty, and he could not bear to think of Britons oppressing Britons. "Who that has an English heart," he once said, "can ever be weary of asserting liberty?"

"I rejoice that America has resisted," he said later.

There were many against Pitt, but he won the day, and the Stamp Act was repealed.

There was great rejoicing in America, and the matter seemed at an end. But the very next year a new bill for taxing the Americans was brought into Parliament. This time the tax was to be paid on tea, glass, lead and a few other things brought into the country.

Once again the colonies were ablaze, and they refused to pay this duty just as they had refused to pay the Stamp Tax. Everywhere there were indignation meetings. But Boston seemed to be the heart of the storm, and to Boston British troops were sent to keep order.

The soldiers had nothing to do, but the very sight of their red coats made the colonists angry. They taunted the soldiers, and worried them every way they knew, and the soldiers were not slow to reply. So at last after eighteen months of bickering one March evening it came to blows. Two or three exasperated soldiers fired upon the crowd of citizens, five of whom were killed and several others wounded.

This was afterwards known as the Boston Massacre. It made the people terribly angry, and next day a great meeting was held in Old South Church. At this meeting the people demanded that the troops should be at once removed from the town. And seeing the temper of the people the Lieutenant Governor withdrew them that same day to a little island in the harbour.

And now finding how useless it was to try to force taxes on unwilling subjects,

185

the Government removed all the taxes except one. King George wanted to show his power. He wanted to prove to the Americans that he had the right to tax them if he liked. So he insisted that there should still be a tax on tea.

"The King will have it so, he means to try the question with America," said Lord North, the easy-going, stupid minister who was now in power.

But to prove that neither the King nor any one else had the right to tax them, without their consent, was exactly for what the Americans were fighting. To them, one tax was as bad as a dozen. It was not a question of money, but a question of right or wrong, of freedom or slavery. So they refused to pay the tax on tea. They refused to buy tea from Britain at all, and smuggled it from Holland. Ships laden with tea came to port, and it was landed. But no one would buy it, and it rotted and mouldered in the cellars. In Boston, however, the people determined that it should not even land. And when three ships laden with tea came into Boston harbour, the people refused to allow them to unload.

"Take your tea back again to England," they said to the captain.

But the captain could not do that, for the customs officers would not allow him to leave until he had landed his cargo. The people were greatly excited. Large meetings were held, and every possible manner of getting rid of the tea was discussed. But at length some of the younger men grew tired of talk. Time was passing. If something were not done, the tea would be landed by force.

That, these bold young men determined, should not be. So about fifty of them dressed themselves as Red Indians, staining their faces brown and painting them hideously. Then, tomahawk in hand, they stole silently down to the ships, and uttering wild war cries sprang on board. They seized the tea chests and with their hatchets burst them open, and poured the tea into the harbour.

There were nearly three hundred and fifty chests, and soon the harbour was black with tea. It was terrible waste, but no one stopped it. From the shore people looked on quietly. And when the work was done the "Red Indians" vanished away as silently as they had come. This was afterwards called the Boston Tea Party. Certainly no greater brewing of tea has ever been known.

When George III heard of the Boston Tea Party he was very angry, and he resolved to punish the people of Boston. "They will be lions," he said, "as long as we are lambs, but if we show them that we mean to be firm they will soon prove very meek."

So he closed the port and forbade any ships to go there, thus cutting off Boston from the trade of the world. He also said that Boston should no longer be the capital of Massachusetts, and made Salem the capital instead.

Boston, of course, was well-nigh ruined by these acts. But instead of looking coldly on her misfortunes, the other colonies rallied to her aid. And grain, cattle and all sorts of merchandise poured into Boston from them.

Boston could not be starved, neither could it be frightened into submitting.

186

Chapter 52 - Paul Revere's Ride - The Unsheathing of the Sword

All the colonies now felt that they must unite in truth, and that they must have some centre to which all could appeal. So a Congress of all the colonies was called at Philadelphia. This is called the first Continental Congress, and to it all the colonies except Georgia sent delegates.

This Congress drew up a Declaration of Rights. They also sent an address to the King in which they declared that they had no wish to separate from Britain.

But the King called the Congress an unlawful and seditious gathering, and would not listen to anything it had to say. Still, far-seeing statesmen with Pitt at their head struggled to bring about a reconciliation.

"I contend, not for indulgence, but for justice to America," he said. "The Americans are a brave, generous and united people, with arms in their hands, and courage in their hearts. It is not repealing this act of Parliament, it is not repealing a piece of parchment, that can restore America to our bosom. You must repeal her fears and her resentments. And you may then hope for her love and gratitude."

But few people listened to Pitt, the bill which he brought into Parliament was rejected with scorn, and the great struggle which was to last for eight years began.

Already in America, men's minds had begun to turn to war, and on every village green the farmers might be seen drilling every evening. Bands of minute men, that is, men who would be ready at a minute's notice, were organised. All sorts of war stores were gathered.

Two of the leaders of the people in all these matters were Samuel Adams and John Hancock. These men Governor Gage, who was also commander of the troops, was ordered to arrest and send to England to be tried as traitors. Gage having heard that both men were staying at the village of Lexington decided to arrest them together.

For this he carefully laid his plans. Eight hundred men were to leave Boston in secret at dead of night. First they were to go to Lexington, and having arrested the "traitors" they were next to march on to Concord to seize the large war stores which were known to be gathered there.

All the preparations were made as silently and as secretly as possible. But the colonists were on the alert. They knew that something was afoot, and guessed what it was.

On the 18th of April Gage gave strict orders that no one was to be allowed to leave Boston that night. But no orders could stop determined men.

And as the moon was rising a little boat was rowed across the Charles river almost under the shadow of the British man-of-war. The boat reached the farther shore and a man booted and spurred, and if ready for a long ride, leaped out upon the bank. This man was Paul Revere.

At ten o'clock the troops also were silently rowed across the Charles River, and in the darkness set out for Lexington. But not far off on the bank of the same river, a man stood waiting beside a saddled horse. Quietly he waited, looking always towards the tower of the Old North Church. It was Paul Revere, and he waited for a signal to tell him which way the red coats were going.

Suddenly about eleven o'clock two twinkling lights appeared upon the tower, and without a moment's loss Paul Revere leaped into the saddle and dashed away. Swiftly he rode, urging his good horse onward with voice and hand.

Near the lonely spot where stood the gallows he passed. Here under a tree, two horsemen waited, and as Revere came nearer he saw that they were British soldiers. Swiftly they darted at him. One tried to seize his bridle, the other to head him off. But Revere was a fearless rider, and knew the countryside by heart. He swerved suddenly, doubled, and was soon clear of his pursuers.

Then on through the darkness he galloped unhindered till he reached Medford. Here he stayed but to rouse the captain of the minute men, and onward he sped once more. Now at the door of every cottage or farmhouse which he passed he loudly knocked, shouting his news "the soldiers are coming," and thundered off again in the darkness.

A little after midnight he reached Lexington and stopped before the house where Adams and Hancock were sleeping. He found it guarded by minute men, and as he excitedly shouted his news, they bade him be quiet.

"Don't make such a noise," said the sergeant, "you will waken the people in the house."

"Noise," cried Revere, "you will soon have noise enough - the regulars are coming."

Hancock was awake, and hearing Revere's voice he threw up his window, shouting to the guard to let him in. So Revere went into the house and told all he knew. When they heard the news, Hancock wanted to stay and fight, if fighting there was to be. But the others would not hear of it, so as day dawned the two men quietly walked away, and were soon on the road to Philadelphia.

Meanwhile the British troops were steadily marching nearer and nearer. At first all was silent: save the clatter and jingle of their arms and the tramp of their feet, there was no sound. No light was to be seen far or near. Then suddenly a bell rang, a shout was heard, lights twinkled here and there. The night was no longer silent and dark. The country was no longer asleep.

The colonel in command of the troops grew anxious. He had expected to take the people completely by surprise, and he had done so. Somehow the secret had leaked out. The whole countryside was up and awake, and fearing lest with his small company of soldiers, he would not be able to do what he had set out to do, he sent back to Boston for more men.

And sure enough, his fears were well founded, for when in the cold grey of early dawn the advance party reached Lexington, they found a little guard of sixty or seventy armed men drawn up to receive them.

"Disperse, ye rebels, disperse," shouted the commander as he rode towards them. But the men stood motionless and silent.

"Why don't you disperse, you villains?" he cried again.

Then seeing words had no effect, he gave the order to fire. The soldiers obeyed, and eight minute men fell dead, and several more were wounded. The minute men returned the fire, but just then more British soldiers appeared in sight. And seeing that it was useless to try to resist so great a force the Americans dispersed.

Thus the terrible war, which was almost a civil war, began. The British now marched on to Concord. They had failed to arrest the men they had been sent to arrest at Lexington. So there was all the more reason to hurry on to Concord, and seize the war stores before there was time to spirit them away. But when about seven o'clock in the morning the troops arrived at Concord the stores for the most part had been already safely hidden. A gun or two they found, and a few barrels of flour. The guns were spiked, the barrels staved in, the court house set on fire.

But meanwhile the minute men had been gathering, and now a force four hundred strong appeared on the further side of a bridge known as the North Bridge. The bridge was held by two hundred British, and when they saw the minute men approach they began to destroy it.

There was a sharp exchange of fire. Then the minute men charged across the narrow bridge, sweeping all before them. The British fled back to the village, and the minute men, hardly knowing what they had done, retired again across the bridge and waited.

The British leader now decided to return to Boston. He had done nothing which he had set out to do. But he saw this his position was one of great danger. Everywhere he was surrounded with enemies. His men were hungry and worn out, so about twelve o'clock the march back to Boston began.

But the return was not easy, for all the way the troops were harassed by the Americans. Every bush, every wall concealed an armed farmer, whose aim was deadly and sure. Man after man fell, and beneath the constant and galling fire coming, it seemed from everywhere and nowhere, the nerves of the wearied, hungry men gave way. Faster and faster the long red line swept along in every growing confusion. There was no thought now of anything but safety, and the march was almost a rout when at length the reinforcements from Boston appeared. These were a thousand strong, and their leader, Lord Percy, seeing the confusion and distress of the British formed his men into a hollow square. Into this refuge the fugitives fled, throwing themselves upon the ground in utter exhaustion, with their tongues hanging out of their mouths "like those of dogs after a chase."

Lord Percy had brought cannons with him, so with these he swept the field, and for a time forced the colonists to retire. But they did not disperse; they still hovered near, and as soon as the retreat again began, there began with it the constant galling fire from every tree or bush, before, behind, on either side. To return the fire was useless, as the enemy were hidden. It was a sort of warfare not unlike that which Braddock had had to meet, a sort of warfare in which the American farmer was skilled, but of which the British soldier knew nothing. So when, at length, as day darkened the British troops reached Boston they were utterly spent and weary. And in a huddled, disorganised crowd, they hurried into shelter.

Chapter 53 - The First Thrust-The Battle of Bunker Hill

The sword was at length unsheathed. There was no more doubt about it. There was to be a war between the Mother Country and her daughter states. And now far and wide throughout the colonies the call to arms was heard and answered. Farmers left their ploughs and seized their rifles, trappers forsook their hunting grounds, traders left their business, and hastened to join the army.

John Stark, a bold trapper learned in Indian ways and famous in Indian warfare, marched from New Hampshire at the head of several hundred men. Israel Putnam, more famous still for his deeds of daring in the Indian wars, came too. He was busy on his farm at Pomfret, Connecticut, when the news of the fight at Lexington reached him. He was already a man of fifty-seven but there and then he left his work and hastened round the neighbouring farms calling out the militia. Then, commanding them to follow him with all speed, he mounted his horse, and turned its head towards Cambridge. Hour after hour throughout the night he rode onward, and as day dawned on the 21st of April he galloped into Cambridge, having ridden a hundred miles in eighteen hours without a change of horse. Handsome young Captain Benedict Arnold, half sailor, half merchant, gathered his men on New Haven green. And when the general of militia bade him wait for regular orders and refused to supply him with ammunition for his men, he threatened to break open the magazine if the ammunition was not forthcoming at once. So, seeing that nothing would restrain him, the general yielded, and Arnold, gallant and gay, with sixty men behind him marched for Cambridge.

Thus day by day men of all classes, and of all ages, poured in from the countryside, until an army of sixteen thousand was gathered around Boston.

Meetings, too, were held throughout the country, when patriots urged the need of arming and fighting. In the Virginian Convention, Patrick Henry, the great orator, thrilled his hearers with his fiery eloquence. "We must fight," he cried, "I repeat it, we must fight! An appeal to arms and to the God of Hosts is all that is left us." Brilliantly, convincingly he spoke, and ended with the unforgettable words:— "Is life so dear, or peace so sweet as to be purchased at the price of chains and slavery! Forbid it, Almighty God! I know not what course others may take, but as for me, give me liberty or give me death!"

"His last exclamation," said one who heard him, "was like the shout of the leader who turns back the rout of battle."

But even yet the leaders of the country hoped to avoid a war. The second Continental Congress met at Philadelphia on the 10th of May and the members talked anxiously of ways and means to restore peace. But it was already too late. For the gathered army was no longer to be restrained, and the very day upon which Congress met a British fortress had been seized by the colonists.

The chain of lakes and rivers connecting the Hudson with the St. Lawrence was felt to be of great importance to the colonists. For if Britain had control of it it would cut the colonies in two, and stop intercourse between New England and the south. It would also give the British an easy route by which to bring troops and supplies from Canada.

Among those who felt the importance of this route was Benedict Arnold, and the day after he arrived at Cambridge he laid his ideas before the Massachusetts Committee of Safety, and asked to be allowed to attack the forts guarding this waterway. His request was granted. He was given the rank of colonel, and authority to raise a company of four hundred men for the purpose.

Arnold set out at once, but he soon found that he was not first in the field. For the people of Connecticut, too, had felt the value of this waterway and Ethan Allen with a hundred and fifty volunteers who went by the name of Green Mountain Boys had set out for the same purpose. These Green Mountain Boys took their name from the district of Vermont which means Green Mountain. That district, under the name of New Hampshire Grants, had been claimed by New York colony. But the Green Mountain Boys had resisted the claim, and by force of arms proved their right to be considered a separate colony. Thus having settled their own little revolution they were now ready to take part in the great one.

At Castleton, Vermont, Arnold met Ethan Allen and his men, and claimed the leadership of the expedition. But the Green Mountain Boys scouted the idea. They would fight under their own leader or not fight at all, they said, and as Arnold had gathered very few of his four hundred men he had to give way. So instead of leading the expedition he joined it as a volunteer.

This matter settled the little company marched on to Lake Champlain, and in the middle of the night they arrived at the southern end, opposite Fort Ticonderoga. Here the lake is hardly more than a quarter of a mile wide and the men began at once to row across. But they had only two or three boats and when day began to dawn only about eighty men had got over. With these Allen decided to attack, for he feared if he waited till daylight that the garrison would be awake and would no doubt resist stubbornly. So placing himself at the head of his men with Arnold beside him, he marched quickly and silently up the hill to the gateway of the fort. When the astonished sentinel saw this body of men creeping out of the morning dusk he fired at their leader. But his gun missed fire and he fled into the fort.

After him dashed the colonists uttering a loud, blood-curdling, Indian yell as they reached the parade ground within the fort. The garrison which consisted of about forty men was completely taken by surprise, and yielded with little resistance. They Allen marched to the door of the commandment's quarters, and striking three blows upon it with his sword hilt, commanded him to come forth and surrender.

As Allen struck, the door was flung open, and half dressed and half awake the commandment appeared.

"In whose name," he demanded, "do you order me to surrender!"

"In the name of the great Jehovah and the Continental Congress," thundered Allen.

Really the Continental Congress had nothing to do with the matter. The commandment could not know that. But he had only to look about him to see that the fort was already in the hands of the enemy. So seeing no help for it he yielded; and all his great stores of cannon and ammunition were sent to supply the needs of the New England army.

Two days after this Crown Point, further down the lake, was also seized, for it was only guarded by twelve men. Here a small ship was found and Arnold's chance to lead came. For he was a sailor, and going on board with his own men he made a dash for St. John's at the northern end of the lake. When he was about thirty miles from the fort the wind dropped, and his ship lay rocking idly on the water. Arnold, however, was not the man to be easily beaten. He had boats enough to carry thirty men, and with these he set off to row to the fort. All night the men bent to the oars, and at six o'clock in the morning they reached St. John's.

Once more the fort was easily taken. For here too, there were no more than twelve men. Arnold, however, was only just in time, for he learned from his prisoners that troops were expected from Canada. He felt therefore that St. John's was no safe place for him and his little band of thirty. So he seized a small ship which lay in the harbour, sank everything else in the shape of a boat, and made off. And when the Canadian troops arrived next day they found the fort deserted alike by friend and foe, and the boats which should have carried them on their way to Ticonderoga at the bottom of the lake.

By these quick bold attacks the control of the great waterway was for a time at least in the hands of the colonists. It was, moreover, rendered useless to the British, for their boats being destroyed they had no means of transporting soldiers southwards until new boats could be built. This caused a long delay, a delay very useful to the colonists.

In the meantime Allen was appointed commandment of Ticonderoga, and Arnold, with a little soreness at his heart returned to Cambridge. He had been appointed leader of the expedition, but had been forced to join it as a volunteer under another leader. His knowledge and dash had crowned the expedition with success, but another received the rewards and praise.

When however the Continental Congress heard what had been done it was rather taken aback. It was not at all sure at first whether it was a case for rewards or reprimands, for it was still vainly hoping for peace. So it ordered that an exact list of all cannon and supplies which had been captured should be made, in order that they might be given back to the Mother Country, "when the restoration of the former harmony between Great Britain and these colonies shall render it prudent and consistent."

Meanwhile the new army grew daily larger. It was still almost entirely made up of New Englanders, but it was now called the Continental Army, and the Continental Congress appointed George Washington to be commander-in-chief.

Washington was now a tall, handsome man, little over forty. He was as modest as he was brave, and he accepted the great honour and heavy duties laid upon him with something of dread.

"Since the Congress desire it," he said, "I will enter upon this momentous duty,

192

and exert every power I possess in their service. But I beg it may be remembered by every gentleman in this room that I this day declare, with the utmost sincerity, I do not think myself equal to the command I am honoured with,"

Meantime things had not been standing still; while Congress had been choosing a commander-in-chief the army had been fighting. By this time, too, new troops had come out from England, and the British force was now ten thousand strong. Feeling sure that the Americans would not stand against such a force, Governor Gage issued a proclamation offering pardon to all who would lay down their arms, except Samuel Adams and John Hancock. These two, he said, were too bad to be forgiven. Instead they prepared to take possession of the hills commanding Boston.

It was at Bunker Hill that the first real battle of the war was fought. For Lexington had after all been a mere skirmish, only of importance because it was the first in this long and deadly war. The forts on Lake Champlain had been taken without the shedding of blood.

The battle is called Bunker Hill although it was really fought on Breed's Hill which is quite close. The mistake of the name was made because the Americans had been sent to take possession of Bunker Hill, but instead took possession of Breed's Hill.

It was during the night that the Americans took up their position on the hill. And when day dawned and the British saw them there, they determined to dislodge them, and the battle began.

Up the hill the British charged with splendid courage, only to be met and driven back by a withering fire from the American rifles. Their front riles were mowed down, and the hillside was strewn with dead and dying. But again and yet again they came on. At the third charge they reached the top, for the Americans had used up all their ammunition, and could fire no longer. Still they would not yield, and there was a fierce hand to hand fight before the Americans were driven from their trenches and the hill was in possession of the British.

For the British, it was a hard won victory, for they lost nearly three times as many men as the Americans, among them some gallant officers. As to the Americans in spite of their defeat they rejoiced; for they knew now what they could do. They knew they could stand up to the famous British regulars.

And now as Washington rode towards Charleston to take command of the army, news of this battle was brought to him.

"Did our men fight?" asked Washington. And when he was told how well, his grave face lighted up.

"Then the liberties of the country are safe," he cried.

So with hope in his heart Washington rode on, and at length after a journey of eleven days reached Cambridge, the headquarters of the army.

The next day, the 3rd of July, the whole army was drawn up upon the plain. And mounted on a splendid white horse Washington rode to the head of it. Under a great elm tree he wheeled his horse, and drawing his sword solemnly took command of the army of the United Colonies. And as the blade glittered in the

193

sunshine, a great shout went up from the soldiers. They were New Englanders, for the most part, but they welcomed their Virginian commander whole heartedly. For were they not all Americans? Were they not all ready to stand shoulder to shoulder for the one great cause?

But the army of which Washington had taken command was, perhaps, the rawest, worst equipped army which ever marched into the field.

The men had neither uniforms, tents, stores nor ammunition, many of them had no arms. There was no organisation, and little discipline. Even the exact numbers composing this army were not known. They were, in fact, as one of Washington's own officers said, "only a gathering of brave, enthusiastic, undisciplined country lads."

But out of this crowd of brave enthusiastic men, Washington set himself to make an army fit to do great deeds. So he worked, and rode, and wrote, unceasingly and unwearyingly. For he had not only to deal with the army but with Congress also. He had to awaken them to the fact that the country had to do great deeds, and that to do them well money, and a great deal of money, was needed.

Meanwhile George III also was making free at preparations. More soldiers he saw were needed to subdue these rebel farmers. And as it was difficult to persuade Britons to go to fight their brothers he hired a lot of Germans, and sent them out to fight the Americans. Nothing hurt the Americans more than this; more than anything else this act made them long to be independent. After this there was no more talk of making friends.

Chapter 54 - The War In Canada

After Bunker Hill there was a pause in the fighting round Boston which gave Washington time to get his raw recruits in hand a little. Then during the summer news came that Sir Guy Carleton, the Governor of Canada, was making plans to retake Ticonderoga, and the colonists determined to invade Canada. General Philip Schuyler was given command of the expedition, and with two thousand men he set out for St. John's, which Arnold had taken, but had been unable to hold, earlier in the year.

This time the colonists found St. John's better guarded, and only at the end of a two months' siege did it yield. By this time Schuyler had become ill, and the command was given to General Richard Montgomery who crossed the St. Lawrence, and entered Montreal in triumph.

Almost at the same time Benedict Arnold set out with twelve hundred men to attack Quebec. He marched through the forest of Maine, then an almost unknown country and uninhabited save by Indians. It was a tremendous march, and one that needed all the grit and endurance of brave, determined men. They climbed hills, struggled through swamps, paddled across lakes and down unknown streams. Sometimes they waded up to their knees in icy waters pushing their canoes before them against the rapid current, or again they carried them over long portages, shouldering their way through forest so dense that they could scarcely advance a mile an hour. At night soaked with rain and sleet they slept upon the snowy ground. Their food gave out, and the pangs of hunger were added to their other miseries. Many died by the way; others, losing heart, turned back. But sick and giddy, starving and exhausted the rest stumbled onward, and at length little more than five hundred ragged half armed, more than half famished men, reached the shores of the St. Lawrence.

They were a sorry little company with which to invade a vast province. But their courage was superb, their hope sublime, and without delay they set out to take the great fortress which had withstood so many sieges, and had only fallen at last before the genius and daring of Wolfe.

Across the St. Lawrence this little company of intrepid colonists paddled, up the path where Wolfe had led his men they climbed, and stood at length where they had stood upon the heights of Abraham. They had no cannon, and half their muskets were useless. Yet Arnold at the head of his spectral little company boldly summoned the town to surrender.

The town did not surrender, the Governor refused to come out and fight. So seeing the uselessness of his summons Arnold marched away about twenty miles, and encamped to wait for Montgomery's arrival from Montreal. He soon arrived. But even with hid men the colonists only numbered about eight hundred, far too small a company with which to besiege a fortress such as Quebec. Still they resolved to take the place by storm.

It was early on the morning of the 1st of January, 1776, that they made the attempt in the teeth of a blinding snow storm. Arnold led the assault on one side of the town, Montgomery on the other. With tremendous dash and bravery the colonists carried the first barricades, and forced their way into the town. But almost at the outset Montgomery was killed. A little later Arnold was sorely wounded, and had to be carried back to the camp. Both leaders gone, the heart went out of the men, and they retreated, leaving many prisoners at the hands of the British.

The great assault had failed, but sick and wounded though he was, Arnold did not lose heart. He still kept up a show of besieging Quebec. "I have no thought of leaving this proud town, " he said, "until I first enter it in triumph. I am in the way of my duty and know no fear." But the only chance of taking Quebec was to take it in the winter, while the St. Lawrence was closed with ice, so that the British ships could not reach it with reinforcements and supplies. Arnold therefore sent to Washington begging for five thousand troops. Such a number it was impossible for Washington to spare from his little army, and only a few reinforcements were sent, most of whom reached Arnold utterly exhausted with their long tramp through the pathless wilderness. Smallpox, too, became rife in the camp, so although there at length two thousand men before Quebec not more that a thousand were fit for duty. Yet what mere men could do they did.

But winter passed and Quebec remained untaken. Then on April morning Captain Charles Douglas arrived off the mouth of the St. Lawrence with a fleet of British ships. He found the river still packed with ice. But Quebec he knew must be in sore straits. It was no time for caution, so by way of experiment he ran

195

his flag ship full speed against a mass of ice. The ice was shivered to pieces, and the good ship sailed unharmed. For nine days the gallant vessel ploughed on through fields of ice, but suffering no serious damage, her stout-hearted captain having no thought but to reach and relieve the beleaguered city.

His boldness was rewarded. Other vessels followed in his track, and at their coming the colonists gave up their attempt to conquer Canada, and marched away.

The attack on Canada had been an utter failure, but Arnold still clung to the hope of commanding the great waterway from the St. Lawrence to the Hudson. At Crown Point he began to build ships, and by the end of September had a little fleet of nine. The British also busied themselves building ships, and on the 11th of October a fight between the two fleets took place on Lake Champlain, between the island of Valcour and the mainland.

The British ships were far larger and more numerous than the American, indeed in comparison with the British the American boats were mere cockle shells, but the colonists put up a gallant fight which lasted five hours, and the sun went down leaving them sadly shattered but still unbeaten.

The British commander, however, felt sure of finishing them off in the morning. So he anchored his ships in a line across the southern end of the channel, between the island and the mainland, thus cutting off all retreat. But Arnold knew his danger, and determined to make a dash for freedom. The night was dark and foggy. The British were so sure of their prey that they kept no watch. So while they slept one by one the American ships crept silently through their lines and sped away.

When day dawned the British with wrath and disgust saw an empty lake where they had expected to see a stricken foe. They immediately gave chase and the following day they again came up with the little American fleet, for many of the ships were so crippled that they could move but slowly. Again a five hours' battle was fought. One ship, the Washington, struck her flag. But Arnold in his little Congress fought doggedly on. Then seeing he could resist no more he drove the Congress and four other small boats ashore in a creek too narrow for any but the smallest one of the British ships to follow. Here he set them on fire, and bade his men leap for the shore, he himself being the last to leave the burning decks. On land he waited until he was certain that the ships were safe from capture, and that they would go down with their flags flying. Then he marched off with his men, and brought them all safely to Ticonderoga.

The attack on Canada had been an utter failure, the little American fleet had been shattered, save for Ticonderoga the coveted waterway was in the hands of the British. Had the British commander known it too he might have attacked Ticonderoga then and there, and taken it with ease. But Arnold was there, and Arnold had made such a name for himself by his dash and courage that Carleton did not dare attack the fort. And contenting himself for the moment with having gained control of Lake Champlain he turned to attack Canada. Arnold had failed to take Quebec, and he has lost his little fleet. But against his failure to take Quebec his countrymen put his wonderful march through pathless forest; against

196

the loss of the fleet the fact that but for Arnold it would never have been built at all. So the people cheered him as a hero, and Washington looked upon him as one of his best officers.

But Arnold's temper was hot if his head was cool, he was ambitious and somewhat arrogant. And while he had been fighting so bravely he had quarreled with his brother officers, and made enemies of many. They declared that he fought not for his country's honour but for the glory of Benedict Arnold. So it came about that he did not receive the reward of promotion which he felt himself entitled to. When Congress appointed several new Major Generals he was passed over, and once again, as after the taking of Ticonderoga, bitterness filled his heart.

Chapter 55 - The Birth of A Great Nation

While these things were happening in the north the British had been forced to march away from Boston.

At first Washington could do little but keep his army before the town, for he had no siege guns with which to bombard it. Nor had he any desire to destroy the town." Burn it," said some, "if that is the only way of driving out the British." Even John Hancock to whom a great part of Boston belonged advised this. "Burn Boston," he said," and make John Hancock a beggar, if the public good requires it." But Washington did not attempt to burn it.

After the taking of Ticonderoga and Crown Point however he got guns. For many of the cannon taken at these forts were put on sledges and dragged over the snow to Boston. It was Colonel Henry Knox who carried out this feat. He was a stout young man with a lovely smile and jolly fat laugh, who greatly enjoyed a joke. He had been a bookseller before the war turned him into a soldier. And now as he felled trees, and made sledges, and encouraged his men over the long rough way he hugely enjoyed the joke of bringing British guns to bombard the British out of Boston.

When Washington got these guns he quietly one night took possession of Dorchester Heights, which commanded both Boston town and harbour. So quick had been his action that it seemed to General Howe, the British commander, as if the fortifications on Dorchester Heights had been the work of magic. But magic or no magic they were, he saw, a real and formidable danger. With siege guns frowning above both town and harbour it was no longer possible to hold Boston. So hastily embarking his troops General Howe sailed away to Halifax in Nova Scotia, and Boston was left in peace for the rest of the war.

By this time there had been fighting in the south as well as in New England. For King George had taken it into his stubborn head that it would be a good plan to attack the southern colonies in spite of the fact that the war in the north was already more that he could manage. Sir Peter Parker, therefore, was sent out from England with a fleet of about fifty ships, and Lord Cornwallis with two thousand men, to attack Charleston in South Carolina. Howe was also ordered to send some soldiers southward, and although he could ill spare them from Boston he sent General Sir Henry Clinton with a small detachment.

According to arrangement the troops from Boston and England were to attack together with the loyalists of the south and the friendly Indians. But everything was bungled. The fleet, the land force, the loyalists and the Indians all seemed to be pulling different ways, and attacked at different times. The assault on Charleston was a miserable failure, and to the delight of the colonists the whole British force sailed away to join Howe in the north, and for more than two years there was no fighting in the southern colonies.

The commander of the colonists in Charleston was General Charles Lee. He was not really an American at all, but an Englishman, a soldier of fortune and adventure. He had wandered about the world, fighting in many lands, and had been in Braddock's army when it was defeated. He never became an American at heart like some other Englishmen who fought on their side. He cared little for them, he cared as little for the cause in which they were fighting, merely seeing in it a chance of making himself famous, and he had a very poor opinion of their fighting qualities. He was a tall, spare man with a hollow-cheeked, ugly face, and a disagreeable manner. He had a great opinion of himself, and boasted to such purpose that the Americans believed him to be a military genius. And in this first tussle with the British in the south he did so well that their belief in him seemed justified. He seemed to the people a hero and a genius rolled in one. In all the war after he did nothing to uphold the fame he gained at Charleston.

South as well as north had now had a taste of war. South as well as north had seen the British sail away, foiled. Every royal governor had by this time been driven from his post, and for six months and more the colonies had practically ruled themselves. What then, said many, was the use of talking any more about allegiance to the mother country? It was time, they said, to announce to all the world that the colonies of America were a free and independent nation.

There was much grave discussion in Congress and throughout the country. Some patriots, even those who longed most ardently to see America a free country, thought that it was too soon to make the claim. Among those was Patrick Henry who had already ranged himself so passionately on the side of freedom." The struggle is only beginning," he said," and we are not yet united. Wait till we are united. Wait until we have won our freedom, then let us proclaim it."

But by degrees all those who hesitated were won over, and on the 4th of July, 1776, the colonies declared themselves to be free.

Many meetings were held in what has since been called Independence Hall at Philadelphia. Much discussion there was, but at length the solemn declaration was drawn up. "We, the Representatives of the United States of America," so it ran," in General Congress assembled, appealing to the supreme judge of the world for the rectitude of our intention, do, in the name, and by the authority of the good people of these colonies, solemnly publish and declare, that these united colonies are, and of right ought to be, Free and Independent States." These are but a few words of the long, gravely worded declaration which was drawn up by Thomas Jefferson, and which is familiar to every American to this day.

John Hancock was President of Congress at this time, and he was the first to sign the declaration. Large, and clear, and all across the page the signature runs, showing, as it were, the calm mind and firm judgment which guided the hand that wrote. It was not until a few days later that it was signed by the other members.

It was on the 4th of July that Congress agreed to the declaration, and so that day has ever since been kept as a national holiday. It was the birthday of the United States as a Nation. But it was not until a few days later that the Declaration was read to the people of Philadelphia from Independence Hall. It was greeted with cheers and shouts of delight. The old bell upon the tower pealed joyfully, and swift riders mounted and rode to bear the news in all directions. The next day it was read at the head of each brigade of the army, and was greeted with loud cheers.

This Declaration of Independence was a bold deed, it might almost seem a rash one. For the British army was still in the land, and the Americans by no means always victorious. But the very fact of the boldness of the deed made them feel that they must be brave and steadfast, and that having claimed freedom they must win it. The Declaration drew the colonies together as nothing else had done, and even those who had thought the deed too rash came to see that it had been wise.

Chapter 56 - The Darkest Hour - Trenton and Princeton

In many places the news of the Declaration of Independence and the news of the victory at Charleston came at the same time, and gave a double cause for rejoicing. It was the last good news which was to come for many a long day. Indeed for months misfortune followed misfortune, until it almost seemed as if the Declaration of Independence had been the rash and useless action some had held it to be.

By the end of June General Howe sailed southward from Halifax, and landed on Staten Island southwest of New York, to await the arrival from England of his brother, Admiral Howe. On July 12th, just eight days after the declaration of independence, Admiral Howe arrived with strong reinforcements of ships and men. But before he began to fight he tried to come to terms with the rebel colonies, and for a second time free pardon was offered to all who would submit and own British rule once more. But the Americans were in no mood to submit, and had no wish for "pardon."

"No doubt," said one, "we all need pardon from heaven, but the American who needs pardon from his Britannic Majesty is yet to be found."

So instead of submitting they made ready to fight. The British also prepared to fight, and the force of the next blow fell upon New York. There were now more than thirty thousand British troops gathered here. It was the largest army which had ever been sent out of England, and King George had never a doubt that this great force, backed by his unconquerable navy, would soon bring the ten or twenty thousand ragged, half starved rebels to their knees.

He little knew the men or the man which who he had to deal. The army was indeed ragged and undisciplined. But as the great Napoleon said later, "In war the man is everything." And Washington was soon to show the world what could be done by brave undisciplined men whose hearts were behind their muskets.

As soon as Washington had gained possession of Boston he left an old general with a small force to guard it, and transported the main body of his army to New York, feeling sure that the next attack would be made there.

Brooklyn Heights on Long Island commanded New York, very much in the same way as Bunker Hill and Dorchester Heights commanded Boston, and Washington knew he must keep possession of those heights, if New York was not to be given up without a blow being struck. He did not want to give it up without striking a blow, for he feared the effect on the spirits of the country. So he send General Putnam with about eight thousand men to occupy the Heights.

In doing this Washington placed his army in a very dangerous position, for the East River was large enough to allow British war ships to sail up it and thus cut his army in two. But he could do nothing else, for if the enemy got possession of the Heights the town was at his mercy.

Howe was not slow to see this, and, having carefully and secretly made his plans, he attacked the forces on Brooklyn Heights in the early morning of August 27th in front, and flank, and rear, all at once.

One division of the Americans was nearly wiped out, many being killed and the rest being taken prisoner. A little band of Marylanders put up a fine but hopeless fight for nearly four hours, the remnant of them at length taking refuge in the fortifications. To make the defeat a disaster for the colonists Howe had but to storm these fortifications. But he refused to do so. Enough had been done for one day, he said. Bunker Hill had taught the British to beware of storming heights. A siege would be less costly, thought Howe.

Within the fortifications the colonists were in a miserable plight. They had little shelter, the rain fell in torrents, and a cold northeast wind chilled them to the bone. They had nothing to eat except dry biscuit and raw pork. They were hungry and weary, wet and cold. Yet one of their miseries was a blessing. For as long as the northeast wind blew Howe could not bring his ships up the East River and cut communications between Long Island and New York. For in those days, it must be remembered, there were no steamers, and sailing vessels had to depend on wind and tide.

Washington, however, knew his danger. He knew that he must withdraw from Long Island. So secretly he gave orders that everything which could be found in the shape of a boat was to be brought to Brooklyn Ferry. They were soon gathered, and at eight o'clock in the evening, two days after the battle of Long Island, quickly and quietly the army was ferried across the wide river to the New York side. All night the rowers laboured, but the work was by no means finished when day dawned. The weather, however, still helped the colonists, for a thick fog settled over the river and hid what was going on from the British. Wounded, prisoners, cannon, stores, horses, were all ferried over, and when later in the day the British marched into the deserted camp they found not so much as a crust of bread.

It was about six in the morning when the last boat put off, and in it was

200

Washington, the last man to leave. For forty hours he had hardly been off his horse, and had never for a minute lain down to rest. He was unwearyingly watchful, and left nothing to chance, and this retreat is looked upon as one of the most masterly in all military history.

Having abandoned Brooklyn Washington knew that he could not hope to hold New York against an attack. But for a fortnight neither Admiral nor General Howe made any attack. Instead they talked once more of peace. It almost seemed as if Lord Howe were on the side of the Americans, as indeed he had always said he was, until he was ordered out to fight against them. "He is either a very slow officer, or else he is our very good friend," said one of them.

The fortnight which he now wasted gave Washington time to decide what it was best to do, and when at last the British began the attack on New York nearly all the stores and cannon had already been removed to Harlem Heights, about ten miles away at the north of Manhattan Island. All the troops, too, had gone except about four thousand under General Putnam, who stayed to keep order, and look after the removal of the last of the stores. When the attack came these were very nearly caught. For the regiment who ought to have guarded the landing place, and have kept the enemy from advancing until Putnam could retire, ran away as soon as they saw the red coats.

In vain their officers tried to rally them; panic had seized them, and they fled like frightened sheep. In the confusion Washington rode up. He was a man of fiery temper, and now when he saw his men show such a lack of courage in the face of the enemy he lost all control. Dashing his had upon the ground, and, drawing his sword, he bade them cease their cowardly retreat. But even Washington could not rally the fleeing men. Then his wrath and despair knew no bounds, and spurring his horse, he rode alone towards the enemy. Death, he felt, was better than such shame. But one of his officers, dashing after him, seized his bridle and turned him back to safety.

Meanwhile Putnam was making frantic efforts to gather his men and march them off to Harlem Heights. It was a day of violent heat, and as the men struggled on, laden with their baggage, their breath came short, and the perspiration trickled down their faces. Every moment they expected to be attacked in the rear.

But the attack did not come. For as Howe and his officers were passing the pleasant country house of Mrs. Robert Murray a servant came out to ask them to lunch. It was a tempting invitation on a hot day, —too tempting to be refused. So a halt was called, and while Howe and his officers enjoyed a pleasant meal, and listened to the talk of a clever, handsome lady, Putnam marched his panting men to safety.

Washington was greatly cast down at what he called the "disgraceful and dastardly" conduct of some of his troops that day. He knew that an attack on Harlem Heights must come, and come soon. But what would be the result? Would his men run away, or would they fight? "Experience, to my extreme affliction," he wrote sadly, "has convinced me that this is rather to be wished for than expected. However, I trust there are many who will act like men, and show themselves worthy of the blessings of freedom."

Washington had no real cause for fear. Next day the test came, and the Americans wiped out the memory of the day before. In wave after wave the British attacked, but again and again the colonists met them, and at last drove them to their trenches; and there was joy in the patriot camp.

Howe still pursued the war very slowly. After the battle of Harlem Heights he left Washington along for nearly a month, during which time the colonist fortified their camp strongly. But the commander-in-chief soon became convinced that the place was little better than a trap, in which Howe might surround him, and force him to surrender with all his army. So he retreated northward to White Plains, and the British settled down in New York, which they held till the end of the war.

And now misfortunes fell thick and fast upon the patriots. They still held Fort Washington on Manhattan Island, and Fort Lee on the opposite side of the Hudson, the garrisons of which were under the command of General Greene. Washington now advised him to abandon the forts, but did not give him absolute orders to do so. It is probably that he would have taken his commander's advice had not Congress interfered and sent orders that Fort Washington was not to be given up, except as a last necessity. Greene, believing that it was possible to hold it, tried to obey Congress. But on the 16th of November, after a fierce fight against tremendous odds, the fort was surrounded, and all the defenders to the number of about three thousand were taken prisoner.

The loss was a bitter blow to Washington, for the men taken prisoners were some of his best soldiers. Four days later Fort Lee was also taken, and although the garrison escaped they left behind them large stores of food, ammunition, baggage of all sorts, as well as cannon, which they could ill spare.

Washington now resolved on a retreat towards Philadelphia, and gloom settled on the ragged little army of patriots. They were weary of retreats and defeats, and felt that their cause was already lost. Winter was fast coming on and many shouldered their arms and marched homeward. And so the once buoyant enthusiastic army melted away to a hungry and dispirited troop of little more than four thousand.

General Lee had at this time but lately returned from his triumphs in South Carolina, and he was more boastful and arrogant than ever. After Washington he was second in command, but he had no doubt in his own mind that he ought to be first. Now he was not slow to let others know what he thought. And while Washington, noble and upright gentleman as he was, trusted Lee as a friend, and believed in him as a soldier, Lee schemed to supplant him.

Washington had left Lee at North Castle with seven thousand men. Now he sent him orders to join him at once, so that if he should have to fight a battle he could have at least some sort of army to fight with. But Lee pretended to misunderstand. He made excuses for delay, he argued, and lied, and stayed where he was. Perhaps he thought that it would be no bad thing if Washington should be defeated and captured. Then he would be commander-in-chief.

But it was Lee who was captured, not Washington. He had in a leisurely fashion at last begun to move, and on the march he spent a night at a wayside inn. The British, hearing of his whereabouts, surrounded the inn and took him prisoner. For more than a year he remained in their hands, a very comfortable captive, and his army, under General John Sullivan, marched to join Washington, who was still retreating southward through New Jersey before the overwhelming force of the British.

It was weary work retreating. But with masterly generalship, and untiring watchfulness, Washington avoided a battle, and slipped through the toils. As the pursued and pursuers neared Philadelphia something like panic laid hold of the city. All day long the rumble of wagons might be heard carrying women and children to places of safety. Congress was hurriedly removed to Baltimore; but hundreds of men seized their rifles and marched to join the army to fight for their country in its darkest hour.

But already the worst was over. Washington's army was now well reinforced. He had the recruits from Philadelphia, he had Lee's army, and he also had two thousand men sent him by Schuyler from the north. So he resolved to make a bold bid for fortune. He resolved to do or die. He gave as the password, "Victory or death," and in the dark of Christmas night, 1771, he and his men crossed the Delaware River above the town of Trenton, where the British lay, together with a large company of the Hessian troops who had been hired to fight the Americans. The river was full of floating ice, which made the crossing dangerous and slow. But through the darkness the men toiled on, fending off the ice blocks as best they could as they steered their boats through the drifting mass. At length, after ten hours' labour, they reached the other side without the loss of one man.

It was four o'clock when the troops started off on their seven-mile march to Trenton over the snowy ground, the icy wind driving the sleet and snow in their faces. But by eight o'clock they had reached Trenton. The British were utterly taken by surprise, and almost at once the Hessians surrendered.

Having sent his prisoners, to the number of nearly a thousand, to the other side of the river, Washington took possession of the town. But he was not long allowed to remain there. For the British commander, Lord Cornwallis, marched to dislodge him with an army of eight thousand men.

Washington let him come, and on the 2nd of January, Cornwallis encamped before Trenton, determined next morning to give battle. He was sure of victory, and in great spirits. "At last we have run down the old fox, and we will bag him in the morning," he said.

But Washington was not to be so easily caught. The two armies were so near that the watchfires of the one could be plainly seen by the other. All night the American watchfires blazed, all night men could be heard working at the fortifications. But that was only a blind. In the darkness Washington and his army quietly slipped away to Princeton. There he fell upon the British reinforcements, who were marching to join Cornwallis at Trenton, and put them to flight.

When day came Cornwallis was astonished to find the American camp empty.

203

And when he heard the firing in the distance he knew what had happened, and hastily retreated to New York, while Washington drew off his victorious but weary men to Morristown in New Jersey. Here for the next few months they remained, resting after their labours, unmolested by the foe.

Chapter 57 - Burgoyne's Campaign - Bennington and Oriskany

As many of the Americans had foreseen, the British had from the first formed the design of cutting the colonies in two by taking possession of the great waterway from the Hudson to the St. Lawrence. Their plans had been long delayed, but in the spring of 1777, they determined to carry them out.

General Burgoyne was now in command of the Canadian troops. He was a genial man of fashion, a writer of plays, and a great gambler. But he was a brave soldier, too, and his men adored him. For in days when it was common to treat the rank and file as a little better than dogs, Burgoyne treated them like reasoning beings.

It was arranged that Burgoyne should move southward with his main force, by way of Lake Champlain to Ticonderoga, and that a smaller force should go by Lake Ontario and seize Fort Stanwix. Howe, at the same time, was in Albany, having, it was to be supposed, swept the whole country free of "rebels."

It was a very fine plan, but it was not carried out as intended - because, although Burgoyne received his orders, Howe did not receive his. For the British minister, who ought to have sent them, went off on a holiday and forgot all about the matter for several weeks. When at length he remembered, and sent the order, Howe was far away from the Hudson, at his old game of trying to run Washington to earth.

Burgoyne, however, knew nothing of this and cheerfully set out from Canada with a well drilled, well equipped, and well fed army of about eight thousand men, and on the 1st of July reached Ticonderoga.

Since this fort had been taken by Ethan Allen it had been greatly strengthened, and the Americans believed that now it could withstand any assault, however vigorous. But while strengthening the fort itself they failed to fortify a little hill near. They had already much experience of the danger of heights commanding a town or fort. But they thought that this hill was too steep and rugged to be a danger. No cannon, it was said, could ever be dragged up to the top of it. When the British came, however, they thought otherwise. They at once saw the value of the hill, and determined that guns should be dragged up it. For forty-eight hours they worked furiously, and when day dawned on the 5th of August both men and guns were on the summit.

The American commander, St. Clair, saw them with despair in his heart. Every corner of the fort was commanded by the guns, and the garrison utterly at the mercy of the enemy. To remain, he knew, would mean the loss of his whole force. So he resolved to abandon the fort, and as soon as the sun set the work was begun. Guns and stores were laden on boats, cannon too heavy to be removed were spiked, and nearly all the garrison had left when a fire broke out in the officers' quarters.

The light of the flames showed the British sentinels what was going on. The alarm was given. The British made a dash for the fort, and as day dawned on July 6, 1777, the Union Jack was once more planted upon its ramparts.

Then a hot pursuit began. At the village of Hubbardton the Americans made a valiant stand, but they were worsted and fled, and five days later St. Clair brought the remnant of his force into Fort Edward, where the main army under Schuyler was stationed.

Burgoyne had begun well, and when King George heard the news he clapped his hands with joy. "I have beat them," he cried, dashing into the queen's rooms, "I have beat all the Americans." But over America the loss cast a gloom. St. Clair and Schuyler were severely blamed and court-martialled. But both were honourably acquitted. Nothing could have saved the garrison from being utterly wiped out; and when men came to judge the matter calmly they admitted that it was better to lose the fort than to lose the fort and garrison also. Meanwhile Burgoyne was chasing hot-foot after the fugitives. As he approached, Schuyler abandoned Fort Edward, for it was a mere shell and impossible of defence for a single day. But as he fell back, he broke up the roads behind him. Trees were felled and laid across them every two or three yards, bridges were burned, fords destroyed. So thoroughly was the work done that Burgoyne, in pursuit, could only march about a mile a day, and had to build no fewer than forty bridges in a distance of little more than twenty-four miles.

Besides destroying the roads Schuyler also made the country a desert. He carried away and destroyed the crops, drove off the sheep and cattle, sweeping the country so bare that the hostile army could find no food, and were forced to depend altogether on their own supplies. Before long these gave out, and the British began to suffer from hunger.

Burgoyne now learned that at the village of Bennington the patriots had a depot containing large stores of food and ammunition. These he determined to have for his own army, and he sent a force of six hundred men, mostly Germans and Indians, to make the capture.

This old trapper, Captain John Stark, was in command of the American force at Bennington. He had fought in many battles from Bunker Hill to Princeton. But, finding himself passed over, when others were promoted, he had gone off homeward in dudgeon. But now in his country's hour of need he forgot his grievances and once more girded on his sword. He led his men with splendid dash and the enemy was utterly defeated, and Stark was made a brigadier general as a reward. It was a disaster for Burgoyne, and on the heels of this defeat came the news that the second force marching by way of Lake Ontario had also met with disaster at Oriskany near Fort Stanwix.

This force had surrounded Fort Stanwix, and General Nicholas Herkimer had marched to its relief.

General Herkimer was an old German of over sixty, and although he had lived all his life in America, and loved the country with his whole heart, he spoke

205

English very badly, and wrote it worse. It must have sadly puzzled his officers sometimes to make out his dispatches and orders. One is said to have run as follows: "Ser, yu will orter yur bodellyen to merchs Immetdielich do ford edward weid for das broflesen and amenieschen fied for en betell. Dis yu will desben at yur berrel." This being translated means:" Sir, you will order your battalion to march immediately to Fort Edward with four days' provisions, and ammunition for one battle. This you will disobey at your peril."

As this doughty old German marched to the relief of Fort Stanwix he fell into an ambush prepared for him by the famous Indian chief, Joseph Brant, who, with his braves, was fighting on the side of the British. A terrible hand to hand struggle followed. The air was filled with wild yells and still wilder curses as the two foes grappled. It was war in all its savagery. Tomahawks and knives were used as freely as rifles. Stabbing, shooting, wrestling, the men fought each other more like wildcats than human beings. A fearful thunderstorm burst forth, too. Rain fell in torrents, a raging wind tore through the tree tops, thunder and lightning added their terrors to the scene.

For five hours the savage warfare lasted. Almost at the beginning a ball shattered Herkimer's leg and killed his horse. But the stout old warrior refused to leave the field. He bade his men take the saddle from his horse and place it at the root of a great beech tree. Sitting there he directed the battle, shouting his orders in his quaint guttural English, and calmly smoking a pipe the while. They were the last orders he was to give. For, ten days after the battle he died from his wound, serenely smoking his pipe, and reading his old German Bible almost to the last.

Soon the noise of the battle was heard at Fort Stanwix, and the garrison, led by Colonel Marinus Willett, sallied forth to the aid of their comrades, put a detachment of the enemy to flight, and captured their stores of food and ammunition, together with five flags. And now for the first time the Stars and Stripes were unfurled.

When Washington had taken command of the army there had still been no real thought of separating from Britain. So for his flag he had used the British ensign with the Union Jack in the corner. But instead of a red ground he had used a ground of thirteen red and white stripes, on stripe for each colony. But when all hope of reconciliation was gone Congress decided that the Union Jack must be cut out of the flag altogether, and in its place a blue square was to be used with thirteen white stars in a circle, one star for each state, just as there was one stripe for each state.

People, however, were too busy doing other things and had no time to see to the making of flags. So the first one was hoisted by Colonel Willett, after the battle of Orskany. He had captured five standards. These, as victor, he hoisted on the fort. To make his triumph complete, however, he wanted an American flag to hoist over them. But he had none. So a soldier's wife gave her red petticoat, some one else supplied a white shirt, and out of that and an old blue jacket was made the first American flag to float upon the breeze.

This, of course, was only a rough and ready flag, and Betsy Ross, a seamstress, who lived in Arch Street, Philadelphia, had the honour of making the first real one. While in Philadelphia Washington and some members of council called upon Betsy to ask her to make the flag. Washington had brought a sketch with him, but Betsy suggested some alterations. So Washington drew another sketch, and there and then Betsy set to work, and very soon her flag also was floating in the breeze.

Chapter 58 - Burgoyne's Campaign - Bemis Heights and Saratoga

After all the fierce fighting at Oriskany neither side could claim a victory. The British had received a check, but were by no means beaten. Fort Stanwix was still besieged, and unless relief came must soon fall into the hands of the enemy.

Colonel Gansewoort, the commandant of the fort, therefore now sent to Schuyler asking for help, and Benedict Arnold, who had but lately arrived, volunteering for the service, was soon on his way with twelve hundred men. Arnold was ready enough to fight, as he was. But he knew that his force was much smaller than that of the British, and, after some thought, he fell upon a plan by which theirs could be made less.

A spy had been caught within the American lines, and was condemned to death. He was an almost half-witted creature, with queer cunning ways, and the Indians looked upon him as a sort of Medicine Man, and feared him accordingly. Knowing this, Arnold thought that he might be useful to him, and promised to spare his life if he would go to the British camp and spread a report among their Indian allies that the Americans were coming down upon them in tremendous force.

The man was glad enough to get a chance to escape being hanged, and his brother being held as hostage, he set out. He acted his part well. Panting and breathless, with his coat torn in many places by bullets, and a face twisted with fear, he dashed into the enemy camp. There he told his eager listeners that he had barely escaped with his life from the Americans (which was true enough) and that they were marching towards them in vast numbers, and showed his bullet-riddled coat as proof of his story.

"How many are they?" he was asked.

In reply the man spread his hands abroad, pointing to the leaves of the trees and shaking his head as if in awe.

The Indians were greatly disturbed, and began to hold a council. While they were still consulting, an Indian, friendly to the Americans, who was in the plot, arrived. He told the same story as the spy, pointing like him to the numberless trees of the forest when asked how many of the enemy were coming.

Then another and still another Indian arrived. They all told the same tale. A mysterious bird had come to warn them, they said, that the whole valley was filled with warriors.

At length the Indians could bear no more. Already many of their best warriors had been slain. They would no longer stay to be utterly wiped out, and they prepared to flee.

In vain the British commander implored them to stay. Bribes, threats, and

207

promises were all alike useless. At last he offered them "fire water." For if only he could make them drunk, he thought, they might forget their fear. But even the much coveted "fire water" had no power to still their terrors. They refused to drink, and with clamour and noise they fled.

The panic spread to the rest of the army. Two battalions of white men followed in the wake of their redskin brothers, and the commander, deserted by the bulk of his army, was forced to join in the general retreat.

It was a humiliating and disorderly flight. The Indians, when they recovered from their terror, had lost every vestige of respect for their white brothers. Soon they became insolent, and amused themselves by playing on their fears. "They are coming! They are coming!" they would cry whenever the weary fugitives lay down to rest. Then they would laugh to see the white men leap up again, fling away their knapsacks and their rifles, so as to make the greater haste, and stumble onward.

At length the shameful retreat came to an end, and, hungry and ragged, a feeble remnant of the expedition reached the shores of Lake Ontario, and passed over into Canada.

Such was the news brought to Burgoyne soon after the defeat at Bennington. It make his dark outlook darker still. No help could ever come to him now from the north, and all his hopes were fixed on Howe's advancing host from the south. But no news of Howe's approach reached him. Day by day the American force round him was increasing. Day by day his own was growing weaker. At last in desperation he decided to risk a battle. For he saw that he must either soon cut his way through the hostile forces or perish miserable.

General Horatio Gates was now in command of the Americans instead of Schuyler. Gates was nothing of a soldier. Indeed it was said of him that all throughout the beginning of the war he never so much as heard the sound of a gun, and that when there was a battle to the fore he always had business elsewhere. Like Lee he was an Englishman by birth. And even as Lee had been jealous of Washington so Gates was jealous of Schuyler, and at last he succeeded in ousting him. He did so at a good time for himself, for all the hard work of this campaign was done, and Gates stepped in time to reap the glory.

Burgoyne thought little of Gates, and called him an old woman. So he was the more ready to give battle. But the Americans were now so thoroughly aroused that they would have fought well without a leader. Besides, Arnold was with them, and Arnold they would have followed anywhere.

The Americans were strongly entrenched on Bemis Heights, and on the day of battle Gates would have done nothing but sit still and let the enemy wear himself out in attacks. But this did not suit Arnold's fiery temper, and he begged hard to be allowed to charge the enemy. Bates grudgingly gave him leave, and with a small force he bore down upon the British. The fight was fierce, and finding his force too small Arnold sent to Gates asking for reinforcements. But Gates, although he had ten thousand troops standing idle, refused to send a man. So, with his always diminishing handful of troops, Arnold fought on till night fell.

Again neither side could claim a victory. But Burgoyne had lost nearly six hundred men, and his position was not one whit the better. Gates took all the credit to himself, and when he sent his account of the battle to Congress he did not so much as mention Arnold's name. Out of this, and his refusal to send reinforcements, a furious quarrel arouse between the two men, and Gates told Arnold that he had no further use for his services and that he could go. Arnold, shaken with wrath, would have gone had not his brother officers with one voice begged him to stay. So he stayed, but he had no longer any command.

Like a caged and wounded lion Burgoyne now sought a way out of the trap in which he was. But turn which way he would there was no escape. He was hemmed in on all sides. So eighteen days after the battle of Bemis Heights he took the field again on the same ground. It was a desperate adventure, for what could six thousand worn and weary men do against twenty thousand already conscious of success?

The British fought with dogged courage. Chafing with impatience Arnold watched the battle from the heights. He saw how an attack might be made with advantage, how victory might be won. At length he could bear inaction no longer, and, leaping on to his horse, he dashed into the fray.

"Go after that fellow and bring him back," shouted Gates; "he will be doing something rash."

The messenger sped after him. But Arnold was too quick, and the battle was well nigh won before Gates' order reached him. As Arnold came his men gave a ringing cheer, and for the rest of the day he and Daniel Morgan were the leaders of the battle, Gates never leaving his headquarters.

Where the bullets flew thickest, there Arnold was to be found. The madness of battle was upon him, and, like one possessed, he rode through flame and smoke, his clear voice raised above the hideous clamour, cheering and directing his men.

The fight was fierce and long, but as the day wore on there could be no more doubt about the end. The British were defeated. Yet so long as daylight lasted they fought on.

Just as the sun was setting Arnold and his men had routed a party of Germans, and a wounded German, lying on the ground, shot at Arnold, killing his horse and shattering his leg - the same leg which had been wounded at Quebec.

As Arnold fell, one of his men, with a cry of rage dashed at the German and would have killed him where he lay. But Arnold stopped him. "For God's sake, don't hurt him." he cried, "he's a fine fellow." So the man's life was spared.

Arnold's leg was so badly shattered that the doctors talked of cutting it off. Arnold, however, would not hear of it.

"If that is all you can do for me," he said, "put me on another horse and let me see the battle out."

But the battle was over, for night had put an end to the dreadful strife.

With this defeat Burgoyne's last hope vanished. To fight again would be merely to sacrifice his brave soldiers. He had only food in the camp for a week, and there was still no sign of help coming from the south. There was nothing left to him but to surrender.

So on October 17th he surrendered to General Gates, with all his cannon, ammunition, and great stores, and nearly six thousand men.

As his soldiers laid down their arms many of them wept bitterly. But there was no one there to see or deride their grief. For the Americans, having no wish to add to the sorrow of their brave foe, stayed within their lines. Then, as the disarmed soldiers marched away, Burgoyne stepped out of the ranks, and, drawing his sword, gave it to General Gates.

"The fortune of war has made me your prisoner," he said.

"It was through no fault of yours," replied Gates, with a grave courtesy, as he handed back the sword.

Chapter 59 - Brandywine - Germantown - Valley Forge

Washington spent the winter of 1776-7 at Morristown. In May he once more led his army out, and while the forces in the north, under Schuyler and then Gates, were defeating Burgoyne, he was holding his own against Howe's far more formidable army further south.

Howe had spent the winter at New York, which from the time of its capture to the end of the war, remained the British headquarters. In the spring he determined to capture Philadelphia, the "revel capital," and began to march through New Jersey. But in every move he made he found himself checked by Washington. It was like a game of chess. Washington's army was only about half the size of Howe's, so he refused to be drawn into an open battle, but harried and harassed his foe at every turn, and at length drove Howe back to Staten Island.

Having failed to get to Philadelphia by land, Howe now decided to go by sea, and , sailing up Chesapeake Bay, he landed in Maryland in the end of August. But there again he found Washington waiting for him. And now, although his army was still much smaller than Howe's, Washington determined to risk a battle rather than give up Philadelphia without a blow.

With his usual care and genius Washington chose his position well, on the banks of the Brandywine, a little river which falls into the Delaware at Wilmington about twenty-six miles from Philadelphia. On both sides the battle was well fought. But the British army was larger, better equipped, and better drilled, and they gained the victory.

This defeat made the fate of Philadelphia certain, and Congress fled once more, this time to Lancaster. Yet for a fortnight longer Washington held back the enemy, and only on the 26th of September did the British march into the city. But before they had time to settle into their comfortable quarters Washington gave battle again, at Germantown, on the outskirts of Philadelphia.

It was a well contested battle, and at one time it seemed as if it might end in victory for the Americans. But Washington's plan of battle was rather a hard one for inexperienced troops to carry out. They were as brave as any men who ever carried rifles, but they were so ignorant of drill that they could not even form into column or wheel to right or left in soldierly fashion. A thick fog, too, which hung over the field from early morning, made it difficult to distinguish friend from foe, and at one time two divisions of the Americans, each mistaking the other for the enemy, fired upon each other.

But although the battle of Germantown was a defeat for the Americans it by no means spelled disaster. Another two months of frays and skirmishes followed. Then the British settled down to comfortable winter quarters in Philadelphia, and Washington marched his war-worn patriots to Valley Forge, about twenty miles away.

Wile the Americans had been busy losing and winning battles, Pitt in England was still struggling for peace and kindly understanding between Britain and her colonies. "You can never conquer the Americans," he cried. "If I were an American, as I am an Englishman, while a foreign troop was landed in my country I would never lay down my arms, —never, never, never!"

But Pitt talked in vain. For the King was deaf to all the great minister's pleadings. In his eyes the Americans were rebels who must be crushed, and Pitt was but the "trumpet of sedition."

But meanwhile all Europe had been watching the struggle of these same rebels, watching it, too, with keep interest and admiration. And now soldiers from many countries came to offer help to the Americans. Among them the best known perhaps are Kosciuszko, who later fought so bravely for his own land, Poland; and Lafayette, who took a large share in the French Revolution.

Lafayette was at this time only nineteen. He had an immense admiration for Washington, and after they met, in spite of the difference in the their ages, they became lifelong friends, and Lafayette named his eldest son after Washington.

But the Americans owed more perhaps to Baron von Steuben than to any other foreigner. Von Steuben was a German, and had fought under Frederick the Great.

Washington had taken up winter quarters at Valley Forge, which is a beautiful little valley. But that winter it was a scene of misery and desolation. The cold was terrible, and the army was ragged and hungry. The men had neither coats, shirts, nor shoes, and often their feet and hands froze so that they had to be amputated. For days at a time they had but one poor meal a day. Even Washington saw no hope of help. "I am now convinced beyond a doubt," he wrote, "that unless some great and capital change takes place this army must inevitably be reduced to one or other of these three things: starve, dissolve, or disperse."

Much of this misery was due to the neglect and folly of Congress. It had sadly changed from the brave days of the Declaration of Independence. It was filled now with politicians who cared about their own advancement rather than with patriots who sought their country's good. They refused to see that money, and still more money, was needed to keep a properly equipped army in the field. They harassed Washington with petty interference with his plans. They gave promotion to useless officers against his wishes and better judgment. There was plenty of food in the country, stores of clothing were ready for the army's use, but they lay by the wayside, rotting, because there was no money to pay men to bring it to the army. Washington wore himself out in fruitless efforts to awaken Congress to a sense of its duty. And at length, utterly despairing of any support, weary of seeing his men suffer and dwindle day by day under the miseries of Valley Forge, he wrote out his resignation as Commander-in-Chief of the army. And it needed all the persuasions of his officers to make him tear it up.

It was to this camp of misery at Valley Forge that Baron von Steuben came. And the ragged, hungry, perishing army he drilled. To these men, brave enough, but all unused to discipline, he taught what discipline meant.

At first it was by no means easy. For the Baron knew little English and the men he tried to teach knew not a word of French or German. So misunderstandings were many, and when one day a young American officer named Walker, who knew French, came to von Steuben and offered to act as interpreter he was overjoyed. "Had I seen an angel from heaven," he cried, "I could not have been more glad."

But even then, between his own mistakes and the men's mistakes, the Baron was often driven distracted, and lost his temper. Once, it is said, utterly worn out, he turned the troops over to Walker. "Come, my friend," he cried, "take them; I can curse them no longer."

But in spite of all hindrances and failings, both men and officers learned so much from von Steuben that when the terrible winter was over the army went forth again to fight far more fit to face the foe than before.

_____

Chapter 60 - War on the Sea

Besides being themselves more fit to fight, the Americans now received other help, for France joined with America in her struggle against Britain. And after this the war was not confined to America only. There was war on the sea, now, as well as on land, and whenever the British and the French navies met there was fighting.

The Americans themselves also carried the war on to the sea. At first they had no fleet, but very soon they began to build ships and before long they had a little fleet of six. Of this fleet Esek Hopkins was made commander-in-chief. He was an old salt, for he had been captain of a trading vessel for thirty years. But as a naval commander he was not a success. He had no knowledge of warfare, he was touchy, obstinate, and could not get on with Congress, which he said was a pack of ignorant clerks who knew nothing at all. The fleet under him only made one cruise. Then he was dismissed, and was succeeded by James Nicholson, the son of a Scotsman from Berwick-on-Tweed.

As the war went on other vessels were added to the first six. But the largest was not bigger than a small British cruiser, and in the end they were nearly all taken, or sunk to prevent them being taken. Still before their end they fought many gallant fights, and did some good work for their country.

The first shot of the Revolution on the water was fired by Captain Abraham Whipple when he chased a tender belonging to the British cruiser Rose, and captured her. This was, however, not the first shot the hardy Captain had fired against the British. For in 1772, before the "Boston Tea Party," even, had taken place, he had seized and burned the British revenue schooner, Gaspé, in Narragansett Bay.

The commander of the Gaspé had been trying to put down smuggling on the coast of Rhode Island. He stopped all vessels, and examined even market boats, to see if they had any smuggled goods. This made the Rhode Island people very angry. They had smuggled as they liked for a hundred years; the British laws against it seemed to them mere tyranny; and they looked upon the commander of the Gaspé as little better than a pirate, who was interfering with their lawful trade. So when one day the people learned that the Gaspé had gone aground a few miles from Providence, and could not be got off before three o'clock in the morning, they determined to attack her.

Abraham Whipple was chosen as captain for the expedition. He and his men boarded the Gaspé, wounded the captain, overpowered the crew, and burned the schooner to the water's edge.

When the British commander-in-chief heard of it he was furious, and he wrote to Whipple.

"Sir," he said, "you, Abraham Whipple, on the 10th of June, 1772, burned his Majesty's ship the Gaspé, and I will hang you at the yardarm."

To this Whipple, nothing daunted, replied: "Sir, always catch a man before you hang him."

Whipple was never caught until 1778, when with his ship the Providence he tried to relieve Charleston, in South Carolina, which was at that time besieged by the British. Then he was not hanged, but kept prisoner until the end of the war.

Lambert Wickes, captain of the Reprisal, was another gallant naval officer. When Benjamin Franklin was sent as United States ambassador to France in 1776 he sailed in the Reprisal, which was the first American warship to visit the shores of Europe.

It might be here interesting to note that besides being minister to France, Franklin had to look after naval affairs in a general way. He used his powers with wisdom, and often with great humanity. Among other things he gave all American naval commanders orders that they were not to attack the great discoverer, Captain Cook, no matter in what part of the ocean they might meet him. They were not merely forbidden to attack him, they were even commanded to offer him any aid they could. For it would not beseem Americans, said Franklin, to fight against one who had earned the admiration of the whole world.

The Reprisal did not return home before it had made its presence felt. For, having landed Franklin, Wickes cruised about the Bay of Biscay and the English Channel, capturing many British merchantmen, and taking them to France, where he sold them.

At this time France was still at peace with Britain, and the British Government complained bitterly to the French at this breach of neutrality. They were, therefore, forced to order the American ships to leave France, and Wickes sailed for home.

On the way the Reprisal was chased by a British warship, and Wickes only saved himself from capture by throwing his guns overboard. He thus escaped one danger, however, only to fall into another, and in a storm off the coast of

Newfoundland the Reprisal went down, and all on board were lost.

But of all the naval commanders on the American side, the Scotsman, John Paul Jones, was the most famous. He was the son of a gardener, and was born at Arbigland in Kirkcudbrightshire. From a child he had been fond of the sea, and when still only a boy of twelve he began his seafaring life on board a ship trading with Virginia. For some years he led a roving and adventurous life. Then after a time he came to live in America, which, he said himself, "has been my favourite country since the age of thirteen, when I first saw it."

His real name was John Paul. But he took the name of Jones out of gratitude to Mr. Jones, a gentleman of Virginia, who had befriended him when he was poor and in trouble.

When the War of the Revolution broke out Jones was a young man of twenty-seven, and he threw himself heart and soul into the struggle on the side of the Americans. He was the first man to receive a naval commission after the signing of the Declaration of Independence. He was, too, the first man to break the American naval flag from the mast. This was not, however, the Stars and Stripes, but a yellow flag with a pine tree and a rattlesnake, and the words, "Tread on me how dares."

Jones became famous at once for his deeds of skill and daring, for it was his sole ambition, he said, "to fight a battle under the new flag, which will teach the world that the American flag means something afloat, and must be respected at sea." But he never liked the yellow flag. It was more fit for a pirate ship, he thought, than to be the ensign of a great nation, and he it was who first sailed under the Stars and Stripes, which he hoisted on his little ship, the Ranger. This was only a vessel of three hundred tons. In it in November, 1777, he crossed the Atlantic, harried the coasts of England and Scotland, and then made his way to France.

From France Jones set out again with a little fleet of four ships. His flagship he called Bonhomme Richard, as a compliment both to France and Franklin. Franklin being the author of "Poor Richard's Almanac," for which Bonhomme Richard was the French translation.

The Bonhomme Richard was the largest vessel of the American navy, but it was only a worn-out old East India merchantman, turned into a man-of-war by having portholes for guns cut in the sides. And, although, Jones did not know it at the time, the guns themselves had all been condemned as unsafe before they were sent on board. The other ships of the squadron were also traders fitted up with guns in the same way, but were all much smaller than the Bonhomme.

With this raffish little fleet Paul Jones set out to do great deeds. His bold plan was to attack Liverpool, the great centre of shipping, but that had to be given up, for he found it impossible to keep his little squadron together. Sometimes he would only have one other ship with him, sometimes he would be quite alone. So he cruised about the North Sea, doing a great deal of damage to British shipping, catching merchantmen, and sending them to France as prizes.

At length one afternoon in September, when he had only the Pallas with him, he sighted a whole fleet of merchantmen off the coast of England and at once gave chase. The merchantmen were being convoyed by two British men-of-war, the Serapis and the Countess of Scarborough, and they at once got between Jones and his prey. Then the merchantmen made off as fast as they could, and the men-of-war came on. Presently the captain of the Serapis hailed the Bonhomme Richard.

"What ship are you?" he shouted.

"I can't hear what you say," replied Jones, who wanted to get nearer.

That made the British captain suspicious. Nearer and nearer the two vessels drew on to each other.

"Hah," he said, "it is probably Paul Jones. If so there is hot work ahead."

Again the Serapis sent a hail.

"What ship is that? Answer immediately, or I shall be obliged to fire into you."

Paul Jones answered this time - with a broadside - and a terrible battle began. The carnage was awful. The decks were soon cumbered with dead and dying. The two ships were so near that the muzzles of the guns almost touched each other. Both were soon riddled with shot, and leaking so that the pumps could hardly keep pace with rising water. Still the men fought on.

Jones was everywhere, firing guns himself, encouraging his men, cheering them with his voice and his example. "The commodore had but to look at a man to make him brave," said a Frenchman, who was there. "Such was the power of one heart that knew no fear."

The sun went down over the green fields of England, and the great red harvest moon came up. Still through the calm moonlit night the guns thundered, and a heavy cloud of smoke hung over the sea. Two of the rotten old guns on the Bonhomme Richard had burst at the first charge, killing and wounding the gunners; others were soon utterly useless. For a minute not one could be fired, and the Captain of the Serapis thought that the Americans were beaten.

"Have you struck?" he shouted, through the smoke of the battle.

"No," cried Jones, "I haven't begun to fight yet."

The next instant the roar and rattle of the musketry crashed forth again. Both ships were now on fire, and a great hole smashed in the side of the Bonhomme.

"For God's sake, strike, Captain," said one of his officers.

Jones looked at him silently for a minute. The he answered: "No," he cried, "I will sink. I will never strike."

The ships were now side by side, and Jones gave orders to lash the Bonhomme Richard to the Serapis. He seized a rope himself and helped to do it. The carpenter beside him, finding the lines tangled rapped out a sailor's oath.

But Jones was calm as if nothing was happening.

"Don't swear, Mr. Stacy," he said. "We may soon all be in eternity. Let us do our duty."

Lashed together now the two ships swung on the waves in a death grapple. The guns on the Bonhomme Richard were nearly all silenced. But a sailor climbed out on to the yards, and began to throw hand grenades into the Serapis. He threw one

215

right into the hold, where it fell upon a heap of cartridges and exploded, killing about twenty men. That ended the battle. With his ship sinking and aflame, and the dead lying thick about him, the British captain struck his flag, and the Americans boarded the Serapis and took possession.

In silence and bitterness of heart Captain Pearson bowed and handed his sword to Jones. But Jones had only admiration for his gallant foe. He longed to say something to comfort him, but he looked so sad and dignified that he knew not what to say. At length he spoke.

"Captain Pearson," he said "you have fought like a hero. You have worn this sword to your credit, and to the honour of your service. I hope your King will reward you suitably."

But Captain Pearson could not answer, his heart was still too sore. Without a word he bowed again and turned away.

While this terrible fight had been going on the Pallas had engaged the Countess of Scarborough, and captured her, and now appeared, not much worse for the fight. But the Bonhomme Richard was an utter wreck, and was sinking fast. So as quickly as possible, the sailors, utterly weary as they were with fighting, began to move the wounded to the Serapis. The crew of the British ship, too, worked with a will, doing their best to save the enemies of the night before. At length all were safely carried aboard the Serapis, and only the dead were left on the gallant old Bonhomme Richard.

"To them," says Jones, in his journal, "I gave the good old ship for their coffin, and in it they found a sublime sepulchre. And the last mortal eyes ever saw of the Bonhomme Richard was the defiant waving of her unconquered and unstricken flag as she went down."

So this strange sea-duel was over. The victorious ship went down, and the victorious captain sailed away in his prize. But the Serapis, too, was little more than a wreck. Her main mast was shot away. Her other masts and spars were badly damaged, and could carry but little sail, and it seemed doubtful if she would ever reach port. But, after a perilous journey, the coasts of Holland were sighted, and the Serapis was duly anchored in the Texel.

With deeds like these the little American navy realised Jones' desire. But beyond that they did little to bring the war to an end. Far more was done by the privateers, which were fitted out by the hundred. They scoured the seas like greyhounds, attacking British merchantmen on every trade route, capturing and sinking as many as three hundred in one year. This kind of warfare paid so well, indeed that farming was almost given up in many states, the farmers having all gone off to make their fortunes by capturing British merchantmen.

As for Paul Jones he never had a chance again of showing his great prowess. When the war was over he entered the service of Russia, and became an admiral. He died in Paris in 1792, but for a long time it was not known where he was buried. His grave was discovered in 1905, and his body was brought to America by a squadron of the navy which was sent to France for the purpose, and reburied at Annapolis with the honour due to a hero.

216

Chapter 61 - The Battle of Monmouth - The Story of Captain Molly

While the Americans were learning endurance in the hard school of Valley Forge the British were having a gay time in Philadelphia. The grave old Quaker town rang with song and laughter as never before. Balls and parties, theatricals and races, followed each other in a constant round of gaiety. And amid this light-hearted jollity Howe seemed to forget all about the war.

Had he chosen he could easily have attacked Valley Forge, and crushed Washington's perishing army out of existence. Or if he grudged to lose men in an attack, he might have surrounded the Americans, and starved them into submission. But he did neither. He was too comfortable in his winter quarters, and had no wish to go out in the snow to fight battles.

Those in power in England had long been dissatisfied with Howe's way of conducting the war. Time and again he had seemed to lose his chance of crushing the rebellion and now this idle and gay winter in Philadelphia seemed the last straw. Such bitter things indeed were said of him that he resigned his commission, and went home, and the supreme command was given to General Clinton.

Now that France had joined with America, Britain was in a very different position than before. She could no longer afford to send out large armies such as Howe had been given to subdue the colonies. For she had to keep troops at home to protect Great Britain from invasion.

She had to send ships and men all over the word, to repel the attacks of the French on her scattered colonies and possessions. Clinton therefore was left with only an army of about ten thousand. And with this force he was expected to conquer the country which Howe had been unable to conquer with thirty thousand.

Clinton knew that his task was a hard one. He saw that the taking of Philadelphia had been a mistake, and that from a military point of view it was worthless. So he decided at once to abandon Philadelphia, and take his army back to New York. And on the morning of the 18th of June the British marched out. A few days later Congress returned, and the city settled back to its quiet old life once more.

It was no easy task for Clinton to cross New Jersey in grilling summer weather, with a small force, an enormous baggage train, and Washington hanging threateningly about is path, harassing him at every step. That he did accomplish it brought him no little renown as a soldier.

For some time, following the advice of his officers, Washington did not make a general attack on the British. But near the town of Monmouth he saw his chance, and determined to give battle.

General Lee had by this time been exchanged, and was now again with Washington's army as second in command, and for this battle Washington gave him command of an advance party of six thousand men. With him were Anthony Wayne and Lafayette.

On the morning of the battle Lee's division was in a very good position. It seemed as if the British might be surrounded with ease, but when Wayne and Lafayette were about to attack Lee stopped them.

"You do not know British soldiers," he said to Lafayette. "We are certain to be driven back. We must be cautious."

"That may be so, General," replied Lafayette, "but British soldiers have been beaten, and may be so again. At any rate, I should like to try."

But for answer, Lee ordered his men to retreat.

At this Lafayette was both angry and astonished, and he hurriedly sent a message to Washington, telling him that his presence was urgently needed.

The soldiers did not in the least know from what they were retreating, and they soon fell into disorder. Then suddenly Washington appeared among them. He was white to the lips with wrath.

"I desire to know, " he said, in a terrible voice, turning to Lee, "I desire to know, sir, what is the reason—whence arises this disorder and confusion?"

Lee trembled before the awful anger of his chief. He tried to make excuses. Then Washington's fury knew no bounds. He poured forth a torrent of wrath upon Lee till, as one of his officers who heard him said, "the very leaves shook on the trees." Then halting the retreating troops, he formed them for battle once more. Later in the day meeting Lee he sent him to the rear.

Soon the battle was raging fiercely. Some of the hottest fighting took place round the American artillery, which was commanded by General Knox. The guns were doing deadly work, yet moving about coolly amidst the din and smoke of battle, there might be seen a saucy young Irish girl, with a mop of red hair, a freckled face, and flashing eyes. She was the wife of one of the gunners, and so devoted was she to her husband that she followed him even to battle, helping him constantly with his gun. His comrades looked upon her almost as one of the regiment, and called her Captain Molly, and she wore an artilleryman's coat over her short red skirt, so that she might look like a soldier.

Captain Molly was returning from a spring nearby with a bucket full of water, when her husband, who was just about to fire, was killed by a shot from the enemy. The officer in command, having no one to take his place, ordered the gun to be removed.

Molly saw her husband fall, heard the command given, and she dropped her bucket and sprang to the gun.

"Bedad no," she cried. "I'll fire the gun myself, and avenge my man's death."

It was not the first time that Molly had fired a gun. She was with her husband at Fort Clinton, when it was taken by the British. As the enemy scaled the walls the Americans retreated. Her husband dropped his lighted match and fled with the rest. But Captain Molly was in no such haste. She picked up the match, fired the gun, and then ran after the others. Hers was the last gun fired on the American side that day.

Now all the long day of Monmouth she kept her gun in action, firing so skillfully and bravely, that all around were filled with admiration, and news of her deeds was carried through the army. Even Washington heard of them.

218

Next day he ordered her to be brought to him, and there and then he made her a sergeant, and recommended her for an officer's pension for life. But now that her husband was dead Molly's heart was no longer with the army. Soon after the battle of Monmouth she left it, and a few years later she died.

All through the long summer day of pitiless heat the battle raged. Again and again the British charged. Again and again they were thrown back, and at length were driven across a ravine. Here Washington would have followed, but the sun went down, and darkness put an end to the fight.

Washington, however, was determined to renew the battle next day, and that night the army slept on the field. He himself slept under a tree, sharing a cloak with Lafayette. But the battle was never renewed, for during the night Clinton marched quietly away. When day dawned he was already too far off to pursue, and at length he got safely into New York.

This was the last great battle to be fought in the northern states, and a few weeks later Washington took up his quarters on White Plains. There for nearly three years he stayed, guarding the great waterway of the Hudson, and preventing the British from making any further advance in the north.

Chapter 62 - The Story of a Great Crime

For his strange conduct at the battle of Monmouth General Lee was court-martialled, and deprived of his command for one year. Before the year was out, however, he quarreled with Congress, and was expelled from the army altogether. So his soldiering days were done, and he retired to his farm in Virginia. He was still looked upon as a patriot, even if an incompetent soldier. But many years after his death some letters that he had written to Howe were found. These proved him to have been a traitor to the American cause. For in them he gave the British commander advice as to how the Americans cold best be conquered.

Thus his strange conduct at the battle of Monmouth was explained. He had always given his voice against attacking the British on their way to New York. And doubtless he thought that if Washington had been defeated, he could have proved that it was because his advice had not been followed. If in consequence Washington's command had been taken from him, he would have been made commander-in-chief and cold have easily arranged terms of peace with the British.

But his plans miscarried. He lived to see American victorious, but died before peace was signed.

Lee was a traitor. But he had never been a real American. He had taken the American side merely for his own glory, and had never done anything for it worthy of record. But now a true American, one who had fought brilliantly and gallantly for this country, turned traitor, and blackened his fair name, blotting out his brave deeds for all time.

When the Americans took possession of Philadelphia again Benedict Arnold was still too crippled by his wound to be able for active service. So the command of Philadelphia was given to him.

There he soon got into trouble. He began to live extravagantly, and grew short of money. He quarreled with the state government, and with Congress, was accused of inviting loyalists to his house, of getting money by dishonest acts, and of being in many ways untrue to his duty. He also married a beautiful young loyalist lady, and that was another offence.

Arnold was arrogant and sensitive. He grew restive under all these accusations, and demanded an enquiry. His demand was granted, and a court-martial, although acquitting him of everything except imprudence, sentenced him to be reprimanded by the Commander-in-chief.

Washington loved his high-spirited, gallant officer, and his reprimand was so gentle and kind that it seemed more like praise than blame. But even Washington's gracious words chafed Arnold's proud spirit. He was hurt and angry. He had deserved well of his country, and he was reprimanded. He had fought gallantly, and had been passed over for others. He had been twice wounded in his country's service, and he was rewarded by jealousy, caviling, and a court-martial.

Soon these feelings of bitterness turned to thoughts of treachery, when exactly is not known. But turn they did, and Arnold began in secret to write letters to General Clinton, the British commander-in-chief.

In the summer of 1780, his wound still making him unfit for active service, Arnold was given command of the fortress of West Point, which guarded the approaches to the Hudson Valley. This fortress he agreed to betray into the hands of the enemy, and thus give them command of that valley for which Burgoyne had made such a gallant and hopeless fight. For a long time Arnold carried on a secret correspondence with Major André, a British officer, and at length a meeting between them was arranged. One September night Arnold waited until all was still and dark in the fort. Then stealthily he crept forth and reached in safety a clump of trees on the bank of the Hudson just beyond the American lines. Here he lay waiting.

Soon through the darkness the British warship, the Vulture, crept up the river. Presently Arnold heard the soft splash of oars, and in a few minutes Major André stepped ashore.

For hours the two conspirators talked until at length all details of the plot were settled. But day had dawned before Arnold returned to West Point, and André set out to regain the Vulture, with plans of the fort, and all other particulars hidden in his boots. By this time, however, the batteries on shore had begun to fire upon the ship, and André, finding it impossible to get on board, decided to go back to New York by land.

It was a dangerous journey, but for a little while he crept on unseen. Then suddenly his way was barred by three Americans, and he found himself a prisoner.

"Have you any letters?" asked his captors.

"No," he answered.

They were not satisfied with his answer, and began to search him. But finding nothing they were just about to let him go when one of them said, "I'm not satisfied, boys. His boots must come off."

220

André made every kind of excuse to prevent them taking off his boots. They were hard to pull off, he said, and it would take a long time. He was already late, so he begged them not to hinder him more. But the more unwilling he was to take off his boots, the more determined were his captors that they should come off.

So they forced him to sit down, his boots were pulled off, and the papers discovered.

Only one of the three Americans could read. He seized the papers and glanced hastily over them.

"By heaven," he cried, "he is a spy!"

It was in vain that André now begged to be set free. First he tried persuasion, and when that failed he tried bribery. But his captors would not listen, and marched him off to headquarters.

Arnold was just about to sit down to breakfast, with some other officers as his guests, Washington being expected every minute to join them, when a letter was handed to him, telling him that a spy had been captured. It was an awful moment for Arnold. If André was captured then all too surely his own treachery was known. He could not stay to face the disgrace. But he made no sign. He calmly folded the letter, and put it in his pocket. Then saying that he had been suddenly called to the fort, he begged his guests to excuse him, and went out, and mounting the horse of the messenger who had brought the letter, he sped away, never staying his flight until he was safe aboard the Vulture.

Very soon after Arnold had escaped Washington arrived. And when the traitorous papers which had been found in André's possession were placed in his hands he was overcome with grief.

"Arnold is a traitor, and has fled to the British," he said. "Whom can we trust now?"

As he spoke the tears ran down his cheeks, bitter tears rung from his noble soul at the thought of this "one more devil's-triumph and sorrow for angels."

The chief sinner had escaped. But he had left his fellow conspirator to pay his debt. For a spy could expect no mercy. André was young, brave, and gay. He had such winning ways with him that even his captors came to love him, and they grieved that such a gay young life must be brought to a sudden and dreadful end. His many friends did their best to save him. But their efforts were all in vain. Nothing could alter the fact that he was a spy caught in the act, and the punishment was death.

So one morning André was led out to die. He begged to shot as a soldier, and not hanged like a felon. But even that was denied him. Calm and brave to the end he met his death.

When Arnold's treachery was known a cry of rage rang through the country. Yet in spite of his foul deed people could not quite forget how nobly he had fought. "Hang him," they cried, "but cut off the leg that was wounded at Saratoga first!"

Arnold, however, was beyond their vengeance, safe in the British lines. There he at once received a commission, and turned his sword against his own country.

221

Thus a brave man cast his valour in the dust, and made his name a scorn and a by-word. But who shall say that the men who belittled his deeds, and followed him with jealousy and carping, were wholly blameless?

Chapter 63 - A Turning Point in the World's History

After nearly four years' fighting the British had utterly failed to subdue the rebel colonies. They had lost one whole army, had poured out treasures of blood and money, and all they had in return was New York and the coast town of Newport. Besides this they were at war with half Europe. For in 1779 Spain declared war against Britain, more indeed from anger against the British than from any love of the Americans. The following year Holland also declared war against Britain, who thus found herself surrounded by foes.

Still, in spite of all, the British stuck doggedly to their task of conquering the Americans. But as Pitt had told them again and again, it was an impossible task. At length, having failed to make any impression in the north they decided to change the seat of war and attack the weaker colonies in the south.

Here for a time they were more successful. Georgia was overrun, then South Carolina, and Charleston, which had made such a brave defence at the beginning of the war, surrendered to the British, with all its stores of food and ammunition.

Things were going badly for the patriots in the south, and Gates, who was still looked upon as a hero, because Burgoyne had surrendered to him, was sent to take command. Now he had a chance to prove of what stuff he was made. He proved it by being utterly defeated at the battle of Camden.

This defeat was a bitter blow. Never since before the battle of Trenton had the patriot cause seemed so much in danger. But the dark days passed, and once more the Americans began to win instead of lose battles. South Carolina was re-conquered, and Cornwallis, who was commander-in-chief of the British army in the south, retired into Virginia, and occupied Yorktown.

Just at this time Washington learned that a French fleet was sailing for Chesapeake Bay, and he determined to make a grand French-American attack on the British in the south. He made his plans very secretly, and leaving General Heath with four thousand men to guard the Hudson, he marched southwards, moving with such quickness that he had reached the Delaware before Clinton in New York knew what he was about. His army now consisted of two thousand Americans, and four thousand French, and this was the only time throughout the war that French and Americans marched together.

On the 6th of October the siege of Yorktown began. It was soon seen that its defenses were of no use against the seventy heavy siege guns of the allied army, and the surrender of Cornwallis was only a matter of time - for he was caught in a trap, just as Burgoyne had been. He could not escape to the south, for Lafayette barred the way to the Carolinas. He could not escape by sea, for the French and British fleets had fought a battle at the entrance of Chesapeake Bay, in which the British ships had been so badly damaged that they were obliged to sail to New York to refit. He could not escape to the north or the east, for Washington's army shut him in.

Still for a few days the British made a gallant stand. But their ammunition was running short, their defenses were crumbling to bits, and on the 19th of October, almost four years to a day after Burgoyne's surrender to Gates, Cornwallis surrendered to Washington.

Two days later the British soldiers marched out with flags furled, while the bands played a tune called "The World Turned Upside Down." To them indeed the world must have seemed turned upside down, for the all-conquering British had been conquered at last, and that by a nation of farmers unskilled in war. Yet they may have found some comfort in the thought that after all they had been beaten by their equals, by men of their own race.

On either side there was the same grit and endurance, the same love of fair play. But added to that the Americans had fought for a great cause. Their hearts were in it, as the hearts of the British had never been. This was their great advantage. This nerved their arm.

For two years after this Clinton still held New York, but there was no more fighting between the regular armies, and the surrender of Cornwallis may be said to have ended the war. When Lord North heard the news he was distracted with grief. He dashed wildly up and down the room, waving his arms and crying over and over again, "O God, it is all over, it is all over."

As for King George, he would not admit that it was all over, and he swore he would rather give up his crown than acknowledge the States to be free. But at length he, too, had to give way, and the treaty of peace was signed in Paris in November, 1782. This Peace, however, was only a first step, for Europe was still at war, and it was difficult to settle matters. But in September of the following year the real peace was signed, and the United States were acknowledged to be free. By this treaty Florida was given back to Spain, the Mississippi was made the western boundary, and the Great Lakes the northern boundary of the United States.

Thus a new great power came into being, and as an English historian has said, "the world had reached one of the turning points of its history."

Part VII STORIES OF THE UNITED STATES UNDER THE CONSTITUTION

Chapter 64 - Washington First In War, First In Peace

After the peace was signed in September, 1783, all the British soldiers left America, and Washington felt that his work was done. So he resolved to give up his post as commander-in-chief, and go back to his pleasant Virginian home.

He was glad at the thought of going back to the home he loved, yet sad at the thought of saying farewell to his officers. For eight years they had worked for him faithfully, together they had faced dark days, together they had been through deep waters. And now that victory was won, Washington's heart was filled with love and gratitude.

It was at Faunces's Tavern in New York that Washington met his officers for the last time. When he came into the long, low room where they were all gathered, he was so moved that he could not speak. Silently he went to the table and filled a glass with wine. Raising it, he turned to the men who stood as silently about him, and with an effort, commanding his voice he spoke.

"With a heart full of love and gratitude," he said, "I now take leave of you, most devoutly wishing that your latter days may be as prosperous and happy as your former ones have been glorious and honourable."

Then having drunk to the toast he set the glass down.

"I cannot come to each of you to take my leave," he said brokenly, "but shall be obliged if each of you will come and take me by the hand."

The General who was nearest to Washington then turned to him and silently grasped his hand.

With tears in his eyes, Washington put his arms about him and kissed him. And thus one after the other his officers silently said good-bye, no one of them trusting himself to speak.

Then still in silence, they followed him to the boat which was to carry him on the first part of his way to Annapolis where Congress was assembled, and where he was to lay down his sword.

His journey was like a royal progress. In every town and village through which he passed the people gathered to cheer and bless him. So he reached Annapolis. There before Congress he resigned his commission. Then with a sigh of relief, a simple citizen once more, he mounted his horse and rode homewards.

But now the colonies which had wrung themselves free from the rule of Britain were not altogether happy. They called themselves the United States, but there was little union. Before the Revolution there had been much jealousy between the various states. For a time, indeed, in the heat of the struggle, they had forgotten these differences. But now that the struggle was over, and peace had come, these jealousies appeared again. Each state had its own government, its own taxes, its own money. So there was great confusion. But no state wanted to give up any of its privileges, and it seemed hopeless to institute one Central Government, for each state thought only of itself, and each one was afraid of giving Congress too much power lest it should usurp the power of the state government.

The states quarreled with each other about their boundaries, some of them made absurd claims to vast territory on the strength of their royal charters, quite forgetting that these charters were now done away with. There were riots everywhere, indeed, never was the State in such danger of shipwreck as now at its very beginning.

Washington from his quiet retreat at first watched the struggle anxiously, but not despairingly. "Everything will come right, at last," he said. "My only fear is that we shall lose a little reputation first."

As time went on, however, he grew more anxious. "I think we have opposed Great Britain," he said, "and have arrived at the present state of peace and independency, to very little purpose, if we cannot conquer our own prejudices."

But Washington had no real need to fear. The men who had fought for their freedom proved themselves worthy of it, and in May, 1787, a meeting of all the states was called at Philadelphia.

Of this Convention, as it was called, Washington was chosen President. It was no easy post, nor was the business for which the members of the Convention were called together a simple business. They had, indeed, a very great task to perform, the task of forming a new constitution or mode of government, which all states would accept. It was not easy to please every one, and also do thoroughly good work. So for four months the Convention sat, discussing this and that, listening now to one side, now to another, weighing, judging and deciding.

But at length the thing was done. In the same hall where the Declaration of Independence had been signed the Constitution had been framed. Then the delegates went home and a copy of the Constitution was sent to each state.

It had been agreed that nine states must accept the Constitution before it could become law. The question now was whether nine would accept it or not. Many hesitated a long time. For it seemed to them that this new Constitution which was going to unite all the states into one was going also to give far too much power into the hands of a few people. It would be a case of tyranny over again, many feared. And, having suffered so much to free themselves from one tyranny, they were not ready to place themselves under a second.

But others at once saw the need of a strong central government and accepted the new Constitution whole-heartedly and almost at once. Delaware had the honour of coming first early in December, 1787, but before the month was gone two more states, Pennsylvania and New Jersey, followed the good example. A week or so later came Georgia and then Connecticut. After a good deal of hesitation Massachusetts also came into line; then Maryland and South Carolina.

Only one more state was now needed to make the union safe. Would that one state come in, the friends of union asked themselves, and they worked their hardest to make people think as they did.

At length their efforts were rewarded and New Hampshire made the ninth, and just four days later the great State of Virginia also came in. New York soon followed and only North Carolina and Rhode Island remained out of the Union. But in time they, too, came in, Rhode Island last of all, and not for fully a year after the first President had been chosen, and the government organised.

The new government required that there should be a Congress to look after the affairs of the nation, with two houses, something after the fashion of the British Parliament. It also required that there should be a President at the head of everything.

There was little doubt as to who should fill that place. George Washington, the man who had led the army to victory, was the man chosen to be first President of the United States.

Other people were indeed voted for, but Washington had more than twice as many votes as John Adams, who came next to him. The others were simply nowhere. So Washington was made President and Adams vice-president.

But Washington had no wish to be President. He was too old, he said (he was only fifty-seven) and besides he was not even a statesman but a soldier. The people, however, would not listen to him. "We cannot do without you," they said. "There is no use framing a new government if the best man is to be left out of it."

So to the entreaties of his friends Washington yielded. But it was with a heavy heart, for he greatly doubted his own powers.

"In confidence I tell you," he wrote to an old friend, "that my movement to the chair of government will be accompanied by feelings not unlike those of a culprit who is going to the place of his execution."

But whatever he felt, his journey to New York was not like that of a criminal, but rather like that of a king. From far and near the people crowded to see him pass. They raised triumphal arches, they scattered flowers at his feet, they sang chants and hymns in his honour. From first to last it was one long triumph. When he reached New York bells rang and cannon boomed, the streets were gay with flags, and crowded with people, and as he passed along cheer upon cheer thundered and echoed over the city.

Next day, the 30th of April, 1789, Washington took his place as President of the United States.

At nine o'clock in the morning the churches were thronged with people praying for the welfare of their President. By twelve these same people were all crowding to the Federal Hall eager to be present at the great ceremony. Soon the space in front of the hall was one closely packed mass of people; every window and balcony was crowded also, and people were even to be seen on the roofs.

A little after noon Washington reached the hall, and as he stepped out on to the balcony a cheer of welcome burst from the gathered thousands. Again and again they cheered, again and again Washington bowed in acknowledgement. He was greatly touched; tears stood in his eyes, and at length utterly overcome he sat down.

Suddenly a deep hush fell upon the swaying crowd and after a slight pause Washington rose again. Then in the grave silence the voice of Robert R. Livingston, the Chancellor of New York, could clearly be heard.

"Do you," he asked, "solemnly swear that you will faithfully execute the office of President of the United States, and will to the best of your ability preserve, protect and defend the Constitution of the United States?"

With his hand upon the Bible which the Secretary of the Senate held beside him Washington replied.

"I do solemnly swear," he said, "that I will faithfully execute the office of President of the United States, and will, to the best of my ability, preserve, protect and defend the Constitution of the United States."

Then bowing his head he kissed the Bible help before him. "So help me God," he murmured.

The Chancellor then stepped forward and in a ringing voice he shouted, "Long live George Washington, President of the United States."

A great answering shout went up from the people, the flag was broken to the breeze, and cannon boomed forth a salute to the first President of the United States.

Again and again Washington bowed his thanks to the cheering people. Then, shaken with emotion, the shouts still sounding in his ears, he turned away and entered the hall to read his address.

Thus the Story of the United States under the Constitution was begun.

Washington was a thorough aristocrat and now that he had been chosen head of the State he felt that he must surround himself with a certain amount of ceremony. Now he no longer walked or rode abroad, but drove about in a fine coach drawn by six white horses. He no longer went to see people, but they came to him on certain days and at appointed times. When he held receptions he dressed himself splendidly in black velvet with silk stockings. He wore a jeweled sword at his side and buckles both at the knee and on his shoes. Instead of shaking hands with people he merely bowed.

All this ceremony and state came easily to Washington. Even as a simple Virginian gentleman he had been used to a certain amount of it. For in those days plain gentleman folk were much more ceremonious than they are today. Besides, kings always surrounded themselves with a great deal of state, and it seemed to Washington that a ruler must do so to keep up the high dignity of his office.

The first President's post was no easy one. The whole machinery of government had to be invented and set going, and first and foremost the money matters had to be set straight.

They were in a great muddle. The war had cost a great deal, so the new government began in debt and nearly every separate state was also in debt. But a clever man named Alexander Hamilton took hold of the money matters and soon put them right.

Among other things he said that the government must take over the war debts of all the states. At once the states made an outcry. "If we allow the government to pay our debts," they said, "we become slaves to the government. If we give up control of our own money matters the government will have too much power over us. We put too much power in the hands of a few." Then they talked of tyranny.

You see many of the people of the United States rightly or wrongly had come to look upon any government as certain to be tyrannous. However, Hamilton got his way in the end. The money matters of the nation were settled satisfactorily, and the separate states bound more securely together.

And now another state joined the union, that of Vermont. Vermont, as you can see if you look on the map, lies between New Hampshire and New York, and there had been bitter disputes between the two over the land which both claimed. In 1765, however, King George III had decided that the land belonged to New York, and must be under the rule of that colony. The people, however, rebelled. And when in 1777 the Governor of New York threatened to drive them all into the Green Mountains if they did not yield peaceably they raised an army of volunteers to whom they gave the name of Green Mountain Boys. They took this name from the word Vermont which meant Green Mountain.

The Green Mountain Boys fought the New York Governor and declared Vermont a separate colony. Now these old quarrels were forgotten. New York no longer claimed the land, and Vermont joined the Union as the fourteenth state.

In the following year another state was added to the Union. This was the State of Kentucky. It was, like several other states, an offshoot of Virginia, and carved out of the territory which Virginia claimed by right of her old charter which gave her all the land between the Atlantic and the Pacific.

Among the early settlers of Kentucky was a famous hunter named Daniel Boone. He was a gentle, kindly man who loved the forest and the loneliness of the wilderness. All the lore of the forest was his, he knew the haunts and habits of every living thing that moved within the woods. He could imitate the gobble of the turkey, or the chatter of a squirrel, and follow a trail better than any Indian. It was with no idea of helping to found a state, but rather from a wish to get far from the haunts of his fellowmen that he moved away into the beautiful wilds of Kentucky.

In those days Kentucky was not inhabited by any tribe of Indians, but it was their hunting ground, and they were very angry when they saw white men come to settle there and spoil their hunting. So Boone had many fierce fights with Indians, and was more than once taken prisoner by them.

Many other settlers followed Boone, and after the Revolution many Virginians moved to Kentucky. These people soon became clamorous for separation from Virginia, and at last in 1792 Kentucky was received into the Union as a separate state.

And now the question of a suitable capital for the United States began to be thought of. The first Congress had met at New York, but it only remained there a short time. Then the seat of government was moved to Philadelphia. Philadelphia, however, was not considered a good place. So it was decided to build a new capital. The Northern States wanted it in the north, the Southern States wanted it in the south, but finally it was agreed upon to have it on the Potomac River almost in the middle, Virginia and Maryland offering the territory. Splendid plans were made, and the building was begun, but for the next ten years Philadelphia still remained the seat of government.

So four busy years went past, and the time of Washington's presidency drew to an end. He rejoiced to think that after his hard work for his country he could now go back to his peaceful home at Mount Vernon, and be at rest. But his friends would not let him go. The government of the United States was not yet firmly on its feet. Only he could make it firm, they said. The people loved him, and would be guided by him when they would not follow any one else, therefore he must stay.

At length Washington yielded to the entreaties of his friends and allowed himself to be elected President a second time.

And now there arose difficulties between the United States and their old friends,

228

the French. For, while the Americans had been hammering away at their Constitution, and making a new nation out of raw material, the French had risen against the tyranny of their king, and had declared France a Republic. And when many of the European countries joined together to fight France, and force them to take back their king, the French people looked to the sister Republic across the Atlantic for help. They had helped the Americans in their struggle, surely now the Americans would help them. But the French went too far. They seemed to lose all sense of right and wrong, they put hundreds of people to death without cause and drowned France in blood.

So, many people who had wished them well at the beginning, turned from them, and although many people in America were ready to fight for the French, Washington determined to keep peace. He was not ungrateful to the French for their help in the American Revolution. But he felt that their wild orgy of blood was wrong, and he saw too, that America was too young a nation to plunge again into war. So he proclaimed the United States to be neutral, that is, that they would take part on neither side in the European War.

When the French heard that America refused to help them, they were greatly hurt. But worse was yet to follow, for Washington, besides refusing to fight for the French, made a treaty with the British, with whom the French were at war.

The War of Independence had left some bitterness between the old country and the new. And as time went on that bitterness increased rather than lessened. The United States felt that Britain hardly treated them with the respect due to an independent nation, and indeed some of Britain's actions were fairly high handed.

During the war a great many Negroes had been carried off into Canada, and Britain would not pay for them. The boundaries between the United States and Canada were still in dispute. Britain made no effort to settle them, but kept possession of such forts as Oswego, Detroit, Niagara, and others. Then, because they were at war with France, the British interfered with, and almost ruined, American trade with the French West Indies. And lastly, what seemed to Americans the worst insult of all, they claimed the right of search. That is, they claimed the right of searching neutral vessels for British seamen and of taking them by force to serve in the British navy. In those early days it was difficult to distinguish an Englishmen from an American by his speech, and thus Americans were often seized and made to serve in the British navy. There were other grievances, but these were chief.

Taken altogether they made the Americans so angry that Washington feared another war, for which he knew the nation was not ready. He decided therefore to make a bid for peace, and sent John Jay to London to arrange matters between the two countries.

Jay did not find British statesmen in any yielding mood, and so the treaty which he arranged, and which goes by his name, was not altogether favourable to the Americans. There was, for instance, nothing in the treaty about paying for the slaves, nor about the right of search. But seeing that he could get no better terms Jay accepted those offered him. Undoubtedly America asked more than Britain

229

could well give. Equally undoubtedly Britain gave less than America had a right to expect.

Washington was not satisfied with the treaty, but he felt that Jay had done his best. He felt, too, that it was either the treaty or war. So rather than have war he signed it.

When, however, the terms of it became known a cry of rage rang through the country. Those who had supported it were hooted at and stoned in the streets, John Jay was burned in effigy, the treaty itself was publicly burned. Even Washington, beloved as he was, did not escape. Taunts and insults were flung at him. He was called a tyrant and a traitor, but in spite of all the opposition Washington stood firm. He held to the treaty, and peace with the old country was kept.

The storm was bitter while it lasted, but at length it died down and the men who had flung insults at Washington saw in time that he had been right. He had kept peace; and as a young nation America stood in need of peace more than anything else.

Washington's second term of office now came to an end. He was utterly weary of public life, and he resolutely refused to stand for President again. It was nearly forty years, now, since he had first begun to work for his country. He felt that his work was done, and all he wanted now was to spend his last days quietly in his beloved home, Mount Vernon.

This time Washington had his way and laid down his office. Then, as second President, the people chose John Adams, who had already been Vice-President.

Chapter 65 - Adams - How He Kept Peace with France

The crowd which gathered to see John Adams take the oath was almost as great as that which had gathered when Washington had first been made President.

But it was upon the old and not upon the new President that all eyes were turned. And when the ceremony was over the people seemed still loath to part from their beloved President, and a great crowd followed him in silence to his home. At the door, before entering, he turned, and with tears running down his cheeks he signed a last farewell to his people. So for a long silent moment he stood upon the doorstep, then he entered the house, and as the door closed upon him a great sob broke from the crowd.

Thus the people took a last farewell of their great and beloved leader.

Almost as soon as John Adams became President in 1797 he found himself plunged into trouble with France. For the Jay Treaty had made the French people very angry. They refused to receive Charles C. Pinckney, who was sent as ambassador, and he had to flee to Holland for refuge. The Americans were very angry at this treatment of their minister and talked of war. But Adams was anxious to keep peace. So he sent two more ambassadors to France and with them Pinckney returned also.

But the French received the three ambassadors with little more courtesy than they had received the one.

230

They now began to demand all sorts of things from the United States; they demanded, among other things, that the Americans should pay them a large sum of money as a bribe. They demanded a large loan also. If they refused, why, then let the Americans beware. With these demands and threats the ambassadors were obliged to leave France. But they were not going to be bullied. So to the French threats they replied by building ships, raising an army, and buying cannon. Everywhere, too, patriotic songs were written and sung, one of them being, "Hail Columbia," by Joseph Hopkinson.

Once more George Washington was asked to become commander-in-chief in 1798, and with a heavy heart he consented. He did not want to leave his quiet home for the horrors and clamour of the battlefield. Still less did he want to fight against his old friends. But at his country's call he rose.

The French, however, were not really anxious to fight the United States. They merely wanted to get money from them, and when they saw the spirit of the nation, they changed their tune and did everything they could to keep peace between the two countries. But the Americans were now so angry with the French that they were determined to fight them. "War with France!" was everywhere the cry.

John Adams, however, like Washington, was determined if possible to keep peace. So without asking any one's advice he sent another friendly mission to France, and the quarrel was quietly settled. Thus peace was kept, but the people were angry with Adams. They declared that he had all sorts of mean reasons for his action. He was sure he had done right. "When I am dead," he said, "write on my tomb, 'Here lies John Adams, who took upon himself the responsibility of peace with France.'" He felt that he could have no better epitaph.

While Adams was President, in 1796, another state was added to the Union. This was Tennessee, which was an offshoot from North Carolina.

For several years Tennessee passed through troublous times. For a few years, indeed, the state was set up as a separate republic, under the name of Franklin. This name was given to it in honour of Benjamin Franklin, the great statesman. But some of the people wanted it called Frankland or Freeland so it was known by both names.

The inhabitants of Franklin now chose a Governor, instituted a Senate and a House of Commons, and made laws for themselves. But very soon this government collapsed, and after a few more troublous years the state entered the Union under the name of Tennessee.

All this time men had been busy building the new capital and toward the end of 1800 the government was removed there. Washington, the great Father of his Country, had just died and it was determined to call the new city by his name.

But when the government arrived at Washington they found the city little more than a wilderness. Only a part of the Capitol was built, and around it there was nothing but desolation. There were neither streets, nor shops, neither business nor society.

The President's house was set down in the midst of an uncultivated field, and

231

beyond that and the unfinished Capitol there were but a few scattered houses and one hotel. Many people were disgusted with the new capital, and it was given all sorts of names, such as the "Capital of Miserable Huts," "The Wilderness City," or the "Mudhole." Every now and again one or other of the members of Congress would suggest that the capital should be removed elsewhere, but there were always some determined to stay. And at length by slow degrees the city grew into one of the beautiful capitals of the world.

Chapter 66 - Jefferson - How the Territory of the United States was Doubled

Adams was an honest and patriotic man, but he never won the love of the people as Washington had done. And when in 1801 his term of office came to an end he went back to his country home. There he spent the rest of his life as a simple citizen.

Jefferson first President inaugurated in Washington

Thomas Jefferson was the next President - the first to be inaugurated in the new capital. He had been Vice-President with Adams, and was already well known in politics. It was he who wrote the Declaration of Independence, and he was in every way one of the greatest statesmen of his time. He was a lanky, sweet-tempered, sandy coloured man. He wore badly fitting clothes, and hated ceremony of all kinds. He was quite determined not to have any fuss over his inauguration, so dressed as plainly as possible, he rode to the Capitol by himself, tied his horse to the palings and walked into the Senate Chamber alone, just like any ordinary man.

This lack of ceremony he kept up throughout all the time he was President. Indeed he sometimes overdid it and offended people. Once the British Minister was to be presented to him and went dressed in his grandest uniform. But to his disgust he found Jefferson in the very shabbiest of clothes, and slippers down at the heel. So the good gentleman went away feeling that the President of the United States had meant to insult not merely himself but the King he represented.

It was while Jefferson was President in 1803 that Ohio joined the Union as the seventeenth state. For a long time there had been a few squatters on the land. But it was only after the Revolution that it really began to be inhabited by white men.

In 1788 about fifty men led by Rufus Putnam, "the Father of Ohio," settled there. They founded a town and called it Marietta in honour of Maria Antoinette, the French Queen. Others followed, and soon villages were sprinkled all along the north bank of the Ohio River.

Then some years later Moses Cleaveland founded the town of Cleveland on the shores of Lake Erie. But all along the banks of the Ohio Indians lived. And they would not let the white men settle on their land without protest. So the new settlers were constantly harassed and in danger of their lives, and many murders were committed.

At length it was decided that this must cease. And as the Indians would listen to no argument General St. Clair with an army of eighteen hundred men marched against them. He did not know the country, and he had no guide. Late one evening in November he encamped in the woods. At dawn the next day he was awakened by the blood-curdling cry of the Indians. The men sprang to arms, but in the night the Indians had completely surrounded them, and the fight was hopeless. For four hours the slaughter lasted; then the white men fled, leaving half their number dead upon the field.

It was one of the worst defeats white men ever suffered at the hands of the Indians. The whole countryside was filled with the horror and the Redmen exulted in their victory. The President tried to reason with them, but they would not listen. The only thing that would satisfy them was that the white men should withdraw beyond the Ohio.

This the white men refused to do, and they sent another large force against the Indians. This time the force was under the command of General Wayne. In a great battle he utterly defeated the Indians. Afterwards he held a grand council with them. And they, knowing themselves defeated, swore peace forevermore with the white men, and acknowledged their right to the land beyond the Ohio.

This was the first great council that the Indians had ever held with the "thirteen fires" of the United States. They kept their treaty faithfully, and not one of the chiefs who swore peace to General Wayne ever again lifted the war hatchet against the Pale-faces.

And now that peace with the Indians was secure, many settlers flocked into the country, and in 1893 Ohio was received into the Union as the seventeenth state.

But the most interesting and important thing which happened during Jefferson's time of office was the Louisiana Purchase in 1803. By this a vast territory was added to the United States.

You remember that at the Peace of Paris after the British had conquered Canada, the French gave up to Spain all their claims to the great tract of land beyond the Mississippi called Louisiana. When France gave up that vast territory to Spain she was weak. But now again she was strong - far stronger than Spain - for the great soldier Napoleon Bonaparte had risen to power. He now looked with longing eyes on the lost province of Louisiana, and by a secret treaty he forced the King of Spain to give back Louisiana to France.

As soon as this treaty was made known there was great excitement in the United States. For if France planted colonies all along the Mississippi the Americans would be shut out from the West, they might even be shut off from the Mississippi, and unable to use it for trade. And to the states bordering upon it this would have been a great misfortune. For in days when there were few roads, and no railways, the Mississippi was the only trade route for the Western States.

Having weighed these matters seriously Jefferson determined if possible to buy new Orleans from the French, and thus make sure of a passage up and down the great river. And he sent James Monroe to Paris to arrange this.

A few months earlier nothing would have induced Napoleon to sell any part of Louisiana, for he dreamed of again founding a New France across the Atlantic. But now war threatened with Britain. He did not love the United States, but he

233

hated Britain. He would rather, he thought, crush Britain than found a New France. To crush Britain, however, he must have money, and the great idea came to him that he could make money out of Louisiana by selling it to the Americans. So he offered it to them for twenty million dollars.

The Americans, however, would not pay so much, and at length after some bargaining the price of fifteen million dollars was agreed upon, and the whole of Louisiana passed to the American Government, and the territory of the United States was made larger by more than a million square miles.

"We may live long," said Livingston, who with Monroe had carried the business through, "we may live long, but this is the noblest work of our lives. It will change vast solitudes into smiling country."

Three greatest events in the History of the United States

And indeed, after the Revolution, and the great Civil War which was to come later, the Louisiana Purchase is the greatest event in American History.

As to Napoleon, he was well pleased with his bargain. For besides getting money to help him in his wars he believed that he had made the United States powerful enough to fight and conquer Britain. And as he hated Britain the idea pleased him. "This increase of territory,' he said, "assures the power of the United States for all time. And I have given England a rival which sooner or later will abase her pride."

As a matter of fact, however, Napoleon had really no right to sell Louisiana. For in his treaty with Spain he had promised not to yield it to any foreign government. And when the Spaniards knew what he had done they were very angry. But Napoleon did not care; he did as he liked.

The flag of Spain had been hauled down, and the flag of France run up with great ceremony. But not for long did the French flag float over New Orleans. In less than three weeks it was hauled down and with firing of cannon and ringing of bells the Stars and Stripes was hoisted.

Chapter 67 - Jefferson - How the Door Into the Far West was Opened

Very little was known of this vast territory which was thus added to the United States. For the most part it was pathless wilderness where no white man had ever set foot. Long before the Louisiana Purchase Jefferson had wanted to send out an exploring party into this unknown west. Now he was more anxious for it than ever. And at length he succeeded in getting an expedition sent out.

The leaders of this expedition were two young officers, Captain Merriwether Lewis and William Clark. From their names the expedition is usually known as the Lewis and Clark Expedition.

They made very careful preparations and in 1804 they set out with about twenty-seven men to explore the river Missouri.

Some years before this a United States Captain, Robert Grey, had discovered a great river in the west coast of America and called it the Columbia, after the name of his ship. And now what Lewis and Clark had set out to do was to reach that river from the east.

It is impossible to tell here of all their thrilling adventures, for they would fill a whole book. I can only give you the merest outline. But some day you will no doubt read the whole story as Lewis and Clark tell it themselves.

The expedition started from the mouth of the Missouri, and at first the explorers passed by the scattered farms and little villages where white men lived. But these were the farthest outposts of civilisation; soon they were left behind, and the little band of white men were in a land inhabited only by Redskins. The current was so swift and the wind so often in the wrong direction that sails were almost useless, and the boats were rowed, punted and towed upstream with a great deal of hard labour. Some of the travelers went in the boats, others rode or walked along the bank. These last did the hunting and kept the expedition supplied with meat.

One of the leaders always went with those on shore. For it was often difficult for the two parties to keep together. Sometimes the river wound about, and those on land could take a short cut, while at other times those on land had to make a wide circuit to avoid marshes or steep precipices. The river was full of fish, and the land swarmed with game. Antelopes, deer, black bear, turkeys, geese, ducks, in fact all sorts of birds and beasts were abundant. There were also great quantities of delicious wild grapes as well as plums, currants and other fruits; so the travelers had no lack of food.

They met many tribes of Indians and they nearly all seemed friendly, for both Lewis and Clark knew well how to treat Indians. When they came into their land they called the chiefs together to a council, and made them a speech telling them that the land was no longer Spanish but American. The Indians would pretend to be pleased at the change, but really they understood nothing about it. But they liked the medals and other trinkets which the white men gave them. And most of them were very anxious to have some of the "Great Father's Milk" by which they meant whiskey. But one tribe refused it.

"We marvel," they said, "that our brothers should give us drink which will make us fools. No man can be our friend who would lead us into such folly."

Until the end of October the expedition kept on, always following the course of the Missouri, north-west. But the weather now became very cold; ice began to form on the river, and the explorers determined to camp for the winter. Not far from what is now the town of Bismarck, North Dakota, they built themselves a little village of log huts and called it Fort Mandan, for the country belonged to the Mandan Indians.

Here they met both French and British fur traders, who in spite of the bitter weather came from Assiniboia, about a hundred and fifty miles north, to trade for furs with the Indians.

The weather was bitterly cold, but the men were fairly comfortable in their log huts, and they had plenty to do. They went upon hunting expeditions to get food, they built boats, and they set up a forge. This last greatly interested the Indians who brought their axes and kettles to be mended, and in return gave the white men grain. Soon the smith was the busiest man in the whole company, the

235

bellows particularly interesting the Redmen.

Indeed everything about the white strangers was so interesting to the Indians that they were nearly always in their huts. On Christmas Day the travelers only got rid of their inquisitive visitors by telling them that it was a great medicine day with the white people, when no strangers were allowed near them, and they must keep away.

The travelers stayed at Fort Mandan till the beginning of April; then the ice being melted on the river they set out again.

Game now became more than ever plentiful, and they had several encounters with huge grizzly bears. The Indians had told the explorers terrible stories about these bears. They themselves had such great respect for them that they never went out to hunt them without putting on their war paint, and making as great preparations as if they were going to fight some enemy tribe.

The white men too soon came to have a great respect for them. "I find," wrote Lewis, in his journal, "that the curiosity of our party is pretty well satisfied with respect to this animal. He has staggered the resolution of several of them."

Later on he added, "I must confess that I do not like the gentlemen, and had rather fight two Indians than one bear."

One day Lewis was on shore, and seeing a herd of buffalo shot one for supper. After it fell he stood looking at it, and forgot to load his rifle again. While standing thus he suddenly saw a large bear creeping towards him. Instantly he lifted his rifle, but remembered in a flash that it was not loaded. He had no time to load, so he thought the best thing he could do was to walk away as fast as he could.

It was in an open plain with not a bush or tree near; and as Lewis retreated the bear ran open-mouthed at full speed after him. Lewis took to his heels and fled. But the bear ran so fast that Lewis soon saw that it would be impossible to escape, for the bear was gaining fast upon him. Then suddenly it flashed across his mind that if he jumped into the river he might escape. So turning short he leaped into the water. Then facing about he pointed his halberd at the bear. Seeing this the bear suddenly stopped on the bank not twenty feet away. Then as if he were frightened he turned tail and ran away as fast as he had come.

Lewis was glad enough to escape so easily, and he made up his mind that never again would he allow his rifle to be unloaded even for a moment.

Other dangers, too, beset the travelers. One day Lewis and his companions were following the boats along the bluffs which rose high above the water's edge. The ground was so slippery that they could only with difficulty keep their feet. Once Lewis slipped and only saved himself by means of the pike which he carried from being hurled into the river a hundred feet below. He had just reached a spot where he could stand fairly safely when he heard a voice behind him cry out: "Good God! Captain, what shall I do?"

He turned instantly and saw that one of his men who had lost his foothold had slipped down to the very edge of the precipice and was now hanging half over it. One leg and arm were over, and with the other he clung frantically to the edge of

236

the cliff.

Lewis saw at once that the man was in great danger of falling and being dashed to pieces below. But he hid his fear.

"You are in no danger," he said in a calm voice. Then he told the man to take his knife out of his belt and dig a hole in the side of the cliff for his right foot. The man, steadied by his leader's calm voice, did as he was told and in a few minutes was able to drag himself up to the top of the cliff. Then on his hands and knees he crawled along till he was again in safety.

After two months the travelers reached the great falls of the Missouri River. Here they had to leave the water, and carry their boats overland until they arrived above the rapids. It was no easy matter and they were all by this time worn and weary. So they camped for a few days, and made a rough sort of cart on which to carry the boats. For they were too worn out to carry them on their shoulders. But the way was so rough that long before the end of the journey the cart broke down.

Then began a most painful march. The country was covered with prickly pear, and the thorns of it pierced the men's moccasins and wounded their feet. The sun was so hot that they had to rest every few minutes, and they were so tired that they fell asleep at every stopping place. Yet there were no grumblers, and in spite of the many hardships they went on cheerfully, and after ten days' hard work they were above the rapids.

They were now right among the Rocky Mountains. These they crossed, and after many more adventures, dangers and hardships at last - on the 8th of November - they arrived within sight of the Pacific.

"Great joy in the camp," wrote Lewis. "We are in view of the ocean, this great Pacific Ocean, which we have been so long anxious to see."

Having at length reached the Columbia River the travelers sailed down it to its mouth, and so reached the shores of the Pacific and the end of their journey.

They spent the winter on the Pacific coast and towards the end of March set out again on their homeward way. The return journey was almost as full of hardships and dangers as the outward one had been. But all were safely overcome and on the 20th of September the explorers arrived once more at St. Louis whence they had set out more than two years before.

Every one was delighted to see them back. They were also surprised, for the whole expedition had long ago been given up as lost. But far from being lost every man of them returned except one who had died not long after they had left St. Louis.

Since they set out, these bold adventurers had marched nine thousand miles over barren deserts, across snow-topped mountains, through wildernesses yet untrodden by the foot of any white man. They had passed among savage and unknown tribes, and kept peace with them. They had braved a thousand dangers, and had returned triumphant over them all. The great journey from sea to sea had been accomplished, and the door into the Far West opened.

Other travelers and explorers trod fast upon the heels of Lewis and Clark.

Hunters, and fur-traders, and settlers followed them, and bit by bit the West became known and peopled. But in the story of that growth the names of Merriwether Lewis and William Clark will always be first, for it was they who threw open the door into the Far West.

Chapter 68 - Jefferson - About An American Who Wanted to be a King

When Jefferson had been chosen President, another man named Aron Burr had run him very close. And, when the final choice fell on Jefferson, Aron Burr became Vice-President. He was much disappointed at not becoming President, and a few years later he tried to be elected Governor of New York. But again, someone else was chosen, and Burr was again very much disappointed, and he began to blame Alexander Hamilton, who for many years had been his constant rival, for all his failure. So he challenged Hamilton to fight a duel.

In those days, duels were still common, for people had not come to see that they were both wicked and foolish. Hamilton did not want to fight, but he knew people would call him coward if he did not. He was not brave enough to stand that. So he fought.

Early one July morning in 1804, the two men met. Burr took steady aim and fired, Hamilton, firing wildly into the air, fell forward dying.

Hamilton had been selfish and autocratic, and many people disliked him. Now when they heard of his death, they forgot that. They only remembered how much the nation owed to the man who had put their money matters right. The whole country rose in anger against Burr, and called him a murderer.

Seeing the outcry against him becoming so great, Burr fled to Philadelphia. But even there, people looked at him askance, so he decided to go for a tour in the West.

His travels took him to Marietta, Ohio, the little town which had been founded by Rufus Putnam; then to Cincinnati and Louisville, and so southward till he reached New Orleans.

There he began to have secret meetings with all the chief men, for Burr was now full of a great idea.

He had failed to get into power in the United States, and his failure had made him bitter. He had killed the man who he thought was his greatest enemy. And that, instead of helping him, had caused the people to cast him out altogether. Now he determined to own an empire for himself, and have nothing more to do with the United States. He had in fact made up his mind to divide the West from the East, and make himself Emperor of the West under the title of Aron I. The Empire was to be kept in the family, and his beautiful daughter Theodosia was to be Queen after him; but it was gravely debated whether her husband could take the title of King or not.

The mad scheme grew daily. Burr's plan was suddenly to seize both President and Vice-President. Then having the heads of government in his power he would next lay hands on the public money and the navy. He would take what ships he wanted, burn the rest, and, sailing to New Orleans, he would proclaim his empire.

238

But Burr dare not let every one know his real intentions, and so he gave out that he meant to lead an expedition against Mexico.

As time went on hundreds of people knew of his conspiracy. It was talked of everywhere. But Jefferson paid no heed. He did not believe that Burr meant any treason against the Union. So the conspirators went on building boats, and arming men, undisturbed.

But things did not go so smoothly as Burr had hoped. He had expected to get help from Britain, and he got none. He had expected help from Spain, and he got none. Still he went on with his scheming. He had even written out his Declaration of Independence it was said, when suddenly the end came. One of Burr's friends betrayed him and at length President Jefferson woke up to what was going on.

At once he issued a proclamation declaring that a conspiracy against Spain was being carried on, and commanding all officers of the United States to seize the persons engaged in the plot. No name was mentioned in the proclamation, but Burr knew his plot was discovered. Once more he had failed; and he fled. He changed clothes with a boatman on the Mississippi, and vanished into the forest.

For a month no one knew where he was, for beneath the battered white felt and homespun clothes of a river boatman no one recognised the dapper politician.

Meanwhile Burr was slowly making his way east hoping to reach the coast, and get away in some ship. He had still many friends, and one night he stopped at a cottage to ask his way to the house of one of these friends. In the cottage were two young men. One of them, named Perkins, looked keenly at the stranger. It seemed to him that his face and clothes were not in keeping, and his boots looked to smart for the rest of his get up.

After the stranger had gone he still thought about it. Then suddenly he said, "That was Aron Burr. Let us go after him and arrest him."

The other man, however, laughed at him, and refused to stir. So Perkins went off alone to find the sheriff, and soon the two were riding posthaste after the stranger.

When they reached the house to which Burr had asked the way, Perkins stayed outside with the horses, and the sheriff went into the house. He was going to arrest a bold bad man, and it would be a great feather in his cap. So in he marched feeling very firm and grand, expecting to find a terrible ruffian of a fellow. But instead of a terrible ruffian the sheriff found a pleasant, delightful gentleman, and a brilliant talker. So the poor sheriff's heart failed him. He really could not arrest this charming gentleman, and instead he stayed to hear him talk.

Meanwhile out in the cold Perkins waited with the horses, and as the hours went past and the sheriff did not return he guessed what had happened. But he was not going to be done out of his capture. So he went off to the captain of the fort, and told him of his discovery. The captain was not so easily charmed as the sheriff, and before the next evening Burr found himself a prisoner in the fort.

There he remained for about three weeks; then he was sent to Richmond, Virginia, to be tried.

It was a journey of about a thousand miles, and in those days there were of course no railways and even few roads. A great part of the way led through pathless forest and wilderness, and the whole journey had to be done on horseback. But Perkins undertook to see the thing through, and with a guard of nine men they set off.

It was a toilsome march. They had to carry food with them, and as often as not had to sleep in the open air. They swam their horses over rivers, and picked their way through swamps, while hostile Indians hung about their track. Every day was the same, but still day after day they pushed on.

Once Burr tried to escape. They were riding through a small town in South Carolina where he knew that he had many friends. So suddenly he leapt from his horse crying out, "I am Aron Burr, a prisoner. I claim your protection."

But as quick as lightning Perkins was off his horse too, and with a pistol in either hand he stood before Burr.

"Mount," he said; "get up."

The two men glared at each other.

"I will not," replied Burr defiantly, heedless of the pistols.

Perkins had no wish to shed blood. Burr was not a very big man. For an instant Perkins measured him with his eye. Then throwing his pistols down, without a word he seized his prisoner, and lifted him into his saddle, as if he had been a child. And almost before the townspeople had realised what had happened the company was well on its way again.

The trial was long and exciting. Most people believed Burr guilty of treason, but it was difficult to prove. So in the end he was set free.

The American people, however, would have nothing more to do with him. The law might say he was innocent, but nevertheless they felt he was a traitor. So he was hunted and hounded from place to place, and at length changing his name he slipped on board a ship and sailed for Europe.

But even there he found no peace. He was turned out of England, and looked upon with suspicion in France. He was often penniless and in want, and after four years of unhappy wandering he returned home.

He found that he and his misdeeds were well nigh forgotten. No one took any notice of him. So taking no more part in public life he quietly settled down in New York.

Under all the blows of fortune Burr never bowed his head. For although every one else might think him a traitor his beautiful daughter Theodosia believed in him and loved him. He as passionately loved her, and in all his wanderings he carried her portrait with him.

But now the worst misfortunes of his life overtook him. For a few weeks after he landed in America, Theodosia wrote to tell him that her little boy had died. This was a great grief to Burr, for he loved his grandson only a little less than his daughter.

The worst was still to come, however. Theodosia set out from Carolina to visit her father. But the ship in which she sailed never came to port. It was never heard of again, and all on board were lost.

Now at length Burr's head was bowed. Life held nothing more for him, and he cared no longer to live. But death passed him by. So for more than twenty years he lived, a lonely forsaken old man. He was eighty years old when he died.

Chapter 69 - Madison - The Shooting Star and the Prophet

Jefferson was twice chosen President. He might, had he wished, have been elected a third time. But like Washington he refused he refused to stand. And as those two great presidents refused to be elected a third time it has become a kind of unwritten law in the United States that no man shall be president longer than eight years.

The next president to be elected was James Madison, who had been Jefferson's secretary and friend. He was a little man always carefully and elegantly dressed. He was kindly natured and learned, and, like Jefferson, he loved peace. He soon, however, found himself and his country at war.

Ever since the Indians had been defeated by General Wayne they had been at peace. But now they again became restless. It was for the old cause. They saw the white people spreading more and more over their land, they saw themselves being driven further and further from their hunting grounds, and their sleeping hatred of the Pale-faces awoke again.

And now a great chief rose to power among the Indians. He was called Tecumseh or Shooting Star. He was tall, straight and handsome, a great warrior and splendid speaker.

Tecumseh's desire was to unite all the Indians into one great nation, and drive the Pale-faces out of the land. In this he was joined by his brother Tenskwatawa or the Open Door. He took this name because, he said, he was the Open Door through which all might learn of the Great Spirit. He soon came to be looked upon as a very great Medicine Man and prophet, and is generally called the Prophet.

Much that the Prophet taught to the people was good. He told them that they ought to give up fighting each other, and join together into one nation, that they ought to till the ground and sow corn; and above all that they should have nothing to do with "fire water." "It is not made for you," he said, "but for the white people who alone know how to use it. It is the cause of all the mischief which the Indians suffer."

The Prophet also told the Indians that they had no right to sell their land, for the Great Spirit had given it to them. And so great was the Prophet's influence that he was able to build a town where the Indians lived peacefully tilling the ground, and where no "fire water' was drunk.

Now about this time General Harrison, the Governor of the Territory of Indiana, wanted more land. So in 1809 he made a treaty with some of the Indians and persuaded them to sign away their lands to him. When Tecumseh heard of it he was very angry. He declared that the treaty was no treaty, and that no land could be given to the white people unless all the tribes agreed to it.

241

The Governor tried to reason with Tecumseh, but it was of no avail. And as time went on it was more and more plain that the Indians were preparing for war.

Tecumseh traveled about rousing tribe after tribe. "Let the white race perish," he cried. "They seize our land, they trample on our dead. Back! whence they came upon a trail of blood they must be driven! Back! back into the great water whose accursed waves brought them to our shores! Burn their dwellings! Destroy their stock! Slay their wives and children! To the Redman belongs the country and the Pale-face must never enjoy it. War now! War for ever! War upon the living. War upon the dead. Dig their very corpses from their graves. Our country must give no rest to a white man's bones. All the tribes of the North are dancing in the war dance."

After speeches like these there could be little doubt left that Tecumseh meant to begin a great war as soon as he was ready. And as time went on the settlers began to be more and more anxious, for murders became frequent, horses and cattle were stolen, and there seemed no safety anywhere.

The Governor sent messages to the various tribes saying that these murders and thefts must cease, and telling them that if they raised the tomahawk against their white fathers they need expect no mercy.

The Prophet sent back a message of peace. But the outrages still went on, and through friendly Indians the Governor learned that the Prophet was constantly urging the Indians to war.

So the Governor determined to give him war, and with nearly a thousand men he marched to Tippecanoe, the Prophet's village. Tecumseh was not there at the time, but as the Governor drew near the Prophet sent him a message saying that they meant nothing but peace, and asking for a council next day.

To this General Harrison agreed. But well knowing the treachery of the Indians he would not allow his men to disarm, and they slept that night fully dressed, and with their arms beside them ready for an attack.

The Governor's fears were well founded. For the day had not yet dawned when suddenly a shot was heard, and a frightful Indian yell broke the stillness.

In a minute every man was on his feet, and none too soon, for the Indians were upon them. There was a desperate fight in the grey light of dawn. The Indians fought more fiercely than ever before, and while the battle raged the Prophet stood on a hill near, chanting a war song, and urging his men on.

Every now and again messengers came to him with news of the battle. And when he was told that his braves were falling fast before the guns of the white men he bade them still fight on.

"The Great Spirit will give us victory," he said; "the Pale-faces will flee."

But the Pale-faces did not flee. And when daylight came they charged the Indians, and scattered them in flight. They fled to the forest, leaving the town deserted. So the Americans burned it, and marched away.

When Tecumseh heard of this battle he was so angry that he seized his brother by the hair of his head and shook him till his teeth rattled. For the Prophet had begun to fight before his plans were complete, and instead of being victorious

242

had been defeated. And Tecumseh felt that now he would never be able to unite all the tribes into one great nation as he had dreamed of doing. The braves too were angry with the Prophet because he had not led them to victory as he had sworn to do. They ceased to believe in him, and after the battle of Tippecanoe the Prophet lost his power over the Indians.

Chapter 70 - Madison - War with Great Britain

The Berlin Decree, 1806, and the Orders in Council,1807

Meanwhile in Europe a terrible war between France and Britain was raging. And the effects of this war were being felt in America. For in order to crush Britain Napoleon declared that the British Isles were in a state of blockade, and forbade any country to trade with Great Britain. In reply the British declared France to be in a state of blockade, and forbade any country to trade with France.

These decrees and others of the same sort hit American trade very hard, and under them the American people began to be restive. Then, added to this, the British still claimed the right to search American vessels for deserters from the British navy. And very often American citizens were carried off and made to serve in the British navy. This right of search perhaps annoyed the Americans even more than the Berlin Decree or the Orders in Council, as the French and British decrees were called, and at length many of them became eager for war.

Napoleon was doing even worse things than the British. But in spite of a good deal of friction France was still looked upon as a friend, while the bitterness against Britain had not yet been forgotten. Then too it was easier to fight Britain than France. For to fight France it would have been necessary to send an army across the sea, while to fight Britain it was only necessary to march into Canada. A good many of the Americans were rather pleased with that idea, hoping that they might conquer Canada and add it to the States.

But Madison hated war and loved peace almost as much as Jefferson who had said "our passion is for peace." But many of the older men who had helped to found the Republic and laboured to keep it at peace had now gone. In their place there had risen some eager young men who earned for themselves the name of War Democrats. They overpersuaded Madison, and on June 18th, 1812, war with Great Britain was declared.

As soon as war was declared Tecumseh, with all the braves he could command, immediately went over to the British side. The British at this time had a very clever General named Brock, and for some time things went ill for the Americans on land.

But on the sea they had much better success. The first great fight was between the American ship Constitution and the British ship Guerriere. The Guerriere was a good deal smaller than the Constitution, but the British captain was so certain that any British ship, no matter how small, could beat any American one, no matter how large, that he cared nothing for that.

It was afternoon when the two ships came in sight of each other, and immediately prepared for a fight. Nearer and nearer they came to each other, but

243

not until they were scarce fifty yards apart did the Constitution open fire. Then it was deadly. The mizzen mast of the Guerriere was shot away; very soon the main mast followed, and in less than half an hour the Guerriere was a hopeless wreck. Then the British captain struck his flag and surrendered.

The Constitution was scarcely hurt, and after this she got the name of Old Ironsides. She sailed the seas for many a long day, and is now kept as a national memorial in the navy yard at Portsmouth, Mass.

The loss of one ship was as nothing to the great sea power of Britain. But it cheered the Americans greatly, and it was the beginning of many like successes. So this way and that, both on land and sea, fortune swayed, now one side winning, now the other.

At the battle of Queenstown, a city in Canada, on the Niagara River, the British won the victory, but lost their great leader Brock, so that victory was too dearly bought.

Yet still the British continued to win, and after one battle the Indians began to torture and slay the American prisoners. The British general did not know how to curb the fiery Redmen, and he let the horrid massacre go on. But when Tecumseh heard of it he was filled with wrath and grief.

With a wild shout of anger he dashed in among the Indians. Two Indians who were about to kill an American he seized by the throat and threw to the ground. Then, brandishing his tomahawk furiously, he swore to brain any Indian who dared to touch another prisoner. And such was the power that this chief had over his savage followers that they obeyed him at once.

Then Tecumseh turned to the British leader. "Why did you permit it?" he asked.

"Sir," replied General Proctor, "your Indians cannot be commanded."

Tecumseh looked at him in utter scorn. "Begone," he said; "you are not fit to command. Go and put on petticoats."

Things went so badly for the Americans that instead of conquering Canada it seemed almost as if they were in danger of losing some of their own territory. For the British had over-run the great peninsula of Michigan and had command of Lake Erie. The Americans, however, determined to get control of Lake Erie. They had no ships there. But that did not daunt them in the least. There was plenty of timber growing in the forest and out of timber ships could be made. So they felled trees, they brought sails and cordage from New York and Philadelphia in wagons and sledges, and worked so fast and well that very soon ten splendid vessels were ready.

Meanwhile the British commander watched the work and determined to pounce upon the ships as they were being launched. But just for one day he forgot to be watchful. The Americans seized the opportunity, and the ships sailed out on to the lake in safety. The squadron was under the command of a clever young officer named Oliver Hazard Perry. He was only twenty-eight, and although he had served in the navy for fourteen years he had never taken part in a battle. His men were for the most part landsmen, unused alike to war and ships. But while the ships were building Perry drilled his men untiringly. So when the fleet was

244

launched they were both good marksmen and seamen.

It was a bright September day when the great battle took place between the British and American fleets. Much of the British fire was directed at the American flag-ship named the Lawrence, and soon nearly all her men were killed, and the ship seemed about to sink.

But Perry was not beaten. Wrapping his flag about his arm, with his few remaining men he jumped into the boats, and rowed to another ship called the Niagara.

Soon after this, two of the British ships got entangled with each other. The Americans at once took advantage of the confusion and swept the British ships from end to end with a terrible fire.

For half an hour longer the fight went on. Then the British Commander struck his flag. For the first time in history Great Britain surrendered a whole squadron, and that to a young man of twenty-eight with little experience of warfare.

Perry at once sent a message to headquarters to tell of his victory. It was short and to the point. "We have met the enemy, and they are ours," was all he said.

This great victory gave the Americans control of the Lakes and made many of the British victories on land useless. Perry's fleet was now used to land soldiers in Canada and General Proctor began to retreat.

At this Tecumseh was disgusted. "You always told us," he said to the British leader, "that you would never draw your foot off British ground. But now, father, we see that you are drawing back. And we are sorry to see our father doing so without seeing the enemy. We must compare our father's conduct to a fat dog that carries its tail erect till it is frightened, and then drops it between its legs and runs away."

But General Proctor would not listen. He continued to run away. At length, however, the Americans overtook him, he had to fight.

In Battle of the Thames, Oct. 5, 1813, the British were defeated and brave Tecumseh was killed. It is not quite known when or by whom he was killed. But when the Indians saw their leader was no longer among them they had no more heart to fight. "Tecumseh fell and we all ran," said one of his braves afterwards. Thus the power of these Indians was broken for ever.

The war still went on, and it was fought not only in the North but all along the coasts and in the South. The Americans marched into Toronto, the capital of Upper Canada, and burned the Parliament House. The British marched into Washington, and burned the Capitol and the President's House, deeds which no one could approve even in the heat of war.

The proper name for the President's house is the Executive Mansion, but it is known, not only in America, but all the world over as the White House. According to one tradition it was only after being burnt by the British that it received this name. For when it was repaired the walls were painted white to cover the marks of fire. According to another tradition the people called it the White House from the beginning in honour of the first President's "consort" Martha

Washington whose early home on the Pamunkey River in Virginia was called the White House.

At sea American privateers did great damage to British shipping, and so daring were they that even the Irish Sea and the English Channel were not safe for British traders.

For two and a half years the war lasted. Then at length peace was made by the Treaty of Ghent. It was signed on Christmas Eve, 1814, and for more than a hundred years there has been peace between Great Britain and the United States of America. Let us hope it will never be broken.

Nothing was altered by this war. No territory changed hands, and as for the things about which the war began, they were not mentioned in the treaty of peace. For the war with France was over, so of course the blockades which had hit American trade so hard were no more in force. On both sides peace was hailed with delight. In America bonfires were lit, bells were rung, and men who were the greatest enemies in politics forgot their quarrels, fell into each other's arms and cried like women. Everywhere too "The Star Spangled Banner" was sung.

It was during this war that this famous song was written. The British were about to attack Baltimore when Francis Scott Key, hearing that one of his friends had been taken prisoner, rowed out to the British fleet under a flag of truce to beg his release. The British Admiral consented to his release. He said, however, that both Key and his friend must wait until the attack was over.

So, from the British fleet, Key watched the bombardment of Fort McHenry which guarded the town. All through the night the guns roared and flashed, and in the lurid light Key could see the flag on Fort McHenry fluttering proudly. But before dawn the firing ceased.

"What had happened," he asked himself, "was the fort taken?"

Eagerly he waited for the dawn. And when at last the sun rose he saw with joy that the Stars and Stripes still floated over the fort. There and then on the back of an old letter he wrote "The Star Spangled Banner." People hailed it with delight, soon it was sung throughout the length and breadth of the States, and at length became the National Anthem.

During Madison's presidency two states were added to the Union. In 1812 Louisiana was added as the eighteenth state.

The State of Louisiana was only a very small part of the Louisiana Purchase, and when it was first proposed that it should join the Union some people objected. Louisiana should be kept as a territory, they said, and they declared that Congress had no power to admit new states except those which were formed out of land belonging to the original thirteen states.

"It was not for these men that our fathers fought," cried a Congressman. "You have no authority to throw the rights, and liberties, and property, of this people into hotch-potch with the wild men on the Missouri, or with the mixed, though more respectable, race of Anglo-Hispano-Gallo-Americans who bask on the sands in the mouth of the Mississippi."

He declared further that if this sort of thing went on it would break up the

Union. But in spite of him and others who thought like him Louisiana became a state in 1812.

In 1816, just about two years after the end of the war with Britain, Indiana was admitted into the Union as the nineteenth state. You know that besides the Constitution of the United States each state has also its own constitution. Thus when a territory wanted to become a state it had to frame a constitution which had to be approved by Congress.

In June, 1816, a convention to frame a constitution was called at Corydon, which was then the capital of Indiana. The weather was warm, and instead of holding their meetings in the State House the members used to meet under a great elm which stood near. Under the cool shadow of its branches the laws for the state were framed, and from that the elm was called the Constitution Elm. It still stands as it stood a hundred years ago, and the people of Corydon do everything they can to protect it, and make it live as long as possible.

Chapter 71 - Monroe-The First Whispers of a Storm-Monroe's Famous Doctrine

Madison was twice elected President. He was chosen for the second time during the war with Britain. In 1817 his second term came to an end and James Monroe took his place.

Monroe was not so clever as the presidents who had gone before him. But he was a kindly, generous man. Every one liked him, and the time during which he was President was called the "era of good feeling."

And indeed men were so glad of this time of peace which had come after such long years of war that they forgot old quarrels and became friends again.

Unfortunately the peace was broken by a war with the Seminole Indians in Florida. Florida still belonged to Spain, and it became a haunt for all sorts of adventurers. These adventurers robbed, and murdered, and created terrible disturbances among the Indians, until along the frontier between Georgia and Florida there was neither safety nor peace for any white man.

So the President at length sent General Jackson, who had won great fame in the War of 1812, to bring the Indians to order. Jackson marched into Florida, and in three months' time had subdued the Indians, brought order out of wild disorder, and in fact conquered Florida.

But this was far more than Monroe had meant Jackson to do. And it seemed as if General Jackson was like to be in trouble with the Government, and the Government in trouble with Spain. However things were smoothed over, and the matter with Spain was put right by the United States buying Florida in 1819. And of this new territory Jackson was made Governor.

Meanwhile more states were being added to the Union.

After the War was over, hundreds of families had found a new home, and a new life, in the unknown wilderness of the West. Indeed, so many people moved westward that the people in the East began to grow anxious. For it seemed to them that soon the eastern states would be left desolate, and they asked their State

Governments to stop the people going west. "Old America seems to be breaking up and moving westward," said one man.

All sorts of stories of the hardships and dangers of the West were spread abroad. But in spite of all that was said the stream still poured westward. The people went in great covered wagons drawn by teams of horses, carrying with them all their household goods, or they rode on horseback taking nothing with them but a few clothes tied up in a handkerchief, while some even trudged the long hundreds of miles on foot.

The rivers, too, were crowded with boats of all sorts, many people going part of the way by river, and the rest on foot. In the East fields were left desolate, houses and churches fell to ruins, while in the West towns and villages sprang up as if by magic, and the untrodden wilderness was turned to fertile fields.

So, as the great prairies of the West became settled, the settlers became eager to join the Union. Thus new states were formed. Mississippi became a state in 1817, the first year of Monroe's presidency. Illinois followed in 1818, Alabama in 1819, and Missouri in 1821. Mississippi, Illinois and Alabama were framed out of original territory but Missouri was framed out of the Louisiana Purchase. All four names are Indian. Mississippi and Missouri are named after the rivers which flow through them, Mississippi meaning Father of Waters and Missouri Great Muddy. For the Missouri is full of yellow mud. Illinois is named after the tribe of Indians who lived there. Their name was really Iliniwok meaning "Men" but white people pronounced it badly and it became changed to Illinois. Alabama means "here we rest."

In 1820 Maine also was admitted as a state. Maine, however, was not newly settled country. Since colonial days it had been a part of Massachusetts. But having become dissatisfied, it separated from Massachusetts, and asked to be admitted to the Union as a separate state.

It was just about the same time that Missouri was also asking to be admitted as a state. And strangely enough the admission of these two states became connected with each other. We must look back a little to see how.

You remember that two hundred years before this, slaves were first brought to Virginia. In those days no one thought that slavery was wrong. So as colony was added to colony they also became slave owners. But gradually many people began to think that slavery was a great evil, and every now and again one colony or another would try to put it down. But these attempts always ended in failure.

In the northern states, however, there were few slaves. For in these northern states there was not much that slaves could do which could not be done just as well by white men. So it did not pay to keep slaves, and gradually slavery was done away with.

But in the South it was different. There it was so hot that white men could not do the work in the rice and cotton fields. And the planters believed that without Negro slave labour it would be impossible to make their plantations pay.

Then, when the power of steam was discovered and many new cotton spinning machines were invented, the demand for cotton became greater and greater; the

Southern planters became more sure than ever that slavery was needful. They also became afraid that the people in the North would want to do away with it, and if the number of the states in which slavery was not allowed increased it would be easy for them to do this. So the Southerners determined that if non-slavery states were admitted to the Union slavery states must be admitted also to keep the balance even.

Now when Maine and Missouri both asked to be admitted as states the Southerners refused to admit Maine as a free state unless Missouri was made a slave state to balance it.

There was tremendous excitement and talk over the matter. Meetings were held in all the large towns. In the North the speakers called slavery the greatest evil in the United States, and a disgrace to the American people.

In the South the speakers declared that Congress had no right to dictate to a state as to whether it should have slavery or not. But even in the South few really stood up for slavery. Almost every one acknowledged that it was an evil. But it was a necessary evil, they said.

In the House and the Senate there were great debates also. But at length an arrangement was come to. Missouri was admitted to the Union as a slave state, but in the rest of the Louisiana Territory north of the degree of latitude 36 degrees slavery was forbidden for all time. This was called the Missouri Compromise; compromise meaning, as you know, that each side gave up something. And in this way a quarrel between the North and South was avoided for the time being.

But it was only for the time being, and wise men watched events with heavy hearts. Among these was the old President Jefferson. "The question sleeps for the present," he said, "but is not dead." He felt sure that it would awake again and shatter the Union, and he thanked God that being an old man he might not live to see it.

In 1821 Monroe was chosen President for a second time and it was during this second term that he became famous throughout all the world. He became so through what is known as the Monroe Doctrine.

During the wars with Napoleon the King of Spain had been so crushed that he was no longer strong enough to govern his colonies. So one after another the Spanish colonies in America had declared themselves free and had set up as independent republics. But Spain of course was anxious to have her colonies back again, and it seemed very likely that the King would ask some of the other great powers in Europe to help him to reconquer them. Monroe however determined to put a stop to wars of conquest between the old world and the new.

So he announced that the Continents of America were no longer to be looked upon as open to colonisation by any European power. And that if any European power attempted to interfere with any American government they would have the United States to reckon with. Those colonies which still belonged to European powers would be left alone, but any attempt to reconquer colonies which had declared themselves to be free would be looked upon as an act unfriendly to the

249

United States.

Such was the famous Monroe Doctrine, and because of it the name of Monroe is better known all over the world than any other United States President except Washington.

The British were quite pleased with Monroe's new doctrine. The other great powers of Europe were not. But they yielded to it and dropped their plans for conquering any part of America. And ever since the doctrine was announced the Continents of America have been left to manage their own affairs.

Chapter 72 - Adams - The Tariff of Abominations

In 1825 Monroe's term of office came to an end and John Quincy Adams became President. He was the son of John Adams who had been second President, and he had been Secretary of State to Monroe. It was said, indeed, that it was really he who originated the famous Doctrine which came to be called by Monroe's name.

He was an honest man and a statesman. He refused to give offices to his friends just because they were his friends, and he refused to turn men out of office simply because they did not agree with him in politics. He wanted to do what was right and just. But he did it from a cold sense of duty. So no one liked him very much. Both House and Senate were against him, and he was not able to do all he would have done for his country.

Adams wanted to do a great deal towards improving the country. He wanted canals to be cut. And as the steam engine had just been discovered, he was eager to have railroads and bridges. But Congress would not help him.

Still, much was done in this direction. Several canals were cut; railroads began to be built, and the rivers were covered with steamboats.

Manufacturers also began to flourish. For during the 1812 war it had been very difficult to get manufactured goods from foreign countries. So Americans had begun to make these things for themselves.

And after the war was over, they went on manufacturing them. At length people began to be proud of using only American made things. And when Adams was inaugurated everything he wore had been manufactured in the States.

The factories were for the most part in the North, and soon the Northerners began to clamour for duties on imported goods. They wanted to keep out foreign goods, or at least make them so dear that it would pay people to buy American made goods.

But the people in the South who did not manufacture things themselves wanted the duties to be kept low. However the manufacturers won the day, and twice during Adams' presidency bills were passed, by which the tariff was made higher. The second bill made the duties so high that many people were very angry and called it the "tariff of abominations." In the South, indeed many people were so angry that they swore never to buy anything from the North until the tariff was made lower. Thus once again North and South were pulling different ways.

Adams would willingly have been President for a second term. But in spite of his honesty and his upright dealings no one liked him. So he was not re-elected.

When he ceased to be President, however, he did not cease to take an interest in politics, and for many years after he was a member of Congress, where he did good service to his country.

Chapter 73 - Jackson - "Liberty and Union, Now and Forever" - Van Buren - Hard Times

In 1829 Andrew Jackson, the great soldier, became President. All the presidents up till now had been well born men, aristocrats, in fact. But Jackson was a man of the people. He had been born in a log cabin on the borders of North and South Carolina. He had very little schooling, and all his life he was never able to write correct English.

When his friends first asked him to stand for President, he laughed. "Do you suppose," he said, "that I am such a fool as to think myself fit for President of the United States? No, sir, I know what I am fit for. I can command a body of men in a rough way, but I am not fit to be President."

However, he did consent to stand. The first time he was unsuccessful, and Adams was chosen instead, the second time he was brilliantly successful.

Jackson's inauguration was a triumph. Hundreds and thousands of the common people came to see the "people's man" become President. Every road leading to the Capitol was so thronged that the procession could hardly make a way through the crowd, and when the President appeared the cheers were deafening.

After the inauguration was over there was a great reception at the White House. The crush was tremendous. People elbowed each other and almost fought for a sight of the new President. They stood on the satin covered chairs in their muddy boots to get a glimpse of him over the heads of others. Glasses were broken, and wine was spilled on the fine carpets. In fact, it was a noisy jollification and many people were shocked. "The reign of King Mob seemed triumphant," said an old gentleman; "I was glad to escape from the scene as soon as possible."

But Jackson did not mind; he liked to see people enjoy themselves. "Let the boys have a good time once in four years," he said.

Jackson was a man of the people, but he was an autocrat too, and he had a will so unbending that even in his soldiering days he had been called Old Hickory. So now, Old Hickory had a Cabinet but he did not consult them. He simply told them what he meant to do. His real Cabinet were a few friends who had nothing at all to do with the government. They used to see him in private, and go in and out by a back door. So they got the name of the Kitchen Cabinet. And this Kitchen Cabinet had much more to do with Jackson's administration than the real Cabinet.

As President, Jackson did many good things. But he did one bad thing. He began what is known as the "spoils system."

Before, when a new President was elected, the Cabinet, secretaries and such people were of course changed also. But Jackson was not content with that. He thought that it was only right that his friends who had helped him to become

251

President should be rewarded. So he turned out all sorts of civil servants, such as post masters, customs officers, and clerks of all sorts. This he did, not because they were dishonest, or useless, or unfit for their positions, but simply because they did not think as he did in politics. And in their places he put his own friends who did think as he did.

In the first year of his "reign" he thus removed two thousand people, it is said. The whole of Washington too, was filled with unrest and suspicion, no man knowing when it would be his turn to go. Many of the government clerks were now old men who had been in the service almost since the government was established. When they were turned out, there was nothing for them to do, nothing but beggary for them to look forward to. In consequence there was a great deal of misery and poverty. But the removals went on.

In time this became known as the "spoils system," because in a speech a senator talking of this matter said, "to the victor belongs the spoils of the enemy."

But something much more serious soon began to call for attention. You remember that the Tariff Bill of 1828 had been called the Tariff of Abominations, and that the people in the South objected to it very much. A feeling had begun to grow up that the interests of the North and the South were different, and that the North had too much power, and the South too little. So some Southern men began to declare that if any state decided that a law made by Congress was not lawful according to Constitution they might set that law at nought in their own state and utterly disregard it.

This was called nullification because it made a law null and void. Wise men saw at once that if this was allowed it would simply break up the Union and every state would soon do just as it liked.

So when a Southern statesman announced this theory of delusion and folly 'Liberty first and Union afterwards,' Daniel Webster answered him.

Webster was a splendid looking man with a great mane of black hair and flashing black eyes. He was, too, a magnificent speaker and a true patriot.

As he spoke men listened in breathless silence, spellbound, by the low clear voice. In burning words Webster called to their love of country. He touched their hearts, he awoke their pride, he appealed to their plain common sense.

"Let us not see upon our flag," he said, "those words of delusion and folly 'Liberty first and Union afterwards'; but everywhere, spread all over in characters of living light, blazing on all its ample folds, as they float over the sea and over the land, and in every wind under the whole heavens, that other sentiment, dear to every true American heart, 'Liberty and Union,' now and for ever, one and inseparable."

Thus Webster ended his great speech, and with a long sigh his hearers awoke from the spell he had laid upon them, awoke to the fact that one of the world's greatest orators stood among them.

"That crushes nullification," said James Madison.

But the South was neither convinced nor crushed.

The President was a Southern man, it was known that he disliked high tariffs, so the Southerners hoped that he would help them. But stern Old Hickory would lend no hand to break up the Union.

On Jefferson's birthday some of the people who believed in nullification gave a dinner to which Jackson was invited and asked to propose a toast. He accepted the invitation, but soon discovered that the dinner was not meant so much to honour the memory of Jefferson as to advocate nullification and all the toasts hinted at it. Presently Jackson was called upon for his toast, and as he rose deep silence fell upon the company. Then in a clear and steady voice the President gave his toast: "Our Federal Union; it must and shall be preserved."

It was a great disappointment to the Nullifiers and after that all hope of help from the President was lost.

However, the people of South Carolina were still determined, and in 1832 they declared that the tariff law of that year was null and void, and no law; and that if the Government tried to force them to regard it they would set up a government of their own.

The whole state was in wild excitement. People talked openly of separating from the Union, a President was chosen and medals were struck bearing the inscription, "First President of the Southern Confederacy."

"If this thing goes on," said Jackson, "our country will be like a bag of meal with both ends open. Pick it up in the middle endwise and it will run out. I must tie the bag and save the country."

So Jackson sent a proclamation to the people of South Carolina begging them to think before they dragged their state into war. For war they should have, he told them plainly, if they persisted in their ways.

But South Carolina replied defiantly talking of tyranny and oppression, and declaring again their right to withdraw from the Union if they wished.

Both sides were so defiant that it seemed as if there might indeed be war. But there was none.

South Carolina found that the other Southern states would not join her as she had expected. So when the Government yielded so far as to reduce the tariff to some extent South Carolina grew quiet again and the danger passed.

Jackson was twice elected President. And at the end of his second term two states were added to the Union. In June, 1836, Arkansas, part of the Louisiana Purchase, became a state. It was still rather a wild place where men wore long two-edged knives called after a wild rascal, Captain James Bowie, and they were so apt to use them on the slightest occasions that the state was nicknamed the Toothpick State.

Arkansas came in as a slave state, and early the following year Michigan came in as a free state. Michigan had belonged at one time to New France, but after the War of Independence Britain gave it up to the United States when it became part of the North West Territory.

During the 1812 war Michigan was again taken by the British. But they only kept it for a short time, for soon after Captain Perry's great victory it was won back again by the Americans.

253

Up to that time there were few settlements in the territory. But gradually more people came to settle, and at length in 1834 there were quite enough people to entitle it to be admitted as a state. And after some squabbling with Ohio over the question of boundaries it was admitted to the Union early in 1837. The state takes its name from the great lake Michigan, being an Indian word meaning "Great Sea."

Michigan was the thirteenth new state to be admitted. Thus since the Revolution the number of states had been exactly doubled.

In 1837 Martin Van Buren became President. He had been Secretary of State and then Vice-President, and had been a great favourite with Jackson who was very anxious that he should become President after him.

Van Buren made very few changes in the cabinet, and his Presidency was very like a continuation of Jackson's "reign."

Yet no two men could be more different from each other than Jackson and Van Buren. Jackson was rugged, quick tempered and iron willed, marching straight to his end, hacking his way through all manner of difficulties. Van Buren was a smooth tongued, sleek little man who, said his enemies, never gave any one a straight answer, and who wrapped up his ideas and opinions in so many words that nobody could be sure what he really thought about any subject.

All the presidents before Van Buren had been of British descent, and they had all been born when the States were still British colonies. Van Buren was Dutch, and he had been born after the Revolution was complete.

This was not a happy time for America, for the whole country began to suffer from money troubles. One reason for this was that people had been trying to get rich too fast. They had been spending more than they had in order to make still more. Great factories were begun and never finished, railroads and canals were built which did not pay. Business after business failed, bank after bank shut its doors, and then to add to the troubles there was a bad harvest. Flour became ruinously dear, and the poor could not get enough to eat.

The people blamed the Government for these bad times. Deputation after deputation went to the President asking him to do something, railing at him as the cause of all their troubles.

But amid all the clamour Van Buren stood calm. "This was not a matter," he said, "in which the Government ought to interfere. It was a matter for the people themselves," and he bade them to be more careful and industrious and things would soon come right.

But the Government too had suffered, for government money had been deposited in some of the banks which had failed. And in order to prevent that in the future Van Buren now proposed a plan for keeping State money out of the banks, so that the State should not be hurt by any bank failing.

This came to be called the Subtreasury System. There was a good deal of opposition to it at first but in 1840 it became law. It is the chief thing to remember about Van Buren's administration. It is also one of those things which become more interesting as we grow older.

254

Chapter 74 - Harrison - The Hero of Tippecanoe

People had grown to dislike Van Buren so much that he had no chance of being elected a second time, and the next President was General Harrison. Never before or since perhaps has there been so much excitement over the election of a President. For Van Buren's friends tried very hard to have him re-elected, and Harrison's friends worked just as hard on his behalf.

Harrison was the general who had led his men to victory at Tippecanoe, and he immediately became first favourite with the people. He was an old man now of nearly seventy, and since he had left the army had been living quietly on his farm in the country.

So one of Van Buren's friends said scornfully that Harrison was much more fit to live in a log cabin and drink hard cider than live in the White House and be President.

It was meant as a sneer, but Harrison's good friends took it up. Log Cabin and Hard Cider became their war-cry, and the election was known as the Log Cabin and Hard Cider campaign. And soon many simple country people came to believe that Harrison really lived in a log cabin, and that he was poor, and had to work for his living even as an old man.

All sorts of songs were made and sung about this gallant old farmer.

"Oh, know ye the farmer of Tippecanoe? The gallant old farmer of Tippecanoe? With an arm that is strong and a heart that is true, The man of the people is Tippecanoe."

That is the beginning of one song and there were dozens more like it.

And while the old farmer of Tippecanoe was said to be everything that was good and honest and lovable, Van Buren on the other hand was represented as being a bloated aristocrat, who sat in chairs that cost six hundred dollars, ate off silver plates with golden forks and spoons, and drove about in an English coach with a haughty smile on his face.

It was a time of terrible excitement, and each side gave the other many hard knocks. But in the end Harrison was elected by two hundred and thirty-four electoral votes to Van Buren's sixty. As Vice-President John Tyler was chosen. "Tippecanoe and Tyler too" had been one of the election cries.

Inauguration day was bleak and cold, rain threatened and a chill wind blew. But in spite of unkind weather Harrison's friends arranged a grand parade. And mounted on a white horse the new President rode for two hours through the streets. Then for another hour he stood in the chill wind reading his address to the people.

All the time he wore no overcoat. Because, it is said, rumours were spread abroad that he was not strong, and he wanted to show that he was. When the long ceremony was at length over he was thoroughly chilled, but no serious illness followed.

It was soon seen, however, that he could not bear the strain of his great office. He had never been strong. Of late years he had been used to a quiet country life, seeing few people and taking things easily.

Now from morning till night he lived in a whirl. He was besieged with people who wanted posts. For the spoils system being once begun, every President was almost forced to continue it. And never before had any President been beset by such a buzzing crowd.

Harrison was a kindly old man, and he would gladly have given offices to all who asked. It grieved him that he could not. But he was honest, too, and he tried to be just in making these new appointments. So his days were full of worry and anxious thought. Soon under the heavy burden he fell ill. And just a month after his inauguration he died.

Never before had a President died in office, and it was a shock to the whole people. Every one grieved, for even those who had been his political enemies and worked hard to prevent his election loved the good old man. Death stilled every whisper of anger against him, and, united in sorrow, the whole nation mourned his loss and followed him reverently to the grave.

Chapter 75 - Tyler - Florida Becomes a State

John Tyler now became President. At first there was some doubt as to what he should be called. Adams, the ex-President, said he should be called "Vice-President acting as President." But that was much too long. Someone else suggested "Regent," but that smacked too much of royalty. But the people did not worry about it; they just called him President, and so the matter settled itself.

One important matter during Tyler's presidency was the settling of the boundary between British America and Maine. The uncertainty of where the border between the two countries really was had caused a good deal of friction, the British accusing the Americans and the Americans accusing the British of encroaching on their territory. Many attempts had been made to settle it, but hey had all failed. And both sides had become so angry over it that it was very nearly a question of war.

But now at last the question was thrashed out between Daniel Webster, the great orator acting for the United States, and Lord Ashburton acting for Britain. Lord Ashburton came out to Washington. The business was carried through in a friendly fashion and settled satisfactorily.

The twenty-seventh state was admitted to the Union during Tyler's time of office. This was Florida. Since Spain had given up Florida to the United States there had been a good deal of unrest among the Indians. And at last the settlers decided that it would be better to send them out of the country altogether.

So the settlers made a treaty with the Indians by which the Indians agreed to accept lands in the West instead of their Florida lands. But when the time came for them to go they refused to move, and a war which lasted seven years was begun.

It was a terrible war and thousands of lives were lost on either side, for the Indians were led by a brave and wily chief named Osceola. But at length they were defeated. They were then removed to western lands as had been agreed; only about three hundred were allowed to remain, and these were obliged to keep to the extreme south of the province.

The war ended soon after Tyler became President. Then land was offered free to settlers who would promise to remain at least five years. Many were glad to get land on such easy terms, and soon the country which had been a refuge for escaped slaves and a haunt for desperadoes became the home of orderly people.

In a very short time these new settlers wished to join the Union, but at first they could not agree as to whether Florida should be made into one or two states. Finally, however, it was decided that it should be one, and in March, 1845, it was admitted to the Union as a slave state.

Chapter 76 - Polk - How Much Land Was Added to the United States

In 1845 Tyler's term expired and James Knox Polk became President. He had been a long time in Congress, and had been Speaker of the House for four years. Yet nobody had heard very much about him, and nearly everyone was surprised when his party succeeded in electing him.

During Polk's term of office three states were admitted to the Union. The first of these was the great State of Texas. After the Louisiana Purchase the United States had claimed Texas as part of Louisiana. But the Spaniards to whom all Mexico belonged disputed their claim, and declared that Texas belonged to them. The dispute went on until the United States bought Florida from Spain. Then in part payment for Florida the Americans gave up all claim to Texas.

But really this agreement could matter little to Spain, for the Mexicans were already in revolt, and in 1821 declared themselves independent.

Meanwhile many Americans began to settle in Texas. The United States Government began to feel sorry that they had given it up, and they tried to buy it from the Mexicans. The Mexicans, however, refused to sell it. But many men in the southern states became more and more anxious to get Texas. Because they saw that if they did not get some more territory free states would soon outnumber slave states. For all the land south of the Missouri Compromise line had been used up, the only part left being set aside as Indian Territory. In the north on the other hand there was still land enough out of which to carve four or five states.

All the Americans who had settled in Texas were slave holders. And when Mexico abolished slavery Texas refused to do so. This refusal of course brought trouble, and at length the Texans, declaring that the government of Mexico was tyrannical, rose in rebellion against Mexico, and declared themselves a republic.

But the Mexicans would not allow this great territory to revolt without an effort to keep it. So they sent an army to fight the Texans. The leader of the Mexican army was Santa Anna, the Mexican President. The leader of the Texans was General Sam Houston.

Sam Houston was an adventurous American who a year or two before had settled in Texas. He had had a varied life. He had been a soldier, a lawyer, a Congressman, and finally Governor of a state. Then he had suddenly thrown everything up, had gone to live among the Indians, and was adopted into an Indian tribe.

While he was living with the Indians wild stories of his doings were spread about. One story was that he meant to conquer Texas, and make himself Emperor of that country. But Houston had really no intention of founding a nation.

In the war with Texas the Mexicans were at first successful, and the terrified people fled before them. But at the battle of San Jacinto the Texans utterly defeated the Mexicans. The rout was complete and the Mexicans fled in every direction, among them their leader, Santa Anna.

Mounted on a splendid black horse he fled toward a bridge crossing a river which flowed near. But when he reached the bridge he found that the Texans had destroyed it. He was being hotly pursued by the enemy. So without pausing a moment he spurred his horse into the river, swam across, and to the surprise of his pursuers climbed the steep cliff of the opposite side, and disappeared.

Darkness now fell and the Texans gave up the pursuit. But next morning they set out again to scour the country in search of fugitives. Meanwhile Santa Anna, having abandoned his horse and changed his clothes in a forsaken cottage, was trying to make his way to the Mexican border. Presently, however, one of the search parties came upon a little man dressed in blue cotton coat and trousers, a leather cap and red woolen slippers. He was a miserable looking object, and when he saw the Texans approach, he tried to hide himself in the grass. He was soon found, however, and when the Texans asked him who he was he said he was a private soldier.

The Texans then told him to follow them to the camp. And when he said he could not walk he mounted on one of their horses, and, riding behind a Texan, he was led into camp.

The Texans had no idea who they had captured until they reached their camp. Then when the Mexican prisoners saw the queer little figure they exclaimed, "The President! the President!" Only then did the Texans discover what a great man they had captured.

Houston had been wounded in the battle, and was lying on a mattress under the tree when Santa Anna was led before him.

"I am General Antonio Lopez de Santa Anna," said the prisoner, "and a prisoner of war at your disposal."

Houston looked at him in silence, and then signed him to sit down on a box which stood near. And there under the spreading branches of the tree a truce was arranged, and Santa Anna wrote letters to his generals telling them to cease fighting.

The Texans wanted to hang Santa Anna for his cruelties during the war, but Houston saved him from their wrath, and after he had signed a treaty acknowledging the independence of Texas he was set free.

Texas now declared itself a republic, and of this new State General Sam Houston - "Old Sam Jacinto," as he was affectionately nicknamed - was chosen

President. The flag chosen for the Republic was blue with a single yellow star in the middle, and from this flag Texas came to be called the Lone Star State.

The Texans had declared themselves a free and independent nation. But as a republic Texas was very small, and the Texans had no intention of remaining a lonely insignificant republic. What they desired was to join the United States. And very soon they asked to be admitted to the Union.

But Texas lay south of the Missouri Compromise line, and although small for an independent republic it was huge for a state, and might be cut up into three or four. Therefore the people in the North were very much against Texas being admitted to the Union as it would increase the strength of the slave states enormously. But the Southerners were determined to have Texas, and at last in 1845 it was admitted as a slave state. The two last states which had been added to the Union, that it, Florida and Texas, were both slave states. But they were soon balanced by two free states, Iowa and Wisconsin.

Iowa is an Indian name meaning "Sleepy Ones." The state was called after a tribe of Indians of that name who were there when the Frenchmen first explored the country. It was the first free state to be carved out of the Louisiana Purchase.

Wisconsin was part of the Northwest Territory and was the last part of it to be organised as a state. Like many other states Wisconsin takes its name from its chief river, which means "Gathering Waters." There are many lead mines in Wisconsin and these had been worked in a poor sort of way by the Indians, and when white people began to work them there was trouble between them and the Redmen.

At different times Red Bird and Black Hawk rose against the whites, but both were defeated. At length the disputes were settled by treaties with the Indians and the land began to be peopled by whites.

Wisconsin is often called the Badger State. It got this name not because badgers are to be found there, but because the lead miners, instead of building houses, used to dig out caves in the hillsides and live in them summer and winter. From this they were nicknamed Badgers, and the state became known as the Badger State.

Besides Texas, another great territory was added to the States at this time, and another boundary dispute between British America and the United States was settled.

For many years both Britain and the United States had claimed the Oregon Territory. The Americans claimed it by right of Captain Gray's discovery of the Columbia River, and also by right of the exploration of Lewis and Clark. The British claimed it by right of the discoveries of Sir Alexander Mackenzie, and also on the ground that it had been occupied by Hudson's Bay Company.

Three times attempts had been made to settle the boundary, but each time the attempts had failed. At length the two countries agreed to occupy it jointly. This arrangement was to come to an end by either country giving a year's notice.

President Polk's appetite for land was huge. He wanted the whole of Oregon for the United States. So in 1846 the joint agreement came to an end, and new efforts for final settlement began.

Many others were as eager as the President to have the whole of Oregon, and "Fifty-four Forty or Fight" became a battle-cry. Fifty-four Forty was the imaginary line or parallel of latitude on the north of the disputed territory. So that the cry "Fifty-four Forty or Fight" meant that these hotspurs demanded the whole of Oregon or war with Great Britain.

On the other hand some people thought a ridiculous fuss was being made over an utterly useless piece of land.

"What do we want with it?" they said. "What are we to do with it? How could a bit of land five thousand miles away ever become part of the United States? It is absurd!"

Steam, said someone, would make it possible. Railways would bring Oregon near to the seat of government.

"Steam!" cried the objectors. "Railways across the Rocky Mountains! Rubbish!"

The British on their side did not want the whole of Oregon, but they wanted the land as far south as the Columbia River.

However in the end both sides gave way a little. It was agreed to halve the country, and the parallel 49 was taken as the boundary. Thus another large territory was added to the States and the northern frontiers peacefully settled from east to west.

But Polk's land hunger was not yet satisfied. He had half of Oregon, he had the whole of Texas, but he wanted more. He waned California, but California belonged to Mexico. He tried to buy it from Mexico, but Mexico would not sell it. Polk, however, was determined to have it. So determined was he that he made up his mind to fight for it, if there was no other way of getting it.

It was easy to find an excuse for war. The boundaries of Texas were very uncertain, and a tract of land lying east of the Rio Grande River was claimed by both Texas and by Mexico. IN 1846 Polk sent an army to take possession of this land.

General Zachary Taylor was in command of this expedition. And when he arrived near the mouth of the Rio Grande and began to build a fort the Mexicans were very angry. They sent him a message ordering him to be gone in twenty-four hours.

Of course Taylor refused to go, and he began to blockade the river, so as to stop trade with Mexico.

The Mexicans then made ready to fight, and next morning they attacked and captured a scouting party of Americans.

When the news reached Washington there was great excitement. "Mexico has passed the boundary of the United States," declared the President, "has invaded our territory, and shed American blood on American soil."

"War exists," he said, "notwithstanding all our efforts to avoid it, exists by the act of Mexico herself."

260

Some of the people, however, did not believe that Mexico was wholly to blame for beginning the war. And a young Congressman named Abraham Lincoln asked the President to state the exact spot on American territory where American blood had been spilled. This was called the "Spot resolution."

But in spite of any protest that was made war was declared, and volunteers came pouring in from every side.

The war lasted for a year and a half, and from the first the Mexicans had the worst of it. Throughout the whole war they never won a battle. Besides General Taylor's army the Mexicans soon had two more to fight. In the north General Kearney marched into New Mexico and took possession of it in the name of the United States. Then he marched into California and claimed that also. In the south the Commander-in-Chief, General Scott, landed at Vera Cruz. And after taking the town he marched triumphantly on, conquering everything on his way till he reached Mexico City, and the war was practically at an end.

It was not, however, until February of the following year that the treaty of peace was signed in Mexico and not till the 4th of July was it proclaimed in Washington. By it a great tract of land was given to the United States, stretching from the borders of Texas to the shores of the Pacific and from the present northern border of Mexico to Oregon.

_____

Chapter 77 - Polk - The Finding of Gold

In return for the great tract of land ceded to the United States Mexico received 15 million dollars. But the Mexicans little knew what a golden land they were parting with, and what a bad bargain they were making. Nine days before the treaty was signed gold was found in California. But news traveled slowly in those days, and the treaty was signed before the Mexicans knew of the great discovery.

Some time before this a Swiss named Sutter had settled in the Sacramento Valley. He had prospered greatly, and had become a regular little potentate, ruling the whole district round.

He had thousands of horses and cattle, and hundreds of men worked for him, both white men and Indians. Now he wanted to build a saw mill and a man named Marshall, a settler from the East, undertook to build it for him.

Marshall was a moody, queer tempered man. But he was a good workman. So about fifty miles from Sutter's fort the saw mill was begun. Now one day while Marshall was walking beside the mill stream inspecting the work he saw something yellow and shining among the loose earth and gravel which was being carried down by the stream. At first he thought little about it, but as again and again he saw these shining grains he at length thought that they might be gold and picked some up.

Next morning he again went to inspect the mill stream and there he found a piece of the shining stuff bigger than any he had found the day before. Marshall picked up the piece, and when he felt it heavy in his hand he began to feel a little excited.

Could it really be gold? he asked himself. Marshall did not know much about gold, but he knew that it was heavy, and that it was fairly soft. So he bit and hammered it with stones, and finding that it was easily beaten out he at last decided that it was indeed gold.

So he mounted his horse and rode off to Sutter to tell him of his wonderful discovery. It was a pouring wet day in January, and when Marshall reached the fort he was soaked through. But he took no thought of that, and marching right into Sutter's office with something of an air of mystery asked for a private talk.

Sutter wondered what had brought Marshall back from the mill, and he wondered still more at the mysterious air.

Soon he understood. For Marshall took out a little bag, and emptying what it held into his hand, held it out to Sutter.

"I believe this is gold," he said.

"It certainly looks like it," said Sutter in surprise.

Then Marshall told how he had found it in the mill stream, and that he believed there were tons of it.

Sutter was a very great man in the countryside, and he had things which no one else dreamed of having. Among these was an Encyclopedia. So he looked up the article on gold and read it carefully. And then the two men tried all the tests they had at command, and at last came to the conclusion that the shining grains which Marshall had found were certainly gold.

Sutter would have been glad to keep the secret for a little time, at least until his mill was finished. But such a secret could not be kept. Soon every one round knew of the great discovery. The sawmill was left unfinished, the workmen went off to dig for gold, and everyone else followed their example.

The towns were deserted, shops and offices were shut up, houses were left half built, fields were left unploughed, horses and cattle roamed about uncared for. High and low, rich and poor, lawyers, doctors, labourers, threw down their tools or their pens, turned the key in the door, and departed for the gold fields.

Some went by sea, and those who could not get passage in ships hired any small craft which they could find. They put to sea in the most rotten or frail little boats, willing to brave any danger if only they might at length reach the land of gold.

Others went by land, some rode on horseback or drove in a wagon, others went on foot all the way, carrying with them nothing but a spade or shovel.

It was a mad rush for wealth. Every one as soon as he heard the wonderful news was seized with the gold fever. When ships came into port the sailors heard the news, and they deserted wholesale, and the ships were left to rock at anchor without a soul on board. Prisoners broke prison and fled to the gold fields. Warders followed, not to take them but to remain and dig. Newspapers could not be issued, because the printers had all run off; every industry was neglected except the making of spades and picks. And the price of these rose and rose till they could not be had for less than ten dollars apiece, and it is said that even fifty dollars was offered for one.

But in some places upon the gold fields picks and shovels were not needed, for all the men had to do was to pick at the seams with their pocket knives to get enough gold to make them rich.

At first it was only from California, Oregon and the Western settlements that men rushed to the gold fields. For although the telegraph had been discovered a short time before this there were neither telegraphs nor railroads in the West. But soon, in a wonderfully short time too, the news spread. It spread to the Eastern States, then to Europe, and from all over the world the rush came.

Every ship that would float put to sea. Many instead of going their usual routes sailed for California, the whale fisheries were neglected and the whalers took to mining. The fleets of all the world seemed to make for the shores of America.

Across the Continent, too long trains of lumbering wagons drawn by oxen slowly wound. They were tented over and were so huge that whole families lived in them, and they were given the name of prairie schooners. All day long they crawled along and as dusk fell they gathered into groups. Fires were lit, tents pitched for the night. Then early next morning the travelers would be astir again, and so day after day through lonely uninhabited wildernesses the caravans moved on.

In one unending stream great tented wagons, carts, carriages, horsemen or even walkers moved along, all going in the same direction, to the golden land of the West.

Many were the dangers these adventurous travelers had to brave. There were dangers from hostile Indians, and from wild animals, from lack of food and water, and above all from sickness. Cholera broke out in these slow-moving trains, and many a man who had set out gaily found a grave by the wayside, and never reached the land of his golden hopes.

The road too was strewn with broken down wagons, and the bones of oxen and horses, and many had to finish their weary journey on foot.

But in spite of all mischances hundreds and thousands reached the gold fields, and all over the Sacramento Valley, or wherever gold was found, little towns sprang up.

These were towns of wooden shanties and canvas tents. And whenever the gold gave out, or news came of some richer mine, the diggers would forsake the little town, and rush off somewhere else. And no sign of life would be left in the once busy valley save the weather-worn huts and the upturned earth. Some men made fortunes almost in a day, many returned home well off. But by far the greater number returned poorer than they came, and with their health shattered by the hardships of the life. Many more never returned at all, but found a nameless grave among the lonely valleys.

Others made fortunes again and again, and lost them as quickly as they made them. For though at first the men who went to the gold fields were for the most part young, and strong, and honest, the greed of gain soon brought all the riff-raff of the towns. Many men joined the throng who had no intention of working, and who but came to lure the gold away from those who had found it.

So gambling saloons, and drinking saloons, sprang up everywhere, and many a man left them poorer if not wiser. Murders became frequent, but men thought little about them. Every man went armed, and if he could not protect himself it was his own fault.

Theft was looked upon as a far worse sin. For everybody lived in frail wooden huts or open tents. They had no means of locking up their gold, and thought nothing of leaving it lying about quite unprotected. But when criminals and lowdown ruffians began to come things were changed; until at last many were afraid to have it known that they possessed gold lest they should be murdered for it.

Among the many who did not make fortunes out of the finding of gold were Marshall and Sutter. Neither of them was lucky as a miner and both of them died in poverty.

Chapter 78 - Taylor - Union or Disunion

Polk had no chance of being re-elected as President. For many people looked upon the war with Mexico as a great wrong, and as a stain upon the flag. So even although it had given to the United States California, and all its untold wealth, Polk was not forgiven for having brought the war about. And while the people were rushing from all corners of the globe to California, a new President was inaugurated.

This new President was no other than General Zachary Taylor, who had become famous during the Mexican war, for people did not blame him for the war. He had only obeyed orders as a soldier must and every one admired his bravery and skill.

He was a rough old soldier, and his men called him Old Rough and Ready. And when he first heard that people wanted to make him President, like Jackson, that other rough old soldier before him, he simply laughed at the idea.

"I am not vain enough to think that I am fit to be President," he said. "I would gladly see some other citizen more worthy chosen for that high office."

Old Rough and Ready was a soldier, and nothing but a soldier. He knew nothing at all about politics, and had never even voted. However when people insisted that he should be President, he began rather to like the idea, and at length consented to be a candidate, and was elected.

Because of the discovery of gold, thousands and thousands of people flocked to California. And although many returned to their homes again, many also remained in California, and made their homes in the new-found sunny land. So it came about that California was peopled faster than any other part of America, and in 1849, less than two years after the discovery of gold, it asked to be admitted to the Union as a state.

But before it was admitted a fierce battle had to be fought, for the Californians wanted the state to be admitted as a free state. Now part of California lay south of the Missouri Compromise Line, so the Southerners were angry, and declared that California must be divided into two, and that the Southern part must come into the Union as a slave state.

The Southerners felt that they had a right to be angry. For they had helped to bring on the Mexican War for the purpose of getting more territory south of the Missouri Compromise Line, so that they should be sure of slave states to balance the free states of the north. They had won the land, and now victory would be turned to defeat if the new states were admitted as free states.

So they threatened, as they had threatened before, to break away from the Union if they were not listened to.

No sooner was Taylor inaugurated than he had to turn his attention to this great matter. The Southerners were determined to use all their power to get their way, and Senator John Caldwell Calhoun, an old man, who for years had been a champion of slavery, determined to speak once more for the cause.

Calhoun was so old and ill that he could hardly walk, and he tottered into the Senate Chamber leaning on the arms of two friends. He was far too feeble to read his speech. So, pale and deathlike, he sat in his chair while a friend read it for him.

"The South must have a share in the new territory," he said. "If you of the North will not do this, then let our Southern States separate and depart in peace."

This was the great statesman's last word to his country. Three weeks later he lay dead. He was the greatest of Southern politicians. He really believed that slavery was a good thing, and that life in the South would be impossible without it. And loving his country deeply, he could not bear to think of its ruin.

"The South! the poor South! he murmured, as he lay dying. "God knows what will become of her."

The next great speech was made by Daniel Webster. Twenty years had come and gone since he made his first great speech for Union. Now thousands turned to him, begging him to reconcile the North and South. And on the day he made his speech, the Senate Chamber was packed from floor to ceiling.

"I speak today," he said, "not as a Massachusetts man, nor as a Northern man, but as an American, having no locality but America. I speak today for the preservation of the Union. Hear me for my cause."

But to the men burning with zeal against slavery his speech seemed lukewarm. "The law of Nature," he said, "settles forever that slavery cannot exist in California." It was a useless taunt and reproach to the slave holders to forbid slavery where slavery could not exist. He blamed the North for having fallen short in its duty to the South, and declared that the South had just cause for complaint.

Many applauded this speech, but to others it was like a blow in the face.

"Webster," cried one, "is a fallen star! Lucifer descending from heaven!"

A third great speech was made four days later by William H. Seward. He spoke whole-heartedly for union.

"Slavery must vanish from the Union," he said, "but it would vanish peacefully." He brushed aside as impossible the thought that any state should break away from the Union. "I shall vote for the admission of California directly," he said, "without conditions, without qualifications, and without compromise."

The Washington Monument

But still the debate went on. Summer came and on the 4th of July 1850, there

265

was a great ceremony for the laying of the foundation stone of the Washington Monument.

The President was present and sat for hours in the blazing sun. Then feeling very tired he went home and drank iced milk and ate some cherries. That night he became very ill, and a few days later he died.

"I have tried to do my duty," he said. Then the brave and honest old soldier laid down his heavy burden and was at rest.

Once again a sad procession left the White House, and wound slowly through the streets lined with soldiers. Behind the funeral car was led the President's old war horse which he would never mount again. The people wept to see it, and the whole nation mourned for the brave old soldier who had tried to do his duty.

Chapter 79 - Fillmore - The Underground Railroad

The Vice-President, Millard Fillmore, now became President. He was the son of very poor parents; he had picked up an education how he could, and he was nineteen before he saw a history, or a map of his own country. But he was determined to become a lawyer. And after a hard struggle he succeeded. Then from step to step he rose, till he had now reached the highest office in the land.

Under the new President the debate over California still went on. But at length the matter was settled, and California was admitted as a free state. This was on the 9th of September, 1850, but the news did not reach California until October. For months the people had been waiting for an answer to their petition. And as the days went past they grew more and more impatient. But at last one morning San Francisco was filled with excitement for the Oregon was seen coming into harbour gaily decorated with flags.

With shouts of joy the people ran down to the wharf for they knew the Oregon would never come in with flags flying in such a way if she were not bringing good news.

And when they heard the news they laughed, and cried, and kissed each other in joy. Cannon were fired and bells rung, shops were shut, and every one went holidaying.

Messengers too were sent in every direction. Stage coaches with six-horse teams ran races to be the first to bring the news to outlying towns and villages. As the coaches dashed through villages men on them shouted the news, and the villagers would shout and laugh in return.

Then, leaping on their horses, they would ride off to tell some neighbour. So throughout the land the news was carried.

By the admission of California to the Union as a free state the non-slave states were greatly strengthened. But in some degree to make up for this, a very strict law about the arrest of runaway slaves was passed. This was called the Fugitive Slave Law and it was bad and cruel. For, by it, if a negro were caught even by some one who had no right to him, he had no chance of freedom. A negro was not allowed to speak for himself, and he was not allowed the benefit of a jury. Also any person who helped a slave to run away, or protected him when he had run away, might be fined.

The North hated the Bill but it was passed. Many people, however, made up their minds not to obey it. For conscience told them that slavery was wrong and conscience was a "higher Law." So when men came to the free states to catch runaway slaves they were received with anger, and everything was done to hinder them in their man-catching work. The Underground Railroad, too, became more active than ever.

This Underground Railroad was not a railroad, and it was not underground. It was simply a chain of houses about twenty miles or so apart where escaped slaves might be sure of a kindly welcome. The railroad was managed by men who felt pity for the slaves and helped them to escape. It went in direct roads across the States to Canada. The escaping slaves moved so secretly from one house to another that it almost seemed as if they must have gone underground. So the system came to be called the Underground Railroad, and the friendly houses were the stations.

Once a runaway slave reached one of these friendly houses or stations he would be hidden in the attic or cellar or some safe place. There he would be fed and cared for until night came again. Then the password would be given to him, and directions how to reach the next underground station. And, with the pole star for his guide, he would set out.

Arriving at the house in the dusk of early morning, before any one was astir he would knock softly at the door.

"Who's there?" would be asked.

Then the runaway would give the password in answer. Perhaps it would be "William Penn," or "a friend of friends," or sometimes the signal would be the hoot of an owl. And hearing it the master of the underground station would rise and let the "passenger" in.

Sometimes the slavers would come alone, sometimes in twos and threes or even more. As many as seventeen were hidden one day at one of the stations.

Thousands of slaves were in this way helped to escape every year. It was a dangerous employment for the station-masters, and many were found out and fined. They paid the fines, they did not care for that; and went on helping the poor slaves.

Most of the people connected with the underground railroad were white, but some were coloured. One of the most daring of these was Harriet Tubman. She helped so many of her countrymen to escape that they called her "Moses" because she had led them out of the land of bondage. She was nearly white, but had been a slave herself. And having escaped from that fearful bondage she now spent her life in trying to free others.

Again and again, in spite of the danger in being caught, she ventured into the Southern States to bring back a band of runaway slaves. And she was so clever and so full of resource that she always brought them safely away. More than once when she saw she was being tracked, she put herself and her little company into a train, taking tickets for them southwards. For she knew that no one would suspect them to be runaway slaves if they were traveling south. Then, when their track was covered, and danger of pursuit over, they all turned north again.

Harriet was both brave and clever, and when the Civil War broke out, she served as a scout for the Northern Army, earning the praise of those who employed her. She lived to be very old, and died not many years ago, happy to know that all her countrymen were free.

But although many slaves tried to run away, all slaves were not unhappy. When they had a kind master they were well taken care of, and lived in far greater comfort that if they had been free. In the more northerly of the slave states, such as Virginia, the slaves were generally household servants, and were treated in the most affectionate manner. It was farther south in the cotton growing districts, where slaves worked in gangs under the whip of the overseer who was often brutal, that the real misery was.

But even with the kindest of masters a slave could never feel safe. For that master might die or lose his money, and have to sell his slaves. Then husband and wife, parents and children might be sold to different masters, and never see each other again. The one would never know whether the other was happy or miserable, alive or dead. Or they might be sold down South to work in the rice swamps or the cotton fields. It was this that the happy, careless slave from the North most dreaded.

It was just at this time when the Fugitive Slave Law was being enforced, and the Underground Railroad was working nightly that "Uncle Tom's Cabin" was written and published. You all know the story of poor old Tom, of funny, naughty Topsy and all the other interesting people of the book. We look upon it now as merely a story-book. But it was much more than that. It was a great sermon and did more to make people hate slavery than any other book ever written.

It was read by hundreds and thousands of people, and soon the fame of it spread to every country in Europe, and it was translated into at least twenty languages. And even today when the work it was meant to do is done, hundreds of boys and girls still laugh at Topsy and feel very choky indeed over the fate of poor old Uncle Tom.

Chapter 80 - Pierce - The Story of "Bleeding Kansas"

In 1853 Fillmore's term of office came to an end and Franklin Pierce became President. He was only forty-eight, and was the youngest President who had been elected so far.

He was the son of a soldier who had fought in the Mexican War. But by profession he was a lawyer and not a soldier.

During the administration of Pierce another territory was added to the United States. This was a strip of land which now forms the south of New Mexico and Arizona. It was bought from Mexico in 1854 and, as James Gadsden arranged the treaty with the President of Mexico, it was called the Gadsden Purchase. With this purchase the territory of the United States as we know it today was completed. Only seventy years had passed since the Peace of Paris. But in these seventy years the country had made mighty strides and had been doubled and trebled. Instead of being merely a strip of land east of the Mississippi it now stretched from ocean to ocean.

The chief interest in this administration was still the slavery question. It had not been settled as some people thought it had been. But it slept, at least, until suddenly a senator names Douglas awoke it again by bringing in a bill to do away with the Missouri Compromise Line.

There was still a great deal of territory of the Louisiana Purchase waiting to be carved into states. Now said Douglas, "why make all this fuss about slavery or no slavery every time a new state wants to be admitted? Do away with this Missouri Compromise, and when there are enough people in a territory to allow of its being admitted as a state, let these people themselves decide whether they wish it to be a free state or a slave state."

The bill which Douglas brought in thus to do away with the Missouri Compromise was known as the Kansas-Nebraska Bill, as Douglas suggested calling the great unorganised territory Nebraska in the north and Kansas in the South.

Douglas was a Northern man, but he wanted to please the Southerners, and get them to vote for him as President. So he brought in this bill. It met the fierce opposition from the North, but it passed. The President alone had power to stop it. But he did not use his power.

Douglas had brought in the bill to make himself popular. But he made a great mistake. All over the North he was hated and cursed because of it. In town after town he was hanged in effigy, and then burned with every mark of scorn. He was reviled as a Judas, and some women living in a little Northern village sent him thirty pieces of silver.

In spite of this bill the Northerners were determined that slavery should not be extended. So even before the President had signed it men were hurring westward into Kansas. Claims were staked out, trees were felled, and huts built as if by magic. Settlers streamed in by hundreds every day. Some came of themselves, others were sent by societies got up to help settlers, and by the end of the year, two or three towns were founded.

But the slave holders were just as determined to make Kansas a slave state. So from Missouri, which was a slave state and bordered upon the Kansas Territory, thousands of slave owners came over the border and settled in Kansas.

They too found several towns, and there began a fierce struggle for the upper hand.

March 30th, 1855 was appointed by the Governor for the election of a council and House of Representatives for the Territory.

The "Free Staters" were already to vote in force. But the election was a farce. For when the day came, five thousand Missourians marched across the border. They were a wild, sunburned, picturesque mob. They had guns on their shoulders, revolvers stuck in their belts and bowie knives in their big top boots.

They took possession of the polling booths, and if the judges would not do as

269

they wished, they were turned out.

"Do you live in Kansas?" asked a Judge

"Yes, I do," replied the Missourian, without a moment's hesitation.

"Does your family live in Kansas?" asked the judge, who knew the man was not speaking the truth.

"It is none of your business," replied the Missourian. "If you don't keep your impertinence to yourself, I'll knock your head from your shoulders."

So the judge gave it up, and every one who liked voted.

There were not three thousand voters in the Territory, but over six thousand votes were recorded, three-quarters of them being those unlawful votes of the Missourians. Thus said a learned gentleman, "It has been maintained by the sharp logic of the revolver and the bowie knife, that the people of Missouri are the people of Kansas!"

The Governor of Kansas was named Reeder. His sympathy was with the South. But he was an honest man, and when he saw the lawless way in which the Missourians were behaving, he resolved to see justice done. And although they threatened to hang him, he ordered new elections in the seven districts which dared to make a protest. But the new elections made little difference. Owing to the fact that so many of the people were disputing its result, this election did not settle the question whether Kansas were to be admitted as a slave or a free state, and it still remained a Territory. And as soon as the legislature met, the "Free State" members were promptly unseated, and the others had things all their own way.

The laws which this legislature drew up with regard to slaves were quite out of keeping with the needs and desires of free America.

If any person were to entice a slave away from his master they were to suffer death. If they hid and protected a slave, they might be imprisoned with hard labour for five years or more. And if any person declared that Kansas was not a slave territory, they were to be imprisoned with hard labour for at least two years.

These were only a few of the laws. But the Governor vetoed them all. That is, he refused to pass them, veto coming from a Latin word meaning "I forbid." This made the slave party angry and they asked the President to remove Reeder and send a new Governor. This the President had power to do, as Texas was still only a Territory and not a state.

The President was now quite on the side of the slave owners. So a new Governor was sent, but the struggle went on just as before. Both sides began to arm, and at length it came to bloodshed.

The town of Lawrence, which was a Free State town, was sacked by a mob of ruffians, and civil war in Kansas was begun.

In Kansas there was an old man named John Brown. He was a fierce old Puritan, and he believed that God had called him to fight slavery. And the only way of fighting it that he thought possible was to slay the slave-holders.

A few days after the sacking of Lawrence he set off with his sons and one or

270

two others to teach the slave-holders a lesson. Blood had been spilled by them, and he was determined that for every free state man who had been murdered he would have a life of a slave-holder in revenge.

So in the dead of night he and his band attacked the farms of sleeping men, and, dragging them from their beds, slew them in cold blood. Before day dawned six or seven men had been thus slain.

When the Free Staters heard of this deed they were shocked. But it roused the Border Ruffians to fury. Armed companies of both sides marched through the country, and when they met, there was bloodshed. For three years Kansas was in a state of disorder and riot. Governor after governor came with friendly feelings to the South. But when they saw the actions of the slave party they resigned rather than support such injustice.

At length the slave party gained their end, but they were defeated. They were defeated by Douglas, that same man who had caused the Missouri Compromise to be done away with. Then he had blackened his name, now he redeemed it.

The President was ready to use all his power to force the admission of Kansas as a slave state. Douglas warned him to beware, and when the President persisted, he rose in his place, and made such a wonderful speech that the bill introduced by the slave-holders was defeated. And when at length Kansas was admitted to the Union in 1861, it was admitted as a free state.

Chapter 81 - Buchanan - The Story of the Mormons

THE President whom Douglas defied over the question of Kansas was not Pierce, for in 1857 his term of office came to an end and James Buchanan was elected as President. Like Pierce, he was a "Northern man with Southern principles," and he threw his lot with the slave-holders.

Like Pierce, he was a lawyer, and in ordinary times might have made a good President and have left an honoured name behind him. But he came into power at a most difficult and dangerous time. He was not big enough or strong enough for the task. And so his name is less honoured perhaps than that of any other President.

Besides Kansas, two more states were admitted into the Union during Buchanan's term of office. These were Minnesota in 1858 and Oregon in 1859. They both became states while the struggle over Kansas was going on. For in them there was no trouble over the slavery question, and they were both admitted as free states. Minnesota was part of the Louisiana Purchase together with the last little corner of the North-West Territory. Oregon was part of the Oregon country. These with Kansas now made thirty-four states. So there were now thirty-four stars in the flag.

It was at this time that what is known as the Mormon War took place.

Mormonism was a new religion founded by Joseph Smith. Joseph Smith was a shiftless, idle, jovial fellow, one of a large family as shiftless and idle as himself. He was very ignorant, but he had a wonderful imagination, and he could never tell the

271

simplest happening of his everyday life without making a great story out of it.

When he grew to be a man he began to dream dreams and see visions, and at length he declared that a messenger from heaven had shown him where to find a golden book. No one else saw this golden book, because Smith had been warned by the angel that great punishment would fall upon him if he showed it to any one. He was, however, allowed to make a "translation" of what was written in the book. This he did, publishing it as "The Book of the Mormons" or "The Golden Bible." But it seems very likely that part of this so-called translation was really copied from a story written by a man named Spaulding which had never been published. A great deal of it was, however, copied from the Bible.

Smith, who was at this time living in the State of New York, now declared that the religion which had been revealed to him was the only true religion. He founded a Church of which he was head or "prophet" and under him were twelve apostles and other dignitaries. A few people soon joined him and gradually their numbers increased until at last they numbered several thousand.

They now became a community by themselves, they moved about from place to place, and at length settled in Illinois where they built a city called Nauvoo.

Smith had many revelations. If he wanted a horse or cart he had a revelation saying that it was to be given to him. If he wanted his followers to do anything, again he had a revelation saying it was to be done. So he ruled like an autocrat and did whatever he chose. And while at Nauvoo he had a revelation which said it was quite lawful for men to marry as many wives as they wanted.

Soon the people of Illinois began to dislike the Latter-day Saints, as they called themselves. For they stole horses and cattle and all sorts of things belonging to other settlers. And once anything was stolen by the Mormons, it was impossible to get it back. For if a stranger went to their city, and showed by his questions that he had come to look for something he had lost, he soon found himself followed by a Mormon who silently whittled a stick with a long sharp knife. Soon the man would be joined by another, also whittling a stick with a long knife. Then another and another would silently join the procession, until the stranger could stand it no longer and hastily departed homeward.

So as time went on the people grew more and more angry with the Mormons. And at length their anger burst into fury, and, in 1844, Smith and one of his brothers were lynched by the mob.

The Mormons were greatly cast down at the death of their Prophet, but they soon found a new leader in Brigham Young, one of the twelve apostles.

But this change of leader brought no peace between the Mormons and their neighbours. Complaints of theft grew more and more frequent. Both sides went about armed, murders were committed, and the settlers burned many of the Mormon farms.

At length the whole of the Mormons were expelled from Illinois, and one March day a great caravan started westward. Slowly day by day they moved onward through unknown wildernesses, making a road for themselves, and building bridges as they went, and only after long trials and hardships they reached the Great Salt Lake.

The land around was treeless and desolate, and the ground so hard that when they tried to plough it the ploughshare broke. Yet they decided to make their dwelling-place amid this desolation, and in 1847 the building of Salt Lake City was begun.

At the beginning, troubles and trials were many. But with hard work and skilful irrigation the desert disappeared, and fertile fields and fair gardens took its place.

The Mormons now laid claim to a great tract of land and called it the State of Deseret. And over this state Brigham Young ruled supreme.

In 1850, however, the United States organized it as a territory and changed the name to Utah. Utah is an Indian word meaning Mountain Home. Of this territory Brigham Young was Governor, but other non-Mormon officials were sent from Washington. Very soon there was trouble between the Mormons and these non-Mormon officials and, one after another, they returned to Washington saying that it was useless for them to remain in Utah. For with Brigham Young as governor it was impossible to enforce the laws of the United States, and that their lives even were in danger.

But when there was talk of removing Young from the post of Governor he was indignant. "I am and will be Governor," he said, "and no power can hinder it until the Lord Almighty says, 'Brigham, you need not be Governor any longer.'"

The Mormons were indignant at the false reports, as they considered them, of their doings which were spread abroad in the East. So they asked the President to send one or two visitors "to look about them and see what they can see, and return and report."

But instead of sending visitors President Buchanan appointed a new Governor, and sent a body of troops to Utah.

Thus began what is called the Mormon War. But there was never a battle fought. Although at first the Mormons prepared to resist, they changed their minds. And the Government troops marched into Salt Lake City without resistance. They found the city deserted, as nearly all the inhabitants had fled away. They soon returned, however, and "peace" was restored. But the submission was only one in form, and for many a long day there was trouble between the Government and the Territory of Utah.

Besides the main body of Mormons who founded Salt Lake City there is another band, followers of Joseph Smith's eldest son also called Joseph. They broke away from the first Mormons because they did not think it right to marry more than one wife, nor could they believe in all that "the prophet" taught his followers. Their chief city is Lamoni in Iowa where they live quiet industrious lives and are greatly respected by their neighbours.

This religion, founded so strangely, has spread very rapidly. In 1830 the church had only six members. Today there are more than three hundred thousand Mormons in the world, most of whom are in the United States.

273

Chapter 82 - Buchanan - The First Shots

Meanwhile a great man was coming into power. This was Abraham Lincoln. He was the son of very poor people and his earliest days were spent in the utmost poverty and want. His home in Kentucky was a wretched little log cabin without doors or windows, and the bare earth for a floor. But in spite of his miserable and narrow surroundings Lincoln grew up to be a great, broad-minded loveable man.

He was very anxious to learn, and he taught himself nearly all he knew, for in all his life he had only two or three months of school. The few books he could lay hands on he read again and again till he almost knew them by heart.

Lincoln grew to be a great, lanky, hulking boy. He had the strongest arm and the tenderest heart in the countryside, and was so upright in all his dealings that he earned the name of Honest Abe.

Everybody loved the ungainly young giant with his sad face and lovely smile, and stock of funny stories.

He began early to earn his living, and was many things in turn. He did all sorts of farm work, he split rails and felled trees. He was a storekeeper for a time, then a postmaster, a surveyor, a soldier. But none of these contented him; he was always struggling towards something better.

While keeping shop he began to study law, and when he was not weighing out pounds of tea and sugar he had his head deep in some dry book. While trying his hand at other jobs, too, he still went on studying law, and at length he became a lawyer.

Even before this he had taken great interest in politics and had sat in the Illinois House of Representatives, and at length in 1846 he was elected to Congress. But he only served one term in the House, after which he returned to his law business and seemed for a time to lose interest in politics.

But the passing of the Kansas-Nebraska Bill aroused him again. As a boy he had been to New Orleans. There he had seen the slave market. He had seen negro parents parted from their children, and sold to different masters. He had seen them chained like criminals, beaten and treated worse than beasts of burden, and from these sights he had turned away with an aching heart. "Boys," he said, to his companions, "let's get away from this. If ever I get a chance to hit that thing, I'll hit it hard."

And he did not forget what he had seen; the memory of it was a constant torment and a misery to him. And now the chance had come, and he hit "that thing" hard.

In 1858 he challenged Douglas, the author of the Kansas-Nebraska Bill, to go round the country with him and make speeches on the great subject of the day: Douglas to take one side of the question and Lincoln the other. It was a bold thing to do, for Douglas was considered the greatest speaker of the time, and Lincoln was scarcely known. But the speeches made Lincoln famous and henceforth many of the men in the North looked upon him as their leader. He wanted to have slavery done away with, but above all he loved his country. "A house divided against itself," he said, "cannot stand. I believe this government cannot endure half-slave, half-free. I do not expect the Union to be divided. I do not expect the House to fall. But I do expect it will cease to be divided. It will become all one thing, or all the other."

He had no bitterness against the South, for he loved his whole country, South as well as North. It was slavery he hated, not the slave-holders. But the slave-holders hated him and his ideas. So when in November, 1860, Lincoln was chosen President the Southern States declared that they would not submit to be ruled by him.

As you know, the new President is always chosen some months before the end of the last President's term. Lincoln was thus chosen in November, 1860, but did not actually become President till March, 1861.

So with Buchanan still President, several of the Southern States declared themselves free from the Union. South Carolina led the rebellion. Amid great excitement, a new declaration of independence was read, and union with the other states was declared to be at an end.

The example of South Carolina was soon followed. Mississippi, Alabama, Florida, Georgia, Louisiana and Texas all declared their union with the States at an end. They then joined together. And calling themselves the Confederate States, they elected a President, drew up a Constitution, and made ready to seize the Union forts and arsenals.

Meanwhile President Buchanan knew not what to do. He tried to steer both ways at once. He said the Southern States had no right to break away from the Union, but he also said that the Government had no power to force them to return. In reality, however, his heart was with the South, and he believed that the Southerners had just cause for anger. So the Southerners soon came to believe that the President would let them go their own way. Some of the Northerners, too, thought a division would be a good thing, or at least that disunion was better than war. "Let the slave states depart in peace," they said. But others would not hear of that, and were ready to fight to the last if only the Union might be preserved.

The country was fast drifting towards war; and soon the first shot was fired. Charleston, the harbour of South Carolina, was guarded by two forts, Fort Moultrie and Fort Sumter. Fort Moultrie was large, needing about seven hundred men to guard it properly, and Major Anderson, who was in command, had only sixty men under him. So, seeing that the people of South Carolina were seizing everything they could, and finding that the President would send him no help, he drew off his little force to Fort Sumter which could be more easily defended.

Again and again Major Anderson asked for more men, and at length an ordinary little passenger vessel was sent with two hundred and fifty men. But when the little ship steamed into Charleston harbour the Southerners fired upon it. And as it had no guns on board or any means of defence it turned and sped back whence it had come. Thus the first shots in the Civil War were fired on Jan. 9th, 1861.

275

Chapter 83 - Lincoln - From Bull Run to Fort Donelson

IN the midst of all this confusion the new President took his seat. The Southerners were so angry that it was feared that Lincoln would never be allowed to become President at all, but would be killed on his way to Washington. Yet he himself felt no fear, and he journeyed slowly from his home to Washington, stopping at many places, and making many speeches on the way. Day by day, however, his friends grew more and more anxious. Again and again they begged him to change his plans and go to Washington by some other way. But Lincoln would not listen to their entreaties. At length, however, they became so insistent that he yielded to them.

So instead of proceeding as he had intended, he left his party secretly, and with one friend turned back, and went to Washington by a different route. The telegraph wires were cut, so that had any traitor noticed this change of plan he could not tell his fellow conspirators. Thus, all unknown, Lincoln stole silently into the capital during the night. And great was the astonishment both of friend and foe when it was discovered that he was there.

Almost the first thing Lincoln had to do was to send relief to Major Anderson at Fort Sumter. So vessels were laden with food and sent off to the gallant little band.

But as soon as the Southerners heard the news they determined to take the fort before help could arrive. Soon a terrible bombardment began. Half a hundred cannon roared against the fort, shells screamed and fell, and the walls were quickly shattered. The barracks took fire, and after two days it became utterly impossible to resist longer.

So Major Anderson yielded, and with his brave company marched out with all the honours of war.

War was now begun in real earnest, although strange to say, in spite of the terrific firing, not a life had been lost on either side.

Both North and South now began to arm. But when the President called for troops four states scornfully refused to obey. These were Arkansas, Tennessee, North Carolina and Virginia, and instead of gathering troops to help the Government they joined the Confederates. Richmond, Virginia, was chosen as the capital and Jefferson Davis was made President of the Confederacy, which included eleven states.

In the west of Virginia, however, the people were loyal to the Union and it was here that the first great battles of the war were fought.

Life in this part of Virginia which lay beyond the Alleghenies was very different from life in Eastern Virginia. Western Virginia was not a land suitable for slaves, and for a long time the people had desired to part from Eastern Virginia. Now during the war they had their wish, and West Virginia became a separate state. In June, 1863, it was admitted to the Union as the thirty-fifth state.

The war which had now begun was the most terrible ever fought on American soil. For far more even than the War of Independence, it was a war of kindred. It made enemies of comrades and brothers. Men who had been dear friends suddenly found themselves changed into ruthless enemies, families even were divided against each other.

For four years this bitter war lasted, and counting all battles great and small there were at least two thousand, so we cannot attempt to follow the whole course of the great struggle.

The first blood was shed, strangely enough, on the anniversary of the battle of Lexington. On that day, 19th April, 1861, some Massachusetts soldiers were passing through Baltimore, when they were attacked by the mob. Pistols were fired from the houses, paving stones and bricks flew about. Several of the soldiers were killed, many more were wounded; and to protect themselves they fired on the mob, several of whom were killed also.

The greatest leader on the Federal side was General Ulysses S. Grant, and next to him came William T. Sherman and Philip H. Sheridan. But it was not until the war had been going on for some time that these soldiers came to the front, and at first all the fortune was on the side of the South.

General Albert S. Johnston was commander-in-chief of the Southern army by the two most famous Southern leaders were Robert E. Lee and Thomas J. Jackson. Jackson is best known by the nickname of Stonewall, which he received at Bull Run in West Virginia, the first great battle of the war.

It seemed as if the Federals were winning the battle, and some of the Confederates were driven backward. But Jackson and his men stood solid.

"See!" cried a general, "there is Jackson standing like a stone wall!" Thus Jackson got a new name, and the Confederates won the day.

"It was one of the best planned battles of the war," said Sherman afterwards, "but one of the worst fought. Both armies were fairly defeated, and whichever stood fast the other would have run."

Less than three weeks after Bull Run, the Federals met with another disaster at Wilson's Creek in Missouri. Here, after a desperate and gallant fight, they were defeated, and General Nathaniel Lyon, their brave leader, was killed.

These defeats were a great shock to the Federals. For they had thought that the war would be a short affair of three months or so, and that the Southern revolt would be easily put down. Now they knew themselves mistaken, and pulling themselves together, prepared for a long and bitter struggle.

For some months, however, after Bull Run and Wilson's Creek no battle of importance was fought. Then in the beginning of 1862 the war was carried into Kentucky where a stern fight for the great navigable rivers which flow through the state began. For just as in the War of Independence the holding of the Hudson Valley had been of importance so now the holding of the Mississippi Valley was of importance. If the Mississippi from Cairo to New Orleans could be strongly held by the Federals, the Confederacy would be cut in two, and thus greatly weakened. "The Mississippi," said Lincoln, "is the backbone of the rebellion; it is the key of the whole situation.

But to get possession of this key was no easy matter. Early in February two forts on the river Tennessee were taken by the Federals under General Grant.

277

Then they marched upon Fort Donelson, a large and very strong fort on the Cumberland river. At the same time Commander Andrew H. Foote sailed up the river with a little fleet of seven gunboats to assist the army.

The weather was bitterly cold, and as the soldiers lay round the fort tentless and fireless, a pitiless wind blew, chilling them to the bone, and making sleep impossible. Foote with his gunboats had not yet arrived, but in the morning the attack on land was begun. Up the hill to the fort the Federals swept, only to be driven back by the fierce Confederate fire. Again and again they charged. Again and again they were driven back, leaving the hillside strewn with dead and dying. At length the dry leaves which covered the hillside took fire. Choked by the smoke, scorched by the flames the men could advance no more, and they sullenly retreated for the last time. The attack had failed.

That night the gunboats arrived, and soon the bombardment from the river began. But the firing from the fort was so fierce and well placed that before long two of the boats were disabled, and floated helplessly down the stream, and the others too withdrew till they were out of range of the Confederate guns.

There was joy that night in Fort Donelson. By land and water the Federals had been repulsed. The Confederates felt certain of victory.

But the Federals were by no means beaten, and next morning they renewed the fight as fiercely as ever. Yet again the Confederates swept all before them, and the right wing of the Federal army was driven from its position and scattered in flight. Victory for the Confederates seemed certain.

During this fight Grant had not been with the troops, for he had gone down the river to consult with Foote, who had been wounded the day before. About noon he returned, and when he heard of the disaster his face flushed hotly. But he was a man who rarely lost his temper, or betrayed his feelings. For a minute he was silent, crushing some papers he held in his hand. Then in his usual calm voice he said, "Gentlemen, the position on the right must be retaken."

And retaken it was.

General Charles F. Smith led the assault. He was an old soldier who had fought under Zachary Taylor in Texas where "Smith's light battalion" had become famous. White haired now, but still handsome and erect, he rode this day in front of his troops, once and again turning his head to cheer them onward. Bullets whizzed and screamed about him, but he heeded them not.

"I was nearly scared to death," said one of his men afterwards, "but I saw the old man's white moustache over his shoulder, and went on."

Hotter and hotter grew the fire, and the men hesitated and wavered. But the old general knew no fear. Placing his cap on the end of his sword, he waved it aloft.

"No flinching now, my lads," he cried. "This is the way. Come on!"

And on they came, inspired by the fearless valour of the old soldier. And when at length they had triumphantly planted their colours on the lost position, no efforts of the enemy could dislodge them.

Meanwhile another division under General Lew Wallace dashed up another hill with splendid elan, and when night fell, although the fort was still untaken, it was

278

at the mercy of the attackers.

Supperless and fireless, the Federals cheerfully bivouacked upon the field, for they well knew that the morrow would bring them victory. But within the fort there was gloom. Nothing was left but surrender. It would be impossible to hold out even for half an hour, said General Buckner, the best soldier, although the youngest of the three generals in command. The other two generals agreed, but declared that they would not stay to be made prisoner. So in the night they silently crept away with their men.

Early next morning General Buckner, left alone in command, wrote to Grant proposing a truce in order to arrange terms of surrender.

Grant's answer was short and sharp. "No terms except unconditional and immediate surrender can be accepted," he said.

Bitter indeed were the feelings of the Confederate leader when he received this reply. But there was nothing left to him but to accept the terms. He was hopelessly outnumbered, and to fight longer would only mean the throwing away of brave lives uselessly. So he accepted what seemed to him the "ungenerous and unchivalrous terms" which Grant proposed, and surrendered the fort with all its guns and great stores of ammunition, and fourteen thousand men.

Up to this time Grand had hardly been heard of. He was a soldier indeed, and had fought in the Mexican War. But eight years before the outbreak of the rebellion he had left the army. During these years he had tried in many ways to make a living, but had succeeded in none, and at the beginning of the war he was almost a ruined man. Now he became famous, and his short and sharp "unconditional surrender" was soon a watchword in the Northern army. His initials too being U. S. he became henceforth known as Unconditional Surrender Grant.

Chapter 84 - Lincoln - The Story of the First Battle Between Ironclads

There was fighting too on sea as well as on land. The South sent out privateers to catch the merchant vessels of the North, and so bring ruin on their trade. But Lincoln replied by proclaiming a blockade of all Confederate ports.

This was a bold thing to do, for the coast to be watched was some three thousand miles long, and the Government had less than fifty ships to blockade it with. When the blockade was proclaimed, too, many of these ships were far away in foreign lands. The greatest navy yard, also, at Norfolk in Virginia, was in the hands of the Confederates, and was therefore not available for the building of new ships.

So at first the blockade amounted to little. But by degrees it took effect. Ships that had been far away returned, others of all sorts and sizes were bought, still others were built with the utmost speed.

Slowly but surely the iron hand of the North gripped the commerce of the South, and before the end of the war the Southern ports were shut off from all the world.

This was a disaster for the Southerners, for they depended almost entirely on their cotton trade with Europe. Now the cotton rotted on the wharves. There were no factories in the South, for manufactures could not be carried on with slave labour. So the Southerners depended entirely on the outside world for clothes, boots, blankets, iron, and all sorts of war material. Now they were cut off from the outside world, and could get none of these things.

But the Southerners did not meekly submit to be cut off from the world. They had hardly any ships of any kind, and none at all meant for war. But they had possession of the Government navy yard at Norfolk. There they found a half-finished frigate, and they proceeded to finish her, and turn her into an ironclad. When finished she was an ugly looking, black monster with sloping sides and a terrible iron beak, and she was given the name of the Merrimac.

At this time there were only about three ironclads in all the world. They belonged to Britain and to France, and had never yet been used in naval warfare. So when this ugly black monster appeared among the wooden ships of the North she created frightful havoc. It was one day in March that the black monster appeared in Hampton Roads where there was a little fleet of five Federal warships.

The Federal ships at once opened fire upon the uncouth thing. But to their surprise their shots fell harmlessly from its sides, and paying no heed to their guns it made straight for the Cumberland, and struck her such a terrible blow with her sharp beak that she sank with all on board. She went down gallantly flying her flag to the last.

The Merrimac then turned upon another ship named the Congress. The struggle between a wooden vessel and an ironclad was a hopeless one from the beginning. But the Congress put up a splendid fight, and only when the ship was afire did she give in.

It was dusk by now and the terrible Merrimac sheered off leaving the Congress a blazing wreck.

The Federals were filled with consternation. This horrible strange vessel would certainly return with daylight. And what chance had any wooden ship against it?

But help was near.

The Government also had been busy ship-building. A Swede named Ericsson had invented a new vessel which would resist cannon. This ship was just finished, and came into Hampton Roads almost immediately after the battle with the Merrimac. And when the Commander heard the news he took up his position beside the burning Congress, and waited for dawn.

This new vessel was called the Monitor, and a stranger vessel was never seen afloat. Its hull, which was ironclad, hardly showed above the water, and in the middle there was a large round turret. It looked, said those who saw it, more like a cheesebox on a raft than anything else.

Like a tiger hungry for prey the Merrimac came back next morning. The captain expected an easy victory, but to his surprise he found this queer little cheesebox between him and his victims. He would soon do for the impertinent little minnow,

280

he thought, and he opened fire. But his shells might have been peas for all the effect they had, and the Monitor steamed on unhurt, until she was close to the Merrimac. Then she fired.

A tremendous duel now began which lasted three hours. The lumbering Merrimac tried to run down her enemy, but the quick little Monitor danced round and round, turning the turret now this way, now that, and firing how she pleased, like a terrier yapping at a maddened bull. And at length the Merrimac gave up the tussle, and sailed away.

This was the first battle ever fought between ironclads and it has been called a draw. But after all the honours were with the little Monitor, for she forced her big opponent to run away.

It might almost be said that this battle saved the Union, for it showed the Confederates that they would not have it all their own way on sea, and that if they were building ironclads the Federals were building them also. And indeed the Government built ships so fast that by the end of the war, instead of having only about forty they had over six hundred ship, many of them ironclad.

Chapter 85 - Lincoln - The Battle of Shiloh and the Taking of New Orleans

With Grant other successes soon followed the taking of Fort Donelson, and many places both in Kentucky and Tennessee fell into the hands of the Federals.

By the beginning of April Grant with an army of forty thousand men lay at Pittsburg Landing on the Tennessee River. At Corinth, about thirty miles to the south, the Confederates were gathered in equal force. But although the Confederates were so near and in such force the Federals took no heed. They had of late won so many easy victories that they had begun to think lightly of the foe. So no attempt was made to protect the Union army. No trenches were dug, and but few scouts were sent out to watch the movements of the enemy. The Confederate leader, General Johnston, therefore determined to creep up stealthily, and attack the Federals where they lay in fancied security.

As secretly as possible he left Corinth, and marched towards Pittsburg Landing. The weather had been wet, the roads were deep in mud, but in spite of dreadful difficulties for two days the army toiled silently on. At length on the night of Saturday the 5th of April they arrived within four miles of the Federal lines.

Here they halted for the night. The men had brought no tents, they dared light no fires lest they should be seen by the foe. So, weary, wet, and shivering they lay on the cold damp ground, awaiting the dawn, while secure in the comfortable shelter of their tents the Federals slept peacefully. So secure indeed did Grant feel his position to be that he was not with his army that night, but at Savannah some miles distant.

At daybreak the Federal camp was astir. Men were washing and dressing, some were cooking or eating breakfast, most of the officers were still abed, when suddenly the sound of shots broke the Sunday stillness, and the wild "rebel yell" rent the air.

A moment later the surrounding woods seemed to open and pour forth an army. With tremendous dash the Confederates flung themselves upon the half dressed, weaponless crowd of men who fled before them, or were bayoneted before they could seize their muskets. Thus the greatest battle that as yet had been fought on the continent of America was begun.

Soon the roar of cannon reached Grant at Savannah. He knew at once that a fierce battle had begun, and flinging himself on his horse he hurried back to the camp. At eight o'clock in the morning he arrived. But already it seemed as if his army was defeated. It was, however, to be no easy victory for the Confederates. Many of the Federals were only raw recruits, but after the first surprise and flight they rallied repeatedly, making many a stubborn stand against the onslaught of the foe, which from the first great charge of early dawn till darkness fell never seemed to slacken.

In many coloured uniforms, with many coloured pennons waving over them, the Confederates charged again and yet again. And with each charge the air was rent with their wild yell, which could be heard far and wide, even above the roar of the cannon. Bit by bit the Union army was pressed back. They fought doggedly as they went while from division to division rode Grant cheering them, directing them, urging them to greater and ever greater efforts.

Some of the fiercest fighting raged round the little log meeting house called Shiloh, and from this meeting house the battle takes its name. Sherman commanded here, and he held his untried men together with marvelous skill, handling them as no other commander on the field could have done, said Grant later.

On the Confederate side through the thickest of the battle rode Johnston. More than once his horse was shot under him, and his clothes were torn to pieces, but still through the fray he rode unharmed. At length a ball hit him in the thigh. He paid no heed. Still his tall soldierly figure dominated the battle, still his ringing voice cheered on his men. Then suddenly the voice grew faint, the tall figure bent, and a deathly whiteness overspread his cheeks.

"General, are you wounded?" asked one of his officers, anxiously.

"Yes," he answered, faintly, "and I fear badly."

They were his last words. Gently he was lifted from his horse and laid on the ground, and in a few minutes he died.

When the sun went down the Confederates claimed the victory. But if victory it was it was too dearly bought with the death of their commander-in-chief. Nor did the Federals own themselves beaten. They were dumbfounded and bleeding, but not shattered. They felt that the struggle was not over, and still facing each other the weary armies lay down to rest on the field, under the lashing rain, each side well aware that with the morrow would come the decisive contest.

All through the night the guns from the river boomed and crashed, and rain fell in torrents, adding to the discomforts of the wearied men, making sleep almost impossible.

When day dawned rain still fell in a cold and dismal drizzle. The Federals,

282

however, rose cheerfully, for the inspiriting news that twenty-five thousand fresh troops had arrived ran through the lines. Before the sun had well risen the battle began again, but now the advantage was on the Federal side.

The Confederates fought bravely still. To and fro rode General Beauregard cheering on his men, but step by step they were driven backward, and by noon were in full retreat. Then as the Federals realized that the day was theirs cheer after cheer went up from their lines.

The second day's fighting had turned the battle of Shiloh into a victory for the Union, although not a decisive one. On the same day, however, the navy captured a strongly fortified island on the Mississippi called Island Number Ten, with its garrison of seven thousand men and large stores of guns and ammunition. This considerably increased the force of the victory of Shiloh, and gave the Federals control of the Mississippi Valley from Cairo to Memphis.

Meanwhile command of the lower Mississippi had also been wrested from the Confederates by General Benjamin F. Butler in command of the army, and Commander David Glasgow Farragut in command of the fleet.

Captain Farragut who was already sixty-three at this time was a Southerner by birth, but he had never faltered in his allegiance to the Union. "Mind what I tell you," he said to his brother officers, when they tried to make him desert his flag, "you fellows will catch the devil before you get through with this business." And so unshaken was his faith that he was trusted with the most important naval expedition of the war, the taking of New Orleans.

New Orleans is about a hundred miles from the mouth of the Mississippi and the Confederates, who were aware even more than the Federals of the importance of the great waterway, had from the very beginning done their utmost to secure it. Seventy-five miles below New Orleans two forts named Jackson and St. Phillips guarded the approaches to the city. These the Confederates had enormously strengthened, and had stretched a great chain between them from bank to bank, to prevent the passage of hostile ships. They had also gathered a fleet of ironclads and gunboats further to defend the city.

But in spite of all these defenses the Federals determined to take New Orleans and on the 18th of April the Union ships began to bombard the forts. The Confederates replied fiercely, and for four days the sky seemed ablaze and the earth shook. Then having succeeded in cutting the chain across the river Farragut determined to sail past the fort and take New Orleans.

At two o'clock in the morning the ships began to move. The night was dark but very still and clear, and soon the noise of slipping anchor cables warned the enemy of what was afoot. Then a very hail of shot and shell fell upon the Federal boats. Burning fire ships too were sent down upon them, and the red light of battle lit up the darkness. Yet through the baptism of fire the vessels held on their way undaunted. The forts were passed, the Confederate fleet disabled and put to flight, and Farragut sailed unhindered up the river.

At his approach, New Orleans was seized with panic. Filled with a nameless fear women and children ran weeping through the streets, business of every kind was at a standstill. The men, mostly grey-haired veterans and boys, turned the keys in their office doors, and hurried to join the volunteer regiments, bent on fighting to the last for their beloved city. Thousands of bales of cotton were carried to the wharves, and there set on fire, lest they should fall into the hands of the enemy. Ships too were set on fire, and cast loose, till it seemed as if the whole river front was wrapped in flames. Thirty miles away the glare could be seen in the sky, and at the sight even strong men bowed their heads and wept. For they knew it meant that New Orleans had fallen, and that the Queen of Southern cities was a captive.

But there was no fighting, for General Lovell who was in command of the city marched away with his army as soon as the Union ships appeared. The citizens who were left were filled with impotent wrath and despair. They felt themselves betrayed. They had been assured that the city would fight to the last. Now their defenders had marched away leaving them to the mercy of the conqueror.

The streets were soon filled with a dangerous, howling cursing mob man of them armed, all of them desperate. Yet calmly through it, as if on parade, marched two Federal officers, without escort of protection of any kind. The mob jostled them, shook loaded pistols in their faces, yelling and cursing the while. But the two officers marched on side by side unmoved, showing neither anger nor fear, turning neither to right nor to left until they reached the city hall, where they demanded the surrender of the city.

"It was one of the bravest deeds I ever saw done," said a Southerner, who as a boy of fourteen watched the scene.

By the taking of New Orleans Farragut won for himself great fame. His fame was all the greater because in his fleet he had none of the newly invented ironclads. With only wooden vessels he had fought and conquered. "It was a contest between iron hearts and wooden vessels, and iron clads with iron beaks, and the iron hearts won," said Captain Bailey who served in the expedition under Farragut.

After taking New Orleans Farragut sailed up the river and took Baton Rouge, the state capital. So at length the Federals had control of the whole lower river as far as Vicksburg. The upper river from Cairo was also secure to the Federals. Thus save for Vicksburg the whole valley was in their hands, and the Confederacy was practically cut in two.

But Vicksburg stood firm for the South. When called upon to surrender the governor refused. "I have to state," he said, "that Mississippians do not know, and refuse to learn, how to surrender to an enemy. If Commodore Farragut, or Brigadier General Butler, can teach them, let them come and try."

At the time soldiers enough could not be spared to help the fleet to take Vicksburg. So for the time being it was left alone.

Chapter 86 - Lincoln - The Slaves are Made Free

The Federals rejoiced greatly at the successes of Grant and the navy, and indeed they had need of success somewhere to keep up their spirits, for on the whole things did not go well. George McClellan was commander-in-chief, and although he drilled his army splendidly he never did anything with it. He was a wonderful organiser, but he was cautious to a fault, and always believed the enemy to be far stronger than he really was.

He was at last dismissed, and was succeeded by one commander-in-chief after another. Not none proved truly satisfactory. Indeed it was not until the last year of the war, when Ulysses Grant took command, that a really great commander-in-chief was found.

At the beginning of the war no matter who was leader the long campaigns in Virginia ended in failure for the Federals. On the Confederate side these campaigns were led first by Joseph E. Johnston, and then by the great soldier, Robert E. Lee.

Lee came of a soldier stock, being the youngest son of "Light Horse Harry Lee," who had won fame during the War of the Revolution. He was a noble, Christian gentleman, and when he made his choice, and determined to fight for the South, he believed he was fighting for the right.

With Lee was Stonewall Jackson, his great "right hand," and perhaps a finer soldier than Lee himself. His men adored him as they adored no other leader. Like Cromwell he taught them to pray as well as to fight. He never went into battle without commending his way to God, and when he knelt long in prayer his men might feel certain that a great fight was coming. He was secret and swift in his movements, so swift that his troops were nicknamed "Jackson's foot cavalry." Yet he never wore his men out. He thought for them always, and however urgent haste might be he called frequent halts on his flying marches, and made the men lie down even if it were only for a few minutes.

To conquer such leaders, and the men devoted to them, was no easy matter, and it was not wonderful that the campaigns in Virginia marked few successes for the Federals. At length the long series of failures ended with a second, and for the Federals, disastrous, battle of Bull Run. This was followed two days later by the battle of Chantilly, after which the whole Federal army fell back to Washington.

Lee, rejoicing at his successes in Virginia, made up his mind then to invade Maryland, which state he believed would readily join the Confederacy. But he was disappointed. For if the Marylanders had not much enthusiasm for the Union cause they had still less for the Confederate, and the invaders were greeted with exceeding coldness. Their unfailing good fortune, too, seemed to forsake the Confederates, and the battle of Antietam, one of the fiercest of the war, although hardly a victory for the Federals, was equal to a defeat for the Confederates. For fourteen hours the carnage lasted, and when at length night put an end to the slaughter thousands lay dead on either side. Next day, having in a fortnight lost half his army, Lee withdrew once more into Virginia.

Lincoln's chief object in carrying on the war was not to free slaves, but to save the Union.

"My first object is to save the Union," he wrote, "and not either to save or destroy slavery. If I could save the Union without freeing any slaves I would do it. If I could save it by freeing all the slaves I would do it. And if I could save it by freeing some, and leaving others alone I would also do that." Gradually, however, Lincoln began to believe that the only way to save the Union was to free the slaves.

Many people were impetuously urging him to do it. But Lincoln would do nothing rash. It was a tremendous step to take, and the question as to when would be the right moment to take it was, for him, one of tremendous importance. So he prepared his Proclamation of Emancipation and bided his time. Following his own good judgment and the advice of one of his Cabinet he resolved not to announce it so long as things were going badly with the North lest it should be looked upon as the last measure of an exhausted government, a cry for help. It was not to be sent forth into the world as "a last shriek in the retreat," but as a companion to victory.

But victory was slow in coming. At length the great battle was fought at Antietam. It was scarce a victory, for the Federals had lost more men than had the Confederates. Yet it had to pass for one. And a few days after it Lincoln issued his Proclamation of Emancipation. In this he declared that in every state which should be in arms against the Government on the 1st of January, 1863, the slaves should be free forever more. This gave the rebel states more than three months in which to lay down their arms and return to their allegiance.

Meanwhile the war went on. In November General Ambrose E. Burnside was appointed commander of the army of the Potomac. He accepted the post unwillingly, for he did not think himself great enough to fill it. It was soon proved that he was right.

On December 13th a great battle was fought at Fredericksburg in Virginia. The weather had been very cold and the ground was covered with frost and snow. But on the morning of the 13th, although a white mist shrouded the land, the sun shone so warmly that it seemed like a September day. Yet though the earth and sky alike seemed calling men to mildness and peace the deadly game of war went on.

The centre of the Confederate army occupied some high ground known as the Maryes Heights, and Burnside resolved to dislodge them. It was a foolhardy attempt, for the hill was strongly held, the summit of it bristled with cannon. Yet the order was given, and with unquestioning valour the men rushed to the attack. As they dashed onward the Confederate guns swept their ranks, and they were mowed down like hay before the reaper. Still they pressed onward, and after paying a fearful toll in dead and wounded they at length reached the foot of the hill. Here they were confronted by a stone wall so thick and strong that their fire had not the slightest effect on it, and from behind which the Confederates poured a deadly hail of bullets upon them.

Here the carnage was awful, yet still the men came on in wave after wave, only to melt away as it seemed before the terrible fire of the Confederates. "It was like snow coming down and melting on warm ground," said one of their leaders afterwards.

Never did men fling away their lives so bravely and so uselessly.

A battery was ordered forward.

"General," said an officer, "a battery cannot live there."

"Then it must die there," was the answer.

And the battery was led out as dashingly as if on parade, although the men well knew that they were going to certain death.

At length the short winter's day drew to a close, and darkness mercifully put an end to the slaughter.

Then followed a night of pain and horror. The frost was intense, and out on that terrible hillside the wounded lay beside the dead, untended and uncared for, many dying from cold ere help could reach them. Still and white they lay beneath the starry sky while the general who had sent them to a needless death wrung his hands in cruel remorse. "Oh, those men, Oh, those men," he moaned, "those men over there. I am thinking of them all the time."

Burnside knew that he had failed as a general, and in his grief and despair he determined to wipe out his failure by another attempt next day. But his officers well knew that this would only mean more useless sacrifice of life. With difficulty they persuaded him to give up the idea, and two days later the Federal army crossed the Rappahannock, and returned to their camp near Falmouth.

With this victory of Fredericksburg the hopes of the Confederates rose high. They believed that the war would soon end triumphantly for them, and that the South would henceforth be a separate republic. There was no need for them, they thought, to listen to the commands of the President of the North, and not one state paid any heed to Lincoln's demand that the slaves should be set free.

Nevertheless on New Year's Day, 1863, Lincoln signed the great Proclamation of Freedom.

He had first held a great reception, and had shaken hands with so many people that his right hand was trembling. "If they find my hand trembling," he said to the Secretary of State, as he took up his pen, "they will say, 'He hesitated,' but anyway it is going to be done."

Then very carefully and steadily he wrote his name. It was the greatest deed of his life. "If my name is ever remembered," he said, "it will be for this act, and my whole soul is in it."

And thus slavery came to an end. From the beginning of the war there had been a danger that France and Britain might help the South. Lincoln had now made that impossible by making the war one against slavery as well as one for Union. For both France and Britain were against slavery, and could not well help those who now fought to protect it.

Now that they were free, many negroes entered the army. At this the Southerners were very angry, and declared that any negroes taken prisoners would not be regarded as soldiers, but simply as rebellious negroes, and would be punished accordingly. But in spite of their anger many black regiments were formed, and proved themselves good soldiers. And before the end of the war the Confederates, too, were making use of Negro Soldiery. But this was cutting the ground from under their own feet, and showing the injustice of slavery. For as a

Southerner said, "If a negro is fit to be a soldier he is not fit to be a slave."

_____

Chapter 87 - Lincoln - Chancellorsville - The Death of Stonewall Jackson

Still the war went on, and still the North suffered many losses. Soon after the battle of Fredericksburg General Burnside resigned the command of the army of the Potomac. His place was taken by General Joseph Hooker, known to his men as "Fighting Joe." He was a tall and handsome man, brave, and dashing almost to rashness. "Beware of rashness, beware of rashness," said Lincoln, when he appointed him. "But with energy and sleepless vigilance go forward, and give us victories."

But not even "Fighting Joe" could bring victory to the North at once. He found the army disheartened, dwindling daily by desertion, and altogether in something like confusion. He was, however, a splendid organiser, and in less than two months he had pulled the army together and once more made it a terrible fighting machine. He declared it to be the finest army in the world, and full of pride in his men, and pride in himself, he set out to crush Lee.

Near the tiny hamlet of Chancellorsville the two armies met, and the four days' fighting which followed is known as the battle of Chancellorsville.

Everything seemed to favour the Federals. They had the larger army, they were encamped in a good position, and above all the men were full of admiration for, and trust in, 'Fighting Joe."

General Hooker's movements had been quick and sure, his plans well laid. But he had expected the enemy to "flee ingloriously" before him.

The enemy, however, did not flee, but showed a stubborn intention of fighting. Then Hooker's courage failed him. He seemed to lose his grip on things, and much to the surprise of his officers he left his high position and took a lower one.

"Great heavens," said General Meade, when he heard the order, "if we cannot hold the top of a hill we certainly cannot hold the bottom of it."

The first day of the battle passed without any great loss on either side. Night came, the fighting ceased, and the weary men lay down to rest. But for Lee and Jackson there was little sleep. Beneath a small clump of pine trees they sat on packing cases, with maps spread out before them. For Jackson was planning one of his quick and stealthy marches, intent on catching the Federals unawares where they least expected it. And Lee, seeing the indecision of the Federal leader, was nothing loath. He had grown bold even to rashness in proportion as Hooker had grown cautious.

"What exactly do you propose to do?" asked Lee, as he studied the map.

"Go around here," replied Jackson, as with his finger he traced a line on the map which encircled the whole right wing of the Federal army.

"With what force do you propose to make this movement?" asked Lee.

"With my whole corps," answered Jackson.

General Lee thought for a few minutes in silence. Then he spoke.

"Well, go on," he said.

He knew that it was a great gamble. The Federal army was twice as large as his

288

own and yet Jackson proposed to cut it in two, and place the whole Federal army between the two halves. If the movement failed it would be a terrible failure. If it succeeded it would be a great success. It was worth the risk. So he said, "Go on."

As for Jackson he had no doubts. At Lee's words he rose, smiling, and eager. "My troops will move at once, sir," he said, and with a salute he was gone.

Soon in the cool and lovely May morning Jackson's men were marching through what was known as the Wilderness. It was a forest of smallish trees, so thickly set that a man could hardly march through it gun on shoulder. The Federals saw the great column of men move off without misgivings, imagining them to be retreating. Soon they were lost to sight, swallowed up by the Wilderness.

Here and there through the wood narrow, unmade roads were cut, and along these hour after hour twenty-five thousand men moved ceaselessly and silently. Through the thick foliage there came to them faint echoes of the thundering guns, while close about them the cries of startled birds broke the stillness, and the timid, wild things of the woods scurried in terror before them. As the day went on the heat became stifling, and dust rose in clouds beneath the tramping feet. Still, choking, hot and dusty the men pressed on.

The soldiers of the right wing of the Federal army were resting about six o'clock that evening. Their arms were stacked, some were cooking supper, others were smoking or playing cards, when suddenly from the woods there came the whirr of wings, and a rush of frightened squirrels and rabbits, and other woodland creatures.

It was the first warning the Federals had of the approach of the enemy. They flew to arms, but it was already too late. With their wild yell the Confederates dashed into the camp. The Federals fought bravely, but they were taken both in front and rear, and were utterly overwhelmed.

Now and again a regiment tried to make a stand, only to be swept away by the terrific onslaught of the Confederates, and leaving half their number dead on the field they fled in panic. Still with desperate courage the Federal leaders sought to stem the onrush of the enemy and stay the rout.

"You must charge into those woods, and hold the foe until I get some guns into position," said General Pleasonton, turning to Major Peter Keenan.

"I will, sir," replied Keenan. Then calmly smiling, at the head of his handful of men he rode to certain death.

Ten minutes later he lay dead with more than half his gallant followers beside him. But his sacrifice was not in vain. For his desperate thrust had held the Confederates until the guns were placed, and the army saved from utter rout.

The sun went down on a brilliant victory for the Confederates. Yet the night brought disaster for them.

Eager to find out what the Federals were doing General Jackson rode out towards their lines in the gathering darkness. It was a dangerous thing to do, for he ran the risk of being picked off by their sharp-shooters. The danger indeed was so great that an officer of his staff tried to make him turn back. "General," he said, "don't you think that this is the wrong place for you?'

289

But Jackson would not listen. "The danger is all over," he said carelessly. "The enemy is routed. Go back and tell Hill to press right on."

Soon after giving this order Jackson himself turned, and rode back with his staff at a quick trot. But in the dim light his men mistook the little party for a company of Federals charging, and they fired. Many of his officers were killed, Jackson himself was sorely wounded and fell from his horse into the arms of one of his officers.

"General," asked some one, anxiously, "are you much hurt?"

"I think I am," replied Jackson. "And all my wounds are from my own men," he added sadly.

As tenderly as might be he was carried to the rear, and all that could be done was done. But Stonewall Jackson had fought his last victorious fight. Eight days later the Conqueror of all men laid his hand upon him, and he passed to the land of perfect Peace.

During these days he seemed to forget the Great War. His wife and children were with him, and thoughts of them filled his heart. But at the end he was once more in imagination with his men on the field of battle.

"Order A.P. Hill to prepare for action," he cried. "Pass the infantry to the front. Tell Major Hawks-"

Then he stopped, leaving the sentence unfinished. A puzzled, troubled look overspread his handsome, worn face. But in a few minutes it passed away, and calm peace took its place.

"Let us cross over the river," he said, softly and clearly, "and rest under the shade of the trees."

Then with a contented sight he entered into his rest.

Stonewall Jackson was a true Christian and a great soldier, and his loss to the Confederate cause was one which could not be replaced. He believed to the end that he was fighting for the right, and, mistaken although he might be, his honour and valour were alike perfect. Both North and South may unite in admiration for him as a soldier, and in love for him as a Christian gentleman.

Chapter 88 - Lincoln - The Battle of Gettysburg

The day after Jackson was wounded the battle of Chancellorsville continued, and ended in a second victory for the Confederates. On the 4th and 5th the fighting was again renewed. Then the Federals retired across the Rappahannock to their former camping ground unmolested, the Confederates being too exhausted to pursue them.

After Fredericksburg the Confederates had rejoiced. After Chancellorsville they rejoiced still more, and they made up their minds to carry the war into the northern states. So leaving part of his army under General J. E. B. Stuart to prevent the Federals pursuing him Lee marched into Pennsylvania. But General Stuart was unable to hold the Federals back, and they were soon in pursuit of Lee.

At Chancellorsville Hooker had shown that although he was a splendid fighting general he was a poor commander-in-chief, and towards the end of June, while the army was in full cry after the foe, General George Gordon Meade was made commander-in-chief. Meade continued the pursuit, and Lee, seeing nothing for it, gave up his plans of invasion, and turned to meet the foe.

The two forces met near the little town of Gettysburg in Pennsylvania, and a great three-days' battle took place.

The fighting began on the first of July when the Federal army was still widely scattered through the country, and Meade himself far in the rear, and again the Confederates triumphed.

Late that night General Meade arrived upon the field, and began to make preparations for the struggle on the morrow. On both sides the commanders and armies seemed to feel that a great turning point of the war had come, and they bent all their energies on winning. Both camps were early astir, yet each side seemed to hesitate to begin the fearful game, and put fortune to the test. So the morning passed quietly, the hot silence of the summer day being broken only now and again by fitful spurts of firing.

Late in the afternoon at length the Confederates attacked, and soon the battle raged fiercely. The fight swung this way and that, first the one side and then the other gaining ground here, losing it there. When night came the position was little changed. The advantage still lay with the Confederates.

Next day there was no hesitation. Both sides knew that the deadly duel must be fought to the close, and at dawn the roll and thud of cannon began. From hill to hill gun answered gun, shells screamed and hissed, and the whole valley seemed to be encircled with flame and smoke. But the Confederates gained nothing. The Federals stood firm.

At length Lee determined to make a mighty effort to smash the center of the Federal line, and split it in two. Collecting about a hundred and fifty guns he massed them along a height named Seminary Ridge, and with these he pounded the Federals on Cemetery Hill opposite. For two hours the terrible cannonade lasted. At first the Federal guns replied vigorously, then they almost ceased. They ceased, not because they had been put out of action, not because ammunition was running short, but because Meade was reserving his strength for the infantry attack he knew must come.

In the Confederate camp there was strained anxiety. Lee had determined to make the attack, but General Longstreet was against it. He did not believe that it could succeed. It was, he felt sure, only the useless throwing away of brave lives, and his heart was wrung with sorrow at the thought. But Lee insisted, and General George E. Pickett's division was chosen to make the attempt.

So Longstreet gave way. But when Pickett came to him for last orders he could not speak; he merely nodded his head, and turned away with a sob.

Pickett, however, knew neither hesitation nor fear.

"Sir," he said firmly, "I shall lead my division forward."

Again Longstreet gave a sign, and Pickett, gallant and gay, rode off "into the jaws of death." Erect and smiling, his cap set rakishly over one ear, his brown-gold hair shining in the sun, he seemed, said Longstreet long after, more like a "holiday soldier" than a general about to lead a desperate and almost hopeless attack.

The Federal lines were a mile away. Towards them, towards the bristling row of guns, the men marched steadily, keeping step as if on parade, their banners fluttering gaily, and their bayonets glittering in the sunshine. Confident and elated they swept on. They were out to win not merely the battle but the war, and they meant to do it.

Half the distance was covered. Then the Federal guns spoke. Crashing and thundering they tore great gaps in the approaching column. Still the men moved on steadily, resistlessly, until they came within musket range. Then on a sudden the whole Federal line became as it were a sheet of flame and smoke, and the first line of the advancing Confederates seemed to crumble away before the fearful fusilade. But the second line came on only faster and yet faster, firing volley after volley, scattering frightful death as they came.

Nothing could stay their impetuous charge. On they came right up to the rifle pits. In a rush they were across them, and over the barricades. Then with a yell of victory they threw themselves upon the guns, bayoneting the gunners. Leaping upon the barricade a man held aloft the Confederate flag, waving it in triumphant joy. The next instant he fell mortally wounded, and the flag, bloodstained and torn, was trampled under foot.

The Confederate success was only the success of a moment. The handful of heroic men who had reached the Federal guns could not hope to hold them. They died gallantly. That was all.

A storm of shot and shell tore its way through the still advancing ranks. It became an ordeal of fire too great for even the bravest to face. The lines at length wavered, they broke, and the men were scattered in flight. Thousands lay dead and dying on the field, many surrendered and were taken prisoner, and of the fifteen thousand gallant soldiers who had set forth so gaily, only a pitiful remnant of thirteen hundred blood-stained, weary men at length reached their own lines.

This gallant and hopeless charge brought the battle of Gettysburg to an end. It brought victory to the Federal side, and the Confederates slowly retired into Virginia once more.

Yet the victory was not very great nor in any way decisive, and the cost of life had been frightful. Indeed, so many brave men had fallen upon this dreadful field that the thought came to the Governor of the state that it would be well to make a portion of it into a soldiers' burial place and thus consecrate it forever as holy ground. All the states whose sons had taken part in the battle willingly helped, and a few months after the battle it was dedicated. And there President Lincoln made one of his most beautiful and famous speeches.

"Fourscore and seven years ago," he said, "our fathers brought forth on this continent a new nation, conceived in liberty, and dedicated to the proposition that all men are equal. Now we are engaged in a great civil war, testing whether that nation, or any nation so conceived, and so dedicated, can long endure. We are met on a great battlefield of that war. We have come to dedicate a portion of that field, as a final resting-place for those who here gave their lives that that nation might live. It is altogether fitting and proper that we should do this. But, in a larger sense we cannot dedicate - we cannot consecrate - we cannot hollow - this ground. The brave men, living and dead, who struggled here, have consecrated it, far above our poor power to add or detract. The world will little note, nor long remember, what we say here, but it can never forget what they did here. It is for us, the living, rather, to be dedicated here to the unfinished work which they who fought here have thus far so nobly advanced. It is rather for us to be here dedicated to the great task remaining before us-that from these honoured dead we take increased devotion to that cause for which they gave the last full measure of devotion - that we here highly resolve that these dead shall not have died in vain- that this nation, under God, shall have a new birth of freedom - and that government of the people, by the people, for the people, shall not perish from the earth."

Chapter 89 - Lincoln-Grant's Campaign-Sheridan's Ride

The victory of Gettysburg which had been so dearly bought was not very great. But hard upon it came the news that on the 4th of July Vicksburg had surrendered to General Grant. And taking both victories together the people of the North felt that now they had cause to hope.

After the capture of New Orleans in April, 1862, Faragut had sailed up the Mississippi, and except for Vicksburg the whole valley was in the control of the Federals. Faragut would have attacked Vicksburg also but his land force was not strong enough, and Halleck, who was then commander-in-chief, did not see the great importance of Vicksburg, and refused to send soldiers to aid him.

The Confederates, however, knew the importance of holding the city, for it was the connecting link between the revolted states which lay east and those which lay west of the great river. Through it passed enormous supplies of food from the West, and great quantities also of arms and ammunition, and other war stores, which came from Europe by way of Mexico.

So while the Federals neglected to take Vicksburg the Confederates improved its fortifications until they were so strong that it seemed almost impossible that it should ever be taken.

At length Grant was given supreme command of the western army, and he, well knowing the importance of Vicksburg, became intent on taking it. Again and yet again he tried and failed. Indeed he failed so often that people began to clamour for his recall. But President Lincoln turned a deaf ear to the clamour and decided always to "try him a little longer" and still a little longer. And Grant justified his trust.

Finding it impossible to take Vicksburg by assault he determined to besiege it. In a brilliant campaign of less than a fortnight he marched a hundred and fifty miles, and fought four battles. Then he sat down with his victorious army before Vicksburg, and a regular siege began.

Vicksburg was now completely surrounded. On the river the fleet kept watch,

293

so that no boats carrying food, ammunition, or relief of any kind could reach the fated city. On land Grant's army dug itself in, daily bringing the ring of trenches closer and closer to the Confederate fortifications. They were so close at last that the soldiers on either side could hear each other talking, and often friendly chat passed between the "Yanks" and the "Johnnies" or Southerners.

"When are you coming into town, Yank?" the Confederates would ask.

"Well, Johnnie, we are thinking of celebrating the 4th of July there," the Northerners would reply.

And at this the Johnnies would laugh as at a huge joke. No 4th of July would the Yanks celebrate in their city.

Regularly, too, the Confederates would pass over the little Vicksburg paper, the Daily Citizen, to their enemies. This paper appeared daily to the last, although paper grew so scarce that it sometimes consisted only of one sheet eighteen inches long and six inches wide. At length printing paper gave out altogether, and the journal appeared printed on the plain side of wall paper.

Day was added to day, and week to week, and still the siege of Vicksburg lasted. All day cannon roared, shells screamed and whistled, and the city seemed enveloped in flame and noise. The streets were places of death and danger, and the people took refuge in the cellars of the houses, or in caves which they dug out of the clayey soil. In these caves whole families lived for weeks together, only creeping out to breathe the air during the short intervals, night and morning, when the guns ceased firing.

Food grew scarcer and scarcer until at length there was nothing left but salt bacon, the flesh of mules, rats, and mouldy pea flour. The soldiers became no longer fit to man the guns, their rations being no more than a quarter of a pound of bacon and the same of flour each day. Water too ran short, and they were obliged to drink the muddy water of the Mississippi.

Like pale specters the people crept about, and many, both soldiers and citizens, died from starvation and disease brought on by starvation. At length Vicksburg seemed little more than one great hospital, encircled by fire, made hideous by noise. Human nature could endure no longer, and on the morning of the 3rd of July white flags appeared upon the ramparts.

Immediately the roar of cannon ceased, and silence fell on city and camp. After the six weeks' inferno it seemed to the racked nerves and aching ears of the inhabitants as if the silence might be felt, as if the peace wrapped them about like a soft robe. The relief was so great that many who had endured the weeks of torture dry-eyed now burst into tears. But they were healing tears.

Under a lonely tree, a few hundred yards beyond the Confederate lines, Grant met General John C. Pemberton, the defender of Vicksburg. The two men had fought side by side in the Mexican War, and had been friends. Now although divided by cruel strife they shook hand as of old. But memories of bygone days did not soften Grant's heart. His terms were hard. Once more he demanded unconditional surrender. And Pemberton, knowing that resistance was impossible, yielded.

294

Next day the surrender was accomplished, and thirty thousand men became prisoners of war. Before noon the Union flag was flying over the Court House. Thus the "Yanks" celebrated the "glorious Fourth" in Vicksburg, as they had said they would do. But there was no noisy rejoicing. The Federals took possession almost in silence, for they had too much admiration for their gallant foe to wish to give them pain. One cheer indeed rent the air, but it was given for the glorious defenders of Vicksburg.

The whole North was now united in passionate admiration for Grant. Cheering crowds followed him in the streets. Fools and wise men alike were eager to know him, to boast that they had spoken to him or touched his hand. Yet at first sight Grant seemed to have little of the hero about him. He was an "ordinary, scrubby looking man, with a slightly seedy look," said one who saw him in those days. "He did not march nor quite walk, but pitched along as if the next step would bring him to his nose." But his eye was clear and blue, he had a determined look, and seemed like a man it would be bad to trifle with.

This shambling, scrubby looking man, with the clear blue eyes, was now the idol of the people. Lincoln too saw his genius as a leader, and willingly yielding to the popular demand made him commander-in-chief of all the United States armies.

Before long Grant had made his plans for the next campaign. It was a twofold one. He himself with one army determined by blow after blow to hammer Lee into submission while Sherman was to tackle the other great Confederate army under Johnston.

In the beginning of May, Grant set out, and on the 5th and 6th the battle of the Wilderness was fought not far from where the battle of Chancellorsville had been fought the year before. Grant had not meant to fight here, but Lee, who knew every inch of the ground, forced the fight on him.

In the tangled underwood of the Wilderness artillery and cavalry were of little use, and the battle became a fierce struggle between the foot soldiers of either army. The forest was so thick that officers could only see a small part of their men, and could only guess at what was going on by the sound of the firing, and the shouts exultant or despairing, of the men who were drive to and fro in the dark and dreary thickets. In the end neither side gained anything except an increased respect for the foe.

Grant's aim was to take Richmond, the Confederate capital, and after the battle of the Wilderness with that aim still before him he moved his army to Spotsylvania. He was hotly pursued by Lee and here on the 10th and 12th of May another stern struggle took place.

The fighting on the 10th was so terrible that on the 11th both armies rested as by common consent. Next day the battle began again and lasted until midnight. It was a hand-to-hand struggle. The tide of victory swung this way and that. Positions were taken and lost, and taken again and after twenty-four hours of fighting neither side had won. Only thousands of brave men lay dead upon the field.

Still intent on Richmond, Grant moved southwards after this terrible battle, followed closely by Lee. Everyday almost there were skirmishes between the two armies, but still Grant pressed onward and arrived at length within a few miles of Richmond. Here at Cold Harbor Lee took up a strongly entrenched position from which it seemed impossible to oust him, except by a grand assault. Grant determined to make that assault.

Both officers and men knew that it could not succeed, but Grant commanded it and they obeyed. Yet so sure were many of the men that they were going to certain death that it is said they wrote their names and addresses on slips of paper which they tacked to the backs of their coats, so that when their bodies were found it might be easily known who they were, and news be sent to their friends.

At half-past four in the grey morning light eighty thousand men rushed upon the foe. They were met with a blinding fire and swept away. In half an hour the attack was over. It was the deadliest half hour in all American history, and eight thousand Union men lay dead upon the field.

"Some one had blundered." Grant had blundered. He knew it, and all his life after regretted it. "No advantage whatever was gained," he said, "to make up for the heavy loss we suffered."

In this terrible campaign he had lost sixty thousand men. He had not taken Richmond. He had neither destroyed nor dispersed Lee's army. Still he hammered on, hoping in the long run to wear out Lee. For the Confederates had lost heavily, too, and they had no more men with which to make good their losses. On the other hand the gaps in the Federal army were filled up almost as soon as made. "It's no use killing these fellows," said the Confederates, "a half dozen take the place of every one we kill."

But the people of the North could not look on calmly at these terrible doings. They cast their idol down, and cried out against Grant as a "butcher." They demanded his removal. But Lincoln refused again to listen to the clamour as he had refused before. "I cannot spare that man," he said, "at least he fights."

Grant was terrible only for a good end. He was ruthless so that the war might be brought the more speedily to a close. And Lincoln, the most tender hearted of all men, knew it. Undismayed therefore Grant fought on. But his army was weary of much fighting, disheartened by ill success, weakened by many losses. New recruits indeed had been poured into. But they were all unused to discipline. Months of drill were needed before they could become good soldiers. In June then Grant settled down to besiege Petersburg, and drill his new men the while, and not till the spring of 1865 did the army of the Potomac again take the field.

Meanwhile there was fighting elsewhere.

On the part of the Confederates there was a constant endeavour to take Washington, and in July of this year the Confederate army actually came within a few miles of the city. There was great alarm in the capital, for it was defended chiefly by citizen soldiers and fresh recruits who had little knowledge of warfare. But just in time Grant sent strong reinforcements from the army of the Potomac and the Confederates marched away without making an attack. They only retired, however, into the Shenandoah Valley, and their presence there was a constant menace to Washington. Early in August therefore General Sheridan was sent to clear the enemy out of the valley, and relieve Washington from the constant fear of attack.

He began his work vigorously, and soon had command of most of the roads leading to Washington. But he knew that General Jubal A. Early who commanded the Confederate troops was a skilful and tried soldier, and, to begin with, he moved with caution. For some weeks indeed both commanders played as it were a game of chess, maneuvering for advantage of position. But at length a great battle was fought at Winchester in which the Confederates were defeated and driven from the field. Three days later another battle was fought at Fisher's Hill, and once again in spite of gallant fighting the Confederates were beaten.

After this battle Sheridan marched back through the valley, destroying and carrying away everything which might be of use to the foe. Houses were left untouched, but barns and mills with all their stores of food and forage were burned to the ground. Thousands of horses and cattle were driven off, and the rich and smiling valley made a desolation, with nothing left in it, as Grant said, to invite the enemy to return.

Having finished this work Sheridan dashed off to Washington, to consult with the Secretary of war about his future movements. The Confederate army had meanwhile encamped again near Fisher's Hill. And Early, hearing of Sheridan's absence, determined to make a surprise attack on the Federal army.

In the darkness of the night they set out, and stealthily crept towards the Federal camp at Cedar Creek. Every care was taken so that no sound should be made. The men were even ordered to leave their canteens behind, lest they should rattle against their rifles. Not a word was spoken as the great column crept onward, climbing up and down steep hillsides, fording streams, pushing through thickly growing brushwood. At length before sunrise, without alarm or hindrance of any kind the Confederates reached the camp of the sleeping Federals.

Each man was soon in his appointed place, and in the cold grey dawn stood waiting the signal. At length a shot rang out, and with their well-known yell the Confederates threw themselves into the camp.

As quickly as might be the Federals sprang up and seized their arms. But they had been taken utterly by surprise, and before they could form in battle array they were scattered in flight.

Before the sun was well up the Federals were defeated, and their camp and cannon were in the hands of the enemy. Meanwhile Sheridan had reached Winchester on his return journey from Washington. He had slept the night there, and had been awakened by the sound of firing. At first he thought little of it, but as the roar continued he became sure that a great battle was being fought-and he was twenty miles away! He set spurs to his horse, and through the cool morning air,

"A steed as black as steeds of night, Was seen to pass, as with eagle flight. As if he knew the terrible need, He stretched away with his utmost speed."

Mile after mile the great black horse ate up the roads. The sound of firing grew louder and louder, and at length men fleeing in rout and confusion came in sight. There was every sign of a complete defeat. Wounded, unwounded, baggage wagons, mule teams, all were fleeing in confusion.

It was a grievous sight for Sheridan. But he refused to accept defeat. Rising high in his stirrups he waved his hat in the air, and shouted cheerily, "Face the other way, boys. We are going back to our camp. We are going to lick them into their boots."

At the sound of his voice the fleeing soldiers paused, and with a mighty shout they faced about. Even the wounded joined in the cheering. The beaten, disheartened army took heart again, the scattered, disorganized groups were gathered, a compact line of battle was formed, and at the end of two hours the men were not only ready but eager once more to grapple with the foe.

Then the second battle of Cedar Creek was fought. At ten o'clock in the morning the Federals had been defeated. By five in the afternoon the Confederates were not only defeated, but utterly routed. Their army was shattered and the war swept out of the Shenandoah Valley for good and all. Then Sheridan marched his victorious troops to join Grant before Petersburg.

Chapter 90 - Lincoln - Sherman's March to the Sea - Lincoln Re-Elected President

Grant's plan of action was twofold, and while he was fighting the second Confederate army under General J.E. Johnston. At the beginning of the campaign Sherman's army was at Chattanooga in Tennessee, and while Grant was fighting the battle of the Wilderness, he began his march to Atlanta, Georgia. Fighting all the way, the Confederate army always retreating before him, he slowly approached Atlanta. At length on September 2nd he entered and took possession of it.

Here for a few weeks the soldiers rested after their arduous labours. The preparation for the next campaign began. All the sick and wounded, extra tents and baggage, in fact every one and everything which could be done without, was sent back to Tennessee. For the order had gone forth that the army was to travel light on this campaign. None but the fit and strong were to take part in it, and they were to carry with them only three weeks' rations.

Where they were going the men did not know. They did not ask. There was no need to trouble, for Sherman was leading them, and they knew he would lead them to victory.

After Richmond, Atlanta had supplied more guns and ammunition and other war material for the Confederacy than any other town, and before he left it, Sherman determined to destroy everything which might be of use to the enemy. So he emptied the town of all its inhabitants, and blew up all the gun and ammunition factories, storehouses, and arsenals. He tore up the railroads all around Atlanta also, and last of all cut the telegraph which linked him to the North. Then cut off as it were from all the world with his force of nearly sixty-six thousand men, he turned eastward toward the sea.

The army marched in four divisions, taking roads which as nearly as possible ran

298

alongside each other, so that each division might keep in touch with the others. Every morning at daybreak they broke camp and during the day marched from ten to fifteen miles. And as they passed through it they laid waste the land. Railroads were torn up and thoroughly destroyed. The sleepers were made into piles and set alight, the rails were laid on the top of the bonfires, and when hot enough to be pliable were twisted beyond all possibility of being used again. Telegraph wires and poles were torn down, factories were burned, only private homes being left untouched.

Foragers quartered the country, sweeping it bare of cattle, poultry, fodder and corn. For both man and beast of the great army fed upon the land as they passed through it, the rations with which they had come provided being kept in case of need. Indeed the troops fed so well that the march, it was said, was like a "continuous Thanksgiving." What they did not eat they destroyed.

Thus right across the fertile land a stretch of waste and desolation was created about sixty miles wide. Yet it was not done in wantonness, but as a terrible necessity of war. It clove the Confederacy from east to west as thoroughly as the Mississippi clove it from north to south. It rifled and well-nigh exhausted the rich granary which fed the Confederate army, and by destroying the railroads prevented even what was left being sent to them. Grant meant to end the war, and it seemed to him more merciful to destroy food and property than to destroy men.

Through all this great raid there was little fighting done. And as the army marched day by day through the sunny land a sort of holiday spirit pervaded it. The work was a work of grim destruction, but it was done in the main with good temper. The sun shone, the men led a free and hardy life, growing daily more brown and sinewy, and at the end of the march of nearly three hundred miles, far from being worn out, they were more fit and strong than when they set forth.

By the second week in December the goal was reached - Savannah and the sea. Here the army joined hands with the navy. Fort McAllister, which defended the south side of the city, was taken by a brilliant assault, and Sherman prepared for a siege of Savannah both by land and water. But in the night the Confederates quietly slipped out of the city, and retreated across the swamps. When their flight was discovered they were already beyond reach of pursuit, and with hardly a blow struck, the city of Savannah fell into the hands of the Federals.

The great march had ended triumphantly on December 21. "I beg to present to you, as a Christmas gift," wrote Sherman to Lincoln, "the city of Savannah with a hundred and fifty-nine heavy guns and plenty of ammunition, and also about twenty-five thousand bales of cotton."

This news followed hard on the news of another victory. For on December 15th and 16th the Federals under General George H. Thomas had fought a great battle at Nashville, Tennessee, in which the Confederates had been defeated. By this battle their strength beyond the Alleghenies was practically crushed, so as the year 1864 closed, the hopes of the Federals rose high.

Early in 1865 still another victory was recorded in the taking of Fort Fisher in

299

North Carolina. This was the last port in the possession of the Confederates. With it, they lost their last link with the outside world, and the blockade which Lincoln had proclaimed nearly four years before was at length complete.

All hope of success now utterly vanished for the Confederates. Even Lee knew it, and he might have advised the South to lay down arms, but Jefferson Davis, the Southern President, doggedly refused to own himself beaten. So the war continued.

On the 1st of February, Sherman set out from Savannah on a second march. This time he turned northward, and carried his victorious army right through the Carolinas. The march was longer by more than a hundred miles than his now famous march to the sea. It was one too of much greater difficulty. Indeed, compared with it, the march to the sea had been a mere picnic.

The weather now was horrible. Rain fell in torrents, and the army floundered through seas of mud. Along the whole way too they were harassed by the foe, and hardly a day passed without fighting of some sort. But, like an inexorable fate, Sherman pressed on, destroying railroads, and arsenals, creating a desert about him until at length he joined forces with Grant.

In the midst of this devastating war while some states were fighting for separation, another new state was added to the Union. This was Nevada. Nevada is Spanish and means snowy, and the state takes its name from the snowy topped mountains which run through it. It was formed out of part of the Mexican territory. Like West Virginia, the other battle-born state, it was true to the Union. And scanty though the population was, it raised more than a thousand men for the Union cause.

Now too, in the midst of war in November of 1864 came the time of electing a new President. Many people were tired of the war. They had expected it to last for a few months, and it had lasted for years, and some of them were inclined to blame Lincoln for it. So they wanted a new President. But for the most part the people loved Lincoln. He was Father Abe to them. And even those who wanted a change agreed with Lincoln himself when he said that "it was not well to swap horses when crossing a stream."

So Lincoln was triumphantly elected and on March 4th, 1865, he was inaugurated for the second time. He made the shortest speech ever made on such an occasion, and he closed this short speech with the most beautiful and unforgettable words.

"With malice towards none, with charity for all, with firmness in the right, as God gives us to see the right, let us strive on to finish the work we are in; to bind up the nation's wounds; to care for him who shall have borne the battle, and for his widow, and for his orphan -to do all which may achieve and cherish a just and lasting peace among ourselves and with all nations."

Chapter 91 - Lincoln - The End of the War - The President's Death

No President ever took up his burden in a more great hearted fashion than Lincoln. No President ever faced the difficulties of his position with so much tenderness, and so much strength. But he felt his burdens lie heavy on his shoulders. Deep lines of pain were graven on his face, and to his sad eyes there came a deeper sadness. Yet he never lost heart, and even in the gravest moments he would pause to tell a funny story.

"I should break down otherwise," he said.

He had no anger against the south, only a deep pity, a deep desire to see the country one again. So, much as he longed for peace, he would listen to no proposal which did not mean peace with union. And, as Jefferson Davis declared that he would rather die than see North and South united, the war continued.

On the 1st of April a great battle was fought at Five Forks, a few miles from Petersburg. In this the Confederates were defeated, and more than five thousand were taken prisoner. The next day, true to his hammering policy, Grant ordered a great assault all along the lines before Petersburg. At daybreak the attack began, and again the Federals were victorious. All that brave men could do the Confederates did. But their valour availed them nothing. They were far outnumbered, and their line was pierced in many places.

That morning President Davis was sitting in church at Richmond when a dispatch from Lee was brought to him. "My lines are broken," it said; "Richmond must be evacuated this evening."

Quickly and silently Jefferson Davis left the church. His day of power was over, and, with his Cabinet and officials, he fled from Richmond.

Soon the news spread throughout the Southern capital, and panic seized upon the people. Warehouses, filled with tobacco and cotton, were set in flames. All that was evil in the city broke loose, the prison was emptied, rogues and robbers worked their will. Soon the streets were filled with a struggling mob of people, some bent on plunder, others on fleeing from the place of terror and turmoil.

The night passed in confusion and horror past description. Then the next day the Federals took possession of the distracted city, and in a few hours the tumult was hushed, the flames subdued, and something like order restored.

Meanwhile, without entering the city, Grant was hotly pursuing Lee and his army. The chase was no long one. Lee's army was worn out, ragged, barefoot and starving. Grant, with an army nearly three times as large, and well equipped besides, soon completely surrounded him north, south, east and west. Escape there was none.

"There is nothing left me but to go and see General Grant," said Lee, "and I would rather die a thousand deaths." But like the brave soldier he was, he faced what seemed worse that death rather than uselessly sacrifice gallant lives.

A few letters passed between the two great leaders, then they met in a private house at Appomattox Court House. The contrast between the two was great. Lee looked the Southern aristocrat he was. White-haired and tall, erect still in spite of his sixty years, he was dressed in splendid uniform, and wore a jeweled sword at his side. Grant, half a head shorter, fifteen years younger, seemed but a rough soldier beside him. He wore only the blue blouse of a private, and carried no sword, nothing betraying his rank except his shoulder straps.

301

It was Lee's first meeting with "Unconditional Surrender" Grant. But this time Grant drove no hard bargain. "I felt like anything rather than rejoicing at the downfall of a foe who had fought so long and valiantly," he said many years after. The war was over, and there was no need of severity. So officers and men alike were all released on the promise that they would not again take up arms against the United States. The officers were allowed to keep their swords, their horses and belongings. The privates also were allowed to keep their horses, for as Grant said, " they would need them for their spring ploughing."

Everything being settled, Lee returned to his men to break the news to them. His face was stern and sad as he faced his worn and ragged troops. As he looked at them words failed him. "Men," he said, "we have fought through the war together, and I have done the best I could for you." Then he ceased. Tears blinded and choked him, sobs burst from the hardy men who had followed him joyfully to death. So they said farewell.

Grant on his side would allow no rejoicing in his camp, no firing of salutes. "The war is over," he said, "the rebels are our countrymen again." And indeed this was the end of the war, although for a week or two the Confederates elsewhere still held out.

When the news was heard throughout the country people went mad with joy. The great day of peace had come at last, and all the world went a-holidaying. People who were utter strangers to each other shook hands in the street, they laughed and cried, bonfires were lit and bells rung. Never had there been such rejoicing in the land. And among those who rejoiced none was more glad than the President.

"I thank God," he said, "that I have lived to see this day. It seems to me that I have been dreaming a horrid dream for five years. But now the nightmare is gone." And already his thoughts were turned to the binding up of the nation's wounds.

It was the 14th of April and he had promised to go to the theatre that evening. He did not want to go, but his presence had been announced in the papers, and thinking that the people would be disappointed if he failed to appear, he went.

It was about nine o'clock in the evening when the President entered his box with his wife and one or two friends. As soon as he appeared the people rose from their seats and cheered and cheered again, and the actors stopped their play until the audience grew calm again.

In a few minutes all was quiet once more, and for an hour the play went on. Then while everyone in the box was intent upon the stage a man crept softly through the door and stood beside the President. Suddenly a sharp pistol shot rang out, and without a groan the great President fell forward, dying.

His wicked work done, the man sprang from the box on to the stage shouting, "Sic semper tyrannis," - "Thus let it ever be with tyrants." As he sprang his foot caught in the flag which draped the box. He fell with a crash and broke a bone in his leg. But in spite of the hurt he jumped up. Then fiercely brandishing a dagger and shouting, "the South is avenged," he disappeared.

The murderer was a man named John Wilkes Booth. He was a second rate and conceited actor having a vast idea of his own importance. With him and the small band of fanatics he ruled the leaders of the South had nothing whatever to do. Indeed, by his act he proved himself to be their worst enemy.

Now hurrying out of the theatre he mounted a horse which was held in readiness, and galloped away through the night.

Meanwhile the dying President was quickly carried into a house near. But nothing that love or science could do availed. The kind grey eyes were closed never to open again, the gentle voice was stilled forever. All night he lay moaning softly, then as morning dawned a look of utter peace came upon his face and the moaning ceased.

Deep silence fell upon every one around the bed. The Secretary of War was the first to break it.

"Now he belongs to the ages," he said.

So the great President passed on his way. And the people mourned as they had mourned for no other man. As to the negroes they wept and cried aloud, and would not be comforted, for "Massa Linkum was dead," and they were left fatherless.

Chapter 92 - Johnson - How The President Was Impeached

The Vice-President, Andrew Johnson, now became President. Like Lincoln, he came of very poor people. He taught himself how to read, but could not write until after his marriage, when his wife taught him. In many ways he thought as Lincoln did, but he had none of Lincoln's wonderful tact in dealing with men, he could not win men's love as Lincoln had done.

"I tell you," said a Confederate soldier, speaking of Lincoln, "he had the most magnificent face and eyes that I have ever gazed into. If he had walked up and down the Confederate line of battle there would have been no battle. I was his, body and soul, from the time I felt the pressure of his fingers."

The Southerners would have found a friend in Lincoln, but now that friend was lost to them. Had he lived much of the bitterness of the time after the war would never have been.

President Johnson had a very hard task before him. He had "to bind up the nation's wounds" and re-unite the North and South. But he had neither the tact nor the strength needed for this great task. At first it was thought he would be too hard on the South. Then it was thought he would be too lenient, and soon he was at loggerheads with Congress.

For the South, this time was a time of bitterness. The Confederate States were divided into five districts, each district being ruled over by an officer with an army of soldiers under him. From the men who had led the rebellion, all power of voting was taken away, while at the same time it was given to negroes.

The negroes were very ignorant. They had no knowledge of how to use their votes. So a swarm of greedy adventurers from the North swooped down upon the South, cajoled the negroes into voting for them, and soon had the government of these states under their control. These men were called Carpet-baggers. For it was said they packed all their belongings into a carpet bag. They had no possessions, no interests in the South. They came not to help the South, but to make money out of it, and under their rule, the condition of the Southern States became truly pitiful.

But at length this wretched time passed. The troops were withdrawn, the carpet-baggers followed, and the government once more came into the hands of better men.

Meanwhile bitterness had increased between the President and Congress. And now in 1867 Congress brought a bill to lessen the President's power. This was called the Tenure of Office Bill. By it, the President was forbidden to dismiss any holder of a civil office without the consent of the Senate. The command of the army was also taken from him, and he was only allowed to give orders to the soldiers through the commander-in-chief.

The President of course vetoed this bill. But Congress passed it in spite of his veto. This can be done if two-thirds of the Members of the House and the Senate vote for a bill. So the Tenure of Office Bill became law.

Now the President has grown to dislike Edwin Stanton, the Secretary of War. he disliked him so heartily indeed that he would no longer speak to him, and so he determined in spite of the Tenure of Office Bill to get rid of a man he looked upon as an enemy. So Stanton was dismissed. But Stanton refused to go. And when his successor, General Thomas, appointed by the President, walked into the War office, he found Stanton still in possession, with his friends round him.

"I claim the office of Secretary of War, and demand it by order of the President," said Thomas.

"I deny your authority, and order you back to your own office," said Stanton.

"I will stand here," said Thomas. "I want no unpleasantness in the presence of these gentlemen."

"You can stand there if you please, but you can not act as Secretary of War. I am Secretary of War, and I order you out of this office, and to your own," cried Stanton.

"I will not obey you, but will stand here and remain here," insisted Thomas.

In spite of his insistence, however, he was at last got rid of.

But it was impossible that things should go on in this fashion. The Senate was angry because its authority had been set at nought, but it could do little but express its wrath. Then the House took the matter in hand. And for the first and only time in the history of the United States the President was impeached before the Senate, "for high crimes and misdemeanors in office."

But Andrew Johnson did not care. The House sat in judgment on him, but he never appeared before it. He knew the impeachment was only make believe on the part of his enemies to try and get rid of him. So he chose lawyers to defend him, but never appeared in court himself.

For ten days the trial lasted. The excitement throughout the country was intense, and on the last day when the verdict was given the court was packed from floor to ceiling, and great crowds, unable to get inside, waited without.

In tense silence each Senator rose and gave his verdict "guilty" or "not guilty". And when the votes were counted it was found that the President was declared guilty. There were forty-eight Senators, and to convict the President it was necessary that two-thirds should declare him guilty. Thirty-five said guilty, and nineteen not guilty. Thus he was saved by just one vote.

Stanton then quietly gave up the post to which he had clung so persistently. Another man took his place, and the President remained henceforth undisturbed until the end of his term.

During Johnson's Presidency another state was admitted to the Union. This was Nebraska. It was formed out of part of the Louisiana Purchase, the name being an Indian one meaning "shallow water." It had been formed into a territory at the time of the famous Kansas-Nebraska Bill, and now in March, 1867, it was admitted to the Union as the 37th State.

This year too, the territory of Alaska was added to the United States. Alaska belonged to Russia by right of Vitus Bering's discovery. It was from this Vitus Bering that the Bering Strait and Bering Sea take their names. The Russians did very little with Alaska, and after a hundred years or more they decided that they did not want it, for it was separated from the rest of the Empire by a stormy sea, and in time of war would be difficult to protect. So they offered to sell it to the United States. But nothing came of it then, and for some years the matter dropped, for the war came and blotted out all thoughts of Alaska.

But now peace had come, and the subject was taken up again, and at length the matter was settled. Russia received seven million two hundred thousand dollars, and Alaska became a territory of the United States.

A party of American soldiers was landed at the town of Sitka. They marched to the governor's house, and there were drawn up beside the Russian troops. Then the Russian Commander ordered the Russian flag to be hauled down, and made a short speech. Thereupon the soldiers of both countries fired a salute. The American flag was run up, and the ceremony was at an end.

Thus another huge territory was added to the United States. But at first many people were displeased at the purchase. It was a useless and barren country, they thought, where the winters were so long and cold that it was quite unfit for a dwelling place for white men. But soon it was found that the whale and seal fisheries were very valuable, and later gold was discovered. It has also been found to be rich in other minerals, especially coal, and in timber, and altogether has proven a useful addition to the country.

Chapter 93 - Grant - A Peaceful Victory

In 1869 General Grant, who had made such a great name for himself during the Civil War, became President. Grant was a brave and honest soldier. He knew little however about politics. But now that Lincoln was gone the people loved him

305

better than any other man. So he became President.

His was a simple trusting soul. He found it hard to believe evil of any one, and he was easily misled by men who sought not their country's good, but their own gain. So mistakes were made during his Presidency. But these may be forgotten while men must always remember his greatness as a soldier, and his nobleness as a victor. He helped to bring peace to his country, and like his great leader he tried after war was past to bind up the nation's wounds.

When Grant came into power the echoes of the great war were still heard. The South had not yet returned into peaceful union with the North, and there was an unsettled quarrel with Britain. The quarrel arose in this way. During the Civil War the British had allowed the Confederates to build ships in Britain; these ships had afterwards sailed out from British ports, and had done a great deal of damage to Union shipping.

The British had declared themselves neutral. That is, they had declared that they would take neither one side nor the other. But, said the Americans, in allowing Confederate ships to be built in Britain, the British had taken the Confederate side, and had committed a breach of neutrality. And for the damage done to their ships the Americans now claimed recompense from the British Government. The ship which had done the most damage was called the Alabama and from this the claims made by America were called the Alabama Claims.

At first, however, the British refused to consider the claims at all. For years letters went to and fro between the two governments, and as the British still refused to settle the matter, feeling in America began to run high.

But at length the British consented to talk the matter over, and a commission of five British and five Americans met at Washington. After sitting for two months this commission formed what is known as the Washington Treaty. By this Treaty it was arranged that the Alabama Claims should be decided by arbitration. A Court of Arbitration was to be formed of five men; and of this court the President of the United States, the Queen of England, the King of Italy, the President of Switzerland, and the Emperor of Brazil, were each to choose a member.

The men chosen by these rulers met at Geneva in Switzerland, and after discussing the matter for a long time they decided that Britain had been to blame, and must pay the United States fifteen million five hundred thousand dollars. Thus the matter was settled in a peaceful way. Fifty years before, a like quarrel might have led to war between the two countries. Even at this time, with less wise leadership on either side, it might have come to war. But war was avoided and a great victory for peace was won.

Besides the Alabama Claims the last dispute about boundaries between the United States and Canada was settled at this time. This also was settled by arbitration, the new-made German Emperor being chosen as arbiter. "This," said President Grant, "leaves us for the first time in the history of the United States as a nation, without a question of disputed boundary between our territory and the possessions of Great Britain."

Grant was twice chosen as President and it was during his second term that Colorado was admitted to the Union as the thirty-eighth state. The new state was formed partly out of the Mexican Concession, partly out of the Louisiana Purchase, and was named after the great river Colorado, two branches of which flow through it. It was admitted as a state in August, 1876.

Chapter 94 - Hayes - Garfield - Arthur

In 1877 Rutherford B. Hayes became President. Ever since the Civil War a great part of the South had been in constant turmoil. Soldiers were still stationed in the capitals of the various states, and the carpet-bag government still continued. But Hayes wished to put an end to this. So he got the principal white people in the South to promise that they would help to keep law and order. Then he withdrew all the troops. Without their aid the carpet- bag government could not stand, and the white men of the South once more began to rule in the South.

President Hayes also tried to lessen the evil of the "spoils system." In this he met a good deal of opposition. But the system of passing examinations was begun for some posts.

After the troublous times that had gone before this was a time of peace, in which for the first time since the War North and South seemed once more united.

In 1881 James Garfield became President. Like other Presidents before him, his boyhood had been one of poverty and hard work. But from doing odd labouring jobs, or tending barge horses on the Ohio Canal, he had gradually worked upwards. He had been barge-boy, farmer, carpenter, school teacher, lawyer and soldier, having in the Civil War reached the rank of general. At thirty-two he entered Congress, and there soon made his mark.

Now he had become President, and as soon as he took up his office he was besieged by office seekers. They thronged his house, they stopped him in the street, button-holed him in railway carriages. They flattered, coaxed, threatened, and made his life a burden.

But in spite of all this worrying the new President determined to do what he could to end the "spoils system," and appoint people only for the sake of the public good. Accordingly he made many enemies.

Among the many office-seekers whom the President was forced to disappoint was a weak-minded, bad young man named Guiteau. Garfield saw plainly that he was quite unfit to fill any government post, and he refused to employ him. Thereupon Guiteau's heart was filled with hate against the President. He brooded over his wrongs till his hate became madness, and in this madness he determined to kill his enemy.

Since he took up office the President had been hard at work. Now in July he determined to take a short holiday in New England, and visit Mrs. Garfield, who had been ill, and had gone away for a change of air.

On Saturday, the 2nd of July, the morning on which he was going to set out, he awoke in excellent spirits. Before he got up one of his sons came into his room. The boy took a flying leap over his father's bed.

307

"There," he said with a laugh, "you are the President of the United States, but you can't do that."

"Can't I?" said the President.

And he got up and did it.

In the same good spirits he drove to the station.

As he walked along the platform a man with an evil look on his face followed him. Suddenly a pistol shot was heard, and a bullet passed through the President's sleeve, and did no harm. It was quickly followed, however, by a second, which hit the President full in the back, and he fell to the ground. The President was sorely wounded, but not killed. A mattress was quickly brought, and he was gently carried to the White House.

Then a message was sent to Mrs. Garfield, telling her what had happened, and bidding her come home. She and her daughter had been happily awaiting the President's coming to them. Now everything was changed, and in sorrow and haste they went to him.

For nearly three months President Garfield lingered on. At times he seemed much stronger, and those who loved him believed he would recover. But by degrees their hopes faded, and in September he died.

Once again the sorrowing nation followed their President to the grave, and once again the Vice-President took office as President.

The new President was named Chester A. Arthur, and on taking office he was less known to the country than any President before him. He came to office in a time of peace and prosperity, and although nothing very exciting happened during his presidency he showed himself both wise and patriotic.

The best thing to remember him for is his fight against the "spoils system." Ever since Grant had been President men who loved their country, and wanted to see it well served, had fought for civil service reform.

Garfield's sad death made many people who had not thought of it before see that the "spoils system" was bad. For it had been a disappointed seeker of spoils who killed him. So at last in 1883 a law was passed which provided that certain appointments should be made by competitive examinations, and not given haphazard. At first this law only applied to a few classes of appointments. But by degrees its scope was enlarged until now nearly all civil service appointments are made through examinations.

Chapter 95 - Cleveland - Harrison - Cleveland

In 1885 Arthur's term of office came to an end, and Grover Cleveland became President. He was the son of a clergyman, and it was intended that he should have a college education. But his father died when he was only sixteen, and he had to begin at once to earn his own living.

Grover Cleveland, however, determined to be a lawyer, and with twenty-five dollars in his pocket he set out from home to seek his fortune. He did two or three odd jobs by the way, but soon got a place as clerk in a lawyer's office in Buffalo.

308

His foot was thus on the first rung of the ladder which he wished to climb. And he climbed steadily, until twenty-six years later he was chosen Mayor of Buffalo. As Mayor he soon made a name for himself by his fearless honesty and businesslike ways. He would not permit unlawful or unwise spending of public money, and he stopped so many extravagant acts of the council that he became known as the "Veto Mayor," and he saved the town taxpayers thousands of dollars a year.

Next he became Governor of New York State. As Governor he continued his same fearless path, vetoing everything which he considered dishonest or in any way harmful.

And as President, Cleveland was just as fearless and honest as before. During the four years of his presidency he used his power of veto more than three hundred times.

As one would expect from such a man Cleveland stood firm on the question of civil service reform. "The people pay for the government," he said, "and it is only right that government work should be well done. Posts should be given to those who are fit to fill them, and not merely to those who have friends to push them into notice."

President Cleveland also tried to get the tariffs on imported goods reduced. He discovered that there was more money in the treasury than the country required. During the war, duties had been made high because the Government required a great deal of money. But after the war was over, and there was no need for so much money these high duties had still been kept on. The consequence was that millions of dollars were being heaped up in the Treasury, and were lying idle. The president therefore thought that the tariffs should be reduced, and he said so. But there were so many people in the country who thought that a high tariff was good that, when in the next presidency, a new tariff bill was introduced, the duties were made higher than ever.

In 1889 President Cleveland's presidency came to an end, and Benjamin Harrison became President. He was the grandson of that William Henry Harrison who died after he had been President for a few weeks.

During President Harrison's term of office six new states were admitted into the Union. The two first of these were North and South Dakota, the name in Indian meaning "allies." It was the name the allied North-Western tribes gave themselves. But their neighbours called them Nadowaysioux, which means "enemies." The white people, however, shortened it to Sioux, and North Dakota is sometimes called the Sioux State.

Both North and South Dakota were formed out of the Louisiana Purchase. In 1861 they had been organised as [585] the territory of Dakota. Seventeen years or so later they were divided into North and South Dakota and were admitted as states in November, 1889.

Two or three days later Montana was admitted. This state was formed partly out of the Louisiana Purchase, and partly out of the Oregon country. The Rocky

Mountains cross the state, and its name comes from a Spanish word meaning "mountainous."

After Lewis and Clark explored the country many fur traders were attracted to it. But it was not until gold was discovered there that settlers came in large numbers. In spite of terrible trouble with the Indians, and much war and bloodshed, year by year the settlers increased, and in 1889 the territory was admitted as a state.

A few days after Montana the State of Washington was admitted to the Union. It was part of the Oregon country, and was of course named after the great "Father of his country," George Washington.

In the following year Idaho became a state. Its name is Indian, meaning "gem of the mountains." This state, like Washington, was formed out of the Oregon country. The first white men who are known to have passed through it were Lewis and Clark. But, as in Montana, it was not until gold was discovered that settlers in any great numbers were attracted there. One very interesting thing about Idaho is that it was the second state to introduce women's suffrage. That is, women within the state have the same right of voting as men.

But the first state to introduce women's suffrage was Wyoming, which was admitted to the Union a few days after Idaho. This state was formed out of parts of all three of the great territories which had been added to the United States. The east was part of the Louisiana Purchase, the west was part of the Oregon country, and the south part of the Mexican cession. It has much fine pasture land and its Indian name means "broad valley."

In 1893 Harrison's term of office came to an end, and for the second time Grover Cleveland was elected President. This is the only time in the history of the United States that an ex-President has again come to office after an interval of years.

Four hundred years had now passed since Columbus discovered America, and it was decided to celebrate the occasion by holding a great World's Fair at Chicago. It was not possible, however, to get everything ready in time to hold the celebration in 1892, which was the actual anniversary, so the exhibition was opened the following year instead.

There had been other exhibitions in America of the same kind, but none so splendid as the Columbian Fair. It was fitting that it should be splendid, as it commemorated the first act in the life of a great nation. In these four hundred years what wonders had been performed! Since Columbus first showed the way across the Sea of Darkness millions had followed in his track, and the vast wilderness of the unknown continent had been people from shore to shore.

Millions of people from all over the world came to visit the White city as it came to be called; and men of every nation wandered through its stately halls, and among its fair lawns and gardens where things of art and beauty were gathered from every clime.

But most interesting of all were the exhibits which showed the progress that had been made in these four hundred years.

There one might see copies of the frail little vessels in which Columbus braved the unknown horrors of the Sea of Darkness, as well as models of the ocean going leviathans of to-day.

During Cleveland's second term of office still another state entered the Union. This was Utah, the state founded by the Mormons. Polygamy being forbidden, it was admitted in 1896 as the forty-fifth state.

Chapter 96 - McKinley - War and Sudden Death

In 1897 William McKinley became President. Like some other Presidents before him he came of very humble people, and had by his own efforts raised himself until at length he held the highest office in the land.

McKinley was a keen protectionist. That is, he believed in putting a heavy duty on foreign goods coming into the country, not in order to get revenue or income for the needs of the Government, but in order to protect the home manufacturer. He wanted to put such a high duty on foreign goods that the home manufacturer could sell his goods at a high price, and still undersell the foreigner. In President Harrison's time McKinley, then a member of Congress, succeeded in getting the tariff made higher than ever before, and the Act then passed was known as the McKinley Tariff Act. And just as President Monroe is known outside America chiefly because of the Monroe Doctrine, so President McKinley is known because of the McKinley Tariff Act.

For many years now the United States had been at peace. But the year after McKinley came into office the country was once more plunged into war.

In days long ago when Englishmen were struggling to found a colony in Virginia, Spain was a great and powerful nation, and her dominions in the New World were vast. But because of her pride and her cruelty Spain lost these dominions one by one, until at length there remained in the Western hemisphere only a few islands, the largest of which was Cuba. But even these were not secure, and again and again the Cubans rose in rebellion against their Spanish oppressors.

The Spaniards waged war against their revolted subjects in most cruel fashion, and the people of the United States looked on with sorrow and indignation at the barbarous deeds which were done at their very doors.

McKinley had been a soldier in the Civil War, and had fought well and gallantly for the flag. But like other soldier Presidents he loved peace more than war. Like Cleveland before him he felt unwilling to plunge the country into war. So he shut his ears, and turned away his eyes from the misery of Cuba.

But there were many Americans in Cuba. They as well as the Cubans were being starved. So ships were sent to Cuba with food for them, and in this way not only they but many Cubans were saved from starvation. Then a United States battleship called the Maine was sent to Cuba, and anchored in the harbour of Havana, to be ready in case of need to help the Americans.

For three weeks the Maine lay rocking at anchor. Then on the night of 15th February, 1898, while every one on board was peacefully sleeping the vessel was blown up, and two hundred and sixty-six men and officers were killed.

311

When the people of the United States heard the news a wave of anger passed over the land. But the President was calm.

"Wait," he said, "wait till we know how it happened."

So grimly the people waited until experts made an examination. What they found made them believe that the Maine had been attacked from outside. There seemed no doubt that the Spaniards had blown up the vessel although they indignantly denied having had anything to do with it.

Now there was no holding the people, and very shortly war was declared. It was short and sharp. In less than four months it was all over. On land and sea the Spaniards were hopelessly beaten, while in the whole campaign the Americans lost scarcely five hundred men in battle, although more than twice that number died of disease.

The war was fought not only in the West Indies but also in the Pacific. For there Spain possessed the Philippine Islands. These islands had been in the possession of Spain ever since their discovery by Magellan more than three hundred and fifty years before, and they had been called the Philippines after King Philip II of Spain. Now the long rule of Spain came to an end.

The first battle of the war was fought in the Bay of Manila, the capital of the Philippine Islands. Here the Spanish fleet was shattered while not an American was killed. A month or two later the town of Manila was taken, and the Philippines were in the power of the Americans.

In the West Indies too the Spaniards were beaten on land and sea and on August 2nd, 1898, she sued for peace.

By the treaty of peace Cuba became a free republic, while Porto Rico and all the other Spanish islands in the West Indies were given to the United States, as well as the Philippines.

But no sooner was the treaty signed than the Filipinos rose in rebellion against American rule. For three years a kind of irregular war went on. Then the leader of the rebellion, Aguinaldo, was captured, and after that the Filipinos gradually laid down their arms. And when they found that the Americans did not mean to oppress them as the Spaniards had done they became more content with their rule.

The winning of these foreign possessions brought something new into the life and history of America. For now America began to own colonies, a thing quite unlooked for, and not altogether welcome to many.

At this time, also, besides those won in the Spanish War another group of islands came under American rule. These were the Hawaiian Islands, also like the Philippines in the Pacific Ocean.

Hawaii was a monarchy, but for a long time the people had been discontented, and Queen Liliuokalani was the last royal ruler of Hawaii. She wanted to be an absolute monarch, and do what she liked. But when she tried to change the constitution to her liking there was a revolution.

It was a peaceful revolution, and not a shot was fired on either side. It was brought about chiefly by the white people who lived in the islands. A company of

312

marines was landed from the United States cruiser Boston which happened to be in the harbour at the time. The Queen was deposed, and a provisional government set up.

Stamford Dole, an American, was chosen head of this new government. Dole then sent to Washington to ask the United States to annex Hawaii. Meanwhile the stars and stripes were hoisted over the Government buildings at Honolulu, the capital of Hawaii.

All this happened just at the end of Harrison's Presidency. He and his advisers were quite willing to annex Hawaii. But before the matter could be settled his term of office ended, and Cleveland took his place. The new President did not feel at all pleased with what had been done, and he sent a commissioner to Honolulu to find out exactly what had happened, and if the people really wanted to be annexed to the United States.

This commissioner came to the conclusion that the Hawaiians did not want to be annexed and that "a great wrong had been done to a feeble but independent State."

Cleveland therefore refused to annex the islands. He even offered to restore the Queen to her throne if she would promise to forgive all those who had helped to dethrone her. At first she would not promise this, but declared that the leaders of the revolution must be beheaded. In the end, however, she gave way.

"I must not feel vengeful to any of my people," she said. "If I am restored by the United States, I must forget myself, and remember only my dear people and my country. I must forgive and forget the past, permitting no punishment of any one."

But when Dole was asked to give up the islands he refused. He and his party were ready to fight rather than allow the Queen to be set again upon the throne. And seeing him thus determined President Cleveland gave up his efforts on behalf of the Queen.

So for several years Hawaii remained a little independent republic with Dole as President. Then when McKinley came into power the United States was again asked to take the islands under protection. And in July, 1898, while the Spanish War was being fought, Hawaii was annexed, and with solemn ceremony the flag was once more hoisted in Honolulu.

A few years later the islands were made a territory. So the people are now citizens of the United States, and send a representative to Congress.

No President perhaps grew in the love of the people as McKinley did. At the end of his four years' office he was loved far more than he had been at the beginning, and he was easily elected a second time. And but a few months of his second term had passed when people began to talk of electing him a third time.

But when McKinley heard of it he was vexed. He told the people that they must put such an idea out of their heads, for he would not be a candidate for a third term on any consideration.

"All I want," he said, "is to serve through my second term in a way acceptable to my countrymen, and then go on doing my duty as a private citizen."

313

But alas! He was not to be allowed even to serve out his second term. Only six months of it had gone when he went to visit the great Pan-American Exhibition at Buffalo. Here he made a speech which seemed to show that he was changing his ideas about high tariffs, and that it was time now, he thought, to lower them.

Next day he held a great reception in one of the buildings of the Exhibition. Crowds of all sorts of people streamed into the hall, eager to see the President and shake hands with him. Among these came a well-dressed young man who seemed to have hurt his hand, for it was covered with a handkerchief.

The man came quite close to the President who held out his hand with a smile. Then quickly the man fired two shots. Not an injured hand but a pistol had been hidden under the handkerchief.

The President did not fall. He walked steadily enough to a chair, and leant his head upon his hand.

"You are wounded," said his secretary.

"Ho, I think not. I am not much hurt," replied the President. But his face was white and drawn with pain; blood flowed from his wounds. Yet in his pain he thought only of others.

His first thought was for his wife, who was an invalid. "Don't let her know," he said. But he thought too of the wretched man who had shot him. "Don't hurt him," he murmured.

At first it was thought that the wounds were not fatal, and that the President would recover. But just as every one believed that the danger was over his strength seemed to fail him, and in little more than a week he died.

There was such a shining goodness and honesty about President McKinley that all who came near him loved and respected him. Now he went to his last resting-place mourned not only by his own people but by Great Britain and nearly every country in Europe besides. Even his murderer had no special hatred of McKinley. He was an anarchist who believed it was a good deed to kill any ruler.

So in the midst of his usefulness a good man was ruthlessly slain.

Chapter 97 - Roosevelt - Taft

Upon McKinley's death Theodore Roosevelt, The Vice-President, became President. He was the youngest of all the Presidents, being only forty-two when he came into office. Mr. Roosevelt was in the mountains with his wife and children when the news that the President was dying was brought to him. At nine o'clock at night he started off on a long drive of thirty-five miles to the railway station. The road was narrow, and steep, and full of mudholes, and the drive through the darkness was one of danger.

A little after five in the morning the station was reached. Here a special train was waiting which carried the Vice-President to Buffalo as fast as might be. But he was too late to see his President in life. For while he was still on his wild drive through the night, President McKinley had passed peacefully to his last rest.

Mr. Roosevelt was the youngest of all presidents, and he brought to the White House a youthful energy and "hustle" such as no President had before. He had strong opinions to which he never hesitated to give voice, and perhaps since Lincoln no President had been so much a dictator.

Perhaps the most interesting thing in Roosevelt's presidency was the beginning of the Panama Canal.

You remember that when Columbus set forth upon the Sea of Darkness his idea was to reach the east by sailing west. And to this day of his death he imagined that he had reached India by sailing westward. But soon men found out the mistake, and then began the search for the North-West Passages by which they might sail past the great Continent, and so reach India.

The North-West Passage, however, proved a delusion. The men turned their attention to the narrow isthmus by which the two vast continents of North and South America are joined. And soon the idea of cutting a canal through this narrow barrier began to be talked of. But time went on and the Spaniards who held sway over the isthmus did no more than talk. Then an adventurous Scotsman was seized with the idea of founding a colony at Darien. He meant to build a great harbour where all the ships of the world would come. Merchandise was to be carried across the isthmus by camels, and soon his colony would be the key of all the commerce of the world.

Such was his golden dream, but it ended in utter failure.

Still the idea grew. Men of many nations began to discuss the possibility of building the canal. And at length the French got leave from the Government of Columbia and work on the canal was begun. But after working for many years the French gave up the undertaking, which was far more difficult, and had cost far more money than they had expected. Meanwhile the Americans had become much interested in the scheme, and they had begun to think of cutting a canal through the isthmus at Nicaragua. Then when the French company went bankrupt they offered to sell all their rights to the canal to the United States. There was a good deal of discussion over the matter. For some people thought that the Nicaragua route would be better. But in the end it was agreed to take over the canal already begun, and go with it.

Everything was arranged when the Colombian Senate refused to sign the treaty. By this treaty they were to receive ten million dollars, besides a yearly rent for the land through which the canal ran. But that sum seemed to them now too small, and they refused to sign the treaty unless the money to be paid down should be increased to twenty-five million dollars.

This the United States was unwilling to do. Everything came down to a standstill, and it seemed as if the Panama scheme would have to be given up, when suddenly a new turn was given to affairs. For the people of Panama rose in rebellion against Colombia, and declared themselves a republic.

The United States at once recognized the new republic, and before a month had passed a treaty between the United States and the Republic of Panama was drawn up and signed, and the work on the great canal was begun.

A good many people, however, were not very pleased at the manner in which the struggle had been ended. They thought that the United States ought not to have taken the part of rebels in such haste. But the President was quite satisfied that he had done the right thing, and that it would have been base not to help the new republic.

In 1902 Mr. Roosevelt had become president "by accident." If it had not been for the tragedy of President McKinley's death he would not have come into power, and the thought grieved him somewhat. So when he was again elected president he was quite pleased. For now he felt that he held his great office because the people wanted him, and not because they could not help having him.

Few Presidents have grown so much in popularity after coming into office as Mr. Roosevelt. People felt he was a jolly good fellow, and throughout the length and breadth of the land he was known as "Teddy."

"Who is the head of the Government?" a little girl was asked.

"Mr. Roosevelt," was the reply.

"Yes, but what is his official title?"

"Teddy," answered the little one.

During this presidency Oklahoma was admitted to the Union as the forty-sixth state. Oklahoma is an Indian word meaning Redman. It was part of the Louisiana Purchase, and had been set aside as an Indian reservation. All the land, however, was not occupied and as some of it was exceedingly fertile the white people began to agitate to have it opened to them. So at length the Indians gave up their claim to part of this territory in return for a sum of money.

This was in 1889 and President Harrison proclaimed that at twelve o'clock noon on the 22nd of April the land would be opened for settlement. Long before the day people set out in all directions to the borders of Oklahoma. On the morning of the 22nd of April at least twenty thousand people had gathered on the borders. And as soon as the blowing of a bugle announced that the hour of noon had struck there was a wild rush over the border. Before darkness fell whole towns were staked out. Yet there was not enough land for all and many had to return home disappointed. The population of Oklahoma went up with a bound but it was not until eighteen years later, in September, 1907, that it was admitted to the Union as a state.

In 1909 William H. Taft became president. Mr. Taft had been Governor of the Philippines, and had shown great tact and firmness in that post. He and President Roosevelt were friends, and Roosevelt did all he could to further his election.

During Mr. Taft's presidency the last two states were admitted to the Union. Ever since the Civil War New Mexico had been seeking admission as a state, and at one time it was proposed to call this state Lincoln. That suggestion, however, came to nothing, and some years later it was proposed to admit New Mexico and Arizona as one state. To this Arizona objected, and at length they were admitted as separate states, New Mexico on the 6th of January and Arizona on the 11th of February, 1912. Both these states were made out of the Mexican Concession and the Gadsden Purchase.

316

Chapter 98 - Wilson - Troubles With Mexico

In 1913 Mr. Taft's term of office came to an end, and Mr. Woodrow Wilson was elected President. He came into office at no easy time. At home many things needed reform and on the borders there was trouble. For two years the republic of Mexico, which had always been a troublous neighbor, had been in a constant state of anarchy. One revolution followed another, battles and bloodshed became common events. Many Americans had settled in Mexico and in the turmoil American lives were lost and American property ruined. While Mr. Taft was in office he tried to protect the Americans in Mexico.

But he could do little, as the Mexicans made it plain that any interference on the part of America would mean war. Mr. Taft avoided war, but the state of things in Mexico went from bad to worse, and when Mr. Wilson became President a settlement with Mexico was one of the problems he had to face. But first of all the new President turned this thoughts to home matters.

Ever since the McKinley Tariff the duties on goods imported into the country had remained high. Many people, however, had come to believe that high tariffs were a mistake, for while they enriched a few they made living dearer than need be for many. These people wished to have tariffs "for revenue only." That is, they thought duties should only be high enough to produce sufficient income for the needs of the government. They objected to tariffs merely for "protection." That is, they objected to tariffs which "protected" the manufacturer at the expense of the consumer.

President Wilson held these opinions strongly, and during the first year of his presidency a bill was passed by which were luxuries, things which only rich people bought, were heavily taxed, while the taxes on foodstuffs and wool, things which the poorest need, were made much lighter. These changes in the tariff brought in much less income for the government, and to make up for the loss an Income Tax was levied for the first time, everyone who had more than 4,000 dollars a year having to pay it. In this way again the burden of taxes was shifted from the poor to the rich.

The President next turned his attention to the banks. Little change had been made in their way of doing business since the Civil War, and for some time it had been felt that to meet the growing needs of trade a change was wanted. Many people had tried to think out a new system, but it was not easy, and they failed. Mr. Wilson, however, succeeded, and in December, 1913, the Currency Bill was passed.

It would take too long, and would be rather difficult, to explain just what this Act was. Shortly it was meant to keep too much money from getting into the hands of a few people, and to give every one with energy and enterprise a chance.

Other Acts connected with the trade of the country followed these, all of which intended to make the life of the weak and poor easier. Of these perhaps the most interesting for us is the Child Labour Act. This Act was meant to keep people from making young children work too hard, and in order to make child labour less profitable to "exploiters" the Act forbids the sending of goods made by children

317

under fourteen from one state to another. If the children are obliged to work at night, or for more than eight hours during the day, the age is raised to sixteen. This Act was signed in September, 1916, but did not come into force until September, 1917. While these things were being done within the country troubles beyond its boarders were increasing. First there was trouble with Mexico.

A few days before Mr. Wilson was inaugurated, Madero, the President of Mexico, was deposed and murdered, and a rebel leader named Huerta at once proclaimed himself President. That he had anything to do with the murder of Madero has never been openly proved, but Mr. Wilson, believing that he had, looked upon him as an assassin, and refused to acknowledge him as head of the neighboring republic. But beyond that Mr. Wilson hesitated to mix himself or his country in the Mexican quarrel, believing that the Mexicans themselves could best settle their own affairs.

"Shall we deny to Mexico," he asked, a little later, "because she is weak, the right to settle her own affairs? No, I say. I am proud to belong to a great nation that says, 'this country which we could crush shall have as much freedom in her own affairs as we have in ours.'"

Whether the President was wise or unwise in his dealings with Mexico we cannot say. The trouble is too close to us. It is not settled yet. But the one thing we can clearly see is that Mr. Wilson loved and desired peace, not only with Mexico but with the whole of America. He wanted to unite the whole of America, both North and South, in bonds of kindness. He wanted to make the small weak republics of South America feel that the great republic of North America was a watchful friend, and not a watchful enemy, eager, and able when she chose, to crush them. Had the United States put forth her strength, Mexico could have been conquered, doubtless, in no long time. But Mr. Wilson took a wider view than those who counseled such a course. Instead of crushing Mexico, and thereby perhaps arousing the jealousy and suspicion of other weak republics, he tried to use the trouble to increase the good will of these republics toward the United States. He tried to show them that the United States was one with them, and had no desire to enlarge her borders at the expense of another. Whether the means he used were wise or not time will show.

For the most part the country was with the President in his desire to keep out of war with Mexico. This was partly because they believed that America was not prepared for war, partly because they knew that war must certainly end in the defeat of the Mexicans. Having defeated them the United States would be forced to annex their territory, and this no one wanted.

But to keep out of war was no easy matter. The wild disorder in Mexico increased daily. Besides Huerta other claimants for the presidency appeared and the country swarmed with bandit forces under various leaders, all fighting against each other.

At length in April, 1914, some United States sailors who had landed at the Mexican port of Tampico were taken prisoner by the Huertists. They were soon set free again, but Huerta refused to apologize in a satisfactory way, and an

318

American squadron was sent to take possession of Vera Cruz. War seemed now certain. But it was averted, and after holding Vera Cruz for more than seven months the American troops were withdrawn. "We do not want to fight the Mexicans," said Mr. Wilson, at the funeral of the sailors who lost their lives in the attack. "We do not want to fight the Mexicans; we want to serve them if we can. A war of aggression is not a proud thing in which to die. But a war of service is one in which it is a grand thing to die."

On the invitation of the United States three of the South American republics, Argentina, Brazil, and Chile, known from their names as the A. B. C. Powers, now joined with the United States in trying to settle the Mexican difficulty. In May, 1914, they held a Mediation Conference at Niagara Falls in Canada. But nothing came of it, and the disorder in Mexico continued as before.

In July, however, there seemed some hope of a settlement. Huerta fled to Europe leaving his friend, Francisco Carbajal, as President. For a month Carbajal kept his post. Then anarchy worse than ever broke loose. Three men, Carranza, Villa, and Zapata, each declaring themselves President, filled the land with bloodshed and ruin.

Once again on the invitation of the United States South America intervened, delegates from six South American republics meeting at Washington to consider what could be done to bring peace to the distracted country. They decided to give the Mexicans three months in which to settle their quarrels, and warned them that if by that time order was not restored United America would be forced to take action.

Soon after this, however, Carranza succeeded in subduing his rivals to a certain extent, and got possession of the greater part of the country. The United States, therefore, recognized him as President of Mexico, and very shortly many of the European powers did the same.

It seemed as if peace might really come at last to Mexico. But although Villa was worsted he was by to means crushed, and he and his undisciplined followers still kept the country in a state of unrest, doing many deeds of violence. In January, 1916, these marauding troops seized and murdered a party of Americans. A little later they crossed frontiers, and were only driven back after a sharp encounter with United States troops.

This brigandage had to be stopped, and, as Carranza seemed unable to subdue the rebels, five thousand American troops entered Mexico intent on punishing Villa and his bandits. But the task was no easy one. Villa was well suited to be a bandit leader, and he was thoroughly at home in the wild and mountainous country. The Americans, however, pressed him hard, and a battle was fought in which he was believed for a time to have been killed. Soon, however, he was discovered to be alive, and as aggressive as before.

Meanwhile President Carranza had grown restless and suspicious of American interferences, and demanded that the United States troops should be withdrawn from Mexican soil. Indeed he became so threatening that Mr. Wilson called out the militia, and ordered a squadron of war vessels to Mexican waters.

Scarcely was this done when the news reached Washington that a skirmish had taken place between Mexican and United States troops, in which forty had been killed, and seventeen taken prisoners.

War was now certain. But once more it was averted. Carranza set his prisoners free and proposed that the two republics should settle their differences by arbitration.

To this Mr. Wilson agreed, and in the beginning of September a Commission composed of delegates from both countries came together. The Commission suggested that both Mexico and the United States should work together to patrol the frontiers, and safeguard them from further raids. But to this Carranza would not agree, and in February, 1917, the United States troops were withdrawn, and Mexico was once more left "to save herself."

Chapter 99 - Wilson -The Great War

The disorder in Mexico was distressing to America, it was disastrous to the Mexicans themselves. But the effect of America as a whole was slight, while the world at large felt it scarcely at all.

In August, 1914, while the Mexican trouble was still grave, the Great War broke out in Europe. This, strange to say, was to prove a far greater menace to the peace of the United States than the war and bloodshed in the turbulent republic on her borders.

In the days of the French Revolution, when France was warring with a sea of foes, Washington had declared the United States to be neutral. He had refused to draw sword even in aid of the friend who only a few years before had helped Americans so generously in their struggle for freedom. He was wise. For in those days America was weak. She was the youngest of the world's great nations, she had hardly "found herself." Had she mixed herself in the European quarrel she would have suffered greatly, perhaps might even have lost her new-found freedom.

All this Washington knew. Gratitude was due to France, but not useless sacrifice, which would merely bring ruin on America, and help France not at all. So Washington declared for neutrality, and maintained it.

Thirty years later Monroe announced his famous Doctrine. That Doctrine in the words of Henry Jefferson was, "First, never to entangle ourselves in the broils of Europe; second, never to suffer Europe to intermeddle with cis-Atlantic affairs." To that doctrine America has remained faithful. But in the ninety years which have passed since it was first announced many changes have taken place. America is no longer weak, but grown to giant's strength, great among the great. The trade of Europe and the trade of America have become interlocked, discoveries and inventions, the wonders of steam and electricity, have made light of the broad Atlantic. Today men come and go from the one continent to the other with greater ease than a hundred years ago they went from Boston to Washington.

By a thousand ties of commerce and of brotherhood the old world is bound to the new. So the war cloud which darkened Europe cast its shadow also over

America, even although at first there was no thought that America would be drawn into the war. Was it possible, men asked, while Europe was at death grips, for America still to keep her "splendid isolation," was it not time for her to take a place, "In the Parliament of man, in the Federation of the world?"

The ties which bind America to Europe bind her to no one country, but to all; bind her equally, it would seem, to France, Britain and Germany. The first founders of the Republic were of British stock, but with the passing years millions of Germans have found a home within her hospitable borders, together with natives of every nation at war. How then could America take sides? No matter which side she took it seemed almost certain to lead to civil war at home. So on the 11th of August, 1914, Mr. Wilson proclaimed the neutrality of the United States.

To the great bulk of the nation this seemed wise, for the nation as a whole loves and desires peace, and realizes the madness and uselessness of war. Indeed America more than the nations of the Old World has come to see the war is an old-fashioned, worn-out way of settling quarrels.

But although the United States might proclaim her neutrality she was none the less entangled in the war. Germany declared a blockage of Britain, Britain declared a blockage of Germany, and these Orders in Council had a far greater effect on American trade than the Berlin Decrees and the Orders in Council in the day of Napoleon. Difficulties arose with both countries. But the difficulties which arose with Britain were such as wise statesmanship might allay. They were concerned with such things as the censoring of mails, and other irritating delays, which interfered with and caused loss of trade. With Germany the difficulties were of a far more serious order, and soon all sane and freedom loving men found it difficult, if not impossible, to remain neutral in spirit.

The German cause had never been a good one. No danger threatened the country. No European nation desired to make war upon them. They went to war wantonly, and without just cause. Soon it became plain that they meant to wage war with a ruthlessness and inhumanity the world had never known. They threw to the winds all the laws of "fair play." Treaties became for them mere "scraps of paper," to be torn if necessity demanded. They marched through Belgium murdering and torturing the people, wantonly destroying the splendid buildings which had been the country's glory and pride. Zeppelins attacked watering places and fishing villages, ruining peaceful homes, slaying women and children, without reason or profit. Submarines waged ruthless war on the seas, attacking alike traders, passenger vessels or hospital ships, belligerent or neutral, without distinction.

As outrage followed outrage the whole world was filled with horror, and one by one Germany's friends turned from her, estranged by her deeds of violence. These were days, as Mr. Wilson said, "to try men's souls," and the burden of guiding the ship of state through the sea of difficulties lay heavy upon him.

At home and abroad his critics were many. Some praised him because he kept the nation steadfastly on the difficult path of peace, others blamed him because it seemed to them he did not sufficiently uphold American honour, and submitted to German insults rather than draw the sword. No great man in a difficult hour can escape criticism. Few, in any, can escape mistakes.

Amid the clash of opinions one thing was clear, that Mr. Wilson was a patriot. And when in 1916 the time came to choose a President he was re-elected for a second term of four years.

In March, 1917, the President entered upon his new term of office well aware that a hard road lay before him and his country. As he took the oath he opened and kissed the Bible at the passage "God is our refuge and strength, a very present help in trouble." His address was imbued with a sense of the dread solemnity of the times.

"I stand here, and have taken the high solemn oath," he said, "because the people of the United States have chosen me, and by their gracious judgement have named me their leader in affairs. I know now what the task means.

"I pray God that I be given wisdom and prudence to do my duty in the true spirit of this great people. I am their servant, and can succeed only as they sustain and guide me by their confidence, and their counsel...

"The shadows that now lie dark upon our path will soon be dispelled. We shall walk with light all about us if we be but true to ourselves-to ourselves as we have wished to be known in the counsels of the world, in the thought of all those who love liberty, justice, and right exalted."

We cannot here follow in detail all the steps by which Germany forced America at length to declare war. It was in a spirit of service that Mr. Wilson took up his office for a second time, of service not only to his own country but to the world. In the cause of that service he saw himself forced to lead his country into war.

Germany had filled America with spies, plotting constantly against her peace and her honour. She had run amuck upon the seas, and by her submarine warfare endangered the lives and welfare of all mankind. She had become a menace to the world's freedom. The President loves peace even as the soul of America loves peace. But both President and people became at length convinced that the only way to restore peace to the world was to defeat the authors of the war.

Having arrived at this grave conclusion there was no turning back, and on the 2nd April, 1917, Mr. Wilson announced his decision at a joint session of the two houses of Congress.

It was not lightly undertaken.

"It is a fearful thing to lead this great peaceful people into war, into the most terrible and disastrous of all wars, civilization itself seeming to be in the balance. But the right is more precious than peace, and we shall fight for the things which we have always carried nearest our hearts - for democracy, for the right of those who submit to authority to have a voice in their own governments, for the rights and liberties of small nations, for a universal dominion of right by such a concert of free peoples as shall bring peace and safety to all nations, and make the world itself at last free.

322

"To such a task we can dedicate our lives and our fortunes, everything that we are and everything that we have, with the pride of those who know that the day has come when America is privileged to spend her blood and her might for the principles that gave her birth and happiness, and the peace which she has treasured. God helping her she can do no other."

In these noble words the President of the United States threw down the gauge of battle. There was in his heart no rancour against the German people, but only a righteous wrath against her criminal rulers who for their own selfish ends had plunged the world in misery. Never in the world's history has a great nation gone to war in so chivalrous a spirit, for so unselfish ends.

"We have no selfish ends to serve," said the President. "We desire no conquest, no dominion. We seek no indemnities for ourselves, no material compensation for the sacrifices we shall freely make. We are but one of the champions of the rights of mankind. We shall be satisfied when those rights have been made as secure as the faith and the freedom of nations can make them."

The voice was the voice of the President, but he spoke from the heart of the people. Brought together from the ends of the earth, speaking many tongues, worshiping God in many ways, diverse in character and in custom, the nation which stands behind the President to-day is one in heart. In the fiery trail of battle America has found her soul, and the American by adoption has proved himself as truly a citizen of the country as the American by birth. Divided by birth and language, by religion and custom, they are one in soul, one in their desire to dedicate themselves to the great unselfish task they have taken in hand, one in the zeal of sacrifice.

Who can say what days of terror and splendour the future may hold? As I write it lies before us a blacker sea of darkness and adventure than that Columbus crossed. But it would seem that for the great Republic it can hold no diviner hour than this. "Greater love hath no man than this, that a man lay down his life for his friends."

There could be found no more splendid close to a splendid story.

"Mine eyes have seen the glory of the coming of the Lord;
He is trampling out the vintage where the grapes of wrath are stored;
He hath loosed the fateful lightning of his terrible swift sword;
His truth is marching on.

He has sounded forth the trumpet that shall never call retreat;
He is sifting out the hearts of men before His judgment seat;
O, be swift, my soul, to answer Him; be jubilant, my feet,—
Our God is marching on.

In the beauty of the lilies, Christ was born across the sea,
With a glory in His bosom that transfigures you and me;
As He died to make men holy, let us die to make me free,
While God is marching on."

Made in the USA
Columbia, SC
02 November 2020